CLAUDE LÉVI-STRAUSS

"There was a time when a reviewer of Claude Lévi-Strauss' works had to introduce the author as the professor of social anthropology at the Collège de France, a member of the Académie Française, the theoretician of myth and kinship, and an authority on South American Indians, but this is no longer necessary. . . . The problem for most readers, however, is to find a work by Lévi-Strauss that can be understood without post-doctoral training in anthropology. . . . This leaves *Tristes Tropiques,* which is both comprehensible to the layman and pleasurable reading. . . . An adventure into the human mind by one of the finest intelligences of our time. It is a feast." —*New Republic*

"The only Lévi-Strauss book that's accessible to the lay reader . . . an exhilarating intellectual experience." —*National Observer*

Claude Lévi-Strauss

TRISTES
TROPIQUES

Translated from the French by

**JOHN AND DOREEN
WEIGHTMAN**

A KANGAROO BOOK
PUBLISHED BY POCKET BOOKS NEW YORK

TRISTES TROPIQUES

Atheneum edition published 1974

POCKET BOOK edition published February, 1977

A previous English translation of this work, from
which chapters 14, 15, 16, and 39 of the French were
omitted, was published in the United States by Criterion
Books and reprinted by Atheneum.

This POCKET BOOK edition includes every word contained in
the original, higher-priced edition. It is printed from brand-
new plates made from completely reset, clear, easy-to-read type.
POCKET BOOK editions are published by
POCKET BOOKS,
a division of Simon & Schuster, Inc.,
A GULF+WESTERN COMPANY
630 Fifth Avenue,
New York, N.Y. 10020.
Trademarks registered in the United States
and other countries.

ISBN: 0-671-80890-7.
Library of Congress Catalog Card Number: 79-162975.
This POCKET BOOK edition is published by arrangement
with Atheneum Publishers. Copyright, ©, 1955, by Librarie
Plon. This English translation copyright, ©, 1973, by Jona-
than Cape Limited. First published in France as *Tristes
Tropiques*. All rights reserved. This book, or portions thereof,
may not be reproduced by any means without permission
of the publisher: Atheneum Publishers,
122 East 42nd Street, New York, New York 10017.
Cover illustration by Howard Koslow.

Printed in the U.S.A.

TO LAURENT

Nec minus ergo ante haec
quam tu cecidere, cadentque.

LUCRETIUS,
De rerum natura, III, 969

CONTENTS

TRANSLATORS' NOTE

Since this book was first published in 1955, it has become
internationally famous under its French title, which—at M.
Lévi-Strauss's request—we have retained for this edition.
The possible English versions, such as 'Sad Tropics', 'The
Sadness of the Tropics', 'Tragic Tropics', etc., do not quite
correspond either in meaning or in implication to 'Tristes
Tropiques', which is at once ironical and poetic, because of
the alliteration, the taut rhythm ($- \cup \cup - \cup$) and the suggestion of 'Alas for the Tropics!'

The present work is an entirely new translation and the
first complete rendering in English. There are some slight
differences between this text and that of the latest French
edition, because the author himself has made minor changes
on reading the English version.

PART ONE

An End to Journeying

1. SETTING OUT

I hate travelling and explorers. Yet here I am proposing to tell the story of my expeditions. But how long it has taken me to make up my mind to do so! It is now fifteen years since I left Brazil for the last time and all during this period I have often planned to undertake the present work, but on each occasion a sort of shame and repugnance prevented me making a start. Why, I asked myself, should I give a detailed account of so many trivial circumstances and insignificant happenings? Adventure has no place in the anthropologist's profession; it is merely one of those unavoidable drawbacks, which detract from his effective work through the incidental loss of weeks or months; there are hours of inaction when the informant is not available; periods of hunger, exhaustion, sickness perhaps; and always the thousand and one dreary tasks which eat away the days to no purpose and reduce dangerous living in the heart of the virgin forest to an imitation of military service . . . The fact that so much effort and expenditure has to be wasted on reaching the object of our studies bestows no value on that aspect of our profession, and should be seen rather as its negative side. The truths which we seek so far afield only become valid when they have been separated from this dross. We may endure six months of travelling, hardships and sickening boredom for the purpose of recording (in a few days, or even a few hours) a hitherto unknown myth, a new marriage rule or a complete list of clan names, but is it worth my while taking up my pen to perpetuate such a useless shred of memory or pitiable recollection as the following: 'At five thirty in the morning, we entered the harbour at Recife amid the shrill cries of the gulls, while a fleet of boats laden with tropical fruits clustered round the hull'?

Nevertheless, this kind of narrative enjoys a vogue which I, for my part, find incomprehensible. Amazonia, Tibet and Africa fill the bookshops in the form of travelogues, accounts of expeditions and collections of photographs, in all

3

of which the desire to impress is so dominant as to make it impossible for the reader to assess the value of the evidence put before him. Instead of having his critical faculties stimulated, he asks for more such pabulum and swallows prodigious quantities of it. Nowadays, being an explorer is a trade, which consists not, as one might think, in discovering hitherto unknown facts after years of study, but in covering a great many miles and assembling lantern-slides or motion pictures, preferably in colour, so as to fill a hall with an audience for several days in succession. For this audience, platitudes and commonplaces seem to have been miraculously transmuted into revelations by the sole fact that their author, instead of doing his plagiarizing at home, has supposedly sanctified it by covering some twenty thousand miles.

What do we learn from these illustrated lectures, and what do we find in the travel books? We are told the exact number of packing-cases that was required, or about the misdemeanours of the ship's dog, and, interspersed among the anecdotes, are scraps of hackneyed information which have appeared in every textbook during the past fifty years and are presented with remarkable effrontery (an effrontery nevertheless perfectly in keeping with the naïvety and ignorance of the audience) as valid evidence or even original discoveries. No doubt there are exceptions, and every period has had its genuine travellers: I could quote one or two among those who enjoy public favour at the present time. But my aim is neither to condemn hoaxes nor to award diplomas of genuineness, but rather to understand a moral and social phenomenon which is especially peculiar to France and, even here, has made its appearance only very recently.

Twenty years or so ago, people travelled very little and it was not halls like the Salle Pleyel, filled to capacity five or six days running, which extended a welcome to tellers of tales. The only place in Paris which catered for this kind of thing was a small, gloomy, icy and dilapidated amphitheatre in an ancient building at the far end of the Jardin des Plantes. There, the Société des Amis du Muséum held —and perhaps still holds—weekly lectures on the natural sciences.

The projector, which was fitted with inadequate bulbs, threw faint images on to an over-large screen, and the lecturer, however closely he peered, could hardly discern their outlines, while for the public they were scarcely distinguishable from the damp stains on the walls. A quarter of an hour after the advertised starting-time, the lecturer would still be desperately wondering if there would be any audience, apart from the handful of regular attenders scattered here and there among the tiered rows. Just when he was about to abandon hope, the lecture-room would fill up to half-capacity with children accompanied by their mothers or nursemaids, some eager for a free change of scene, others weary of the dust and noise outside. To this mixture of moth-eaten ghosts and restless infants the lecturer was privileged—as the supreme reward for so much effort, care and hard work—to reveal his precious store of memories, which were permanently affected by the chill of the occasion, and which, as he spoke in the semi-darkness, he felt slipping away from him and falling one by one like pebbles to the bottom of a well.

Such, then, was the anthropologist's return—only a shade more dismal than the ceremony which had marked his departure; this was a banquet given by the Comité France-Amérique in a mansion on what is now the Avenue Franklin Roosevelt; the building was uninhabited, and a professional caterer, hired for the occasion, would arrive two hours before and set up camp with his stoves, plates and dishes, and yet a desolate odour still hung about the place, in spite of a hurried attempt at ventilation.

We all met there for the first time, we who were as unaccustomed to the solemnity of such a setting as to the dusty boredom it exhaled. We sat round a table which was far too small for the vast room, where there had been no time to do more than sweep the middle part which we were occupying. We were all young teachers who had only recently started work in provincial lycées and, thanks to a somewhat perverse whim on the part of Georges Dumas, we were about to be translated from our damp and remote winter quarters, redolent of rum toddy, musty cellars and stale wood embers, to tropical seas and luxury liners —all of which experiences, moreover, were doomed to have only a very remote resemblance to the inevitably false picture we were already conjuring up, as travellers are always fated to do.

I had been a pupil of Georges Dumas at the time when he was writing his *Traité de psychologie*. Once a week—I cannot remember whether it was on Thursday or Sunday

mornings—a group of philosophy students met at the
Sainte Anne Hospital, in a room with one wall, the one
opposite the windows, completely covered with gay paintings by lunatics. In that room, one already had the sensation of being exposed to a peculiar kind of exotic experience; there was a platform on which Dumas ensconced his
sturdy, angular frame, crowned by a knobbly head resembling a large root that has been bleached and stripped
through a long stay on the sea bed. His waxy complexion
created a unity between his face, his short, white bristling
hair and his goatee beard, which was also white and
sprouted in all directions. This curious piece of vegetable
flotsam, still bushy with little roots, was suddenly humanized by the flashing of coal-black eyes, which emphasized
the whiteness of the head. The opposition was continued by
the contrast between the white starched shirt with a
turned-down collar and the broad-brimmed hat, the loosely
tied bow and the suit, all of which were invariably black.
There was not much to be learned from his lectures; he
never prepared them, since he was aware of the physical
charm exercised over his audience by the expressive movements of his lips, which were twisted in a constantly flickering grin, and above all by his voice, which was at once
hoarse and melodious. It was a real siren's voice, with
strange inflections recalling not only his native Languedoc
but, even more than any regional peculiarities, certain very
archaic musical modes of spoken French, so that the voice
and the face conjured up, in two different sense registers,
the same single, rustic and incisive style—the style characteristic of those sixteenth-century humanists, who were
simultaneously doctors and philosophers, and of whom he
seemed to be, both physically and mentally, a descendant.

The second hour, and occasionally the third too, were
devoted to the presentation of various patients; this was the
occasion for some extraordinary performances involving
the crafty practitioner and certain inmates who, after years
of confinement, were well used to this kind of drill, knew
what was expected of them, and could produce symptoms
when required or would put up just enough resistance to
give their tamer the opportunity for a dazzling display of
skill. The onlookers were not taken in, but willingly sur-
rendered to the pleasure of watching these demonstrations
of virtuosity. When a student attracted the attention of the
master, he was rewarded by having a patient entrusted to

him for a private interview. No contact with savage Indian
tribes has ever daunted me more than the morning I spent
with an old lady swathed in woollies, who compared herself to a rotten herring encased in a block of ice: she appeared intact, she said, but was threatened with disintegration, if her protective envelope should happen to melt.

At once a scientist and something of a practical joker, as
well as the instigator of broad works of synthesis which remained subordinated to a rather disappointing critical positivism, Georges Dumas was a man of great nobility; he
gave me proof of this later, just after the armistice and
shortly before his death, when he was living in retirement
in his native village of Lédignan. Although almost blind, he
made a point of writing me a kind and discreet letter, which
could have had no other object than to affirm his solidarity
with the first victims of the political events of the time.

I have always regretted not having known him in his
youth when, dark and sun-tanned like a conquistador and
full of enthusiasm for the scientific possibilities opened up
by the psychological theories of the nineteenth century, he
had embarked on the spiritual conquest of the New World.
His relationship with Brazilian society was to be a case of
love at first sight; by virtue of this mysterious phenomenon,
two fragments of the Europe of four hundred years ago—
certain essential elements of which had been preserved,
on the one hand, in a Protestant family of southern France
and, on the other, in an extremely refined and rather decadent bourgeois society leading a slow existence in a tropical
environment—came together, recognized their affinity and
were almost fused one with the other. Georges Dumas's
mistake was that he never realized the profoundly archaic
nature of this coincidence. The only part of Brazil which
succumbed to his charm (and a brief period of power was
to give this part the illusion of being the true Brazil) consisted of landowners who were gradually transferring their
capital to partly foreign-owned industrial investments and
who were trying to provide themselves with an ideological
cover in the form of an urbane parliamentarianism; it was
precisely these landowners who were bitterly referred to as
the *gran fino* (the upper crust) by our students, who were
themselves either of recent immigrant origin or the children
of minor resident landowners who had been ruined by the
fluctuations in world trade. Strangely enough, the founding
of São Paulo university, Georges Dumas's greatest achieve-

ment, was to allow these students of humbler origin to
begin their social ascension by obtaining qualifications
which opened the way to administrative posts. Consequently, our university mission helped to form a new elite
which was to turn away from us to some extent because
Dumas and, following him, the Quai d'Orsay refused to
understand that this elite was our most valuable creation,
even though it was trying to overthrow the feudal landlords, who had certainly made it possible for us to come to
Brazil, but had done so partly so that we could give them a
cultural front and partly so that we could provide them
with entertainment.

But on the evening of the Franco-American dinner,
neither my colleagues nor myself—nor our wives who accompanied us—had any inkling of the involuntary role we
were to play in the evolution of Brazilian society. We were
too busy watching each other, and trying to avoid possible
social blunders, for we had just been warned by Georges
Dumas that we would have to prepare ourselves to lead the
same kind of life as our new masters, that is, become
habitués of the Automobile Club, casinos and racecourses.
This seemed extraordinary to young teachers who had
previously been used to earning 26,000 francs a year, and it
still seemed so even when we were given thrice that salary
because so few people wanted to go abroad.

'The main thing', Dumas had told us, 'is to be well
dressed.' And, to reassure us, he added with rather touching
innocence that we could rig ourselves out very economically
at a shop called 'A la Croix de Jeannette', not far from Les
Halles, where he had always had very satisfactory service
when he was a young medical student in Paris.

2. ON BOARD SHIP

At any rate, we never suspected that for the next four or five years—with very few exceptions—our little group was destined to provide the total complement of first-class passengers on the cargo-cum-passenger liners of the Compagnie des Transports Maritimes plying between France and South America. We had the choice between second-class berths on the only luxury liner using this route, or first-class berths on less grand boats. Social climbers opted for the first alternative and paid the difference out of their own pockets, in the hope of hobnobbing with ambassadors and thus gaining certain doubtful advantages. The rest of us took the cargo-cum-passenger boats, on which the journey lasted six days longer, with calls at several ports, but where we enjoyed supremacy.

I wish now that I had been able, twenty years ago, to appreciate fully the unheard-of luxury and regal privilege of being among the eight or ten passengers who, on a boat built to accommodate 100 or 150, had the deck, the cabins, the smoking-room and the dining-room all to themselves. During the nineteen days at sea, all this space, which seemed almost limitless through the absence of other people, became our province; it was as if the boat were our appanage, moving with us. After two or three crossings, we felt quite at home on board, and knew beforehand the names of all the excellent Marseilles stewards with heavy moustaches and stoutly soled shoes, who smelt strongly of garlic as they served us with chicken suprême and turbot fillets. The meals, which had been planned along Pantagruelian lines, were made even more copious by the fact that there were so few of us to eat them.

The end of one civilization, the beginning of another, and the sudden discovery by our present-day world that it is perhaps beginning to grow too small for the people inhabiting it—these truisms are brought home to me less tangibly by figures, statistics and revolutions than by the fact that when, a few weeks ago, after a lapse of fifteen

9

years I was toying with the idea of recapturing my youth by revisiting Brazil in the same way, I was told on the telephone that I would have to book a cabin four months in advance.

I had fondly imagined that since the introduction of passenger air services between Europe and South America, only one or two eccentric individuals still travelled by boat. Alas, it is an illusion to suppose that the invasion of one element disencumbers another. The sea has no more regained its tranquillity since the introduction of Constellations than the outskirts of Paris have recovered their rustic charm since mass building developments began along the Riviera.

Between the marvellous crossings of the 'thirties and this latest projected one which I hastily abandoned, there had been another in 1941, which I had not suspected at the time of being so extraordinarily symbolic of the future. After the armistice, thanks to the friendly interest shown by Robert H. Lowie and A. Métraux in my anthropological writings, and to the diligence of relatives living in the United States, I was invited to join the New School of Social Research in New York as part of the Rockefeller Foundation's plan for rescuing scholars endangered by the German occupation. The problem was how to get to America. My first idea had been to say that I was returning to Brazil to carry on with my pre-war researches. In the cramped ground-floor premises in Vichy where the Brazilian embassy had taken up its quarters, a brief, and for me tragic, scene was enacted, when I went to ask about renewing my visa. The ambassador, Luis de Souza-Dantas, with whom I was well acquainted and who would have behaved no differently had I been a stranger, picked up his seal and was about to stamp the passport when one of his counsellors interrupted him with icy politeness and pointed out that new regulations had been introduced depriving him of the power to do so. For a few seconds his arm remained poised in mid-air. With an anxious, almost beseeching, glance, the ambassador tried to persuade his subordinate to look the other way so that the stamp could be brought down, thus allowing me at least to leave France, if not to enter Brazil. But all in vain; the counsellor continued to stare at the hand, which eventually dropped on to the table alongside the document. I was not to have my visa; my passport was handed back to me with a gesture of profound regret.

I went back to my house in the Cévennes, not far from Montpellier where, as it happened, I had been demobilized during the retreat, and from there I set off to explore possibilities in Marseilles. According to port gossip, a boat was about to leave for Martinique. By dint of inquiring from dock to dock and in one grimy office after another, I finally discovered that the boat in question belonged to the same Compagnie des Transports Maritimes for which, during all the preceding years, the French university mission to Brazil had provided such a faithful and exclusive clientele. One day in February 1941, when an icy wind was blowing, in an unheated and practically closed-down office, I came upon an official, whose task it had been in the old days to pay his respects to us on behalf of the company. Yes, the boat did exist and was due to sail, but there was no question of my taking it.—Why?—I could not be expected to understand; it was difficult for him to explain; things would not be as they had been in the past.—What would they be like? —It would be a very long, very distressing voyage and he could not even imagine me on board.

The poor man still saw me as a minor ambassador of French culture, whereas I already felt myself to be potential fodder for the concentration camp. Besides, I had just spent the two previous years, first in the heart of a virgin forest, then moving from one billet to another in the course of a disorderly retreat which had taken me from the Maginot Line to Béziers by way of Sarthe, Corrèze and Aveyron; I had travelled in cattle-trucks and slept in sheep-folds, so that the official's scruples struck me as being rather misplaced. I had a vision of myself resuming my wandering existence on the high seas, sharing the toil and the frugal meals of a handful of sailors who had ventured forth on a clandestine boat, sleeping on deck, and forced during long and empty days into a salutary intimacy with the sea.

Finally I got my ticket for the *Capitaine Paul-Lemerle*, but I did not begin to understand the situation until the day we went on board between two rows of helmeted *gardes mobiles* with sten guns in their hands, who cordoned off the quayside, preventing all contact between the passengers and their relatives or friends who had come to say goodbye, and interrupting leave-takings with jostling and insults. Far from being a solitary adventure, it was more like the deportation of convicts. What amazed me even more than the

way we were treated was the number of passengers. About
350 people were crammed on to a small steamer which—as
I was immediately to discover—boasted only two cabins
with, in all, seven bunks. One of the cabins had been allocated to three ladies and the other was to be shared by four
men, including myself. For this extraordinary favour I was
indebted to M.B. (and I take this opportunity of thanking
him), who was unable to tolerate the idea that one of his
former first-class passengers should be transported like livestock. The rest of my companions, men, women and children, were herded into the hold, with neither air nor light,
and where the ship's carpenters had hastily run up bunk
beds with straw mattresses. Of the four privileged males,
one was an Austrian metal-dealer, who was no doubt well
aware of the price he had paid for the privilege; another
was a young 'béké'—a wealthy Creole—whom the war had
cut off from his native Martinique and who was felt to be
worthy of special treatment since he was the only person on
board who could reasonably be presumed to be neither a
Jew nor a foreigner nor an anarchist; lastly, there was an
extraordinary North African character who maintained that
he was going to New York for a few days only (a weird
claim, given the fact that we were going to spend three
months getting there) and who had a Degas in his suitcase.
Although he was no less a Jew than I was, he seemed to be
persona grata with all the policemen, detectives, gendarmes
and security agents of the various colonies and protec-
torates—an amazing mystery which I never managed to
elucidate.

The riff-raff, as the gendarmes called them, included,
among others, André Breton and Victor Serge. André
Breton, who was very much out of place *dans cette galère*,
strode up and down the few empty spaces left on deck;
wrapped in his thick nap overcoat, he looked like a blue
bear. A lasting friendship was about to develop between us,
through an exchange of letters which lasted for quite some
time during that interminable voyage and in which we discussed the relationships between aesthetic beauty and absolute originality.

As for Victor Serge, I was intimidated by his status as a
former companion of Lenin, at the same time as I had the
greatest difficulty in identifying him with his physical presence, which was rather like that of a prim and elderly
spinster. The clean-shaven, delicate-featured face, the clear

voice accompanied by a stilted and wary manner, had an almost asexual quality, which I was later to find among Buddhist monks along the Burmese frontier, and which is very far removed from the virile and superabundant vitality commonly associated in France with what are called subversive activities. The explanation is that cultural types which occur in very similar forms in every society, because they are constructed around very simple polarities, are used to fulfil different social functions in different communities. Serge's type had been able to realize itself in a revolutionary career in Russia, but elsewhere it might have played some other part. No doubt relationships between any two societies would be made easier if, through the use of some kind of grid, it were possible to establish a pattern of equivalences between the ways in which each society uses analogous human types to perform different social functions. Instead of simply arranging meetings on a professional basis, doctors with doctors, teachers with teachers and industrialists with industrialists, we might perhaps be led to see that there are more subtle correspondences between individuals and the parts they play.

In addition to its human load, the boat was carrying some kind of clandestine cargo. Both in the Mediterranean and along the west coast of Africa, we spent a fantastic amount of time dodging into various ports, apparently to escape inspection by the English navy. Passengers with French passports were sometimes allowed to land: the others remained parked within the few dozen square centimetres available to each. Because of the heat, which became more intense as we approached the tropics, it was impossible to remain below and the deck was gradually turned into dining-room, bedroom, day-nursery, wash-house and solarium. But the most disagreeable feature was what is referred to in the army as the sanitary arrangements. Against the rail on either side—port for the men, starboard side for the women—the crew had erected two pairs of wooden huts, with neither windows nor ventilation; one contained a few shower sprinklers which only worked in the morning: the other was provided with a long wooden trough crudely lined with zinc and leading directly into the sea, for the obvious reason. Those of us who were averse to crowds and shrank from collective squatting, which was in any case rendered unsteady by the lurching of the ship, had no choice but to get up very early; and throughout the entire trip a kind of race developed between the fastidious passengers, so that towards the end it was only at about three o'clock in the morning that one could hope for relative privacy. Finally, it was no longer possible to go to bed at all. Except for the time difference of two hours, the same was true for the shower-baths, where the idea uppermost in every mind was, if not to protect one's modesty, at least to succeed in finding a place in the crowd under the insufficient supply of water, which seemed to turn to steam through contact with so many clammy bodies, and hardly touched the skin. In either case, there was a general urge to complete the operation quickly and get out, for the unventilated huts were made of planks of unseasoned, resinous pine which, after being impregnated with dirty water, urine and sea air, began to ferment in the sun and give off a warmish, sweet and nauseous odour; this, added to other smells, very soon became intolerable, especially when there was a swell.

When, after a month at sea, we sighted the Fort de France lighthouse in the middle of the night, it was not the prospect of an edible meal, a bed with sheets and a peaceful night's sleep which caused the passengers' hearts to swell with anticipation. All those who, previously, had enjoyed what are called the amenities of civilization, had suffered not so much from hunger, fatigue, sleeplessness, overcrowding and the disrespect in which they had lived for the past four weeks, as from the enforced filth, which was made still worse by the heat. There were young and pretty women on board; flirtations had begun and sympathies had ripened. For them, to appear in a favourable light before the final separation was more than mere coquettishness: it was an account to be settled, a debt to be honoured, a proof they felt they owed of the fact that they were not fundamentally unworthy of the attentions bestowed on them. With a touching delicacy of feeling, they had taken these attentions only, as it were, on credit. So there was not only an element of farce but also a slight hint of pathos in the cry which arose from every pair of lungs. Instead of the call 'Land! Land!' as in traditional sea stories, 'A bath, at last a bath, a bath tomorrow!' could be heard on every side, while at the same time people embarked on a feverish inventory of the last piece of soap, the unstained towel, or the clean blouse which had been carefully preserved for this great occasion.

This hydrotherapeutic dream implied an exaggeratedly optimistic view of the civilized amenities to be expected after four centuries of colonization (bathrooms are few and far between at Fort de France), but the passengers were soon to learn that their filthy, overcrowded boat was an idyllic refuge, in comparison with the welcome they were to receive almost as soon as the ship docked. We fell into the hands of soldiers suffering from a collective form of mental derangement, which would have repaid anthropological study, had the anthropologist not been obliged to use his entire intellectual resources for the purpose of avoiding its unfortunate consequences.

Most French people had experienced a peculiar war, a *drôle de guerre;* but no superlative could do justice to the war as it had been experienced by the officers stationed in Martinique. Their one assignment, which was to guard the gold of the Bank of France, had degenerated into a kind of nightmare, for which the excessive drinking of punch was only partly responsible; other factors, which played a more insidious but no less essential part, were their isolated situation, their remoteness from metropolitan France, and a historical tradition rich in pirates' tales, so that it was easy to replace the old, one-legged, gold-earringed characters by North American spies or German submarines on secret missions. There had thus developed an obsidional excitement which had driven most individuals into a state of panic, although no fighting had as yet occurred—and for the best of reasons, since no enemy had ever been sighted. The conversation of the native inhabitants revealed the same kind of mental processes, only on a more prosaic level: 'There's no more salt cod, the island's done for' was a frequently heard comment, while some people explained that Hitler was none other than Jesus Christ, who had come back to earth to punish the white race for having failed to follow his teachings during the previous two thousand years.

At the time of the armistice, the non-commissioned officers, far from joining the Free French, felt themselves in harmony with the Vichy government. They proposed to remain 'uninvolved'; their physical and moral state, which had been undermined for months, would have rendered them unfit for active service, supposing they had at any time been up to it; their sick minds found a kind of security in replacing the Germans, their real enemy, but one so far

away as to have become invisible and as it were abstract,
by an imaginary enemy who had the advantage of being
close at hand and tangible—the Americans. Besides, two
United States warships cruised continuously outside the
harbour. A clever assistant-commander of the French
forces used to lunch on board every day, at the same time
as his superior officer deliberately stirred up hatred and
bitterness against the Anglo-Saxons among his troops.

They needed enemies on whom they could vent their
feelings of aggressiveness, which had been accumulating for
months; they needed someone to blame for the defeat of
France, in which they felt they had no share since they had
not taken part in the fighting, but for which, in another
sense, they felt obscurely guilty (they themselves, in fact,
had provided a consummate example and the most extreme
instance of the unconcern, illusions and apathy which had
overcome part, at least, of France). In this respect, our
boat offered a particularly apposite collection of specimens.
It was rather as if the Vichy authorities, in allowing us to
leave for Martinique, had sent them a cargo of scapegoats,
on whom these gentlemen could relieve their feelings. The
soldiers in tropical kit, complete with helmets and guns,
who took up their positions in the captain's cabin to interview each one of us individually, seemed to be less concerned with conducting pre-disembarkation interrogations
than with giving a display of invective to which we could
only listen. The non-French passengers found themselves
classed as enemies; those who were French were rudely
denied this distinction, at the same time as they were accused of having abandoned their country in a cowardly
fashion. The indictment was not only a contradiction in
terms; it sounded strange, coming from men who had been
living under the protection of the Monroe Doctrine ever
since the outbreak of war.

There was no question of baths. It was decided that
everybody was to be interned in a camp called Le Lazaret
on the far side of the bay. Only three people were allowed
to land: the 'béké', who was in a category by himself, the
mysterious Tunisian, who was able to show some document
or other, and myself—as a special favour granted to the
ship's captain by the naval authorities; he and I had discovered we were old friends, since he had been chief officer
on one of the boats in which I had travelled before the war.

3. THE WEST INDIES

At two o'clock in the afternoon, Fort de France was a dead
town; it was impossible to believe that anyone lived in the
ramshackle buildings which bordered the long market-place
planted with palm trees and overrun with weeds, and which
was more like a stretch of waste-ground with, in its middle,
an apparently forgotten statue, green with neglect, of
Joséphine Tascher de la Pagerie, later known as Joséphine
de Beauharnais. As soon as we had booked into a deserted
hotel, the Tunisian and I, still shaken by the morning's
events, jumped into a hired car and headed for Le Lazaret.
We wanted to comfort our companions, and more especially
two young German women who had given us to understand
during the crossing that they would be in a great hurry to
deceive their husbands, once they were able to wash. In this
respect, the business of Le Lazaret increased our disappointment.

While the old Ford was churning its way up steep tracks
in bottom gear and I was rediscovering with delight a host
of vegetable species that were familiar to me since my stay
in Amazonia but that I was to learn here to call by new
names—*caïmite* instead of *fruta do condé* (which has the
shape of an artichoke and a pear-like flavour), *corrosol* and
not *graviola*, *papaye* for *mammão*, *sapotille* (sapodilla) for
mangabeira, etc.—I reflected on the painful scenes which
had just taken place and tried to link them with other
experiences of a similar kind. For my companions, who
had been plunged into an adventurous journey after leading
often uneventful existences, the mixture of spitefulness and
stupidity they had encountered appeared as an unheard-of,
unique and exceptional phenomenon—in fact, as the impact
on their private persons and on the persons of their jailors
of an international catastrophe such as had never before
occurred in history. But I had seen something of the world
and during the preceding years had found myself in far
from ordinary situations, so that for me this kind of experience was not entirely unfamiliar. I knew that, slowly

17

and gradually, experiences such as these were starting to ooze out like some insidious leakage from contemporary mankind, which had become saturated with its own numbers and with the ever-increasing complexity of its problems, as if its skin had been irritated by the friction of ever-greater material and intellectual exchange brought about by the improvement in communication. In that particular French territory, the sole effect of war and defeat had been to hasten the advance of a universal process, to facilitate the establishment of a lasting form of contamination which would never entirely disappear from the face of the earth but would re-emerge in some new place as it died down elsewhere. This was not the first occasion on which I had encountered those outbreaks of stupidity, hatred and credulousness which social groups secrete like pus when they begin to be short of space.

Only a little while previously, a few months before the outbreak of war, in the course of my return journey to France, I had visited Bahia and had walked through the upper town, going from one church to another; there are said to be 365 of them, one for each day of the year, and they vary in style and interior decoration as the days and seasons differ. I was absorbed in photographing their architectural details, and as I moved from place to place I was followed by a group of half-naked nigger-boys who kept pleading, 'Tira o retrato! Tira o retrato!' ('Take a photo of us!'). Finally, touched by such a charming form of begging —they preferred a photo they would never see to a few coppers—I agreed to take a snap to please them. I had barely gone a hundred yards further when a hand descended on my shoulder: two plain-clothes inspectors who had been following me step by step informed me that I had just committed an unfriendly act towards Brazil: the photograph, if used in Europe, might possibly give credence to the legend that there were black-skinned Brazilians and that the urchins of Bahia went barefoot. I was taken into custody, but fortunately was detained only for a short time, because the boat was about to leave.

That boat, as it happened, brought me nothing but bad luck; a few days earlier I had met with a similar experience, just after joining the ship and while it was still at the quayside in the port of Santos. I had hardly gone on board when a commander of the Brazilian navy in full uniform accompanied by two marines with fixed bayonets imprisoned me in my cabin. In this case, it took four to five hours to clear up the mystery. The Franco-Brazilian expedition, of which I had been in charge for the past year, was subject to the official regulations governing the sharing out, between the two countries, of the material collected. The operation had to be carried out under the supervision of the National Museum of Rio de Janeiro, which had immediately notified all the ports in the country that, should I attempt to make a sinister get-away with bows, arrows and feathered head-dresses exceeding the share allotted to France, I must at all costs be taken into custody. However, when the expedition returned, the Rio museum changed its mind and decided to hand over Brazil's share to a scientific institute in São Paulo; I was accordingly informed that the shipment of the French share should take place through Santos and not through Rio, but as it had been forgotten that a different decision had been taken the year before, I was detained as a criminal by virtue of obsolete instructions, which had slipped the minds of their originators but were still remembered by those commissioned to carry them out.

Fortunately, at that time, every Brazilian official still had inside him a concealed anarchist, who was kept alive by the shreds of Voltaire and Anatole France which impregnated the national culture even in the depths of the bush. (Once, in a village in the interior, an old man overcome by emotion had exclaimed, 'Ah Monsieur, you are French! Ah, France! Anatole, Anatole!' as he clasped me in his arms; he had never seen a Frenchman before.) So, being sufficiently experienced to know that I should not be sparing in the expression of my feelings of deference towards the Brazilian State in general and the naval authorities in particular, at the same time I took pains to touch on certain sensitive spots; and, to good effect, since, after a few hours spent in a cold sweat (the ethnographical material was packed in the crates along with my personal effects and my books, because I was leaving Brazil for good, and there was a moment of panic when I thought that everything might be scattered on the quayside just when the boat was weighing anchor), I myself dictated to the official a report in which, in scathing terms, he took credit for having allowed me to leave with my luggage, thus saving his country from an international conflict and subsequent humiliation.

But perhaps I would not have behaved so brazenly had

I not still been influenced by the memory of an incident
which had shown South American policemen in a very
comic light. Two months previously, I had been forced to
change planes in a large village in Lower Bolivia; I was
stranded there for several days in the company of Dr. J. A.
Vellard, while waiting for a connection which failed to arrive. In 1938, the air services were very different from what
they are today. In remote regions of South America, which
had skipped certain stages in civilization, the aeroplane had
at once become a kind of local bus for village people who,
until then, had had to spend several days trekking to the
nearest fair either on foot or on horseback, since there were
no roads. Now, a flight which lasted only a few minutes
(but which, to be exact, often took place more than a few
days late) made the transporting of their hens and ducks
quite easy. The passengers, as often as not, were obliged to
squat among the fowls, since the tiny planes were crammed
with a motley assortment of barefooted peasants, farmyard
animals and packing-cases which were either too heavy or
too bulky to be carried along the forest tracks.

So, for the lack of anything better to do, we wandered
through the streets of Santa Cruz de la Sierra, which had
been transformed by the rainy season into muddy torrents.
These were forded by means of huge stones placed at
regular intervals, like the studs of some pedestrian crossing
that no vehicle could ever get past. A patrol spotted our
unfamiliar faces, which provided sufficient reason for
arresting us and shutting us up, until such time as we could
explain our presence, in a room richly furnished in an old-
fashioned style. It was in the former palace of the provincial governor, and the panelled walls were interspersed with
glass-fronted bookcases, filled with heavy, richly bound
volumes. The effect was broken only by a notice-board,
also glass-fronted and framed, containing an extraordinary
inscription, done in beautiful copperplate, and which I
translate literally from the Spanish: 'Under pain of severe
sanctions, it is strictly forbidden to tear out pages from the
archives and to use them for particular or hygienic purposes. Any person infringing this rule will be punished.'

Honesty compels me to admit that my situation in Martinique improved thanks to the intervention of a highly
placed official belonging to the Ponts et Chaussées who,
beneath a rather cool and reserved exterior, concealed feelings very different from those which normally prevailed in

official circles. I may have been helped too by my frequent visits to the offices of a religious newspaper, where the Fathers of some Order, the name of which I forget, had stored chests full of archaeological remains dating from the Indian occupation; I devoted my leisure hours to making an inventory of them.

One day, I went into the assize court, which happened to be in session; this was my first, and has to date remained my only, visit to a law court. The person on trial was a peasant, who had bitten off a piece of one of his opponent's ears during a quarrel. The accused, the plaintiff and the witnesses expressed themselves volubly in the Creole dialect, the crystalline freshness of which seemed positively uncanny in such surroundings. Their statements were translated for three judges, who were suffering from the heat, since they were wrapped in red, fur-trimmed robes which had lost their crispness in the humid atmosphere. The grotesque garments hung limply round their bodies like bloodstained bandages. It took exactly five minutes to pass a sentence of eight years' imprisonment on the hot-tempered peasant. Justice always has, and always will be, associated in my mind with doubt, scrupulousness and respect. That the fate of a human being could be settled in so short a time and in such an offhand manner filled me with amazement. I could not bring myself to believe that what I had just witnessed had actually happened. Even today, no dream, however fantastic or far-fetched, can inspire me with such a feeling of incredulity.

My fellow-passengers owed their release to a difference of opinion between the naval authorities and the local tradesmen. While the former looked upon them as spies and traitors, the latter considered that their internment at Le Lazaret, even though it was not free of charge, was depriving the town of a source of financial profit. The second view prevailed and, for a fortnight, everyone was free to spend their last French notes, under the close supervision of the police who wove around each individual, and more especially around the women, a web of temptations, provocations, enticements and reprisals. Meanwhile, the Dominican consulate was besieged for visas, and there were any number of false rumours about the arrival of hypothetical boats which were supposed to get us out of our quandary. The situation changed again when the tradespeople in the villages, who were jealous of the big town, argued that they too were entitled to their share of refugees. From one day to the next, everyone was billeted in the inland villages. I was again spared, but being anxious to follow my fair friends to their new abode at the foot of Mont Pelé, I was able—thanks to this final piece of manœuvering on the part of the police—to enjoy some unforgettable walks across the island, which seemed so much more classically exotic than the South American mainland. It was like a deep arborized agate set in a ring of black, silver-flecked beaches, and in the valleys, which were brimful with a milk-white mist, one could only just sense the presence—more perceptible to the ear, through the sound of dripping moisture, than to the eye—of the huge, soft, feathery fronds of the tree-ferns, rising above the living fossils of their trunks.

Although up till then I had fared better than my companions, I was none the less preoccupied by a problem to which I must now refer, since the writing of this book depended on its being solved and this, as will appear, proved to be no easy task. My sole wealth was a trunk full of documents relating to my fieldwork: it included linguistic and technological card-indexes, a travel diary, anthropological notes, maps, diagrams and photographic negatives—in short, thousands of items. The suspicious load had crossed the demarcation line in France only at considerable risk to the professional smuggler who had agreed to transport it. From the reception I had received in Martinique, I concluded that the customs men, the police and the naval intelligence officers must not be allowed even a glimpse of what they would inevitably interpret as instructions in code (the notes on native dialects), or diagrams of fortifications, or invasion plans (the maps, sketches and photos). I therefore resolved to declare that my trunk was in transit, and so it was deposited, still sealed, in the storerooms of the customs house. This meant, as I was later informed, that I would have to leave Martinique on a foreign boat, to which the trunk would be directly transferred (and I had to make a great effort to achieve even this compromise). If I intended to go to New York on the *D'Aumale* (a veritable ghost-ship, which my companions waited for during a whole month before it actually materialized one fine morning, all newy painted like a huge toy from another century), the trunk would have to enter Martinique officially, and then be taken out again. I coudn't have this, and so I boarded an immaculately white Swedish banana boat bound for

Puerto Rico. For four days, I enjoyed a quiet and almost solitary crossing, like a throwback to happier times, for there were only eight passengers on board. It was a good thing I made the most of it.

After the French, I had to contend with the American police. On landing in Puerto Rico, I discovered two things: during the two months which had elapsed since we left Marseilles, the immigration laws in the United States had been altered, and the documents I had with me from the New School for Social Research no longer complied with the new regulations; then, what was more important, the suspicions I had supposed would be aroused in the Martinique police by my anthropological documents, and against which I had so wisely protected myself, were entertained to the highest possible degree by the American police. After being accused, at Fort de France, of being a Jewish Freemason in the pay of the Americans, I had the somewhat bitter compensation of discovering that, from the American point of view, there was every likelihood that I was an emissary of the Vichy Government, and perhaps even of the Germans. While waiting for the New School (which I wired immediately) to satisfy the new legal requirements, as well as for the arrival of a F.B.I. specialist capable of reading French (and, knowing that three-quarters of my notes consisted not of French words but of terms belonging to practically unknown dialects of central Brazil, I shuddered at the thought of the time it would take to discover an expert), the immigration authorities decided to intern me, at the shipping company's expense, in an austere, Spanish-type hotel, where I was fed on boiled beef and chick-peas, while two extremely dirty and ill-shaven native policemen took it in turns to guard my door day and night.

I remember that it was in the courtyard of this hotel that, one evening, Bertrand Goldschmidt, who had arrived on the same boat and who was later to become one of the directors of the Atomic Energy Commission, explained the principle of the atomic bomb to me and revealed (this was in May 1941) that the major powers had embarked on a scientific race, the winner of which would be sure of victory.

After a few days, my last travelling companions settled their personal difficulties and set off for New York. I remained alone in San Juan, escorted by my two policemen,

who, at my request, accompanied me as often as I wanted
to the three places which were not out of bounds—the
French consulate, the bank and the immigration offices. To
go anywhere else, I had to ask for special permission. One
day, I was allowed to go to the university, and my attendant policeman tactfully remained outside and waited
for me at the door, so as to avoid humiliating me. And since
both he and his companion were bored, they occasionally
broke the rules and allowed me, on their own initiative, to
take them to the cinema. It was only during the forty-eight
hours which elapsed between my release and my boarding
the ship that I was able to visit the island, escorted by M.
Christian Belle, who was French consul at the time and
who turned out to be—rather to my surprise, given the
unusual circumstances—a fellow-specialist in American
Indian matters and full of stories of the voyages he had
made along the South American sea-board. Shortly before,
the morning press had announced the arrival of Jacques
Soustelle, who was touring the West Indies in order to persuade the French residents to support General de Gaulle;
again I had to obtain special permission in order to meet
him.

And so, it was at Puerto Rico that I first made contact
with the United States; for the first time I breathed in the
smell of warm car paint and wintergreen (which, in French,
used to be called *thé du Canada*), those two olfactory poles
between which stretches the whole range of American comfort, from cars to lavatories, by way of radio sets, sweets
and toothpaste; and I tried to guess what the girls in the
drugstores with their lilac dresses and mahogany hair were
thinking about, behind their mask-like make-up. It was
here, too, but from the rather special angle of the Greater
Antilles, that I first perceived certain features of the typical
American town; the flimsiness of the buildings, and the
desire to create an eye-catching effect, made it look like
some world exhibition that had become permanent, except
that, in this instance, one might have imagined oneself to
be in the Spanish section.

The accidents of travel often produce ambiguities such
as these. Because I spent my first weeks on United States
soil in Puerto Rico, I was in future to find America in
Spain. Just as, several years later, through visiting my first
English university with a campus surrounded by Neo-Goth-
ic buildings at Dacca in Western Bengal, I now look upon

Oxford as a kind of India that has succeeded in controlling the mud, the mildew and the ever-encroaching vegetation.

The F.B.I. inspector arrived three weeks after the beginning of my stay at San Juan. I rushed to the customs office and opened my trunk; it was a solemn moment. A polite young man came forward and picked out a card-index entry at random. His gaze narrowed and he turned fiercely towards me: 'It's in German!' As it happened, it was a reference to the classic work, *Unter den Naturvölkern Zentral-Brasiliens* (Berlin, 1894), written by von den Steinen, my illustrious and distant predecessor in the central Mato Grosso. My explanation immediately cleared things up and the expert, for whom we had waited so long, lost interest in the whole business. Everything was all right, O.K.; I could enter American territory; I was free.

It is time to stop. Each of these minor adventures recalls other incidents to mind. Some, like the one I have just related, are connected with the war, but others, which I recounted earlier, relate to the pre-war period. And I could add others of more recent date, if I drew on my travels in Asia of the last few years. But today my nice F.B.I. inspector would not be so easily satisfied. Everywhere the atmosphere is becoming equally oppressive.

4. THE QUEST FOR POWER

One trifling incident, which has remained in my memory like an omen, was, for me, the first instance of one of those dubious scents or veering winds which herald some profound disturbance. After deciding not to renew my contract with the University of São Paulo so as to be able to make a long trip into the interior, I had gone on ahead of my colleagues and was travelling back to Brazil a few weeks before they did; so, for the first time for four years, I was the only academic on board; for the first time, too, there were a great many passengers: some foreign businessmen, but chiefly a whole French military mission on its way to Paraguay. The familiar crossing was thus made unrecognizable, as was the once serene atmosphere on board ship. The officers and their wives made no distinction between a transatlantic crossing and a colonial expedition, or between their duties as instructors to what was, after all, a very modest army and the occupation of a conquered country. To prepare themselves, mentally at least, for their task, they turned the deck into a parade-ground, and the civilian passengers were reduced to the status of natives. We did not know where to turn to escape such noisy and high-handed behaviour, which even caused uneasiness among the ship's officers. However, the leader of the mission had a very different attitude from that of his subordinates; he and his wife were both discreet and considerate persons; and they came up to me one day in the secluded corner where I was escaping from the din, and asked about my past work and the object of my mission. Also, they managed indirectly to convey the fact that they were no more than powerless and clear-sighted onlookers. The contrast was so glaring that it seemed to hide some mystery or other; three or four years later I remembered the incident, when I came across the officer's name in the newspapers and understood that his personal position was, indeed, paradoxical.

It was perhaps then, for the first time, that I understood something which was later confirmed by equally demoralizing experiences in other parts of the world. Journeys, those magic caskets full of dreamlike promises, will never again yield up their treasures untarnished. A proliferating and overexcited civilization has broken the silence of the seas once and for all. The perfumes of the tropics and the pristine freshness of human beings have been corrupted by a busyness with dubious implications, which mortifies our desires and dooms us to acquire only contaminated memories.

Now that the Polynesian islands have been smothered in concrete and turned into aircraft carriers solidly anchored in the southern seas, when the whole of Asia is beginning to look like a dingy suburb, when shanty-towns are spreading across Africa, when civil and military aircraft blight the primeval innocence of the American or Melanesian forests even before destroying their virginity, what else can the so-called escapism of travelling do than confront us with the more unfortunate aspects of our history? Our great Western civilization, which has created the marvels we now enjoy, has only succeeded in producing them at the cost of corresponding ills. The order and harmony of the Western world, its most famous achievement, and a laboratory in which structures of a complexity as yet unknown are being fashioned, demand the elimination of a prodigious mass of noxious by-products which now contaminate the globe. The first thing we see as we travel round the world is our own filth, thrown into the face of mankind.

So I can understand the mad passion for travel books and their deceptiveness. They create the illusion of something which no longer exists but still should exist, if we were to have any hope of avoiding the over-whelming conclusion that the history of the past twenty thousand years is irrevocable. There is nothing to be done about it now; civilization has ceased to be that delicate flower which was preserved and painstakingly cultivated in one or two sheltered areas of a soil rich in wild species which may have seemed menacing because of the vigour of their growth, but which nevertheless made it possible to vary and revitalize the cultivated stock. Mankind has opted for monoculture; it is in the process of creating a mass civilization, as beetroot is grown in the mass. Henceforth, man's daily bill of fare will consist only of this one item.

In the old days, people used to risk their lives in India or in the Americas in order to bring back products which now seem to us to have been of comically little worth, such

as *brasil* or brazilwood (from which the name Brazil was
derived)—a red dye—and also pepper which had such a
vogue in the time of Henry IV of France that courtiers
used to carry the seeds in sweetmeat boxes and eat them
like sweets. The visual or olfactory surprises they provided,
since they were cheerfully warm to the eye or exquisitely
hot on the tongue, added a new range of sense experience
to a civilization which had never suspected its own in-
sipidity. We might say, then, that, through a twofold reversal, from these same lands our modern Marco Polos now
bring back the moral spices of which our society feels an
increasing need as it is conscious of sinking further into
boredom, but that this time they take the form of photographs, books and travellers' tales.

Another parallel seems to me to be even more significant.
Intentionally or unintentionally, these modern seasonings
are falsified. Not, of course, because they are of a purely
psychological nature, but because, however honest the narrator may be, he cannot—since this is no longer possible—
supply them in a genuine form. For us to be willing to accept them, memories have to be sorted and sifted; through
a degree of manipulation which, in the most sincere writers,
takes place below the level of consciousness, actual experience is replaced by stereotypes. When I open one of these
travel books, I see, for instance, that such and such a tribe
is described as savage and is said still to preserve certain
primitive customs, which are described in garbled form in
a few superficial chapters; yet I spent weeks as a student
reading the books on that tribe written by professional
anthropologists either recently or as much as fifty years
ago, before contact with the white races and the resulting
epidemics reduced it to a handful of pathetic rootless individuals. Another community, whose existence is said to
have been discovered by a youthful traveller who completed his study in forty-eight hours, was in fact seen (and
this is an important point) outside its habitual territory in
a temporary camp, which the writer naïvely assumed to be
a permanent village. Moreover, the means of approach to
the tribe are carefully glossed over, so as not to reveal the
presence of the mission station which has been consistently
in touch with the natives for the past twenty years, or of
the local motor-boat service reaching into the heart of the
territory. But the existence of the latter can be deduced by
a practised eye from small details in the illustrations, since

the photographer has not always been able to avoid including the rusty petrol-cans in which this virgin people does its cooking.

The emptiness of such claims, the naïve credulity with which they are received and which in fact helps to prompt them, and even the element of praiseworthiness which to some extent redeems so much wasted effort (doubly wasted because its only effect is to extend the degeneration that it tries to conceal)—all this implies powerful psychological motives, both in the authors and their public, on which the study of certain native institutions can serve to throw light. Anthropology itself can help to elucidate the vogue which wins it so much harmful collaboration.

Among a great many North American tribes, the social prestige of the individual is determined by the circumstances surrounding the ordeals connected with puberty. Some young men set themselves adrift on solitary rafts without food; others seek solitude in the mountains where they have to face wild beasts, as well as cold and rain. For days, weeks or months on end, as the case may be, they do not eat properly, but live only on coarse food, or fast for long periods and aggravate their impaired physical condition by the use of emetics. Everything is turned into a means of communication with the beyond. They stay immersed for long periods in icy water, deliberately mutilate one or more of their finger-joints, or lacerate their fasciae by dragging heavy loads attached by ropes to sharpened pegs inserted under their dorsal muscles. When they do not resort to such extremes, they at least exhaust themselves by performing various pointless tasks, such as removing all their body hairs, one at a time, or stripping pine branches until not a single needle remains, or hollowing out blocks of stone.

In the dazed, debilitated and delirious state induced by these ordeals they hope to enter into communication with the supernatural world. They believe that a magic animal, touched by the intensity of their sufferings and their prayers, will be forced to appear to them; that a vision will reveal which one will henceforth be their guardian spirit, so that they can take its name and derive special powers from it, which will determine their privileges and rank within their social group.

Have we to conclude that, in the opinion of these natives, nothing is to be expected from society? Both institutions

and customs seem to them like a mechanism the monotonous functioning of which leaves nothing to chance, luck or
ability. They may think that the only means of compelling
fate is to venture into those hazardous marginal areas where
social norms cease to have any meaning, and where the
protective laws and demands of the group no longer prevail; to go right to the frontiers of average, ordered living,
to the breaking point of bodily strength and to the extremes
of physical and moral suffering. In this unstable border
area, there is a danger of slipping beyond the pale and
never coming back, as well as a possibility of drawing from
the vast ocean of unexploited forces surrounding organized
society a personal supply of power, thanks to which he who
has risked all can hope to modify an otherwise unchange-
able social order.

However, this interpretation is probably still too superficial, since among these Indians of the North American
plains and plateau, individual beliefs are not at variance
with collective doctrine. The dialectic as a whole springs
from the customs and philosophy of the group. It is from
the group that individuals learn their creed; belief in guardian spirits is a group phenomenon, and it is society as a
whole which teaches its members that their only hope,
within the framework of the social order, is to make an
absurd and desperate attempt to break away from it.

It is obvious that this 'quest for power' enjoys a renewed
vogue in contemporary French society, in the unsophisticated form of the relationship between the public and 'its'
explorers. Our adolescents too, from puberty onwards, are
free to obey the stimuli which have been acting upon them
from all sides since early childhood, and to escape, in some
way or other, from the temporary hold their civilization
has on them. The escape may take place upwards, through
the climbing of a mountain, or downwards, by descending
into the bowels of the earth, or horizontally, through travel
to remote countries. Or again, the desired extreme may be
a mental or moral one, as is the case with those individuals
who deliberately put themselves into such difficult situations that, in our present state of knowledge, they leave
themselves no possibility of survival.

Society shows complete indifference to what might be
called the rational outcome of such adventures. They
neither involve new scientific discoveries, nor make any
new contribution to poetry and literature, since the ac-

counts are, for the most part, appallingly feeble. What counts is the attempt in itself, not any possible aim. As in the native example just given, a young man who lives outside his social group for a few weeks or months, so as to expose himself (sometimes with conviction and sincerity, sometimes, on the contrary, with caution and craftiness— but such differences are not unknown in native societies) to an extreme situation, comes back endowed with a power which finds expression in the writing of newspaper articles and bestsellers and in lecturing to packed halls. However, its magic character is evidenced by the process of self-delusion operating in the society and which explains the phenomenon in all cases. The fact is that these primitive peoples, the briefest contact with whom can sanctify the traveller, these icy summits, deep caverns and impenetrable forests—all of them august settings for noble and profitable revelations—are all, in their different ways, enemies of our society, which pretends to itself that it is investing them with nobility at the very time when it is completing their destruction, whereas it viewed them with terror and disgust when they were genuine adversaries. The savages of the Amazonian forest are sensitive and powerless victims, pathetic creatures caught in the toils of mechanized civilization, and I can resign myself to understanding the fate which is destroying them; but I refuse to be the dupe of a kind of magic which is still more feeble than their own, and which brandishes before an eager public albums of coloured photographs, instead of the now vanished native masks. Perhaps the public imagines that the charms of the savages can be appropriated through the medium of these photographs. Not content with having eliminated savage life, and unaware even of having done so, it feels the need feverishly to appease the nostalgic cannibalism of history with the shadows of those that history has already destroyed.

Can it be that I, the elderly predecessor of those scourers of the jungle, am the only one to have brought back nothing but a handful of ashes? Is mine the only voice to bear witness to the impossibility of escapism? Like the Indian in the myth, I went as far as the earth allows one to go, and when I arrived at the world's end, I questioned the people, the creatures and things I found there and met with the same disappointment: 'He stood still, weeping bitterly, praying and moaning. And yet no mysterious sound reached his ears, nor was he put to sleep in order to be transported, as he slept, to the temple of the magic animals. For him there could no longer be the slightest doubt: no power, from anyone, had been granted him . . .'

Dreams, 'the god of the savages', as the old missionaries used to say, have always slipped through my fingers like quicksilver. But a few shining particles may have remained stuck, here and there. At Cuiaba, perhaps, where the gold nuggets used to come from? At Ubatuba, now a deserted port, but where the galleons used to be loaded two hundred years ago? In the air over the Arabian deserts, which were pink and green with the pearly lustre of ear-shells? In America or in Asia? On the Newfoundland sandbanks, the Bolivian plateaux or the hills along the Burmese frontier? I can pick out at random a name still steeped in the magic of legend: Lahore.

An airfield in a featureless suburb; endless avenues planted with trees and lined with villas; an hotel, standing in an enclosure and reminiscent of some Normandy stud farm, being just a row of several identical buildings, the doors of which, all at ground level and juxtaposed like stable-doors, led into identical apartments, each with a sitting-room in the front, a dressing-room with washing facilities at the back, and a bedroom in the middle. Two miles of avenue led to a provincial-looking square, with more avenues branching off, and dotted with occasional shops—a chemist's, a photographer's, a bookseller's or a watchmaker's. Caught in this vast and meaningless expanse, I felt that what I was looking for was already beyond my reach. Where was the old, the real Lahore? In order to get to it, on the far side of these badly laid out and already decrepit suburbs, I still had to go through two miles of bazaar, where, with the help of mechanical saws, cheap jewellery was being manufactured out of gold the thickness of tin-plate, and where there were stalls displaying cosmetics, medicines and imported plastic objects. I wondered if I was at last discovering the real Lahore in dark little streets, where I had to flatten myself against the wall to make way for flocks of sheep with blue-and-pink dyed fleece and for buffaloes—each as big as three cows—which barged into one in friendly fashion, and, still more often, for lorries. Was it when I was gazing at crumbling woodwork, eaten away with age? I might have got some idea of its delicate fretting and carving had the approach to it not been made impossible by the ramshackle electrical supply system, which spread its festoons of wire from wall to wall, like a spider's web all through the old town. From time to time, for a second or two and over the space of a few yards, an image or an echo would seem to surge up from the past: for instance, the clear, serene tinkling in the little street where the gold and silver beaters worked, as if some genie with a thousand arms were absent-mindedly striking a xylophone. Immediately beyond, I again found myself in a vast network of avenues, which had been driven through the ruins of 500-year-old houses, damaged in recent riots —but they had in any case been so often destroyed and repaired that they were of an ageless and indescribable decrepitude. In exploring all this, I was being true to myself as an archaeologist of space, seeking in vain to recreate a lost local colour with the help of fragments and debris.

Then, insidiously, illusion began to lay its snares. I wished I had lived in the days of *real* journeys, when it was still possible to see the full splendour of a spectacle that had not yet been blighted, polluted and spoilt; I wished I had not trodden that ground as myself, but as Bernier, Tavernier or Manucci did . . . Once embarked upon, this guessing game can continue indefinitely. When was the best time to see India? At what period would the study of the Brazilian savages have afforded the purest satisfaction, and revealed them in their least adulterated state? Would it have been better to arrive in Rio in the eighteenth century with Bougainville, or in the sixteenth with Léry and Thevet? For every five years I move back in time, I am able to save a custom, gain a ceremony or share in another belief. But I know the texts too well not to realize that, by going back a century, I am at the same time forgoing data and lines of inquiry which would offer intellectual enrichment. And so I am caught within a circle from which there is no escape: the less human societies were able to communicate with each other and therefore to corrupt each other through contact, the less their respective emissaries were able to perceive the wealth and significance of their diversity. In short, I have only two possibilities: either I can be like some traveller of the olden days, who was faced with a stupendous spectacle, all, or almost all, of which eluded him, or worse still, filled him with scorn and disgust; or I can be a modern traveller, chasing after the vestiges of a vanished reality. I lose on both counts, and more seriously than may at first appear, for, while I complain of being able to glimpse no more than the shadow of the past, I may be insensitive to reality as it is taking shape at this very moment, since I have not reached the stage of development at which I would be capable of perceiving it. A few hundred years hence, in this same place, another traveller, as despairing as myself, will mourn the disappearance of what I might have seen, but failed to see. I am subject to a double infirmity: all that I perceive offends me, and I constantly reproach myself for not seeing as much as I should.

For a long time I was paralysed by this dilemma, but I have the feeling that the cloudy liquid is now beginning to settle. Evanescent forms are becoming clearer, and confusion is being slowly dispelled. What has happened is that time has passed. Forgetfulness, by rolling my memories along in its tide, has done more than merely wear them down or consign them to oblivion. The profound structure it has created out of the fragments allows me to achieve a more stable equilibrium, and to see a clearer pattern. One order has been replaced by another. Between these two cliffs, which preserve the distance between my gaze and its object, time, the destroyer, has begun to pile up rubble. Sharp edges have been blunted and whole sections have collapsed: periods and places collide, are juxtaposed or are inverted, like strata displaced by the tremors on the crust of an ageing planet. Some insignificant detail belonging to the distant past may now stand out like a peak, while whole layers of my past have disappeared without trace. Events without any apparent connection, and originating from incongruous periods and places, slide one over the other and suddenly crystallize into a sort of edifice which seems to have been conceived by an architect wiser than my personal history. 'Every man', wrote Chateaubriand, 'carries within him a world which is composed of all that he has seen and loved, and to which he constantly returns, even when he is travelling through, and seems to be living in, some different world.'* Henceforth, it will be possible to bridge the gap between the two worlds. Time, in an unexpected way, has extended its isthmus between life and myself; twenty years of forgetfulness were required before I could establish communion with my earlier experience, which I had sought the world over without understanding its significance or appreciating its essence.

---

* *Voyages en Italie*, entry dated December 11th.

PART TWO

Travel Notes

---

5. LOOKING BACK

My career was decided one day in the autumn of 1934, at nine o'clock in the morning, by a telephone call from Célestin Bouglé, who was then head of the Ecole Normale Supérieure. For a few years past, he had shown himself to be well disposed towards me, but in a rather remote and reserved way: first, because I was not a *normalien,* and then, more especially, because even if I had been, I did not belong to his 'stable', whose interests he jealously furthered. No doubt, he had been unable to find any better candidate, since he asked me bluntly: 'Do you still want to study anthropology?'—'Most certainly.'—'Then apply for a post as a teacher of sociology at the University of São Paulo. The suburbs are full of Indians, whom you can study at the weekends. But you must give Georges Dumas a firm answer before midday.'

Brazil and South America did not mean much to me. However, I can still remember, with absolute clarity, the pictures conjured up by this unexpected proposal. I imagined exotic countries to be the exact opposite of ours, and the term 'antipodes' had a richer and more naïve significance for me than its merely literal meaning. I would have been most surprised if anyone had told me that an animal or vegetable species could have the same appearance on both sides of the globe. I expected animal, tree or blade of grass to be radically different, and its tropical nature to be glaringly obvious at a glance. In my imagination, I associated Brazil with clumps of twisted palm trees concealing bizarrely designed kiosks and pavilions, and I assumed the atmosphere to be permeated with the smell of burning perfumes, an olfactory detail which had no doubt crept in through an unconscious awareness of the similarity of sound between 'Brésil' and 'grésiller' (to splutter in burning), and which is more responsible than any actual experience for the fact that, even now, I think of Brazil first and foremost as a burning perfume.

Considered in retrospect, these images no longer seem so

arbitrary. I have learnt that the truth of a situation is to be found not in day-to-day observation but in that patient and piecemeal process of distillation which the linguistic ambiguity suggesting the idea of a perfume perhaps encouraged me to practise in the form of a spontaneous pun, the vehicle of a symbolic interpretation that I was not yet in a position to formulate clearly. Exploration is not so much a covering of surface distance as a study in depth: a fleeting episode, a fragment of landscape or a remark overheard may provide the only means of understanding and interpreting areas which would otherwise remain barren of meaning.

At the time, Bouglé's wild promise about Indians was to set me different problems. I suppose he had been led to believe that São Paulo was a native town, at least as regards its suburbs, through confusion with Mexico City or Tegucigalpa. He was a philosopher who had once written a book entitled *The Caste System in India,* without ever pausing to consider whether it would not be better to go to India first and see the situation for himself ('in the flux of events, it is institutions which survive' was his lofty assertion in the preface to the 1927 edition). He did not believe that the conditions in which the natives happened to be living could have serious implications for anthropological research. It is well known, moreover, that he was not the only official sociologist to display such indifference; indeed, examples of it are still to be found.

Be that as it may, I was too ignorant myself not to accept illusions which fitted in so conveniently with my plans, especially since Georges Dumas's ideas on the subject were just as vague. He had known southern Brazil at a time when the extermination of the native communities had not yet been completed, and, what is more important, the people he liked to frequent—dictators, feudal landlords and patrons of the arts—could hardly enlighten him in this connection.

I was therefore very surprised when, at a luncheon party to which I had been taken by Victor Margueritte, I heard the Brazilian Ambassador in Paris voice the official view: 'Indians? Alas, my dear sir, they all disappeared years ago. This is a very sad, very shameful episode in the history of my country. But the sixteenth-century Portuguese colonists were greedy, brutal men. One can hardly blame them for sharing the general barbarousness of the times. They would capture Indians, bind them to the mouths of their cannons and blow them to pieces. That is how the Indians were all got rid of. As a sociologist, you will discover fascinating things in Brazil, but forget about the Indians. You won't come across a single one . . .'

When I recall these remarks today, I find them quite incredible, even coming from a *gran fino* of 1934, and even given the fact that, at the time, the Brazilian elite (happily it has changed since then) could not bear any allusion to Indians or more generally to the primitive conditions of the interior, except to admit—or even suggest—that an Indian great-grandmother might be responsible for their slightly exotic cast of countenance, and not the few drops, or pints, of black blood which, unlike their ancestors of the imperial period, they already felt it incumbent upon them to try to conceal. Yet, in Luis de Souza-Dantas's case, there could be no doubt about his Indian ancestry, and he could well have prided himself on it. But, since he was an expatriate, who had opted for France in his teens, he had completely forgotten what his own country was really like, and the truth had been replaced in his memory by a kind of conventional, official idealization. In connection with such details as he still did recollect, I suppose he preferred to cast a slur on the Brazilians of the sixteenth century, so as to divert attention from the favourite pastime of the men of his parents' generation, and even of the period of his own youth, which was to collect the infected garments of smallpox victims from the hospitals and hang them, together with other gifts, along the paths still frequented by the Indian tribes. This produced the following remarkable result: in 1918, the maps of the state of São Paulo, which is as big as France, showed it as being two-thirds 'unknown territory inhabited only by Indians'; by the time I arrived in 1935, there was not a single Indian left, apart from a few families who used to come to the Santos beaches on Sundays to sell so-called curios. Fortunately, although there were no Indians in the suburbs of São Paulo, some were still to be found three thousand kilometres inland.

I cannot leave this period without pausing to bestow a friendly glance on another world of which I caught a glimpse, thanks to Victor Margueritte (the person who introduced me to the Brazilian embassy). He had remained on friendly terms with me after I had worked for him briefly as his secretary during my later student years. My

function had been to supervise the publication of one of his
books—*La patrie humaine*—by visiting a hundred or so
Parisian personalities to present them with inscribed copies
on behalf of 'le Maître' (he insisted on being given the
title). I also had to draft press notices and items for the
news columns suggesting to the critics suitable lines they
might take. Victor Margueritte has remained in my memory, not only because of the tactful manner in which he
behaved towards me, but also (and this is the case with
everything which makes a lasting impression on me) because of the contradiction between the man and his work.
His writings may appear naïve and crude, in spite of a
certain magnanimity of feeling, but the memory of the
man deserves to remain. His face had the somewhat feminine charm and delicacy of a Gothic angel, and his behaviour was marked by such instinctive nobility that his
faults—and vanity was not the least of them—could never
shock or irritate, since they seemed, in fact, to be an additional sign of his exceptional temperament and intellectual
ability.

He lived in the 17th *arrondissement* in a large, old-fashioned bourgeois flat, where, by now almost blind, he was
actively fussed over by his wife. In her case, age (which
removes the confusion, only possible in youth, between
physical and moral characteristics) had changed what had
once no doubt been admired as 'piquancy' into ugliness
and testiness.

He saw very few people, because he believed that the
young had failed to appreciate him, and because he had
been repudiated in official circles. But the main reason was
that he had set himself on such a high pedestal that he
found it increasingly difficult to find anyone with whom
he could communicate. Although I was never able to discover whether this had come about spontaneously or
through deliberate choice, he had, along with a few others,
shared in the founding of an international brotherhood of
supermen, consisting of five or six members, including
Keyserling, Ladislas Reymond, Romain Rolland, and, I
think, for a time Einstein. The basis of the connection was
the fact that every time one of the members published a
book, the others, scattered throughout the world, would
immediately hail it as one of the highest expressions of
human genius.

But what was most touching about Victor Margueritte

was the naïve way in which he tried to take upon himself the whole heritage of French literature. This was made easier for him through his having been born into a literary family; his mother had been a full cousin of Mallarmé, and so his affectation was buttressed with anecdotes and memories. Zola, the Goncourts, Balzac and Hugo were spoken about as if they were uncles and grandparents whose inheritance had been entrusted to his care. And when he exclaimed impatiently, 'They say I have no style! But what about Balzac; did he have a style?' one would have imagined oneself in the presence of a descendant of a line of kings, who was justifying a misdemeanour of his own by quoting the famous and ebullient temperament of one of his ancestors, which the ordinary mortal thinks of not as a personal characteristic but as the officially recognized explanation of some great upheaval in contemporary history, with the result that he is delighted to find it embodied in a living person. Other writers have been more talented; but few, no doubt, have been able to entertain, with such elegance, their aristocratic conception of their profession.

6. THE MAKING
OF AN ANTHROPOLOGIST

I was studying philosophy with a view to sitting the *agréga-tion* competitive examination, but this was the result less of a genuine vocation than of a dislike for the other subjects I had sampled up till then. When I reached the top or 'philosophy' class in the lycée, I was vaguely in favour of a kind of rationalistic monism, which I was prepared to justify and support; I therefore made great efforts to get into the section taught by Gustave Rodrigues, who had the reputation of being 'advanced'. He was, it is true, a militant member of the S.F.I.O., but on the philosophical level all he had to offer was a mixture of Bergsonism and Neo-Kantism which I found extremely disappointing. He expounded his dry dogmatic views with great fervour and gesticulated passionately throughout his lessons. I have never known so much naïve conviction allied to greater intellectual poverty. He committed suicide in 1940 when the Germans entered Paris.

It was in that class that I first began to learn that every problem, whether serious or trifling, may be solved by the application of an always identical method, which consists in contrasting two traditional views of the question; the first is introduced by means of a justification on common-sense grounds, then the justification is destroyed with the help of the second view; finally, both are dismissed as being equally inadequate, thanks to a third view which reveals the incomplete character of the first two; these are now reduced by verbal artifice to complementary aspects of one and the same reality: form and subject-matter, container and content, being and appearance, continuity and discontinuity, essence and existence, etc. Such an exercise soon becomes purely verbal, depending, as it does, on a certain skill in punning, which replaces thought: assonance, similarity in sound and ambiguity gradually come to form the basis of

42

those brilliantly ingenious intellectual shifts which are thought to be the sign of sound philosophizing.

Five years of study at the Sorbonne boiled down to acquiring skill in this form of mental gymnastics, the dangers of which are nevertheless obvious. In the first place, the technique by which intellectual balance is maintained is so simple that it can be applied in the case of any problem. To prepare ourselves for the examination and for the supreme ordeal of the *leçon d'agrégation* (the oral part, which consists in dealing with a question drawn from a hat, after a few hours' preparation), my fellow-students and I set ourselves wildly unlikely subjects. I was confident that, at ten minutes' notice, I could knock together an hour's lecture with a sound dialectical framework, on the respective superiority of buses and trams. Not only does this method provide a key to open any lock; it also leads one to suppose that the rich possibilities of thought can be reduced to a single, always identical pattern, at the cost of a few rudimentary adjustments. It is rather as if music could be reduced to a single melody, once the musician has realized that this melody can be read either in the treble or the bass clef. In this sense, our philosophical training exercised the intelligence but had a desiccating effect on the mind.

I can see an even graver danger in confusing the advancement of knowledge with the growing complexity of intellectual structures. We were asked to produce a dynamic synthesis, by starting from the least adequate theories and progressing towards the most subtle; but at the same time (since all our teachers were obsessed with the historical approach), we had to explain how the latter had gradually emerged from the former. Basically, it was not so much a system of discovering what was true and what was false as of understanding how mankind had gradually overcome certain contradictions. Philosophy was not *ancilla scientiarum*, the servant and auxiliary of scientific exploration, but a kind of aesthetic contemplation of consciousness by itself. It was seen as having evolved, in the course of the centuries, ever higher and bolder structures, as having solved problems of balance or support and as having invented logical refinements, and the result was held to be valid, in proportion to its technical perfection or internal coherence. The teaching of philosophy might be compared to instruction in a form of art history which proclaimed that Gothic was necessarily superior to Romanesque, and,

within the Gothic, the flamboyant style more perfect than
the primitive, but which did not raise any questions about
what was beautiful and what was not. The signifier did not
relate to any signified; there was no referent. Expertise replaced the truth. After years of this training, I now find
myself intimately convinced of a few unsophisticated beliefs, not very different from those I held at the age of
fifteen. Perhaps I see more clearly the inadequacy of these
intellectual tools; at least they have an instrumental value
which makes them suitable for the service I require of them.
I am in no danger of being deceived by their internal complexity, nor of losing sight of their practical purpose through
becoming absorbed in the contemplation of their wonderful
elaborateness.

However, I suspect that there were more personal causes
for the disgust which quickly made me abandon philosophy
and turn to anthropology, since it offered a way of escape.
After spending a happy year at the Mont de Marsan lycée,
teaching and preparing my course of lessons as I went
along, I was dismayed to discover at the beginning of the
next school year, after being transferred to Laon, that I
would have to repeat the same course for the rest of my
life. A peculiar feature—no doubt a weakness—of my
mental make-up is that I find it difficult to concentrate
twice on the same subject. Normally the *agrégation* is held
to be an inhuman ordeal, at the end of which, one is entitled, if one so wishes, to be left in peace for ever. In my
case, it was just the opposite. I passed the *agrégation* at the
first attempt and as the youngest candidate in my year, and
I had been in no way exhausted by my foray through doctrines, theories and hypotheses. My torment was to begin
later: I realized that I would be physically incapable of
delivering my lessons, unless I evolved a new course every
year. This handicap proved to be still more embarrassing
when I found myself having to act as an oral examiner:
as the questions cropped up at random, according to the
accidents of the draw, I was no longer sure what answers
the candidates were supposed to give. The dimmest of
them seemed to say all there was to be said. It was as if the
subjects were melting away before my eyes, through the
mere fact that I had once applied my mind to them.

Today I sometimes wonder if anthropology did not attract me, without my realizing this, because of a structural
affinity between the civilizations it studies and my particular

way of thinking. I have no aptitude for prudently cultivating a given field and gathering in the harvest year after year: I have a neolithic kind of intelligence. Like native bush fires, it sometimes sets unexplored areas alight; it may fertilize them and snatch a few crops from them, and then it moves on, leaving scorched earth in its wake. At the time, however, I was incapable of achieving any awareness of this deeper motivation. I knew nothing about anthropology, I had never attended any course and when Sir James Frazer paid his last visit to the Sorbonne to give a memorable lecture—in 1928, I think—it never occurred to me to attend, although I knew about it.

It is true that, from my earliest childhood, it had been my hobby to collect exotic curios. But it was an antiquarian interest, the direction of which was governed by the cost of things I could afford. As an adolescent, I was still so uncertain about what I wanted to do that the first person to give an opinion, André Cresson, one of my early philosophy teachers, suggested that law studies would be most suited to my temperament; I remember him with gratitude because of the half-truth concealed in his mistake.

So I gave up the idea of competing for the Ecole Normale Supérieure and enrolled as a law student, while at the same time studying for the *licence* in philosophy; I adopted this solution because it was so easy. A strange fatality hangs over the teaching of law. It is caught between theology, which at that time it resembled in spirit, and journalism, towards which it was beginning to swing as a result of the recent reforms, and so it seems unable to find any basis for itself that is at once solid and objective; it loses one of these virtues in trying to gain or retain the other. The jurist, who is himself an object of study for the social scientist, always makes one think of an animal trying to show the magic lantern to the zoologist. Fortunately, in those days, it was possible to get through examinations after only a couple of weeks' work, thanks to manuals which had to be learned by heart. But I was put off by the people studying law even more than by the barrenness of the subject. I doubt whether the distinction is still valid, but around 1928 the various first-year students could be divided into two distinct species, one might almost say two distinct races: law and medicine on the one hand, the arts and the sciences on the other.

However unattractive the terms extrovert and introvert

may be, they are no doubt the most appropriate ones for the expression of the contrast. On the one hand there was 'youth' (in the sense in which traditional folklore uses this term to signify a certain age group), noisy, aggressive, anxious to assert itself even at the cost of the worst kind of vulgarity, and politically to the extreme Right (of the period); on the other, prematurely aged adolescents, discreet, withdrawn, usually Left-wing, and whose aim was to be admitted to the ranks of the adults they themselves were busily trying to become.

There is a quite simple explanation for the difference. The extroverts, who are studying to enter the professions, behave as they do to celebrate their release from school and the fact that they already accept a definite place in the system of social functions. Finding themselves in an intermediary state between the undifferentiated role of the schoolboy and the specialized activity for which they are intended, they feel themselves to be in a marginal situation and claim contradictory privileges appropriate to both positions.

In the case of arts and science students, the usual openings—teaching, research and various miscellaneous careers—are quite different in kind. The student choosing them does not bid farewell to the world of childhood: on the contrary he is trying rather to remain with it. The teaching profession, after all, offers adults their only possibility of remaining at school. The arts or science student is characterized by an attitude of refusal towards the demands of the group. An almost monklike tendency inspires him to withdraw either temporarily or more permanently into study and to devote himself to the preservation and transmission of a heritage independent of the passing moment. As for the future scholar or researcher, his aim is commensurable only with the time-span of the universe. Nothing could be more mistaken, then, than to lead them to believe that their choice is a form of commitment; even when they think it is, the commitment does not consist in their accepting a particular datum and identifying themselves with one or other of its functions and in accepting the personal opportunities and risks it involves, but in judging it from the outside, as if they themselves were not part of it; their commitment is just their own special way of remaining uncommitted. In this respect, teaching and research are not to be confused with training for a profession. Their greatness and their misfortune is that they are a refuge or a mission.

In this opposition between, on the one hand, the professions, and, on the other, ambiguous activities which can be classed either as a mission or a refuge, partake of both, but are always rather more definitely one than the other, anthropology certainly occupies an exceptional position. It is the most extreme form of the second term of the contrast. While remaining human himself, the anthropologist tries to study and judge mankind from a point of view sufficiently lofty and remote to allow him to disregard the particular circumstances of a given society or civilization. The conditions in which he lives and works cut him off physically from his group for long periods; through being exposed to such complete and sudden changes of environment, he acquires a kind of chronic rootlessness; eventually, he comes to feel at home nowhere, and he remains psychologically maimed. Like mathematics or music, anthropology is one of the few genuine vocations. One can discover it in oneself, even though one may have been taught nothing about it.

To these individual peculiarities and social attitudes must be added other promptings of an essentially intellectual nature. It was during the decade from 1920 to 1930 that psychoanalytical theories became known in France. They taught me that the static oppositions around which we were advised to construct our philosophical essays and later our teaching—the rational and the irrational, the intellectual and the emotional, the logical and the pre-logical— amounted to no more than a gratuitous intellectual game. In the first place, beyond the rational there exists a more important and valid category—that of the meaningful, which is the highest mode of being of the rational, but which our teachers never so much as mentioned, no doubt because they were more intent on Bergson's *Essai sur les données immédiates de la conscience* than on F. de Saussure's *Cours de linguistique générale*. Next, Freud's work showed me that the oppositions did not really exist in this form, since it is precisely the most apparently emotional behaviour, the least rational procedures and so-called pre-logical manifestations which are at the same time the most meaningful. Rejecting the Bergsonian acts of faith and circular arguments which reduced beings and things to a state of mush the better to bring out their ineffability,

I came to the conclusion that beings and things could retain
their separate values without losing the clarity of outline
which defines them in relationship to teach other and gives
an intelligible structure to each. Knowledge is based
neither on renunciation nor on barter; it consists rather in
selecting *true* aspects, that is, those coinciding with the
properties of my thought. Not, as the Neo-Kantians
claimed, because my thought exercises an inevitable influence over things, but because it is itself an object. Being 'of
this world', it partakes of the same nature as the world.

However, this intellectual development, which I under-
went along with other members of my generation, was
given a particular colouring in my case by the intense interest geology had inspired in me ever since childhood. I
count among my most precious memories not so much
some expedition into an unknown region of central Brazil
as a hike along the flank of a limestone plateau in Languedoc to determine the line of contact between two geological
strata. It was sometimes quite different from a walk or a
simple exploration of space. It was a quest, which would
have seemed incoherent to some uninitiated observer, but
which I look upon as the very image of knowledge, with the
difficulties it involves and the delights it affords.

Every landscape appears first of all as a vast chaos, which
leaves one free to choose the meaning one wants to give
it. But, over and above agricultural considerations, geographical irregularities and the various accidents of history
and prehistory, the most majestic meaning of all is surely
that which precedes, commands and, to a large extent, explains the others. A pale blurred line, or an often almost
imperceptible difference in the shape and consistency of
rock fragments, are evidence of the fact that two oceans
once succeeded each other where, today, I can see nothing
but barren soil. As I follow the traces of their age-old
stagnation despite all obstacles—sheer cliff faces, landslides,
scrub or cultivated land—and disregarding paths and
fences, I seem to be proceeding in meaningless fashion. But
the sole aim of this contrariness is to recapture the master-
meaning, which may be obscure but of which each of the
others is a partial or distorted transposition.

When the miracle occurs, as it sometimes does; when, on
one side and the other of the hidden crack, there are
suddenly to be found cheek-by-jowl two green plants of
different species, each of which has chosen the most favour-

able soil; and when at the same time, two ammonites with unevenly intricate involutions can be glimpsed in the rock, thus testifying in their own way to a gap of several tens of thousands of years suddenly space and time become one: the living diversity of the moment juxtaposes and perpetuates the ages. Thought and emotion move into a new dimension where every drop of sweat, every muscular movement, every gasp of breath becomes symbolic of a past history, the development of which is reproduced in my body, at the same time as my thought embraces its significance. I feel myself to be steeped in a more dense intelligibility, within which centuries and distances answer each other and speak at last with one and the same voice.

When I became acquainted with Freud's theories, I quite naturally looked upon them as the application, to the individual human being, of a method the basic pattern of which is represented by geology. In both cases, the researcher, to begin with, finds himself faced with seemingly impenetrable phenomena; in both cases, in order to take stock of, and gauge, the elements of a complex situation, he must display subtle qualities, such as sensitivity, intuition and taste. And yet, the order which is thus introduced into a seemingly incoherent mass is neither contingent nor arbitrary. Unlike the history of the historians, that of the geologist is similar to the history of the psychoanalyst in that it tries to project in time—rather in the manner of a *tableau vivant*—certain basic characteristics of the physical or mental universe. I can take the simile of the *tableau vivant* further: the game called 'charades' provides a simple illustration of a procedure which consists in interpreting each action as the unfolding in time of certain eternal truths, the concrete aspect of which the charades are meant to re-create on the moral level, but which in other fields are referred to specifically as laws. In all these instances, the arousing of aesthetic curiosity leads directly to an acquisition of knowledge.

When I was about sixteen, I was introduced to Marxism by a young Belgian socialist, whom I had got to know on holiday, and who is now one of his country's ambassadors abroad. I was all the more delighted by Marx in that the reading of the works of the great thinker brought me into contact for the first time with the line of philosophical development running from Kant to Hegel; a whole new world was opened up to me. Since then, my admiration for

Marx has remained constant, and I rarely broach a new sociological problem without first stimulating my thought by rereading a few pages of *The 18th Brumaire of Louis Bonaparte* or the *Critique of Political Economy*. Incidentally, Marx's quality has nothing to do with whether or not he accurately foresaw certain historical developments. Following Rousseau, and in what I consider to be a definitive manner, Marx established that social science is no more founded on the basis of events than physics is founded on sense data: the object is to construct a model and to study its property and its different reactions in laboratory conditions in order later to apply the observations to the interpretation of empirical happenings, which may be far removed from what had been forecast.

At a different level of reality, Marxism seemed to me to proceed in the same manner as geology and psychoanalysis (taking the latter in the sense given it by its founder). All three demonstrate that understanding consists in reducing one type of reality to another; that the true reality is never the most obvious; and that the nature of truth is already indicated by the care it takes to remain elusive. For all cases, the same problem arises, the problem of the relationship between feeling and reason and the aim is the same: to achieve a kind of *superrationalism,* which will integrate the first with the second, without sacrificing any of its properties.

I was therefore opposed to the new metaphysical tendencies which were then emerging. Phenomenology I found objectionable in that it postulated a kind of continuity between experience and reality. I agreed that the latter encompasses and explains the former, but I had learned from my three sources of inspiration that the transition between one order and the other is discontinuous; that to reach reality one has first to reject experience, and then subsequently to reintegrate it into an objective synthesis devoid of any sentimentality. As for the intellectual movement which was to reach its peak in existentialism, it seemed to me to be anything but a legitimate form of reflection, because of its overindulgent attitude towards the illusions of subjectivity. The raising of personal preoccupations to the dignity of philosophical problems is far too likely to lead to a sort of shop-girl metaphysics, which may be pardonable as a didactic method but is extremely dangerous if it allows people to play fast-and-loose with the mission incumbent

on philosophy until science becomes strong enough to replace it: that is, to understand being in relationship to itself
and not in relationship to myself. Instead of doing away
with metaphysics, phenomenology and existentialism introduced two methods of providing it with alibis.

Between Marxism and psychoanalysis, which are social
sciences—one orientated towards society, the other towards the individual—and geology, which is a physical
science—but which has also fostered and nurtured history
both by its method and its aim—anthropology spontaneously establishes its domain: for mankind, which anthropology
looks upon as having no limits other than those of space,
gives a new meaning to the transformations of the terrestrial globe, as defined by geological history: this meaning is the product of the uninterrupted labour which goes
on all through the ages in the activities of societies as
anonymous as telluric forces, and in the minds of individuals whom the psychologist sees as particular case histories.
Anthropology affords me intellectual satisfaction: as a form
of history, linking up at opposite ends with world history
and my own history, it thus reveals the rationale common
to both. In proposing the study of mankind, anthropology
frees me from doubt, since it examines those differences
and changes in mankind which have a meaning for all men,
and excludes those peculiar to a single civilization, which
dissolve into nothingness under the gaze of the outside
observer. Lastly, it appeases that restless and destructive appetite I have already referred to, by ensuring me a virtually
inexhaustible supply of material, thanks to the diversity of
manners, customs and institutions. It allows me to reconcile
my character with my life.

This being so, it may seem strange that for so long I
should have remained deaf to the message which, even
during my lost years at school, was being transmitted to me
through the works of the leading French sociologists. As it
happened, the revelation did not occur until 1933–4, when
by chance I came across Robert H. Lowie's *Primitive Society*, which was by no means a recent work. The point
was that instead of presenting me with ideas taken from
books and immediately changed into philosophical concepts, it described the writer's actual experience of native
societies, and presented the significance of that experience
through his involvement. My mind was able to escape from
the claustrophobic, Turkish-bath atmosphere in which it

was being imprisoned by the practice of philosophical reflection. Once it had got out into the open air, it felt refreshed and renewed. Like a city-dweller transported to the mountains, I became drunk with space, while my dazzled eyes measured the wealth and variety of the objects surrounding me.

So started that long and intimate acquaintance with Anglo-American anthropology—carried on first, at a distance, through the medium of books, and later maintained by personal contact—which was to give rise to serious misunderstandings. In Brazil, to begin with, where the university professors expected me to join in teaching the kind of Durkheimian sociology towards which they themselves inclined, both because of the positivist tradition which is still very much alive in South America, and because of their desire to provide a philosophical basis for that moderate liberalism, which is the usual ideological weapon used by oligarchies to combat personal power. I arrived in a state of open revolt against Durkheim and against any attempt to use sociology for metaphysical purposes. At a time when I was doing my best to widen my horizons, I was hardly in a mood to rebuild the prison walls. Since then I have often been criticized for showing too slavish an obedience to Anglo-American thought. This is absolute nonsense. Apart from the fact that, at this moment, I am probably more faithful than anyone else to the Durkheimian tradition—and abroad everybody is aware of this—the authors to whom I willingly proclaim my debt, Lowie, Kroeber and Boas, seem to me to be as far removed as possible from the James or Dewey kind of American philosophy which has been out of date for so long, or from what is now called logical positivism. Since they were Europeans by birth and had been trained in Europe or by European professors, they represent something quite different: a synthesis reflecting, on the level of knowledge, that other synthesis which Columbus had made objectively possible four centuries earlier: the synthesis of a strong scientific method with the unique experimental field offered by the New World at a time when American anthropologists not only had the best available libraries, but could leave their universities and visit native communities as easily as we could go to the Basque country or the Riviera. What I am praising is not an intellectual tradition but an historical situation. It must have been an extraordinary advantage to have access to communities which had never yet been the object of serious investigation and which were still quite well preserved since their destruction had only just begun. Let me quote an anecdote to illustrate what I mean. An Indian, through some miracle, was the sole survivor after the massacre of certain savage California tribes. For years he lived unnoticed in the vicinity of large towns, still chipping stones for the arrow-heads with which he did his hunting. Gradually however, all the animals disappeared. One day the Indian was found naked and dying of hunger on the outskirts of a suburb. He ended his days peacefully as a porter at the University of California.

7. SUNSET

These lengthy and superfluous cogitations are leading up to the fact that one morning, in February 1934, I arrived in Marseilles in order to take ship for Santos. Later there were to be many other departures, and all of them have blended together in my memory, which has retained only a few distinct recollections: first, the peculiar gaiety of winter in the South of France; under a very pale blue sky, which was even more impalpable than usual, the biting air afforded the almost unbearable pleasure that one gets, when thirsty, from gulping down some iced, fizzy liquid. Contrasting with it were the heavy odours clinging about the corridors of the moored and overheated ship, a mixture of sea smells, whiffs of cooking from the galleys and the tang of fresh paint. I also remember the satisfaction and reassurance—I might almost say the serene happiness—of being dimly conscious in the middle of the night of the throbbing of the engines and the rustling of the water against the hull, as if movement were creating a sort of stability more perfect in essence than immobility; indeed, when one was suddenly wakened up at night by the sensation of having stopped in some port, motionlessness aroused a feeling of insecurity and discomfort, and one was disturbed by the alteration in what one had become used to as the natural course of things.

These ships called at many ports. Indeed, the first week of the trip was spent almost entirely ashore, while the cargo was being loaded or unloaded, and we sailed during the night. Each morning, on awakening, we found ourselves docked in a new port: Barcelona, Tarragona, Valencia, Alicante, Malaga, and sometimes Cadiz; or again, Algiers, Oran and Gibraltar, before the longest stretch leading to Casablanca, and lastly to Dakar. Then we started on the main crossing, either directly to Rio and Santos, or more infrequently with a resumption towards the end of the slower movement along the coast, and stops at the Brazilian ports of Recife, Bahia and Victoria. The air gradually became warmer, the Spanish sierras went slowly by on the horizon and, off the African coast, which was too low and swampy to be directly visible, the spectacle was prolonged for days on end by mirages representing hillocks and cliff faces. It was the opposite of a voyage. More than a means of transport, the ship seemed to us to be a dwelling-place and a home, in front of which the revolving stage of the world would halt some new setting every morning.

However, the anthropological approach was still so foreign to me that I did not think of taking advantage of these opportunities. I have learned since then what a useful training in observation such short glimpses of a town, an area or a culture can provide and how—because of the intense concentration forced upon one by the brevity of the stay—one may even grasp certain features which, in other circumstances, might have long remained hidden. I found other sights more attractive and, with the beginner's lack of sophistication, I watched enthralled from the empty deck as, every day, for the space of a few minutes, in all quarters of a horizon vaster than any I had ever seen before, the rising and the setting of the sun presented the beginning, development and conclusion of supernatural cataclysms. If I could find a language in which to perpetuate those appearances, at once so unstable and so resistant to description, if it were granted to me to be able to communicate to others the phases and sequences of a unique event which would never recur in the same terms, then—so it seemed to me—I should in one go have discovered the deepest secrets of my profession: however strange and peculiar the experiences to which anthropological research might expose me, there would be none whose meaning and importance I could not eventually make clear to everybody.

I wonder if, after all these years, I could ever again achieve such a state of grace. Would I be able to relive those feverish moments when, notebook in hand, I jotted down second by second the expressions which would perhaps enable me to fix those evanescent and ever-renewed forms? I am still fascinated by the attempt and often find myself risking my hand at it.

Written on board ship

For scientists, dawn and twilight are one and the same phenomenon and the Greeks thought likewise, since they had a single word with a different qualifying adjective according to whether they were referring to morning or evening. This confusion is a clear expression of the predominant interest in theoretical speculation and betrays remarkable neglect of the concrete aspect of things. It may well be that any given point of the earth oscillates with an indivisible movement between the zone of incidence of the solar rays and the zone in which sunlight misses it or returns to it. But in fact no two phenomena could be more different from each other than night and morning. Daybreak is a prelude, the close of day an overture which occurs at the end instead of the beginning, as in old operas. The face of the sun foretells the immediate nature of the weather; it is dark and lowering if there is to be rain during the early hours of the morning, but rosy, buoyant and frothy if the light is to be clear. But dawn is no guarantee of the nature of the rest of the day. It starts the meteorological process and declares: it is going to rain, it is going to be fine. Sunset is quite a different matter; it is a complete performance with a beginning, a middle and an end. And the spectacle offers a sort of small-scale image of the battles, triumphs and defeats which have succeeded each other during twelve hours in tangible form; but also at a slower speed. Dawn is only the beginning of the day; twilight is a repetition of it. That is why men pay more attention to the setting than to the rising sun; dawn only supplies them with information supplementary to that given by the thermometer or barometer and—in the case of the less civilized—by the phases of the moon, the flight of birds or the movement of the tides. A sunset, on the other hand, elevates them and combines in mysterious patterns the accidents of wind, cold, heat or rain in which their physical beings have been buffeted. The operations of consciousness can also be read in these fluffy constellations. When the sky begins to brighten with the glow of sunset (just as, in certain theatres, the beginning of the performance is indicated, not by the triple knocking customary in France, but by the sudden switching on of the footlights), the peasant pauses as he walks along the country path, the fisherman lets his boat float idly and the savage blinks, as he sits over his now paler fire. Remembering is one of man's great pleasures, but not in so far as memory operates literally, since few individuals would agree to relive the fatigues and sufferings that they nevertheless delight in recalling. Memory is life itself, but of a different quality. And so, it is when the sun declines towards the polished surface of calm water, like alms bestowed by some heavenly miser, or when its disc outlines mountain summits like a hard, jagged leaf, that man is eminently able to receive, in a short-lived daydream, the revelation of the opaque forces, the mists and flashing lights that throughout the day he has dimly felt to be at war within himself.

Very sinister struggles must, then, have taken place within the souls of men, since the insignificance of external events in no way justified any extravagant atmospheric display. Nothing notable had occurred during the day. Towards four o'clock in the afternoon —precisely at that point when the sun, now in mid-career, is losing its clearness of outline, but not yet its brightness, and everything is blurred in a thick golden light which seems to have been deliberately accumulated so as to conceal some preliminary—the *Mendoza* changed course. At each rocking motion caused by the slight swell, the heat began to make itself felt more insistently, but the curve followed by the boat was so imperceptible that the change of direction might have been taken for a slight increase in the normal roll. As a matter of fact, no one paid any attention to it, since nothing more closely resembles a purely geometrical transfer from A to B than a crossing on the high seas. No landscape is present to testify to the slow transition along lines of latitude or the crossing of isotherms or rain-curves. Fifty kilometres along a land road can produce the impression of a change of planet, but five thousand kilometres of ocean present an unchanging spectacle, at least to the unpractised eye. No worry about the itinerary to be followed or the direction to be taken, no knowledge of the invisible lands present beyond the convex horizon, nothing of that kind nagged at the passengers' minds. It seemed to them that they had been shut within a narrow space for a predetermined number of days, not because a particular distance had to be covered, but rather so that they could expiate the privilege of being transported from one end of the earth to the other, without their limbs having to make the slightest effort, since they had, in any case, been made too soft by sleeping in in the mornings and by lazy meals which, for a long time now, had ceased to bring any sensual enjoyment but were looked forward to as a diversion (provided they were exorbitantly protracted) with which to fill the emptiness of the days.

Moreover, there was no sign that any effort was being made. One realized, of course, that somewhere in the depths of that big box there were engines, with men around them making them work. But they did not care to be visited, nor did the passengers care to visit them, nor did the officers care to show the latter to the former or the former to the latter. One could only wander idly about the body of the ship where the work of some solitary sailor putting a few dabs of paint on to a ventilator or the economical movements of the stewards in blue overalls propelling a damp cloth along the first-class corridors offered the only proof of the regular recession of nautical miles, which could be heard vaguely lapping against the rusty hull.

At 5.40 p.m. the sky, to the west, seemed to be cluttered with a complex structure, which was perfectly horizontal in its lower part, like the sea, and indeed one might have thought that it had become detached from the sea through some incomprehensible movement upwards from the horizon, or had been separated from it through the insertion between them of a thick, invisible layer of crystal. Hooked to the top, and hanging towards the depths of the sky, as if through the effect of an inverted force of gravity, were drifting scaffoldings, bulging pyramids and frothy bubblings immobilized in the form of mouldings representing clouds, but which real clouds resemble when they have the polished surface and bulbous relief of carved and gilded wood. This confused mass which concealed the sun stood out in dark colours, with only a few touches of brightness, except towards the top where spurts of flame could be seen rising.

Still higher in the sky, streaks of dappled blondness were decomposing into nonchalant twists which seemed devoid of matter and purely luminous in texture.

On looking along the horizon towards the north, one

could see how the main structure grew narrower and
rose up in a scattering of clouds, behind which there
emerged, in the far distance, a higher bar with a flam-
ing top; on the side nearest the sun—which, however,
remained invisible—its light edged these remnants with
a strong border. Further to the north, the variegated
forms dwindled away and there was only the bar itself,
dull and flat, dissolving in the sea.

To the south, the same bar appeared again, but surmounted by great flagstones of cloud, which rested
like cosmological dolmens on the smoking tips of the
supporting mass.

If one turned one's back completely on the sun and
looked towards the east, one could see two superimposed groups of clouds which were drawn out sideways and seemed to stand out against the light, because
the sun's rays fell behind them lighting up a whole
area of hillocky, bloated but ethereal ramparts, all
glistening, like mother-of-pearl, with pink, mauve and
silvered gleams.

Meanwhile, behind the celestial reefs which cluttered
the sky to the west, the sun was slowly advancing; at
each new stage in its fall, one or other of its rays
would pierce the opaque mass or would find its way
through along a path which, at the moment when the
beam of light appeared, cut the obstacle into a pile of
circular sectors, different in size and luminous intensity. At times, the light would be withdrawn, as if a fist
had been clenched and the cloudy mitten would allow
no more than one or two stiff and gleaming fingers to
appear. Or an incandescent octopus would move out
from the vaporous grottoes and then there would be a
fresh withdrawal.

There are two quite distinct phases in a sunset. At
first, the sun acts as an architect. Only later (when its
rays are reflected and not direct) does it become a
painter. As soon as it disappears behind the horizon,
the light weakens, thus creating planes of vision which
increase in complexity with every second. Broad daylight is inimical to perspective, but between day and
night there is room for an architecture which is as
fantastic as it is provisional. With the darkness, everything is flattened out again, like some marvellously
coloured Japanese toy.

The first phase began at 5.45 p.m. precisely. The sun was already low, but was not yet touching the horizon. At the instant when it appeared below the cloud structure, it seemed to burst like an egg-yolk and splash light all over the shapes to which it was still attached. This spilling of light was soon succeeded by a withdrawal; the surrounding area became dulled and, in the void between the upper edge of the ocean and the lower edge of the clouds, there appeared a misty cordillera, which at one moment was still gleaming and indefinable and at the next dark and clear-cut. At the same time, from being flat it became voluminous. The solid little black objects moved in a lazy, migratory way across a broad, red-hot zone which rose slowly from the horizon into the sky and began the colour phase.

Little by little, the profound structures of the evening withdrew. The mass which had occupied the western sky throughout the day appeared laminated like a sheet of metal illuminated from behind, first by a golden, then a vermilion, then a cherry, glow. Contorted clouds, which would eventually disappear, were already being melted by the glow, scoured by it and carried upwards in a whirl of wisps.

Innumerable networks of vapour suddenly appeared in the sky; they seemed to be distributed in all directions horizontally, obliquely, perpendicularly and even spirally. The sun's rays, as they gradually declined (like a violin bow which is placed at different angles to touch different strings), made each network in turn explode into a spectrum of colours that one would have said was the arbitrary and exclusive property of each. At the moment when it showed itself, each network had the clearness of outline, the exactness and fragile stiffness of spun glass, but then it slowly dissolved, as if its substance, overheated through exposure in a flame-filled sky, were darkening in colour, losing its individuality and spreading out in an ever-thinner layer until it disappeared from the scene, at the same time revealing another, freshly spun network. At the end, all that was left were blurred blues running into each other, just as liquids of different colours and densities, poured one over the other into a transparent bowl, slowly begin to blend, in spite of their apparent stability.

After that, it became very difficult to follow the spectacle which seemed to be repeated, at intervals of minutes or sometimes even seconds, in distant parts of the sky. Towards the east, as soon as the sun's disc had touched the opposite horizon, there suddenly materialized, at a great height and with acid-mauve tints, clouds which until then had been invisible. The vision quickly amplified and was enriched with new details and shades of colour, and then it all began to fade sideways, from right to left, as if someone were rubbing it out slowly and surely with a duster. After a few seconds, the cleansed slate of the sky rose again above the cloudy ramparts. But the latter were taking on a white or grey cast, while the sky grew pink.

In the direction of the sun, a new bar now rose up behind the previous one, which had hardened into a uniform, confused cement block. Now it was the other which was crowned with flame. When its red effulgence began to fade, the dappled effects in the depths of the sky, which had not yet played their part, slowly acquired volume. Their lower sides became golden and burst; their tops, which had been glistening, changed to browns and purples. At the same time, it was as if their substance were being viewed under a microscope: one could see that it was made up of innumerable tiny filaments, which supported their plump forms like a skeleton.

By now, all direct rays from the sun had completely disappeared. The sky no longer held anything but pink and yellow colours: shrimp, salmon, flax, straw; and then this discreet richness could be felt fading away too. The heavenly landscape was re-created in a range of whites, blues and greens. Yet small corners of the horizon still enjoyed ephemeral and independent life. To the left, a hitherto unperceived veil suddenly came into view, like a whimsical mixture of mysterious greens; these gradually changed into reds, at first intense, then dark, then purple, then coal-black, and then the veil was no more than an irregular charcoal mark on grainy paper. Behind, the sky was an alpine yellowy green and the bar still remained opaque with rigid outlines. In the western sky, little horizontal

streaks of gold still sparkled for a moment or two, but
to the north it was almost night: the hillocky ramparts appeared as whitish protuberances under a lime-
washed sky.

Nothing is more mysterious than the series of always identical but unpredictable processes by which
night follows day. Its mark appears suddenly in the
sky, attended by uncertainty and anguish. No one can
foresee the form that the resurgence of night will
adopt on this unique occasion. Through some incomprehensible alchemy, each colour succeeds in changing
into its complementary colour, although we know perfectly well that, to achieve the same effect, a painter
would have to open a fresh tube and squeeze it on to
his palette. But for night, there can be no limit to the
mixing of colours, since night is the beginning of a
false spectacle: the sky changes from pink to green,
but this is because certain clouds, without my noticing
it, have become bright red and so, by contrast, make
the sky seem green, although it was undoubtedly pink,
but so pale a pink that the shades could not withstand
the extreme intensity of the new colour, which, however, had not struck me, since the transition from gold
to red causes less surprise than the transition from pink
to green. And so night comes on as if by stealth.

Thus, the night began to replace a vision of gold
and scarlet by its negative, in which the warm tones
were replaced by whites and greys. The photographic
plate of night slowly revealed a seascape above the sea,
an immense screen of clouds, in front of an oceanic
sky, tapering off into parallel peninsulas, as a flat,
sandy coast might be seen from a swerving, low-flying
plane, stretching its arrows into the sea. The illusion
was increased by the last glimmerings of daylight
which, as they struck the cloudy points at a very
oblique angle, made them stand out in relief as if they
were solid rocks—such as those that, at other times,
are sculpted with light and shade—as if the sun could
no longer use its shining engraving tools on porphyry
and granite, but only on weak and vaporous substances, although in its decline it retained the same
style.

Against this background of cloud which resembled
a coastal landscape, as the sky gradually became less

cluttered, there could be seen appearing beaches, lagoons, swarms of little islands and sandbanks, all flooded by the inert ocean of sky, which peppered the dissolving mass with fiords and inland lakes. And because the sky bordering on those cloudy arrows had the appearance of an ocean, and because the sea normally reflects the colour of the sky, the heavenly picture was a reconstitution of a distant landscape on which the sun would set once more. Besides, one had only to look at the real sea far below to escape from the mirage: it was no longer the scorching sheet it had been at midday or the graceful, shimmering surface that had appeared after dinner. The light-rays, which were now almost horizontal, illumined only the sides of the waves that were turned towards them and left the rest in shadow. The water therefore stood out in relief, with clear, emphatic shadows, which seemed to have been hollowed out of metal. All transparency was gone.

Then, by a very usual, but as always imperceptible and immediate, transition, evening gave way to night. All was changed. In the sky, which was opaque at the horizon, then a sickly yellow rather further up and blue at its highest point, the last clouds engendered by the closing day were in process of scattering. Soon they were no more than hollow, feeble shadows, like the flats of some stage set, which are suddenly revealed in all their shoddy, provisional fragility when the lights have been extinguished, so that one can see that the illusion they created depended not on themselves but on some trick of lighting or perspective. A little while before, they had been alive and had changed with every second that passed; now they congealed in a painful, immutable form, in the midst of a sky the growing darkness of which would soon confuse them with itself.

PART THREE

The New World

---

8. THE DOLDRUMS

At Dakar, we had said goodbye to the Old World and, without sighting the Cape Verde islands, had reached the fateful latitude seven degrees north, where in 1498, during his third voyage, Columbus, who was heading in the right direction for the discovery of Brazil, changed course towards the north-west and so managed, by some miracle, to arrive two weeks later at Trinidad and the coast of Venezuela.

We were approaching Le Pot-au-Noir (the Doldrums), which was greatly feared by the old navigators. The winds peculiar to both hemispheres stop on either side of this area, and the sails would hang for weeks on end without a single breath of wind to stir them into life. The air is so still that one might think oneself in some confined space instead of out on the open sea; dark clouds, with no breeze to disturb their balance, are affected only by gravity, and slowly disintegrate as they drift down towards the sea. Were they less sluggish, their straggling tips could trail across the polished surface of the sea which, lit indirectly by the rays of an invisible sun, has a dull, oily sheen, much brighter than the sky, which remains inky black, so that the normal relationship of luminosity between air and water is reversed. If one looks at the vista the wrong way up, a more likely seascape appears, in which sky and sea have changed places. Across the horizon, which appears closer because of the passivity of the elements and the relative dimness of the light, occasional squalls can be seen lazily moving, like blurred, short-lived columns which still further diminish the apparent distance between the sea and the overcast sky. Between these adjoining surfaces the boat slips along with a kind of anxious haste, as if it had only a short period of grace in which to escape being smothered. From time to time, a squall approaches the ship, loses its outlines, invades the whole of space and lashes the deck with its wet thongs. Then, having passed beyond it resumes

its visible form, while its presence as a volume of sound
dies away.

All sign of life had disappeared from the sea. In front of
the ship, black ripplings of dolphins, more solid and rythmi-
cal than the breaking of the foam against the prow, had
gracefully preceded the white tips of the retreating waves;
now no jet from a blower-dolphin cut across the horizon,
nor was the sea any longer intensely blue and peopled by
fleets of nautili, with their delicate mauve-and-pink membranes outstretched as sails. And, when we got to the far
side of the oceanic depths, would all the marvels seen by
the old navigators still be there to greet us? When the latter
travelled through these unexplored regions, they were less
concerned with discovering a new world than with verifying
the past of the old. They confirmed the existence of Adam
and Ulysses. When Columbus landed on the coast of the
West Indies after his first voyage, he may have thought that
he had reached Japan, but he was still more certain of having rediscovered the earthly paradise. The four hundred
years which had elapsed since then could never wipe out
the tremendous time-gap which kept the New World outside the commotions of history during ten or twenty thousand years. Something would no doubt survive, but on a
different level. I was soon to learn that, although South
America was no longer an Eden before the Fall, thanks to
its aura of mystery, it still remained a golden age, at least
for those who had money. Its privileged position was beginning to melt away like snow in the sun. All that is left
today is one small precious patch; at the same time as it
has become accessible only to the privileged few, it has
changed in character: from being eternal it has become
historic; from being metaphysical it has become social. The
earthly paradise glimpsed by Columbus was to be per-
petuated, and at the same time debased, in a gracious life-
style reserved solely for the rich.

The inky sky over the Doldrums and the oppressive atmosphere are more than just an obvious sign of the near-
ness of the equator. They epitomize the moral climate in
which two worlds have come face to face. This cheerless
sea between them, and the calmness of the weather whose
only purpose seems to be to allow evil forces to gather
fresh strength, are the last mystical barrier between two
regions so diametrically opposed to each other through
their different conditions that the first people to become

aware of the fact could not believe that they were both equally human. A continent barely touched by man lay exposed to men whose greed could no longer be satisfied by their own continent. Everything would be called into question by this second sin: God, morality and law. In simultaneous yet contradictory fashion, everything would be verified in practice and revoked in principle: the Garden of Eden, the Golden Age of antiquity, the Fountain of Youth, Atlantis, the Hesperides, the Islands of the Blessed, would be found to be true; but revelation, salvation, customs and law would be challenged by the spectacle of a purer, happier race of men (who, of course, were not really purer or happier, although a deep-seated remorse made them appear so). Never had humanity experienced such a harrowing test, and it will never experience such another, unless, some day, millions of miles from our own world, we discover some other globe, inhabited by thinking beings. We have at least the advantage of knowing that the distance can in theory be bridged, whereas the early navigators feared they might be venturing into the void.

In order to grasp the absolute, total and intransigent nature of the dilemmas by which the men of the sixteenth century felt themselves to be faced, one must remember certain incidents. In what used to be called Hispaniola (today Haiti and Santo Domingo) the native population numbered about one hundred thousand in 1492, but had dropped to two hundred a century later, since people died of horror and disgust at European civilization even more than of smallpox and physical ill-treatment. Commission after commission was sent out to determine the nature of the inhabitants. If they were really men, could they be the descendants of the ten lost tribes of Israel? Were they Mongols who had ridden there on elephants? Or Scotsmen brought over several centuries before by Prince Modoc? Had they always been pagans or were they lapsed Catholics who had once been baptised by Saint Thomas? There was some uncertainty about whether they were men, and not diabolical creatures or beasts. This was King Ferdinand's attitude, since in 1512 he imported white slave girls into the West Indies with the sole aim of preventing Spaniards marrying natives 'who were far from being rational creatures'. The colonists' reaction to Las Casas's attempts to abolish forced labour was one of incredulity rather than

indignation: 'So,' they exclaimed, 'are we even to be deprived of our beasts of burden?'

Of all these commissions the most deservedly famous was
that of the monks of the Order of Saint Jerome, which is
moving, both because of a conscientious approach, which has
been singularly lacking in colonial undertakings since 1517,
and because of the light it throws on the mental attitudes
of the period. In the course of what was tantamount to a
psycho-sociological inquiry, conceived according to the
most modern standards, the colonists were required to answer a series of questions, the purpose of which was to find
out if, in their opinion, the Indians were or were not 'capable of living on their own, like Castilian peasants'. All the
replies were negative: 'At a pinch, their grandchildren may
be able to: but the natives are so completely depraved that
even this is very doubtful: witness the fact that they shun
the Spanish and refuse to work without pay while carrying
perversity to the point of giving away their possessions;
they do not agree to spurn those of their comrades who have
had their ears cut off by the Spanish.' And the unanimous
conclusion was: 'It would be better for the Indians to become human slaves than to remain free animals . . .'

Evidence given a few years later adds the finishing touch
to the indictment: 'They eat human flesh, and have no form
of justice; they go about naked, eat fleas, spiders and raw
larvae . . . They do not have beards, and if by chance hair
grows on their faces, they lose no time in plucking it out'
(Ortiz addressing the Council of the Indies, 1525).

At the same period, and on a neighbouring island (Puerto
Rico, according to the testimony of Oviedo), the Indians
would capture white men and drown them. Then, for
several weeks, they would mount guard round the drowned
bodies in order to find out whether or not they were subject
to decay. Two conclusions emerge from a comparison between these different processes of investigation: the whites
trusted to social science, whereas the Indians had confidence
in natural science; and while the whites maintained that the
Indians were beasts, the Indians did no more than suspect
that the whites might be gods. Both attitudes show equal
ignorance, but the Indians' behaviour certainly had greater
human dignity.

Difficulties of intellectual comprehension gave an additional note of pathos to the moral problem. Everything was
puzzling for those early explorers: Pierre d'Ailly's *Image*

of the World refers to a newly discovered and supremely happy race of men, *gens beatissima,* consisting of pygmies, macrobiotics and even people without heads. Pierre Martyr quotes descriptions of monstrous beasts: snakes like crocodiles; animals with the body of an ox and a proboscis like that of the elephant; four-legged fish with ox-heads, their backs studded with thousands of warts and tortoise-like shells, as well as man-eating *tyburons*. But these, after all, are only boas, tapirs, manatees or hippopotamuses and sharks (in Portuguese, *tubarão*). Conversely, however, apparent mysteries were accepted as part of the natural course of things. In order to justify the sudden change of course which made him miss Brazil, Columbus, in his official reports, recorded wildly improbable circumstances which have never occurred since then and seem especially unlikely in a permanently humid zone. A burning heat made it impossible to inspect the holds, so that the water and wine casks exploded, the grain stores burst into flame, and bacon and dried meat roasted for a week; the sun was so hot that the crew thought they would be burnt alive. In that happy age everything was still possible, as it is again today, no doubt, thanks to flying saucers!

It was more or less in the area where we were now sailing that Columbus encountered mermaids. Actually he saw them at the end of his first voyage in the Caribbean Sea, but they would not have looked out of place off the Amazon delta. 'The three mermaids', he relates, 'raised their bodies above the surface of the water and, although they were not as beautiful as they appear in pictures, their round faces were definitely human.' The manatees have round heads and their breasts are at the front; since the females hold their young close with their paws as they suckle them, it is not surprising that they should have been taken for mermaids, especially at a period when people went as far as to describe (and even draw) the cotton plant as a sheep tree, that is a tree bearing not fruit but whole sheep hanging by their backs with wool ready to be shorn.

Similarly, when Rabelais, in the Fourth Book of *Pantagruel,* basing himself no doubt on stories told by some navigator who had returned from the West Indies, gives the first caricatural account of what present-day anthropologists call a kinship system, he embroiders freely on very flimsy evidence, for there cannot be many kinship systems in which an old man could call a little girl 'father'. In all such instances, the sixteenth-century consciousness was lacking in an element more important than knowledge: a quality indispensable to scientific thought. The men of that time were not sensitive to the harmonious arrangement of the universe; just as today, on the aesthetic level, a peasant who has observed certain external features of Italian paintings or African sculpture, but fails to perceive their significant harmony, would be unable to distinguish between a fake and a real Botticelli, or between a Pahouin statuette and cheap junk. The mermaids and the sheep tree constitute something different from, and more than, just objective mistakes; on the intellectual level they are to be considered rather as lapses in taste; a defect in minds which, in spite of the great gifts and refinement they displayed in other fields, were deficient in powers of observation. This should not cause us to censure them: rather should we respect them for the results they obtained in spite of such shortcomings.

The deck of a ship bound for North or South America offers modern man a finer acropolis for his prayer than Athens did to Renan. No longer can we worship, as he did, the anaemic goddess of a confined civilization. Over and above those heroes—navigators, explorers and conquerors of the New World—who (before the era of journeys to the moon) undertook the only total adventure open to man, my thoughts turn to the survivors of a rearguard which paid so cruelly for the honour of keeping the gates wide open. I mean the Indians, whose example, through Montaigne, Rousseau, Voltaire and Diderot, enriched the substance of what I was taught at school. Hurons, Iroquois, Caribs and Tupi—I was now on my way to them!

The first glimmerings perceived by Columbus, and which he took to be the coast, came from a species of marine glow-worm which lays its eggs between sunset and the rising of the moon; no land could yet have been in sight. But what I saw during a sleepless night spent on deck, watching and waiting for America, were definitely the lights of the mainland.

From the day before, we had been conscious of the New World although it was not visibly present; the coast was too far away, in spite of the fact that the boat had veered in a southerly direction so as to follow a course parallel to the shore from Cabo São-Agostin to Rio. For two days at least, perhaps three, we were to hug the American coast. Nor was it the huge sea birds—shrill-voiced tropicbirds or tyrannical petrels—which attacked gannets and forced them to disgorge their prey in full flight, that told us we were at our journey's end, since these birds venture a long way from land, as Columbus learned to his cost, because he hailed their appearance as a sign of his victory when he was still only halfway across the Atlantic. As for the flying fish—which shot themselves into the air with a flick of their tails on the water and were carried along on their outspread fins, like silver sparks flashing in all directions above the blue crucible of the sea—for some days past they had become increasingly rare.

The traveller approaching the New World is first conscious of it as a scent very different from the one suggested back in Paris by the connotations of the word Brazil, and difficult to describe to anyone who has not experienced it.

At first, it seemed that the sea smells of the preceding weeks had ceased to circulate so freely; they had come up against an invisible wall: thus immobilized, they no longer claimed the traveller's attention, which was now drawn towards smells that were of a quite different nature and that nothing in his past experience enabled him to define: they were like a forest breeze alternating with hot-house scents, the quintessence of the vegetable kingdom, and held a peculiar freshness so concentrated as to be transmuted into a kind of olfactory intoxication, the last note of a powerful chord, sounded separately as if to isolate and fuse the successive intervals of diversely fruity fragrances. This can only be appreciated by someone who has buried his face in a freshly cut tropical red pepper, after having previously, in some *botequin* of the Brazilian *sertão*, inhaled the aroma of the black, honeyed coils of the *fumo de rolo*, made from tobacco leaves, fermented and rolled into lengths several yards long. In the blend of these closely allied scents, he can recognize an America which, for thousands of years, was alone in its possession of their secrets.

But when, at four o'clock in the morning of the following day, the New World at last appeared on the horizon, its visible image seemed worthy of its perfume. For two days and two nights an immense cordillera came into view: immense not in height but because of the identical recurring pattern, which made it impossible to distinguish any beginning or break in the ragged chain of ridges. The polished stone walls of these mountains rose up several hundred metres above the waves in a crazy jumble of eccentric shapes, such as can sometimes be observed in sandcastles undermined by the tide, but which one would never expect to find on such a vast scale, at least on our planet.

This impression of enormous size is peculiar to America, and can be felt everywhere, in town and country alike: I have experienced it along the coast and on the plateaux of central Brazil, in the Bolivian Andes and the Colorado Rockies, in the suburbs of Rio, the outskirts of Chicago and the streets of New York. Everywhere it makes the same powerful impact; the particular scene may be reminiscent of other scenes, the streets are just streets, the mountains just mountains, the rivers just rivers. The feeling of unfamiliarity comes simply from the fact that the relationship between the size of human beings and the size of the objects around them has been so distended as to cancel out any possibility of a common measure. Later, when one has become accustomed to America, one almost unconsciously makes the adjustment which restores a normal correspondence between the different terms; it involves a barely perceptible effort, of which you are only vaguely made aware by the mental click which occurs as the plane touches down. But the congenital lack of proportion between the two worlds permeates and distorts our judgments. Those who maintain that New York is ugly are simply the victims of an illusion of the senses. Not having yet learnt to move into a different register, they persist in judging New York as a town, and criticize the avenues, parks and monuments. And no doubt, objectively, New York is a town, but a European sensibility perceives it according to a quite different scale, the scale of European landscapes; whereas American landscapes transport us into a far vaster system for which we have no equivalent. The beauty of New York has to do not with its being a town, but with the fact, obvious as soon as we abandon our preconceptions, that it transposes the town to the level of an artificial landscape in which the principles of urbanism cease to operate, the only significant values being the rich velvety quality of the light, the sharpness of distant outlines, the awe-inspiring precipices between the skyscrapers and the sombre valleys, dotted with multicoloured cars looking like flowers.

Having said this, I feel rather embarrassed in speaking about Rio de Janeiro, which I find off-putting in spite of its oft-extolled beauty. I don't quite know how to make the point. It seems to me that the landscape in which Rio is set is out of proportion to its own dimensions. The Sugar Loaf Mountain, the Corcovado and the much-praised natural features appear to the traveller entering the bay like stumps sticking up here and there in a toothless mouth. Since these eminences are almost always swathed in a thick tropical mist, they seem totally unable to fill the horizon, for which in any case they would be inadequate. If you want a satisfactory view you must look at the bay from the landward side and look down upon it from the heights. On the seaward side, the optical illusion is the opposite of the one which obtains in New York; here, it is nature which has the appearance of an unfinished building-site.

Also, it is impossible to gauge the size of Rio bay by means of visual landmarks: the slow advance of the boat, as it manœuvres to avoid the islands, the coolness and the scents which come suddenly down from the tree-clad slopes, establish by anticipation a kind of physical contact with the flowers and rocks, which do not yet exist as objects, but give the traveller a foretaste of the specific character of the continent. And again Columbus springs to mind: 'The trees were so high that they seemed to touch the sky; and, if I understand correctly, they never lose their leaves; for I have seen them as fresh and green in November as they are in May in Spain; some even were in flower, while others bore fruit . . . Wherever I turned, I could hear the nightingale singing, accompanied by thousands of birds of different species.' That is America; the continent makes an inescapable impact. Its presence is made up of all those signs of activity which at dusk enliven the hazy horizon of the bay; but, for the newcomer, the movements, forms and lights are not indicative of provinces, hamlets and towns; they do not signify forests, prairies, valleys and landscapes; they do not express the activities and labours of individuals who are strangers to each other, being each enclosed within the narrow confines of his family and profession. The whole scene exists as a unique and global entity. Surrounding one overwhelmingly on all sides is not the inexhaustible diversity of beings and things, but a single, awe-inspiring presence: the New World.

9. GUANABARA

The bay at Rio eats right into the heart of the city: you land in the centre, as if the other half, like the fabled town of Ys, had already been engulfed by waves. And in a sense this is true, because the first settlement, which was no more than a fort, was situated on the rocky island that the ship passes before docking and which still bears the name of the founder: Villegaignon. I walked up the Avenida Rio-Branco, once a site occupied by Tupinamba villages, but in my pocket I carried Jean de Léry, the anthropologist's breviary.

Almost 378 years ago to the day, he had arrived here with ten other Genevans, Protestants sent by Calvin at the request of Villegaignon, a former schoolfriend of his, who had been converted to the Protestant religion hardly a year after settling in the bay of Guanabara. Villegaignon was a strange character, who had tried every profession in turn, and who had been involved in all sorts of affairs. He had fought against the Turks, the Arabs, the Italians, the Scots (it was he who had abducted Mary Stuart so that she could marry Francis II) and the English. He had been in Malta, Algiers and at the battle of Cerisole. He had almost reached the end of his adventurous career and his interest seemed to be centred on military architecture when, as a result of a professional disappointment, he decided to go to Brazil. But there too, his plans remained in keeping with his restless and ambitious spirit. His primary aim may have been to found a colony, but no doubt he was also keen to carve out an empire for himself; and his immediate objective was to provide a refuge for persecuted Protestants wishing to leave France. He himself was officially a Catholic but probably a freethinker, and he secured the patronage of Coligny and the Cardinal of Lorraine. After a recruitment campaign among both Protestants and Catholics, with forays into public places to take in rakes, wantons and runaway slaves, he finally succeeded on July 12th, 1555, in getting six hundred people on board two boats;

they were a motley collection of pioneers representing all parts of the community, as well as criminals fresh from prison. He had overlooked only two items: women and supplies. They had some trouble in getting away, and were twice forced back to Dieppe. They finally set off on August 14th, and then more trouble started; fighting broke out on the Canary Islands, the water supply on board became polluted, and there was a scurvy epidemic. On November 10th, Villegaignon anchored in the bay of Guanabara, where for several years the French and the Portuguese had been vying with each other in wooing the natives.

The privileged position enjoyed by the French at that time on the Brazilian coast raises some curious problems. It dated back at least to the beginning of the century, a period marked by numerous French expeditions, in particular the one led in 1503 by Gonneville, who brought back an Indian son-in-law from Brazil. About the same time (in 1500), the island of Santa Cruz was discovered by Cabral. Perhaps we should go still further back. Since the French promptly gave the name *Brésil* to the new territory (at least as early as the twelfth century, *Brésil* had been the closely guarded and secret name of the mythical continent which was the source of wood dyes), and since a large number of terms—*ananas, manioc, tamandua, tapir, jaguar, sagouin, agouti, ara, caïman, toucan, coati, acajou,* etc.—were taken over directly by French from the Indian dialects without first passing through the Iberian languages, there is perhaps some truth in the traditional Dieppe belief that Brazil was discovered by Jean Cousin, four years before Columbus's first voyage. Cousin had a certain Pinzon as a member of his crew, and it was other Pinzons who gave fresh heart to Columbus at Palos, when he seemed on the point of giving up. Again it was a Pinzon who commanded *La Pinta* during the first voyage and with whom Columbus never failed to confer whenever there was a question of changing course; finally, it was through abandoning the route that another member of the Pinzon family was to follow a year later to Cabo São-Agostino, thus becoming the first official discoverer of Brazil, that Columbus narrowly missed an additional claim to fame. But for some miracle, the question will never be settled, because the Dieppe records, including Cousin's account, disappeared in the seventeenth century during the fire started by the English bombardment. However, as I set foot on Brazilian

soil for the first time, I could not help recalling all those
ludicrous and tragic incidents which testified to the close
relations existing between the French and the Indians four
hundred years ago: Norman interpreters, who went native,
married Indian women and became cannibals; poor Hans
Staden, who spent several anguished years, expecting every
day to be eaten alive and each time saved by some stroke
of luck, and trying to pass himself off as French because of
his extremely un-Iberian red beard, and getting the following
ripost from King Quoniam Bébé: 'I have already captured
and eaten five Portuguese; all claimed to be French but all
were lying!' There must indeed have been a continuous
relationship between the French and the Indians to allow
the frigate *La Pèlerine*, in 1531, to take back to France,
along with three thousand leopard skins and three hundred
monkeys of different species, six hundred parrots which
'already knew a few words of French . . .'

Villegaignon founded Fort Coligny on an island right in
the centre of the bay; Indians built it, and kept the small
colony provided with food; but they soon wearied of giving
without receiving anything in return, and fled, abandoning
their villages. In the Fort, famine and disease became the
order of the day. Villegaignon began to give rein to his
tyrannical nature and, when the convicts revolted, he had
them massacred. The epidemic spread to the mainland; the
few Indians who had remained faithful to the mission became infected, and eight hundred died.

Villegaignon, who was now undergoing a spiritual crisis,
was indifferent to temporal matters. He was converted
through his contact with Protestants, and he appealed to
Calvin to send missionaries who would enlighten him about
his new faith. So it was that, in 1556, an expedition was
sent out, of which Léry was a member.

At this point, history took such a strange turn that I am
surprised no novelist or scenario-writer has as yet made
use of it. What a marvellous film it would make! A handful
of Frenchmen, after braving every imaginable danger in
their attempt to escape from religious strife in France and
establish a new community where Catholic and Protestant
alike could live under a free and tolerant government, now
found themselves alone on a continent as unfamiliar as a
different planet, knowing nothing of the geographical circumstances or the natives, incapable of growing food to
keep themselves alive, stricken with sickness and disease

and depending for all their needs on an extremely hostile community whose language they could not understand, and were caught in a trap of their own making. The Protestants tried to convert the Catholics, and vice versa. Instead of working for survival, they spent weeks in foolish discussions: How should the Last Supper be interpreted? Should the wine be diluted with water before consecration? The Eucharist and the question of baptism gave rise to veritable theological tournaments, after which Villegaignon was either converted or returned to his former faith.

Things came to such a pass that an emissary was dispatched to Europe to consult Calvin and ask him to settle the controversial issues. Meanwhile the disputes became even fiercer, and Villegaignon began to lose control of his faculties; Léry relates how his moods and outbreaks of severity could be predicted by the colour of his clothes. When, in the end, he turned against the Protestants and started to starve them out, the latter ceased to play any part in the life of the community and moved over to the mainland, where they formed an alliance with the Indians. The idyllic relationship which then sprang up between the French and the Indians inspired that masterpiece of anthropological literature, Jean de Léry's *Le voyage faict en la Terre du Brésil*. The story had a sad ending: after considerable trials, the Genevans managed to return home on a French boat; they were no longer able, as on the outward voyage when they had carried their full complement, lightheartedly to *dégraisser* (take the surplus fat off)—that is, pillage—boats they encountered on the way; famine reigned on board. They ate the monkeys and the parrots, which were so precious that one Indian woman, a friend of Léry's, refused to part with hers unless she were given a cannon in return. The exchange rate for the rats and mice in the holds, the only form of food left, reached four écus each. The water supply ran out. In 1558, the crew landed in Brittany, half dead with hunger.

On the island, the colony began to break up in an atmosphere of terror and executions. Villegaignon, hated by all, considered as a traitor by some and as a renegade by others, feared by the Indians and himself terrified of the Portuguese, abandoned his dream. Under the command of his nephew, Bois-el-Comte, Fort Coligny fell into the hands of the Portuguese in 1560.

The first thing I did in Rio, where I could now roam

at will, was to try and recapture the flavour of those distant happenings. I was actually to get some inkling of it
later, during an archaeological excursion to the far end of
the bay organized by the National Museum in honour of a
Japanese scholar. A steamer landed us on a marshy beach,
where the hull of an old wreck lay rusting away: no doubt
it did not date from the sixteenth century, but it introduced an historical dimension into those empty spaces,
where there was nothing else to show the passage of time.
The distant town had disappeared from view behind the
low clouds and a fine drizzle, which had never stopped since
dawn. Beyond the black mud alive with crabs, beyond the
mangroves whose swollen shapes could equally well indicate growth or decay, lay the forest with the dripping silhouettes of a few isolated straw huts belonging to no particular period. Further away still, the tops of the mountain
slopes were swathed in white mist. As we drew nearer to
the trees, we reached the object of our visit—a gravel pit
where peasants had recently discovered fragments of pottery. I felt the thick earthenware, which was unmistakably
of Tupi origin, because of the white outer coating edged
with red and the delicate black tracery, representing, so it
is said, a maze intended to confuse the evil spirits looking
for the human remains which used to be preserved in these
urns. I was told that we could have reached the site by car,
since it was barely fifty kilometres from the town centre,
but that the rain might have blocked the track and kept
us stranded there for a week. That would have brought
us even closer to a past which was powerless to change this
melancholy spot, where Léry perhaps wiled away weary
hours of waiting by watching the quick movements of a
brown hand as it used a spatula dipped in black varnish
to make those 'thousand charming patterns such as guil-
loches, love-knots and other amusing designs', which I was
now trying to decipher on the back of a softened fragment
of pottery.

The first contact with Rio was different. For the first
time in my life, I was on the other side of the Equator in
the tropics, in the New World. By what major sign, I wondered, was I about to recognize this three-fold mutation?
What voice would provide me with evidence of it, what
note as yet unheard would be the first to strike my ear?
My initial observation was a trivial one: I felt I was in
a drawing-room.

As I strolled, more lightly clad than usual, over the winding and uneven surface of the black-and-white mosaic pavement, I noticed something special about the narrow, shady streets which cut across the main avenue: the transition between the buildings and the roadway was less obvious than in Europe. However lavish the display in their windows, the shops extended right out into the street, so that one hardly noticed whether one was outside or in. In fact, the street was not just a thoroughfare; it was a place where people lived. Bustling and peaceful at the same time, busier and better protected than Western streets, it eventually suggested a term of comparison. The change from one hemisphere to the other, and from one continent and climate to another, had, in the first instance, done little more than render superfluous the thin glass covering which, in Europe, serves to create the same conditions artificially. My first impression of Rio was of an open-air reconstruction of the Gallerias of Milan, the Galerij in Amsterdam, the Passage des Panoramas, or the concourse of the Gare Saint-Lazare.

Travel is usually thought of as a displacement in space. This is an inadequate conception. A journey occurs simultaneously in space, in time and in the social hierarchy. Each impression can be defined only by being jointly related to these three axes, and since space is itself three-dimensional, five axes are necessary if we are to have an adequate representation of any journey. I felt this immediately on landing in Brazil. I was, undeniably, on the other side of the Atlantic and the Equator and very close to the Tropic of Capricorn. This was brought home to me by several things: the steady, humid heat which freed my body of its usual weight of wool, and abolished the contrast between house and street (a contrast which, in retrospect, I discovered to be one of the constants of Western civilization), only to replace it, however, as I was soon to learn, by the different contrast between man and the bush, which does not exist in our entirely humanized landscapes. There were also palm trees, new kinds of flowers and, in front of the cafés, piles of green coconuts, which were split open to give a sweet liquid, with a fresh subterranean flavour.

But I noticed other changes too; from being poor I had become rich, first because my material circumstances had changed, and secondly because the prices of local produce were incredibly low. A pineapple cost twenty sous, a bunch of bananas two francs, chickens, spit-roasted by an Italian shopkeeper, four francs each. It was like the palace of Dame Tartine in the nursery rhyme.* Finally, the state of open-mindedness which accompanies arrival at a new port of call, and the unsolicited opportunities that one feels obliged to take advantage of, create an ambiguity conducive to the suspension of one's usual self-discipline and produce an almost ritual outburst of prodigality. Of course, the effect may sometimes be quite the opposite, as I know from experience, through having arrived penniless in New York after the armistice; but whether it is a question of 'more' or 'less', entailing improvement or a deterioration in one's material circumstances, only by a miracle can it happen that a journey does not bring about some change or other in this respect. Not only does a journey transport us over enormous distances, it also causes us to move a few degrees up or down in the social scale. It displaces us physically and also—for better or for worse—takes us out of our class context, so that the colour and flavour of certain places cannot be dissociated from the always unexpected social level on which we find ourselves in experiencing them.

There was a time when travelling brought the traveller into contact with civilizations which were radically different from his own and impressed him in the first place by their strangeness. During the last few centuries such instances have become increasingly rare. Whether he is visiting India or America, the modern traveller is less surprised than he cares to admit. In choosing his goals and itineraries, he feels especially free to select a particular date of European penetration, or a particular rate of influx of mechanization, rather than another. The search for the exotic boils down to the collecting of earlier or later phases of a familiar pattern of development. The traveller is like an antiquary obliged, by the dearth of material, to abandon his collection of Negro art and to fall back on bargaining for quaint pieces of junk as he tours the flea markets of the inhabited world.

These differences are already discernible in the heart of any town. Just as each plant flowers in its particular season, so each district bears the mark of the centuries which

---

* TRANSLATORS' NOTE: The nearest English equivalent is Queen Pippin's hotel, which is made of sweet things, whereas Dame Tartine's palace is mostly savoury.

saw its growth, its maximum development and its decline. In the pattern of urban vegetation, there are coincidences and chronological sequences. In Paris, the area of the Marais reached its zenith in the seventeenth century, but is now decrepit; the 9th *arrondissement*, a later-flowering species, attained its peak during the Second Empire, but its now shabby buildings are today occupied by a humble variety of fauna who, like insects, find in them a suitable setting for their modest forms of activity. The 17th *arrondissement* remains frozen in its defunct splendour, like a huge chrysanthemum nobly holding its withered head erect long after its allotted span of life. Not long ago the 16th *arrondissement* was resplendent, but now its bright blooms are obscured by the sprouting of office blocks and apartment buildings which are gradually making it indistinguishable from the Parisian *banlieue*.

When we compare towns which are geographically and historically remote from each other, these cyclical differences are complicated by discrepancies in rates of change. As soon as one moves away from the centre of Rio, which has a pronounced turn-of-the-century look, one finds quiet streets, and long boulevards planted with palms, mangoes and trimmed purple-wood trees and bordered by antiquated villas standing in their own grounds. They reminded me (like the residential districts of Calcutta that I was to see later) of Nice or Biarritz under Napoleon III. The tropics are less exotic than out of date. It is not so much their vegetation which testifies to their identity as minor architectural details, and the suggestion of a way of life which gives one the impression that, instead of covering vast distances, one has moved back imperceptibly in time.

Rio de Janeiro is not built like any ordinary town. It was constructed originally along the belt of flat, marshy land bordering the bay and then worked its way in between the steep hills which enclose the bay on all sides, like fingers bent in a tight, ill-fitting glove. Narrow urban developments, some of them twenty or thirty kilometres long, follow the base of granite rocks so steep that no form of vegetation can cling to them; only here and there, on some isolated coign of vantage or in some deep cleft, has a clump of forest been able to develop, and is truly virgin since it remains inaccessible, in spite of being so near. When flying through these cool, deep corridors, you seem

almost to brush against the branches as the plane floats
down between lush tapestries before landing where they
meet the ground. Although so lavishly provided with hills,
Rio treats them with a contempt which is partly to be explained by the shortage of water at the summits. In this
respect, Rio is the opposite of Chittagong, in the Bay of
Bengal; there, each small, cone-shaped mound, rising
above the marshy plain and with its orange-coloured clay
glistening through the green grass, is occupied by a solitary
bungalow, a rich man's fortress to protect him against the
oppressive heat and squalor of the swamps. Rio is just the
opposite: the globular domes, formed of granite in solid
blocks like cast-iron, throw back the heat with such intensity that the air currents circulating along the bottom of
the gorges never manage to rise. Perhaps the problem has
now been solved by urbanization, but in 1935 the al-
timeter unfailingly indicated the place each individual
occupied in the social scale: the higher you lived, the
lower your status. The poor were perched high up on the
hillsides, in *favellas*, where a population of Negroes clad
in well-washed rags composed lively guitar-melodies which,
at carnival time, came down from the hills and invaded the
town, together with their inventors.

The town changed horizontally as well as vertically. As
soon as you embarked on one of the urban tracks winding
between the hills, the landscape took on a suburban aspect.
Botafogo, at the end of the Rio-Branco avenue, was still a
smart part of the town, but after Flamengo, you might have
thought you were in Neuilly. As for the area near the
Copacabana tunnel, twenty years ago it was like Saint
Denis or Le Bourget but with a slightly more rustic air
reminiscent of the French suburbs before the 1914 war.
Copacabana, which now bristles with skyscrapers, in those
days was only a small provincial town with its various
trades and shops.

My last memory of Rio, which dates from just before
my final departure, is of a hotel on the slopes of the Corcovado, where I went to visit some American colleagues.
It could only be reached by a funicular railway of rather
rudimentary construction, set among loose stones and
rocks; one had an impression of something halfway between a garage and a mountain shelter, with control posts
manned by watchful stewards, who might have been fun-
fair attendants. After being hoisted by this contraption

over stony stretches of dirty wasteland, and at times up
almost vertical cliffs, one was rewarded by finding at the
top of the hill a small residence dating from the imperial
period, a single-storied house *(terrea)*, with stuccoed, ochre-
distempered walls. Dinner was served on a platform which
did duty as a terrace and which overlooked a jumble of
concrete buildings, cheap villas and other urban clusters.
In the distance, instead of the factory chimneys which one
might have expected as the final touch in such a heterogeneous landscape was a gleaming, satin-smooth tropical
sea, and over it a monstrous moon.

I went back on board. The boat set sail with all its lights
blazing and crackling. It paraded in front of the sea, which
writhed as it seemed to inspect a floating section of some
street of ill fame. Towards evening there was a thunder-
storm and the water glistened in the distance like a beast's
underbelly. At the same time, the moon was hidden by
ragged patches of cloud, which the wind blew into zigzags,
crosses and triangles. These weird shapes were lit up as if
from within, and against the dark background of the sky
they looked like a tropical version of the Aurora Borealis.
From time to time a reddish fragment of moon could be
glimpsed through these smoky apparitions, as it appeared,
disappeared and reappeared, like an anguished lantern
drifting across the sky.

10. CROSSING THE TROPIC

The coast between Rio and Santos offers further tropical landscapes of dream-like beauty. The coastal chain, which at one point reaches an altitude of more than two thousand metres, slopes down to the sea, and fragments it with little islands and creeks. Beaches of fine sand, bordered by coconut palms or by dark forests bursting with orchids, are enclosed within walls of sandstone or basalt which make them inaccessible except from the sea. Every hundred miles or so there is a little port whose ruined, eighteenth-century houses, once nobly proportioned stone-built mansions erected by shipowners, captains and vice-governors, are now occupied by fishermen. Angra dos Reis, Ubatuba, Parati, São Sebastião and Villa Bella were all places where the gold, diamonds, topazes and chrysolites from the Minas Geraes, the 'general mines' of the kingdom, ended up after several weeks' journey by mule-train through the mountains. When one tries now to find the trails along the *espigões*, the line of ridges, it is difficult to imagine that the traffic was so heavy that the recovery of the shoes lost on the way by the animals constituted a special occupation.

Bougainville describes the precautions which surrounded the mining and transport. Almost immediately on extraction, the gold had to be handed over to the 'Foundation Houses' situated in each district: Rio dos Mortes, Sabara and Serro Frio. There the taxes owing to the crown were collected, and the gold due to the individuals operating the mines was handed over to them in bars stamped with their weight, title and number, as well as with the king's arms. A central warehouse, situated halfway between the mines and the coast, carried out a further check. There a lieutenant commanding fifty soldiers deducted one-fifth, the toll charge for each man and beast, which was shared between the king and the detachment. So it was not at all surprising that the mule-trains from the mines, as they passed this inevitable check-point, should be 'stopped and searched very thoroughly indeed.'

The individual operators then took the gold bars to the Rio de Janeiro mint, where they were exchanged for coins, half-doubloons worth eight Spanish piastres, out of which the king claimed one piastre per half-doubloon for alloyage and the striking of money. And Bougainville adds: 'The mint . . . is one of the finest in existence; it is provided with all the necessary facilities for working at the greatest possible speed. Since the gold comes down from the mines at the same time as the fleets arrive from Portugal, the mining must be done promptly and money is produced with amazing rapidity.'

The system was even more rigorous in the case of diamonds. According to Bougainville, the contractors 'are obliged to give an accurate account of all diamonds discovered and to hand them over to the steward appointed for this purpose by the king. He at once places them in an iron-bound box with three locks. He closes it with one key, the viceroy with another and the *provador* of the Hacienda Reale with the third. The box is then placed in a second one, bearing the seals of the three persons mentioned and also containing the three keys belonging to the first box. The viceroy has no authority to inspect the contents. His function is to deposit the second box in yet a third strong-box, which he dispatches to Lisbon, after affixing his seal to the lock. The box is opened in the presence of the king, who chooses the diamonds he wants and pays the contractors according to an agreed rate.'

Of all this intense activity, which, in the year 1762 alone, accounted for the transport, checking, minting and dispatch of 119 *arrobes* of gold (more than one and a half tons), nothing now remains along this coast, which has reverted to its paradisal state, except a few lonely and majestic buildings, in front of which the galleons used to moor, and whose walls are still lapped by the waves coming up the bays. One would like to think that these awesome forests, virgin bays and precipitous rocks had remained unknown except to a few barefooted Indians clambering down from the high plateaux, whereas in fact, only some two hundred years ago, they provided a location for workshops in which the destiny of the modern world was forged.

After gorging itself on gold, the world became hungry for sugar, but sugar itself consumed slaves. First the exhaustion of the mines—which had been preceded, it is true, by the

destruction of the forests providing fuel for the crucibles—
then the abolition of slavery and lastly a growing world
demand turned the attention of São Paulo and its port,
Santos, towards the cultivation of coffee. After being yellow,
then white, gold became black. But in spite of all these
changes which made Santos one of the centres of international trade, the landscape retains a discreet beauty. As the
boat slowly made its way between the islands, for the first
time I experienced the impact of the tropics. We were
encompassed by a channel of greenery. It was as if we
had only to stretch out our hands to grasp the plants which,
in Rio, had been kept out of reach in their lush seclusion
high up on the hillsides. In this more modest setting, it was
possible to establish contact with the landscape.

The Santos hinterland, an inundated plain, variegated
with lagoons and marshes and crisscrossed by innumerable
rivers, straits and canals, the pattern of which is perpetually blurred by a pearly vapour, seems like the earth itself,
emerging on the first day of creation. The banana plantations covering it are of the freshest and tenderest green
imaginable; it is a sharper hue than the greenish gold of
the jute fields in the Brahmaputra delta with which my
memory is fond of associating them. But the very delicacy
of the tint, its uncertain fragility compared with the serene
sumptuousness of the other colour, helps to create a primeval atmosphere. For half an hour, you drive among
banana plants, which are huge vegetables rather than dwarf
trees, sap-filled trunks terminating in a profusion of rubbery
leaves above a multi-fingered hand emerging from an
enormous brown-and-pink lotus. Then the road rises to a
height of eight hundred metres, right to the top of the serra.
As everywhere along this coast, steep inclines have put
beyond man's reach a virgin forest so rich that, to find its
equal, one would have to travel several thousand miles
north towards the Amazonian basin. While the car groaned
as it took corners which could not even be described as
hairpin bends, since the road curved up in a continuous
spiral through a mist reminiscent of mountain highlands
under other climes, I was free to examine the trees and
plants arranged in tiers like specimens in a museum.

This forest is different from Western forests because of
the contrast between foliage and trunk. The foliage is
darker, its shades of green suggesting the mineral rather
than the vegetable kingdom, and, in the former, jade and

tourmaline rather than emerald and peridot. The trunks, on the other hand, stand out like white or greyish skeletons against the dark background of the foliage. Being too near the edge to contemplate the forest as a whole, I concentrated on the details. Plants lusher than those to be found in Europe had stems and leaves which appeared to have been cut out of metal, so assured was their bearing and so proof against the ravages of time their highly significant shapes. Looked at from the outside, tropical nature seemed to be of quite a different order from the kind of nature we are familiar with; it displayed a higher degree of presence and permanence. As in the Douanier Rousseau's paintings of exotic landscapes, living entities attained the dignity of objects.

Once before I had had a similar impression. It was when I spent my first holiday in Provence, after years devoted exclusively to Normandy and Brittany. A form of vegetation that I had looked upon as vague and uninteresting was replaced by another, in which each species suggested a particular significance. It was rather as if I had been transported from an ordinary village to an archaeological site in which every stone, instead of being simply a component part of a house, bore witness to the past. I tramped excitedly over the rocky ground, repeating to myself that each sprig to be found there was called thyme, origan, rosemary, basil, cistus, sweet bay, lavender, arbutus, caperplant or lentisk, and that each was an aristocrat of the vegetable kingdom which had been entrusted with its particular mission. And I perceived the heavy resinous scent as being both proof and justification of a more valid form of plant life. What the flora of Provence had conveyed to me by its fragrance this tropical vegetation now brought home to me by its shapes. Instead of presenting a world of scents and customs, a herbarium of recipes and superstitions, it was a vegetable company like a troop of accomplished dancers, each of whom had remained poised in the most telling posture, as if to express an intention which was all the clearer through having nothing more to fear from life; a motionless ballet disturbed only by the mineral unrest of bubbling springs.

When we reached the top, everything changed again; gone was the damp tropical heat, and the heroic entanglements of creepers and rocks. Instead of the vast shimmering prospect down to the sea that one enjoys for the last time from the vantage point of the serra, there was, in the opposite direction, a bare, uneven plateau, offering its ridges and ravines under an uncertain sky. A fine Breton drizzle started to fall. We had reached an altitude of nearly one thousand metres, although the sea was still so near. From the top of this eminence the highlands begin forming a series of tiers of which the coastal chain is the first and the most difficult to scale. The landscape slopes away gradually in a northerly direction. Its descent to the Amazon basin, into which it finally collapses through huge faults three thousand kilometres to the north, is interrupted in only two places by lines of cliffs: Serra de Botucatu and Chapada do Mato Grosso, respectively 500 and 1,500 kilometres from the coast. I would have to go beyond both before discovering, along the great rivers of Amazonia, a forest similar to the one clinging to the coastal wall. The major part of Brazil, the area contained between the Atlantic, the Amazon and Paraguay, is a kind of tableland sloping downwards away from the sea: a springboard crinkly with undergrowth and surrounded by a damp circle of jungle and marsh.

Around me, erosion had eaten away the constantly evolving landscape, but man is chiefly responsible for its chaotic aspect. First, the ground was cleared for cultivation, but after a few years, the land became exhausted and was washed away by the rains from around the coffee-shrubs. The plantations were then moved further afield, where the ground was still virgin and fertile. That careful and reciprocal relationship between man and the earth which, in the Old World, established the age-old bond whereby one fashioned the other, has never existed here, where the ground has been violated and destroyed. A rapacious form of agriculture appropriated what was readily available and then moved on, after wresting some profit from the soil. The area of activity exploited by the pioneers has been justly described as a fringe. Since they ruin the soil almost as soon as they clear it for cultivation, they seem doomed to occupy only a moving strip, which, on one side, eats into virgin territory while, on the other, it leaves behind areas drained of their goodness. Like a bush fire, driven forward through consuming what it feeds on, the agricultural blaze has swept through the State of São Paulo in the space of a hundred years. After being lit in the middle of the nineteenth century by the *mineiros,* who had abandoned their exhausted mines, it moved from east to west, and I was soon to catch up with it on the other side of the Parana river, as it drove through a confused jumble of felled trunks and uprooted families.

The road from Santos to São Paulo runs through territory that was one of the earliest parts of the country to be thus exploited. It looks like an archaeological site illustrating obsolete forms of agriculture. Once-wooded hills and slopes show their outlines through a thin covering of coarse grass. Here and there can be detected the dotted lines formed by the mounds once planted with coffee-shrubs; they protrude from the grassy hillsides like withered breasts. In the valleys, vegetation has regained possession of the ground, but it is no longer the noble architecture of the primitive forest; it is the *capoeira,* that is, the secondary forest, sprouting as a continuous thicket of slender trees. Here and there can be seen the hut of some Japanese settler who is trying to reactivate a patch of ground by archaic methods in order to grow vegetable crops.

The European traveller is disconcerted by the landscape which does not correspond to any of his traditional categories. We are unacquainted with virgin nature since our landscape is manifestly subservient to man. It may occasionally appear wild, not because it really is so, but because interaction has occurred at a slower rate (as in forest) or again—in mountainous regions—because the problems arising were so complex that man, instead of evolving a systematic response, has reacted over the centuries with a multitude of *ad hoc* adjustments; the general solutions which sum up these adjustments, and which were never clearly sought for or thought of as such, then appear from the outside as having a primitive character. They are taken as representing the authentic wildness of the landscape, whereas they are the outcome of a series of unconscious efforts and decisions.

But even the most rugged landscapes of Europe have a kind of order, to which Poussin, for instance, gave incomparable expression. If you go into a mountainous area, observe the contrast between the arid slopes and the forests; and the way the latter rise in stages above the plains, with a variety of colours due to the predominance of some particular species according to the aspect or the slope. Only if one has travelled in America does one realize that this sublime harmony, far from being a spontaneous manifestation of nature, is the result of agreements painstakingly evolved during a long collaboration between man and the landscape. Man naïvely admires the effects of his past achievements.

In the inhabited regions of America—and this is true of the North as well as the South (with the exception of the Andean plateaux, Mexico and Central America, where the denser population and more continuous effort bring the situation into line with Europe)—there are only two alternatives: either nature has been so ruthlessly mastered that it has been turned into an open-air factory rather than a rural area (I am thinking of the cane-sugar fields in the West Indies and the maize fields in the corn belt), or—as in the case that I am now referring to—the territory has been sufficiently inhabited by man for him to have had time to lay it waste but not long enough for slow and continuous co-habitation to have raised it to the dignity of a landscape. On the outskirts of São Paulo, and later in the State of New York, in Connecticut and even in the Rockies, I gradually became familiar with a form of nature wilder than our own, because less densely populated and less highly cultivated, but which was devoid of any real freshness; it was degraded rather than wild.

These vast nondescript areas as large as provinces were once, and for a short time, occupied by man. Then he moved on, leaving behind him a battered landscape, cluttered with traces of his past activities. And on these battlefields, where he grappled for several decades with an unknown land, a monotonous vegetation is slowly re-emerging in a confusion which is all the more deceptive since it preserves, beneath a falsely innocent exterior, memories and patterns of former conflicts.

11. SÃO PAULO

Some mischievous spirit has defined America as a country which has moved from barbarism to decadence without enjoying any intermediary phase of civilization. The formula could be more correctly applied to the towns of the New World, which pass from freshness to decay without ever being simply old. Once, a Brazilian girl-student, after her first visit to France, came to see me with tears in her eyes: Paris, with its blackened buildings, had struck her as being dirty. Whiteness and cleanliness were the only criteria by which she could judge a town. But those excursions outside time prompted by the contemplation of monumental architecture and that ageless life characteristic of the most beautiful cities, which have become objects of contemplation and reflection rather than mere instruments of urban functioning: these are things beyond the scope of American towns. In the cities of the New World, whether it be New York, Chicago or São Paulo (and the last two have often been compared), it is not the absence of traces of the past which strikes me; this lack is an essential part of their significance. Unlike those European tourists who sulk when they cannot find another thirteenth-century cathedral to add to their 'bag', I am happy to adapt myself to a system with no temporal dimension, in order to interpret a different form of civilization. But then I fall into the opposite error: since these towns are new and derive their being and their justification from their newness, I find it difficult to forgive them for not remaining new. In the case of European towns, the passing of centuries provides an enhancement; in the case of American towns, the passing of years brings degeneration. It is not simply that they have been newly built; they were built so as to be renewable as quickly as they were put up, that is, badly. When new districts are being created, they are hardly integral elements of the urban scene; they are too gaudy, too new, too gay for that. They are more like stands in a fairground or the pavilions of some international exhibition, built to last only a few months. After that lapse of time, the fair closes and the huge gewgaws lapse into decay; the façades begin to peel, rain and soot leave their grimy trails, the style goes out of fashion, and the original layout disappears through the demolitions caused by some new building fever. The contrast is not between new towns and old towns, but between towns with a very short evolutionary cycle and towns with a slow evolutionary cycle. Certain European cities sink gently into a moribund torpor; those of the New World live feverishly in the grip of a chronic disease; they are perpetually young, yet never healthy.

What struck me first when I visited New York or Chicago in 1941, and when I arrived in São Paulo in 1935, was not the newness of these places but their premature ageing. It did not surprise me to find that these towns lacked ten centuries of history, but I was staggered to discover that so many of their districts were already fifty years old and that they should display the signs of decrepitude with such a lack of shame, when the one adornment to which they could lay claim was that of youth, a quality as transitory for them as for living creatures. Rusty old iron, red trams wtih the appearance of fire-engines, mahogany bars with polished brass rails; brick-built warehouses in deserted streets, where there was only the wind to sweep away the rubbish; rustic parish churches standing at the foot of offices and stock-exchanges built in cathedral style; mazes of seedy buildings looming over intersecting valleys of trenches, swing-bridges and footbridges; a town being piled ever higher, since the vestiges of old buildings are constantly used as a basis for the new. Such was Chicago, the very image of the Americas. No wonder the New World cherishes in it the memory of the 1880s; the only antiquity to which it can lay claim in its thirst for renewal is this modest gap of half a century, too short to be a criterion for our ancient societies, but enough to give it, with its lack of temporal perspective, some little opportunity to sentimentalize about its transient youth.

In 1935, the citizens of São Paulo boasted that, on an average, one house per hour was built in their town. At that time, they were talking of villas; I am assured that the rate remains the same, but that the unit is no longer the villa but the block of flats or offices. The town is developing so fast that it is impossible to obtain a map of it; a new edition would be required every week. It has been said that if you take a taxi to an appointment made several weeks ahead, you are in danger of arriving before the builders have finished. This being so, to revive memories which go back nearly twenty years is like looking at a faded photograph. But at least they may be of some documentary interest; I offer my recollections, such as they are, for the municipal archives.

São Paulo was said, at the time, to be an ugly town. No doubt the buildings in the centre were pompous and old-fashioned: the pretentious poverty of their ornamentation was made still worse by the shoddiness of the general structure. The statues and garlands were not made of stone but of plaster daubed yellow to give the impression of a patina. By and large, the town displayed that monotonous and arbitrary colouring typical of badly constructed buildings, because the architect has fallen back on paint not as a protection but as a means of hiding the underlying defects.

In the case of the stone buildings, the extravagances of the style of the 1890s were partly offset by the heaviness and density of the material; they were limited to the incidental detail. Elsewhere, the bloated, contorted patterning was reminiscent of the scrolls and crusts of leprosy. The garish colours caused the shadows to stand out more blackly; the narrowness of the streets made it impossible for the thin layer of air to 'create an atmosphere', so that one had a feeling of unreality, as if one were not dealing with a town but with a *trompe-l'œil* hastily erected to serve as a background for a film or a stage play.

And yet I never thought that São Paulo was ugly: it was a 'wild' town, as are all American towns, with the possible exception of Washington, D.C., which is neither wild nor domesticated, but is dying of boredom and captivity in the cage of radiating avenues in which Lenfant enclosed it. São Paulo, at that time, was untamed. Originally built on a terrace in the form of a spur facing northwards at the junction of two small rivers—the Anhangabahu and the Tamanduatehy, which later flow into the Tiete river, a tributary of the Parana—it was at first a mere outpost in Indian territory, a missionary centre where, as early as the sixteenth century, Portuguese Jesuits tried to bring natives together and initiate them into the virtues of civilization. On the slope which leads down to the Tamanduatehy and overlooks the working-class districts of Braz and Penha, there still remained, in 1935, a few small provincial streets and *largos,* grassy squares surrounded by low, tiled and whitewashed houses with small barred windows. On one side, there would be an austere parish church, whose only ornamentation was the double bracket marking out a baroque pediment on the upper part of the façade. Far away to the north, the silvery waters of the Tiete meandered through *varzeas*—swamps gradually being turned into cities —and were bordered by an irregular series of suburbs and building developments. Immediately behind was the business centre, which still remained faithful to the style and aspirations of the 1889 Exhibition. There was the Praça da Sé, the cathedral square, halfway between a building site and a ruin. Then the famous Triangle, of which São Paulo was as proud as Chicago of its Loop: a commercial area at the point of intersection of three streets, Direita, São Bento and Quinze de Novembro. These thoroughfares bristled with street signs and were crowded with merchants and employees whose dark city suits proclaimed not only their allegiance to European or North American standards, but also their pride in the fact that, although their town stands right on the tropic, its altitude (eight hundred metres above sea-level) spared them the heaviness of tropical heat.

In São Paulo, in January, the rain does not 'come'; it is engendered by the surrounding humidity, as if the universally permeating vapour had materialized into beads of water, which fall thick and fast yet seem to be retarded by their affinity with the steamy atmosphere through which they are passing. The rain does not descend in vertical or oblique lines, as in Europe: it is more like a pale flickering, made up of a multitude of tiny globules of water pouring down through a moist atmosphere, a kind of cascade of clear tapioca soup. Nor does the rain stop through clouds moving away; it stops when, as a result of the draining off of a certain amount of liquid, the stationary air has rid itself of a surplus of humidity. Then the sky clears and patches of light blue appear between the pale yellow clouds, while Alpine torrents course through the streets.

At the northern tip of the terrace, vast roadworks were in progress; this was the beginning of the Avenida São João, a thoroughfare several kilometres long which was being laid out parallel to the Tiete and following the old route to the North towards Ytu, Sorocaba and the rich plantations of Campinas. It started at the extreme tip of the spur, and then ran downhill through the rubble remaining from demolished areas. To the right lay Florencio de Abreu street, leading to the station between Syrian bazaars, which kept all the inland areas supplied with cheap goods, and peaceful workshops where harness-makers and other craftsmen continued—but for how much longer?—to produce high saddles in tooled leather, horse blankets in a thick cotton weave and harnesses decorated with embossed silver, intended for the planters and peons living in the nearby bush. Then the avenue, after skirting the foot of a skyscraper—the only one in São Paulo at that time, and as yet unfinished—the pink Predio Martinelli, cut through the Campos Elyseos, formerly a residential area inhabited by the rich, where painted wooden villas were falling to pieces in gardens full or eucalyptus and mango trees; then came the working-class street of Santa Ifigenia, along which lay a red-light district, consisting of hovels with raised entresols, from the windows of which the prostitutes hailed their clients. Finally, on the outskirts of the town, the lower-middle-class residential areas of Perdizes and Agua-Branca were making headway and merging to the south-west into the green and more aristocratic slopes of Pacaembu.

To the south, the terrace continued to rise; modest avenues ran up it and were joined at the top, on the ridge of the hill, by the Avenida Paulista, along which stood the once-grandiose residences that were inhabited by the millionaires of the previous half-century and whose architectural style recalled casinos in watering-places. Right at the end, to the east, the avenue looked down to the plain, over the new district of Pacaembu where cube-shaped villas were dotted here and there along winding avenues variegated with the violet-blue blossom of the jacaranda trees, between grassy mounds and banks of ochre-coloured earth. But the millionaires had left the Avenida Paulista. As the town expanded, they had followed it down the south side of the hill towards quiet neighbourhoods with winding streets. Their Californian-style mansions, in micaceous cement and with wrought-iron balustrades, could be glimpsed standing well back in their ample grounds, which had been carved out of the surrounding shrubland to provide a residential estate for the rich.

Cow pastures lay at the foot of concrete blocks, a whole area could suddenly spring into being like a mirage, and avenues bordered by palatial houses would stop suddenly on either side of ravines where, between the banana trees, flowed muddy torrents, which served both as sources of water and as sewers for the mud-walled, bamboo-frame shanties housing a black population similar to the one which, in Rio, camped up the hillsides. Goats ran along the slopes. Some exceptional areas af the town managed to combine every feature. For instance, at the end of two divergent streets leading to the sea, one found oneself at the edge of the deep valley of the Anhangabahu river, spanned by a bridge, which was one of the town's chief thoroughfares. Below was a park laid out in the English style: there were lawns embellished with statues and pavilions, as well as the main buildings of the town, rising vertically from the two slopes—the municipal theatre, the Esplanada hotel, the Automobile Club and the offices of the Canadian company responsible for the lighting system and public transport. Their heterogeneous shapes confronted each other in a frozen jumble. These incongruous buildings were like large herds of mammals assembled at nightfall round a waterhole, hesitant and motionless for a few minutes, since they are impelled, by a need more pressing than fear, to allow a temporary mingling of their antagonistic species. Animal evolution takes place at a much slower rate than that of urban life; if I could see the same scene today, I would perhaps discover that the hybrid herd had vanished, trampled down by a more vigorous and homogeneous race of skyscrapers established on these banks, which may have themselves been fossilized in asphalt to carry a motor-road.

Sheltering in this stony fauna, the elite of São Paulo, like its favourite orchids, constituted a more languid and exotic flora than it was aware of itself. Botanists tell us that tropical species include more varieties than those of the temperate zones, although each variety may comprise only a small number of individuals. The local *gran fino* had carried this specialization to extremes.

Society, being limited in extent, had allocated various roles to its different members. All the occupations, tastes and interests appropriate to contemporary civilization could be found in it, but each was represented by only a single individual. Our friends were not really persons in their own right, but rather functions which had been selected less for their intrinsic importance than for their availability. There was the Catholic, the Liberal, the Legitimist and the Communist; or, on another level, the gourmet, the book-collector, the pedigree-dog (or -horse) lover, the specialist in old or modern painting; and also the expert in local history, the surrealist poet, the musicologist and the painter. These vocations did not spring from any genuine desire to go more deeply into a given branch of knowledge; if two individuals, through some wrong move or some effect of jealousy, happened to occupy the same field or different but too closely adjacent fields, their one thought was to destroy each other, which they did with remarkable persistence and ferocity. On the other hand, between neighbouring domains cultural visits were exchanged, and there was a great display of mutual respect, since each individual was concerned not merely with defending his speciality but also with perfecting that sociological minuet, the performance of which seemed to provide Paulist society with inexhaustible enjoyment.

It must be admitted that certain parts were played with extraordinary brio, thanks to a combination of inherited wealth, innate charm and acquired craftiness which made the frequenting of São Paulo drawing-rooms at once such a delightful and disappointing pastime. But necessity, which demanded that all functions should be fulfilled so that the microcosm might be completed and the great game of civilization go on, also led to certain paradoxes: the Communist might turn out to be the rich heir to the local feudal estates, and an extremely prim society might go so far as to allow one of its members, but only one—since there had to be an avant-garde poet—to appear in public with his young mistress. Some functions were ensured only in a makeshift manner: the criminologist was a dentist who had got the police to adopt a method of identification by using plastercasts of jaws instead of fingerprints; and the monarchist's life was devoted to collecting pieces of household ware belonging to all the royal families in the world—his drawing-room walls were covered with plates, except for the necessary space reserved for the safe in which he kept the letters from the ladies-in-waiting of the various queens expressing their interest in his requests for august crockery.

This specialization on the social level went hand in hand with an appetite for all types of learning. Cultured Brazilians devoured manuals and works of vulgarization. French ministers, instead of boasting about France's as yet unequalled prestige abroad, would have been wiser to try to understand the reasons behind it. Unfortunately, even at

that date, it was due not so much to the wealth and originality of a diminishing scientific and intellectual inventive-
ness as to the ability, which many French scholars and
scientists still possessed, to give an easily intelligible account of difficult problems, to the solution of which they
themselves had made a small contribution. In this sense,
the predilection of South America for France could be
partly explained by a secret connivance based on the same
inclination to be consumers, and to help others to be consumers, rather than producers. The great names venerated
in Brazil—Pasteur, Curie and Durkheim—belonged to a
sufficiently recent past to justify a large credit balance; but
France was paying the interest on this credit in very small
coin, which was all the more appreciated in that her extravagant clients themselves preferred to spend rather than
invest. France was merely sparing them the trouble of
realizing their assets.

It is sad to note that even this role of intellectual broker,
which France was then gradually taking on, seems now to
have become too burdensome for her. We French appear
to remain prisoners of an attitude towards science and
learning inherited from the nineteenth century, when each
area of the intellectual field was sufficiently circumscribed
to allow a man endowed with those traditionally French
qualities—a broad, general culture, quickness and clarity
of thought, a logical mind and literary ability—to achieve
a complete grasp of it and, working in isolation, to rethink
it in his own way and offer his own synthesis. Whether one
applauds the fact or deplores it, modern science and learning no longer admit of this artisan-like approach. Where
once a single specialist could win fame for his country, we
now need an army of specialists, and we haven't got them;
private libraries have become museographic curiosities, but
in France public libraries, being without adequate premises,
without prestige, without research assistants and even without a sufficient number of seats for their readers, discourage
rather than help research work. In short, today scientific
and intellectual creation is a collective and largely anonymous enterprise, for which we are as ill-prepared as it is
possible to be, since we have been too exclusively concerned with unduly prolonging the facile successes of our
old virtuosi. And how long can the latter go on believing
that an impeccable, correct style will make up for the absence of a score?

Younger countries have learned the lesson. In Brazil, for instance, where there had been some brilliant, if far from numerous, individual successes—Euclides da Cunha, Oswaldo Cruz, Chagas and Villa-Lobos—culture had remained, until quite recent times, the plaything of the rich. And it was because the oligarchy felt the need of a civic and secular public opinion to counterbalance the traditional influence of the Church and the army, as well as personal political rule, that they undertook to make culture available to a wider audience by creating the University of São Paulo.

I still remember that, when I arrived in Brazil to take part in the founding of the university, I regarded the lowly status of my Brazilian colleagues with a mixture of pity and condescension. Watching these poorly-paid professors, who were obliged to undertake odd jobs on the side in order to make a living, I felt proud to belong to a country of long-established culture, where a member of the professional classes could feel secure and respected. Little did I imagine that, twenty years later, my hard-working pupils would occupy university chairs, in some fields more numerous and better equipped than their French equivalents, and provided with libraries such as we would be delighted to possess.

Yet these men and women of all ages who crowded into our lecture-rooms with a mixture of enthusiasm and suspiciousness had a lot of leeway to make up. There were young people anxious to obtain the posts that would be available to those who acquired the diplomas we awarded; there were also lawyers, engineers and established politicians who feared that they might soon have to compete against people with university degrees, if they did not have the wisdom to graduate themselves. They were all tainted with a destructive, man-about-town mentality, partly inspired by an out-of-date French tradition in the 'vie parisienne' style of the previous century, which had been introduced by a few Brazilians akin to the stereotype in Meilhac and Halévy's *opéra-bouffe*, but much more a symptom of a social evolution which had occurred in Paris in the nineteenth century and which São Paulo (and Rio de Janeiro) were then reliving in their own way: I mean the increased rate of differentiation between town and country, with the former developing at the expense of the latter, so that the newly urbanized community was anxious to have no truck with rustic naïvety, symbolized in twentieth-century Brazil by the *caipira*—the country bumpkin—as it had been, in the Parisian *théâtre du boulevard,* by the character from Arpajon or Charentonneau. I can recall an instance of this rather questionable humour.

In the middle of one of those streets which led from the centre of São Paulo and still had a rustic look although they might be three or four kilometres long, the Italian colony had erected a statue of Augustus Caesar. It was a life-size bronze reproduction of an antique marble statue, of no great artistic significance, it is true, but deserving of some respect in a town where there was nothing to remind one of any historical event dating back to before the previous century. Nevertheless, the people of São Paulo decided that the arm raised in the Roman salute meant 'This is where Carlito lives.' In the direction indicated by the imperial hand stood the home of Carlos Pereira de Souza, a former minister and an influential politician. It was one of those vast single-storeyed houses, built of bricks and mud and covered with a layer of greyish lime-wash that had been flaking off for the past twenty years, but with scrolls and rose-windows meant to suggest the grandeur of the colonial period.

The general opinion was that Augustus was wearing shorts, which was only half a joke since most of the passersby had never heard of the Roman kilt. These broad pleasantries were going the round within the hour after the inauguration ceremony, and were repeated with plenty of back-slapping at the Odeon cinema's 'elegant' performance, which took place the same day. Thus did the São Paulo middle classes (who had, incidentally, instituted a weekly cinema show at higher prices so as to avoid contact with the plebeian mob) try to get their own back for having, through their own negligence, allowed the establishment of an aristocracy of Italian immigrants, who had arrived half a century earlier to sell ties in the streets and were now the owners of the most flamboyant residences along the 'Avenida' as well as the donors of the much-discussed bronze.

Our students wanted to know everything but, whatever the field of interest, only the most recent theory seemed to them to be worthy of being memorized. They were indifferent to all the intellectual feasts of the past, which in any case they only knew of by hearsay since they did not read the original works, and were always ready to enthuse over new dishes. But in their case fashion is a more appropriate metaphor than cooking: ideas and theories held no intrinsic interest for them; they were merely instruments of prestige and the important thing was to be the first to know about them. To share a theory with other people already acquainted with it was like appearing in a dress that had already been worn; it entailed a loss of face. On the other hand, there was keen competition to obtain, through the absorption of quantities of popularizing journals, sensation-mongering periodicals and manuals, exclusive rights to the most recent model in the intellectual field. My colleagues and I, who were the products of a stringent system of academic training, often felt embarrassed. We had been taught to respect only fully matured ideas, and we found ourselves exposed to attacks by students who, while completely ignorant of the past, were always a few months ahead of us with the latest information. Yet although they had no taste for learning nor any sense of method, they felt it their duty to be erudite, and so, whatever the subject, their essays consisted of a general outline of the history of mankind from the time of the anthropoid apes, followed by a few quotations from Plato, Aristotle and Comte, and ending with a paraphrase of some turgid polygrapher whose work was all the more prized since his very obscurity made it unlikely that anyone else had had the idea of plagiarizing him.

They looked upon the university as if it were tempting but poisoned fruit. To instruct these young people, who had seen nothing of the world and, being often very poor, had no hope of ever visiting Europe, we had been brought over, like wise men from a far country, by members of the upper class, who were loathed for two reasons: first, because they represented the dominant elite, and secondly because of their cosmopolitan existence, which gave them an advantage over all those who had had to stay behind at home, but also cut them off from the life and aspirations of their own country. We appeared suspect through being associated with them, but we were bearers of the apples of knowledge, so that the students alternately shunned us or wooed us, listened with interest or turned a deaf ear. Each of us could measure his influence by the size of the court which grew up around him. The various groups of disciples waged a war of prestige, of which their favourite professors were the symbols, the beneficiaries or the victims. It took the concrete form of *homenagens,* that is, expressions of homage to the master, by means of luncheon-parties or tea-parties, which were all the more touching since they involved genuine sacrifices. In the course of these festivities, the standing of personalities and the subjects they specialized in rose and fell like stocks and shares, according to the prestige of the establishment, the number of people present and the importance of the social luminaries or official personalities who agreed to attend. And since each major nation had its 'embassy' at São Paulo, in the form of a place of refreshment—the English teashop, the Viennese or Parisian *pâtisseries* and the German brasserie—subtle implications were conveyed by the choice of one or the other.

Should any of my former charming pupils, now my respected colleagues, happen to read these lines, I hope they will not take offence. When I think of them, as it their custom, by their Christian names, which sound so quaint to European ears but which, in their diversity, show that their parents were not afraid to cull delightful appellations from any period of human history—Anita, Corina, Zenaïda, Lavinia, Thaïs, Gioconda, Gilda, Oneïda, Lucilla, Zenith and Cecilia, or Egon, Mario-Wagner, Nicanor, Ruy, Livio, James, Azor, Achilles, Decio, Euclides and Milton—I remember that early, tentative period with a complete absence of irony. On the contrary, it taught me a lesson, because it showed how precarious are the advantages conferred by time. In thinking about Europe as it then was and as it is today, and in watching these young Brazilians, in the space of a few years, bridge an intellectual gap that one might have expected to hold up development for decades, I have come to understand how societies decline or come into being; and to realize that those great historical upheavals, which, when one reads about them in the textbooks, appear to be the outcome of anonymous forces working in profound obscurity, can also, in a moment of lucidity, be brought about by the vigorous determination of a handful of talented young people.

PART FOUR

The Earth
and Its Inhabitants

---

12. TOWNS AND COUNTRYSIDE

In São Paulo, it was possible to be a Sunday anthropologist, but not among suburban Indians, about whom I had been given false promises, since the suburbs were inhabited by Syrians and Italians. The nearest anthropological curiosity was a primitive village about fifteen kilometres away, whose ragged inhabitants had fair hair and blue eyes which betrayed their recent Germanic origin. In the 1820s, groups of German colonists had settled in the least tropical areas of the country, and near São Paulo they had more or less merged with, and become indistinguishable from, the impoverished local peasantry, whereas further south, in the state of Santa Catarina, the small towns of Joinville and Blumenau still retained the atmosphere of the previous century among their monkey-puzzle trees. The houses had steeply sloping roofs and the streets German names, and only German was spoken there. Outside the beer parlours, old men with side-whiskers and moustaches sat smoking long pipes with porcelain bowls.

There were also a lot of Japanese around São Paulo, but they were more difficult to approach. They were recruited by immigration agencies which paid their passages, guaranteed them temporary accommodation when they arrived, then allocated them to inland farms which were half villages and half military camps. All public services were laid on: schools, workshops, hospitals, shops and entertainments. The immigrants spent long periods there, in an isolation that was partly voluntary and partly encouraged by the system, paying back their debt to the company and handing over their earnings to its safe keeping. The company undertook to take them back after several years, to die in the land of their ancestors or, if in the meantime they had succumbed to malaria, to repatriate their bodies. The whole vast project was organized so as to give them the feeling of never having left Japan. But it is not certain that it was inspired solely by financial, economic or humanitarian motives. A close look at the map makes clear the

107

strategic intentions that may have lain behind the establishment of the farms. The fact that it was extremely difficult
to gain access to the offices of the Kaigai–Iju–Kumiai, or
to the Brazil–Takahoka–Kumiai, and even more so to
get inside the agricultural centres themselves and the almost clandestine network of hotels, hospitals, brickworks
and sawmills ensuring the self-sufficiency of the colony,
proved the existence of deeply laid plans which had two
very different but interconnected consequences: the segregation of the colonists at carefully selected points, and the
pursuit (coincidental with the opening up of the land) of
archaeological research intended to stress certain analogies
between pre-Columbian remains and those of the Japanese
neolithic period.

In the centre of the town, certain markets in the working-
class districts were run by coloured people. Or, to be more
accurate—since the term 'coloured' is virtually meaningless
in a country where the great variety of races, and the almost total absence of prejudice, at least in past times,
encouraged cross-breeding of every kind—one could practise distinguishing there between the *mestiços,* black crossed
with white, the *caboclos,* white crossed with Indian, and
the *cafusos,* Indian crossed with black. The produce on sale
contained no admixture of styles: there were *peneiras,* a
typically Indian kind of sieve for manioc flour, consisting of
loose latticework made from split bamboos and encircled
with laths, and *abanicos,* fire fans, also inherited from the
Indian tradition, which provide amusing objects of study.
Each type represents an ingenious solution to the problem
of transforming, through plaiting, the permeable and dishevelled structure of a palm leaf into a rigid and continuous
surface capable of creating a current of air when vigorously
shaken. As there are several ways of solving the problem
and several kinds of palm leaf, it is possible to combine
leaves and methods to produce every conceivable form,
and one can make a collection of specimens illustrating
these miniature technological solutions.

There are two main species of palm: in the one, the
small leaves are distributed symmetrically along a central
stem; in the other, they spread out fanwise. The first type
suggests two methods: either all the leaves are turned back
on to the same side of the stem and plaited together, or
each group is plaited separately by folding the leaves at
right-angles and threading the ends of one set through the

lower halves of the others, and vice versa. In this way, two kinds of fan are obtained—the wing shape or the butterfly shape. The second type admits of several possibilities which are always, in varying degrees, combinations of the other two, and the resulting fan, which can be shaped like a spoon, a bat or a rosette, is structurally similar to a kind of large flattened hair-bun.

Another particularly attractive object to be found in the markets of São Paulo was the *figa*. A *figa*, or fig, was an ancient Mediterranean talisman in the shape of a forearm ending in a clenched fist, but with the tip of the thumb emerging between the joints of the middle fingers. It was probably a symbolic representation of coitus. The *figas* on sale in the markets were ebony or silver charms, or large objects as big as signs, crudely carved and painted in gaudy colours. I used to hang gay garlands of them from the ceiling of my house, an ochre-washed villa in the style current in Rome about 1900, which was situated near the upper part of the town. The approach to it was through a bower of jasmine and behind was on old-fashioned garden, at the end of which I had asked the owner to plant a banana tree to give me the feeling of being in the tropics. A few years later, this symbolic banana tree had become a small forest, where I harvested my own fruit.

Lastly, on the outskirts of São Paulo, there was a form of rustic folklore to be observed and recorded: May festivities, when the villages were decorated with green palms; commemorative battles, in the Portuguese tradition, between

FIG 1. An ancient *figa*, found at Pompeii (the top of the thumb is missing)

mouros and *cristãos;* the procession of the *nau catarineta,* a cardboard ship rigged with paper sails; and a pilgrimage to distant parishes concerned with the protection of lepers, where, amid the rank stench of *pinga*—a kind of alcohol made from sugar-cane, very different from rum, and drunk either neat or with lime-juice—bards of mixed blood, in knee-boots and cheap finery and exceedingly drunk, beat drums and challenged each other in the singing of satirical songs. There were also beliefs and superstitions which it was interesting to chart, such as the curing of styes by the laying on of a gold ring or the classification of all food-stuffs into two incompatible groups—*comida quente* and *comida fria,* hot food and cold food—and other maleficent combinations—fish and meat, mangoes with alcoholic beverages, or bananas with milk.

However, in inland areas of the state, it was even more fascinating to concentrate, not on vestiges of Mediterranean traditions, but on the peculiar social forms favoured by a society in the making. The subject was still the same; it was a question of past and present, but whereas classical anthropological inquiry tries to explain the latter by means of the former, here it was the fluid present which seemed to be recapitulating certain very old stages of European evolution. As in France during the Merovingian period, you could see communal and urban life emerging in a country-side made up of latifundia.

The groupings which were developing were not like modern towns—whose features have been so effaced that it is becoming difficult to discover in them the stamp of their particular history—fused into an increasingly homogeneous form in which only administrative distinctions are noticeable. On the contrary, you could examine the towns as a botanist examines plants, recognizing from each one's name, appearance and structure which great family it belonged to in that kingdom that man has added to nature: the urban kingdom.

During the nineteenth and twentieth centuries, the moving ring of the pioneer fringe had slowly travelled from east to west and from south to north. About 1836, only the north, that is, the region between Rio and São Paulo, was firmly inhabited, and the movement was beginning to reach the central zone of the state. Twenty years later, colonization was starting in the north-east in the Mogiana and Paulista areas; by 1886 it had penetrated to Araraquara,

Alta Sorocabana and the Noroeste. In these last areas, as late as 1935, the rate of increase in the population corresponded to the rate of increase in coffee production, whereas in the old lands of the north the drop in coffee production had anticipated the drop in population by half a century. The demographic decline began to be felt only from 1920 onwards, whereas the exhausted plantations were being abandoned as early as 1854.

This cyclical utilization of space corresponded to an historical evolution which left an equally fleeting imprint. It was only in the large coastal towns—Rio and São Paulo—that urban expansion seemed sufficiently firmly based to appear irreversible: São Paulo had 240,000 inhabitants in 1900, 580,000 in 1920, was nearing the million mark in 1928 and by now has passed it. But, in the inland districts, different species of urban communities appeared and disappeared; the provinces were being simultaneously populated and depopulated. As the inhabitants moved from one place to another without necessarily increasing in number, they changed in social type; and the observation side by side of fossilized towns and embryonic cities made it possible, on the human level and within an extremely short stretch of time, to study transformations as striking as those found by palaeontologists comparing various geological strata in order to follow the phases in the evolution of organized beings over millions of years.

As soon as one left the coast, it had to be constantly borne in mind that, in a century, Brazil had been changing more than it had been developing.

During the imperial period, the country was thinly populated, but the distribution was comparatively even. Although the towns on the coast or near it remained small, those further inland were livelier than they are today. An historical paradox too often forgotten is that the general inadequacy in communications favoured the worst means of transport: when there was no other possibility but to go on horseback, people were less reluctant to make their journeys last months rather than days or weeks, or to explore areas where only the mule could venture. All over the interior of Brazil, the pace of life was slow but steady; there were regular boat services on the rivers, the trips being made in short stages spread over several months; and tracks (such as the one between Cuiaba and Goyaz) which had been completely forgotten by 1935 had still been in

intensive use a hundred years earlier by mule-trains num-
bering between fifty and two hundred animals.

Except in the case of the most remote areas, the state
of neglect into which central Brazil had fallen by the beginning of the twentieth century in no way reflected a
primitive situation: it was the price that had been paid for
the increase in population and trade in the coastal areas,
the result of the modern way of life which was developing
there. The inland areas, on the other hand, being difficult
to open up to progress, retrogressed instead of following
the general trend at their own slow pace. Similarly, the
introduction of steamships, by shortening distances, killed
ports-of-call, once famous the world over; and we may ask
whether air travel, by encouraging us to leapfrog over
places where we used to stop, is not going to have a similar
effect. After all, there is no harm in dreaming that mechanical progress may spontaneously yield a compensation on
which we can pin our hopes; it may restore some small
measure of solitude and oblivion, in exchange for the privacy it has so massively destroyed.

On a smaller scale, the interior of the state of São Paulo
and the neighbouring regions illustrated these transformations. There was, or course, no trace of the fortress towns
which had once ensured possession of a province, and
which were the original form of so many Brazilian towns
along the coasts and rivers: Rio de Janeiro and Victoria;
Florianopolis on its island; Bahia and Fortaleza on the
cape; Manaus and Obidos on the banks of the Amazon; or
Villa Bella de Mato Grosso, the ruins of which survive near
the Guaporé and are periodically occupied by the Nambikwara Indians. It was formerly the famous garrison town
of a *capitão de mato*—a captain of the bush—at the Bolivian frontier, that is, on the symbolic line that Pope Alexander VI drew across the as yet undiscovered New World
in 1493, in order to decide between the rival claims of the
Spanish and Portuguese crowns.

Towards the north and west, a few mining towns, now
deserted, were still to be seen, and their ruined monuments
—churches built in the flamboyant baroque style of the
eighteenth century—contrasted in their splendour with the
surrounding desolation. These towns had hummed with activity as long as the mines were being worked; now sunk
in lethargy, they yet seemed to have anxiously retained
vestiges of the wealth which brought about their ruin in

every hollow and fold of their wreathed columns, scrolled pediments and draped statues. The price paid for the mining of the subsoil had been the destruction of the countryside, especially of the forests which supplied wood for the foundries. The towns just wasted away, having, like a fire, exhausted their substance.

The State of São Paulo contains memories of other events too; for instance, the struggle, going back to the sixteenth century, between Jesuits and planters, each group defending a different method of settlement. The Jesuits, on their lands, were determined to wrest the Indians from their savage way of life and organize them into a kind of communal existence under Jesuit control. In certain remote regions of the State, these first Brazilian villages can still be recognized by the name *aldeia* or *missão,* and even more clearly by their spacious and functional plan: the church is at the centre, overlooking a rectangular open space of beaten earth now overgrown with grass, the *largo da matriz,* and is surrounded by streets intersecting each other at right-angles and lined with low houses standing where once the native huts had stood. The *fazenderos,* or planters, were jealous of the temporal power of the missions, which put a check on their tax extortions, and deprived them of slave labour. They launched punitive expeditions, which broke up the association between natives and priests. This rivalry explains a feature peculiar to Brazilian demography: village life, inherited from the *aldeias,* was preserved in the poorest regions, whereas, where the soil was rich and thus the object of fierce possessiveness, the people had no choice but to group themselves round the master's house, in identical straw or mud huts, so that the owner could keep an eye on his employees. Even today, along certain railway lines there is no communal life, and so stations have been built at regular intervals and given names running in alphabetical order—Buarquina, Felicidade, Limão, Marilia, etc. (around 1935 the *Paulista* company had got as far as the letter P)—and for hundreds of kilometres the train stops only at certain halts, called 'keys' each serving a *fazenda* around which the entire local population is concentrated—Chave Bananal, Chave Conceição, Chave Elisa . . .

On the other hand, in some instances, the planters would decide, for religious reasons, to hand over land to a parish. This would cause the creation of a *patrimonio,* a township placed under the protection of a saint. Other *patrimonios*

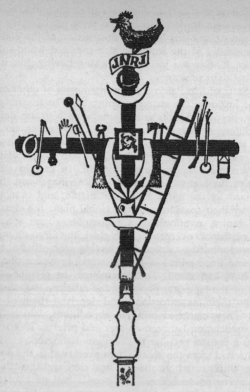

FIG 2. A cavalry cross, from a country district of the State of São Paulo, decorated with various items representing the instruments of the Passion

were secular in character, if they were the result of a landowner deciding to become a *povoador,* 'populator', or even a *plantador de cidade,* a planter of a town. In such a case, he would call the town by his own name, Paulopolis or Orlandia; or, prompted by a political motive, he might place it under the patronage of a famous person, Presidente-Prudente, Cornelio-Procopio, Epitacio-Pessoa . . . Even in the course of their short life-cycle, such townships still managed to change their names several times, each change being indicative of some phase in their development.

To begin with, they might be simply localities known by a nickname: for instance, one might be called *Batatas*, Potatoes, because a small patch of these vegetables grew in the middle of the bush; another, *Feijão-Cru*, Raw Bean, because there was not enough fuel to heat the billy-can in that inhospitable spot; or again, *Arroz-sem-Sal*, Rice-without-Salt, because provisions had run out by the time it had been reached. Then one day, a 'colonel'—this was a title freely bestowed on important landowners and political agents—would try to establish his authority over a few thousand acres that had come into his hands; he would recruit, hire or round up a floating population, and Feijão-Cru would become Leopoldina or Fernandopolis. Later, the town, which had been thus brought into being through ambition or personal whim, might decline and disappear: all that would remain would be the name and a few hovels inhabited by a diminishing community ravaged by malaria and hookworm. Sometimes, however, the town would take root; it developed a collective consciousness and tried to forget that it had been the plaything or instrument of a particular man. A new population fresh from Italy, Germany and half-a-dozen other countries might feel the need to give itself roots, and would make up another name from the dictionary, usually a Tupi name, which would endow it, or so it thought, with a kind of pre-Columbian prestige: Tanabi, Votuporanga, Tupão, or Aymoré . . .

Dead also are the river towns, which were killed by the railway, although here and there traces still remain of a now-defunct cycle. At first, there would be sheds and an inn on the river-bank, so that the canoe crews could spend the night with no fear of being ambushed by Indians. Then, the coming of small steamers gave rise to the *portos de lenha*, about thirty kilometres distant from each other, where the slender-funnelled paddleboats stopped to replenish their stocks of wood. Finally, there were the river ports at each end of the navigable stretches and, at those places which were impassable owing to rapids or waterfalls, the porterage points.

In 1935, two types of towns still retained their traditional appearance together with a degree of vitality. These were the *pousos*, villages situated at crossroads, and the *boccas de sertão*, 'the mouths of the bush', situated at the ends of tracks. Lorries were already beginning to replace the old means of transport—mule-trains or ox-carts. They

followed the same tracks, the precarious state of which
forced them to travel for hundreds of kilometres in first or
second gear, so that they went at about the same pace as
the beasts of burden and had to use the same stops, where
drivers in oil-stained overalls rubbed shoulders with leather-
clad *tropeiros*.

The tracks did not live up to expectations. They were of
various origins; some were former caravan routes, which
had been used for the transport of coffee, sugar-cane, alcohol and sugar in one direction, and salt, rice, beans and
flour in the other. From time to time they were intersected
by a *registro*, right in the heart of the bush: this was a
wooden barrier surrounded by a few huts, where a ragged
peasant representing some dubious authority demanded a
toll charge. This meant that there was also a network of
more secret tracks—the *estradas francas*—for the avoidance
of dues. Lastly, there were the *estradas muladas*, mule
tracks, and the *estradas boiadas*, ox-cart tracks. Along the
latter, it was quite common to hear, for two or three hours
on end, the monotonous and agonizing screech—and it was
enough to drive you mad if you weren't used to it—caused
by the rubbing of the axle of a slowly approaching cart.
These carts, of an antique Mediterranean design which had
scarcely changed since protohistoric times, had been imported in the sixteenth century. They consisted of a heavy
body with wickerwork sides, set directly on an axle which
was fixed to solid hubless wheels. The animals pulling them
spent more energy on overcoming the shrill resistance of
the axle to the body of the cart than on moving the whole
contraption forward.

Also, the tracks were the largely accidental result of a
levelling process brought about by the recurrent action of
animals, carts and lorries moving approximately in the
same direction but each trying to follow the path best suited
to the circumstances created by rainfall, soil subsidence or
growth of vegetation. They formed an intricate maze of
gullies or bare slopes, which sometimes came together to
provide a road a hundred yards or so wide, like an avenue
in the middle of the bush, which reminded me of the
drailles in the Cévennes, or sometimes diverged in all directions to the horizon so that it was impossible to tell which
of these Ariadne's threads one had to follow so as not to
find oneself lost in sandy or marshy wastes, after covering
some thirty kilometres in several hours of dangerous and

Fig 3. A detailed view of the axle of an ox-cart

laborious effort. During the rainy season, the tracks became impassable canals of slimy mud, but later, the first lorry which managed to get through left deep ruts in the wet earth which, after three days of drought, took on the consistency and strength of cement. The vehicles which followed had no other choice but to engage their wheels in these grooves and carry on, which was possible if they had the same gauge and the same ground clearance as the first lorry. If the gauge was the same but the chassis lower, one might suddenly find oneself hoisted up on to the raised mound in the middle of the track and the vehicle would remain stuck on a solid ridge which had to be broken down with pickaxes. If the gauge was different, one had to drive for days on end, with the wheels on one side running in a groove, while the others were raised at an angle, so that the vehicle was in danger of overturning at any moment.

I can still remember one journey, for the sake of which René Courtin sacrificed his new Ford. Jean Maugüé, René and myself had decided to go as far as the car could take us. Our trip ended, in fact, 1,500 kilometres from São Paulo in the hut of a family of Karaja Indians, on the banks of the Araguaya; during the return journey, the front springs broke and we drove for a hundred kilometres with the engine resting directly on the axle, and then, for a further six hundred kilometres, with it held up by means of a strip of iron fashioned by a village craftsman. But what I remember most clearly is the hours of anxious driving through the dark—there are very few villages along the borders of the São Paulo and Goyaz States—without knowing when the particular rut we had chosen to follow might lead us astray. Suddenly the *pouso* emerged out of the darkness, which seemed studded with flickering stars. These were electric bulbs fed by a tiny motor, the throbbing of which had been vaguely audible at intervals for hours but had remained indistinguishable from the nocturnal sounds of the bush. The inn offered us its iron beds or hammocks, and we rose at dawn to wander through the *rua direita* of the *cidade viajante,* or posting station, with its houses and bazaars, and its square occupied by *regatões* and *mascates* —tradespeople, doctors, dentists and even itinerant lawyers.

One can imagine the town, on fair days, bustling with activity. Hundreds of peasants from remote areas leave their huts for the occasion, bringing all their family with them. The journey takes several days, but it allows them, once a year, to sell a calf, a mule, a tapir or puma skin, a few sacks of maize, rice or coffee, and to bring back in exchange a piece of cotton fabric, salt, lamp oil and a few rifle bullets.

In the background lies the plateau, covered with undergrowth interspersed with occasional shrubs. Recent erosion —deforestation occurred only half a century ago—has pitted its surface here and there, as if it had been cautiously chipped with an adze. Differences in level of a yard or two indicate the beginning of terraces and mark out incipient ravines. Not far from a stream—which is wide but not deep, and much more like a fitful flooding than a river properly established in its bed—two or three parallel avenues run past the plots of luxuriant vegetation surrounding the tiled, adobe *ranchos,* lime-washed in a glistening creamy whiteness which is intensified by the brown frames of the shutters and the glare from the purple earth. Immediately adjoining the first houses, which look like covered markets because of their façades with large, paneless windows, almost always thrown wide open, are meadows of coarse grass, close-cropped by the livestock. In anticipation of the fair, the organizers have prepared stocks of fodder, such as sugar-cane tops or young palms pressed together by means of branches tied together with grass ropes. The visitors camp in between the cube-shaped blocks, alongside their carts, whose solid wooden wheels are studded with nails around the rims. During the journey, new wickerwork sides and a roof made of ox skins secured by rope have provided shelter, but here they are completed by an awning made of palms, or a tent of white cotton fabric, extending outwards from the back of the cart. Rice, black beans and dried meat are being cooked in the open air: naked children gambol among the hooves of the oxen, which are chewing sugar-canes, with the pliable stems hanging from their mouths like jets of green water.

A few days later, there is not a soul left. The visitors have vanished back into the bush. The *pouso* drowses in the sunshine. Rustic existence will consist solely of bustle in the *villas de domingo,* which remain shut up all week. On Sunday riders meet there, at this intersection of the tracks, with its drinks-stall and its few huts.

13. PIONEER ZONE

Scenes of this kind are to be found again and again in the inland districts of Brazil, as one moves away from the coast towards the north or west, where the bush extends as far as the Paraguay marshes or the gallery-forest along the tributaries of the Amazon. Villages become increasingly fewer and the areas between them greater: sometimes these consist of open spaces, the *campo limpo*, the 'clean' savannah; sometimes they are covered in undergrowth, and are called *campo sujo*, the 'dirty' savannah, or *cerrado* and *caatinga*, which are two kinds of scrubland.

Towards the south, that is in the direction of the State of Parana, the increasing distance from the Tropic, the altitude and the volcanic origin of the subsoil account, in various ways, for the differences in landscape and ways of living. One can find there remnants of native communities still living near the civilized centres, as well as the most modern forms of inland colonization. So, it was to this area of Norte-Parana that I organized my first trips.

It took only a little more than twenty-four hours to reach the vast temperate and humid forest of coniferous trees which lay beyond the river Parana marking the border of the State of São Paulo and which, by its very denseness, had for so long kept the planters out. Until about 1930, it had remained virtually untouched, except for bands of Indians who still wandered through it and a few pioneers, usually poor peasants, who grew maize in small clearings.

When I arrived in Brazil the region was being opened up, chiefly because of the influence of a British firm to which the government had granted an initial concession of some three million acres, on the understanding that it undertook to build roads and a railway. The English proposed to resell the land in lots to immigrants, mainly from Eastern and Central Europe, and to retain ownership of the railway, the viability of which would be ensured by the transport of agricultural produce. By 1935, the experiment was well under way, and the railway was steadily cutting

through the forest. It was fifty kilometres long at the beginning of 1930, 125 at the end, 200 in 1932 and 250 in
1936. Every fifteen kilometres or so, a station was built
alongside a patch of cleared ground one kilometre square,
which was intended to become a town. Settlement was in
progress so that, in covering the route, one passed through
a succession of places, starting at Londrina, the senior town
which already had three thousand inhabitants, then Nova
Dantzig with ninety, Rolandia with sixty and the last,
Arapongas, which in 1935 possessed one house with a
single inhabitant. He was a middle-aged Frenchman, who
wore military leggings left over from the 1914–18 war and
a straw boater, as he thus tried to make his fortune in the
wilderness. Pierre Monbeig, who has expert knowledge of
this pioneer fringe, tells me that, by 1950, Arapongas had
ten thousand inhabitants.

As one travelled through the country on horseback or by
lorry, following the newly marked-out roads which kept to
the ridges, like the Roman roads in Gaul, it was impossible
to detect any sign of life. The oblong lots of land were
bounded at one end by the road and at the other by the
stream running along the bottom of each valley. But the
work of settlement had begun down below, near the water;
although the *derrubada*, or clearing, was gradually moving
up the slope, the road itself, the symbol of civilization, remained enclosed within the thick covering of forest which,
for a few months or a few years more, would continue to
clothe the tops of the hills. But down in the valleys, the
first harvests, always fabulous in this *terra roxa*, or purple,
virgin land, were showing between the trunks and stumps
of felled trees. The winter rains would rot both trunks and
stumps into fertile humus, and then almost immediately
would wash it away down the slopes, together with the soil
which had fed the vanished forest, since there were no
longer any tree-roots to hold it back. In ten, twenty or
thirty years' time, this land of Canaan might well be reduced to an arid and devastated landscape.

For the moment, the immigrants could think only of the
hard-won joys of abundance; Pomeranian or Ukrainian
families, who had not yet had time to build themselves
houses, and camped, along with their cattle, in wooden
shelters on the river-banks, were enthusiastic about the
miraculous soil, so rich that its mettle had to be broken,
like that of a wild horse, before maize and cotton could

reach fruition, instead of running riot in luxuriant vegetation. A German farmer wept with joy as he showed us the
clump of lemon trees he had grown from a few pips. These
northerners were amazed not only by the fertility of the
land, but even more so perhaps by the exotic crops, which
they had heard of previously only in fairy-tales. Since the
area is at the junction of the tropical and temperate zones,
a few yards' drop in level corresponds to appreciable climatic differences, so that it was possible for them to grow
everything side by side, plants from their home countries
together with American species. Delighted to be able to
indulge in such agricultural entertainment, they juxtaposed
wheat and sugar-cane, flax and coffee . . .

These young cities were totally nordic; the new immigrants joined the old—Germans, Poles, Russians and to
a lesser degree Italians who, rather less than a century before, had settled around Curitiba in the southern part of
the State. The houses, made from planks or roughly fashioned tree-trunks, were reminiscent of central and eastern
Europe. Long horsedrawn waggons with four-spoked wheels
replaced the Iberian ox-carts. And here too, the contours
of a rapidly emerging future world were more exciting
than such unexpected survivals. Day by day, featureless
space was acquiring an urban structure; it was changing, as
an embryo divides into cells, which in turn form specialized
groups, each with its own function. Londrina was already
an organized town with its main street, business centre,
artisans' district and residential area. But what mysterious
forces were at work fashioning the no-man's-land from
which Rolandia, and still more so Arapongas, had yet to
emerge? Certain types of inhabitants would be compelled
in one direction, others in another, and each district would
be obliged to fulfil a particular function or vocation. In
these rectangular spaces arbitrarily cleared in the heart of
the forest, the streets too run at right-angles and are, in the
first instance, all alike; they are simply geometrical lines,
with no intrinsic quality of their own. However, some are
central and others peripheral; some parallel, and others
perpendicular, to the railway line or the road; the former
follow the direction of trade, the latter cut across it and, as
it were, interrupt it. Business and commerce choose the
first, which are necessarily much frequented; and, for the
opposite reason, private houses and certain public services
prefer the second or are forced back on to them. The com-

bination of the two contrasts—between central and peripheral, on the one hand, and parallel and perpendicular, on the other—gives rise to four different modes of urban life which mould the character of the future inhabitants, encouraging some and discouraging others, prompting success or causing failure. What is more, the townspeople will be of two types—the gregarious, who are attracted to the areas with the most advanced degree of urbanization, and the non-gregarious, who are concerned for their individual freedom—and this will give rise to a new kind of counterpoint, which adds its complexities to the first.

Finally, we must take into account those mysterious factors which are at work in so many towns, driving them westwards and condemning their eastern districts to poverty or decay. Such factors may be no more than a manifestation of that cosmic rhythm which, since the beginning of the human race, has imbued mankind with the unconscious belief that to move with the sun is positive, and to move against it negative, one direction expressing order, the other disorder. We gave up sun worship a long time ago and we have lost the habit of associating the points of the compass with magic qualities, colours and virtues. But however hostile our Euclidean minds may have become to the qualitative conception of space, we cannot prevent the major astronomical and meteorological phenomena conferring almost imperceptible but ineradicable properties on certain areas. Nor can we alter the fact that, for all men, the east-west direction denotes achievement, while the inhabitants of the temperate regions of the northern hemisphere look upon the north as the seat of cold and darkness, and the south as that of heat and light. No hint of all this transpires in the rational behaviour of any particular individual. But urban life offers a strange contrast. While representing the most complex and refined form of civilization, through the exceptionally large concentrations of human beings it brings together within a small space, and through the duration of its cycle, it provides a melting pot for the precipitation of unconscious attitudes, which are almost imperceptible in single instances but which, because of the number of individuals who exemplify them for the same reason and in the same manner, become capable of producing important consequences, such as the growth of towns from east to west and the polarization of luxury and poverty along the east–west axis, a phenomenon which

would be incomprehensible if we did not accept the fact
that towns have the advantage, or the limitation—because
of that magnifying ability they share with microscopes—
of showing, on the plate of the collective conscience, the
swarming, microbial mass of our ancestral and still-living
superstitions.

But are they really superstitions? I see these preferences
rather as denoting a kind of wisdom which savage races
practised spontaneously and the rejection of which, by the
modern world, is the real madness. Savages have often succeeded in achieving mental harmony with a minimum of
effort. What wear and tear, what useless irritation, we could
spare ourselves if we agreed to accept the true conditions
of our human experience and realize that we are not in a
position to free ourselves completely from its patterns and
rhythm! Space has its own values, just as sounds and perfumes have colours, and feelings weight. The search for
such correspondences is not a poetic game or a practical
joke (as some critic has had the audacity to say it is, in
connection with Rimbaud's 'sonnet des voyelles', which is
now a classic text for linguists who know the basis, not of
the colour of phonemes—which is a variable depending on
the individual—but of the relationship between them, which
admits of only a limited scale of possibilities); it offers absolutely virgin territory for research where significant discoveries are still to be made. If, like the aesthete, fish
divide perfumes into light and dark, and bees classify
luminosity in terms of weight—darkness being heavy and
brightness light—the work of the painter, the poet or the
musician, like the myths and symbols of the savage, ought
to be seen by us, if not as a superior form of knowledge, at
least as the most fundamental and the only one really
common to us all; scientific thought is merely the sharp
point—more penetrating because it has been whetted on the
stone of fact, but at the cost of some loss of substance—
and its effectiveness is to be explained by its power to
pierce sufficiently deeply for the main body of the tool to
follow the head.

The sociologist can help towards the creation of this total
and concrete humanism. The major manifestations of social
life have something in common with works of art, namely
that they come into being on the level of the unconscious,
because they are collective, and *although* works of art are
individual. However, this is a minor difference, and really

only an apparent one, since social phenomena are produced *by* the public and works of art *for* the public; it is the public which endows them with a common denominator and determines the conditions of their creation.

So it is not in any metaphorical sense that we are justified in comparing—as has so often been done—a town with a symphony or a poem; they are objects of a similar nature. The town is perhaps even more precious than a work of art in that it stands at the meeting point of nature and artifice. Consisting, as it does, of a community of animals who enclose their biological history within its boundaries and at the same time mould it according to their every intention as thinking beings, the town, in both its development and its form, belongs simultaneously to biological procreation, organic evolution and aesthetic creation. It is at one and the same time an object of nature and a subject of culture; an individual and a group; reality and dream; the supremely human achievement.

In these synthetic towns of southern Brazil, the hidden and stubborn determination behind the way the houses were laid out, the streets given specialized functions and the various districts different styles, seemed all the more significant in that it was both a continuation and a contradiction of the whim to which they owed their existence. Londrina, Nova Dantzig, Rolandia and Arapongas—which had come into being through a decision taken by a team of engineers and financiers—were slipping quietly back into the concrete diversity of a realistic order of things, as Curitiba had done a century earlier, or as Goiania is perhaps doing at the present time.

Curitiba, the capital of the State of Parana, appeared on the map through the government's decision to create a town. The site was bought from a landowner and resold in lots that were sufficiently cheap to cause an influx of population. The same method was used later to provide the State of Minas with its capital, Bello Horizonte. In the case of Goiania, the gamble was a greater one, since the aim was, in the first instance, to create a federal capital for Brazil, *ex nihilo*.

About one third of the way, as the crow flies, between the southern coast and the course of the Amazon, lie vast plateaux which have been forgotten by man for the last two hundred years. At the time of the caravans and the river-steamers, it was possible to cross them in a few weeks to get from the mines to the north. After reaching the banks of the river Araguaya, the traveller could go down by boat as far as Belem. The only evidence of this old provincial way of life was Goyaz, the tiny capital of the State of Goyaz, which lay a thousand kilometres from the coast and was virtually cut off from it. In a verdant setting overlooked by the irregular crests of palm-studded hills, streets of low houses ran down between gardens and squares where horses grazed in front of churches with ornate windows, which were half barns, half houses with belfries. Colonnades, stuccoed walls and pediments, always freshly painted with a wash that was like egg-white ringed with cream, ochre, blue or pink, recalled the baroque style of the Iberian pastorals. A river flowed between mossy embankments which, in places, had collapsed under the weight of the creepers, banana trees and palms growing among the deserted houses; but the lush vegetation seemed not so much to brand them as ruins as to add a silent dignity to their dilapidated façades.

I do not know whether one should regret or rejoice at the absurdity, but the administration decided to forget Goyaz, with its countrified setting, its calades and old-fashioned charm. It was all too small and too old. A completely virgin territory would have to be found for the establishment of the gigantic scheme that was now envisaged. This territory was discovered a hundred kilometres to the east, in the form of a plateau covered with nothing but coarse grass and thorn bushes, as if it had been struck by a plague which had destroyed all the fauna and stunted the vegetation. No railway or road led to it; only tracks fit for carts. A symbolic square, a hundred kilometres long on each side, was marked out on the map of the area. This was to be the site of the federal district, in the centre of which the future capital would be built. As there was no irregularity of surface to worry the architects, they could work on the site as if it were a drawing-board. The plan of the town was marked out on the ground; they drew the boundary, and inside it, the different areas, residential, administrative, business, industrial, even the one devoted to entertainment. The latter is always important in a pioneer city: there was a time, about 1925, when, in Marilia, which had been founded in a similar way, out of the six hundred newly built houses, nearly a hundred were brothels, most of them specializing in those *Francesinhas* who, together with French nuns, were the most active agents of French influence abroad in the nineteenth century. The Quai d'Orsay was well aware of this, since, in 1939, it was still spending a substantial fraction of its secret funds on the dissemination of so-called naughty magazines. Certain of my former colleagues will not contradict me if I mention that the founding of the University of Rio Grande do Sul, the most southerly state in Brazil, and the preference shown there for French teachers is to be explained by the fact that a future dictator had been given a taste for French literature and French freedom by a young lady of easy virtue, whom he had known in Paris as a young man.

From one day to the next, the papers were full of notices announcing the founding of the city of Goiania. A detailed plan was given, as if the town were a hundred years old, and alongside it were enumerated the advantages the inhabitants could look forward to—roads, railway, water supply, sewers and cinemas. If I remember rightly, at the beginning, in 1935–6, there was even a period when land was offered free to those prospective buyers who agreed to pay the legal expenses of the purchase. Solicitors and speculators were the first occupants.

I visited Goiania in 1937. On an endless plain, half vacant lot and half battlefield, bristling with electric cable poles and survey posts, were a hundred or so new buildings, scattered in all directions. The largest was the hotel, a cube of cement which, in the surrounding flatness, looked like an air-terminal or a small fort; one felt tempted to describe it as a 'bastion of civilization', not in a metaphorical but in a literal sense, which in the circumstances took on strongly ironical overtones. Nothing could be more barbaric or inhuman than this appropriation of the desert. The clumsy and unlovely building was the opposite of Goyaz; neither history, nor the passage of time nor custom had filled its emptiness or softened its stiffness; like a station or a hospital, it was a place of transit not of residence. Only the fear of some disaster could justify the existence of this block-house. A disaster had, in fact, occurred, and the silence and immobility all around was its ominous aftermath. Cadmus, the civilizer, had sown the dragon's teeth. Out of this land scorched and burnt by the monster's breath, one expected to see men sprouting.

14. THE MAGIC CARPET

Today, the memory of that big hotel in Goiania coincides with my recollections of other hotels which, at the opposite poles of luxury and poverty, bear witness to the absurdity of the relationships which man consents to have with the world, or rather, which are increasingly forced upon him. I rediscovered the Goiania hotel, but enlarged out of all proportion, in another no less arbitrary town, Karachi, where political calculations and the systematic uprooting of communities had, in a period of three years up to 1950, increased the population from 300,000 to 1,200,000; it, too, was in the heart of the desert, since Karachi stands at the eastern tip of that arid plain which stretches from Egypt to India and has stripped the living skin off a vast area of our globe.

Originally a fishing village, then as a result of the English colonial presence, a small port and trading centre, Karachi had been promoted to the rank of capital in 1947. In the long avenues of the former compound, lined by collective or individual barrack-like structures—the latter, private residences of officials or officers—each one standing separately in its patch of dusty vegetation, hordes of refugees slept out in the open and were leading a wretched existence on the pavement, bloody with the spittle of betel chewers, while the Parsee millionaires were busy building Babylonian palaces for western businessmen. For months on end, from dawn till dusk, a procession of men and women in rags filed past (in Moslem countries, the segregation of women is not so much a religious practice as a mark of bourgeois prestige, and the poorest members of the community are not even entitled to have a sex), each carrying a basket full of newly mixed concrete, which he or she tipped into the shuttering, before going back, without a pause, to the mixers to reload for another round. Each wing was in use almost before it was finished, since a room with board could be let at more per day than a woman worker earned in a month; in this way, the cost of building

128

a luxury hotel could be regained in nine months. So, the work had to be done quickly, and the foremen were not much concerned about whether the different blocks were all exactly in line. There had probably been no change since the days when the Satraps compelled slaves to pour mud and pile up bricks for the building of their rickety palaces; the line of women basket-carriers, silhouetted against the sky on top of the scaffolding, could indeed have served as a model for the friezes on one of those palaces.

Cut off from native life (which in this desert was itself an artificial effect of colonization) by a few miles made impassable by an intolerable monsoon-like, but never re-solved, humidity, and even more so by the fear of dysen-tery ('Karachi tummy'), a community of businessmen, industrialists and diplomats languished in the heat and boredom of these bare cement cells which served as bed-rooms and which seemed to be designed in this way not only for reasons of economy but still more to facilitate the process of disinfection that took place each time one of them was vacated by the human specimen who had been immobilized there for a few weeks or months. And my memory at once leapfrogs over another three thousand kilometres to link this picture with another, connected with the temple of the goddess Kali, the oldest and most revered sanctuary in Calcutta. On the banks of a stagnant pond, and in an atmosphere redolent with that mixture of physi-cal deformity and fierce commercial exploitation in which the popular religious life of India is conducted, not far from bazaars overflowing with pious colour plates and painted plaster divinities, stands the 'Rest-House', the modern shelter built by the religious organizers to house the pilgrims. It is a long cement hall, divided into two parts, one for the men and the other for the women, and each lined with platforms, also made of bare cement, in-tended for use as beds. I was asked to admire the gutters and the water-cocks. As soon as the human cargo has got up and been dispatched to its devotions, during which it begs for the healing of its ulcers, cankers, scabs and run-ning sores, the whole building is washed out by means of hoses so that the stalls are clean and fresh for the next batch of pilgrims. Nowhere, perhaps, except in concentra-tion camps, have human beings been so completely iden-tified with butcher's meat.

However, this was not meant as anything more than a

temporary lodging. A little further on, at Narrayanganj, the jute workers earn their living inside a gigantic spider's web formed by whitish fibres hanging from the walls and floating in the air. They then go home to the 'coolie lines', brick troughs with neither light nor flooring, and each occupied by six or eight individuals; they are arranged in rows of little streets with surface drains running down the middle, which are flooded thrice daily to clear away the dirt. Social progress is now tending to replace this kind of dwelling by 'workers' quarters', prisons in which two or three workers share a cell three metres by four. There are walls all around, and the entrance gates are guarded by armed policemen. The communal kitchens and eating-quarters are bare cement rooms, which can be swilled out and where each individual lights his fire and squats on the ground to eat in the dark.

Once, during my first teaching post in the Landes area, I had visited poultry yards specially adapted for the cramming of geese: each bird was confined to a narrow box and reduced to the status of a mere digestive tube. In this Indian setting, the situation was the same, apart from two differences: instead of geese, it was men and women I was looking at, and instead of being fattened up, they were, if anything, being slimmed down. But in both instances, the breeder only allowed his charges one form of activity, which was desirable in the case of the geese, and inevitable in the case of the Indians. The dark and airless cubicles were suited neither for rest, leisure nor love. They were mere points of connection with the communal sewer, and they corresponded to a conception of human life as being reducible to the pure exercise of the excretory functions.

Alas, poor Orient! In Dacca, that secretive city, I visited various middle-class households. Some were as luxurious as the antique shops on Third Avenue in New York; others, belonging to comfortably off people, were as full of cane pedestal-tables, fringed tea-cloths and china as a suburban villa in Bois Colombes. Some, in the old style, were like our poorest peasant cottages, and the cooking was done on a stove of beaten earth, at the far end of a muddy little courtyard. On the other hand, there were three-roomed flats for well-to-do young married couples in buildings indistinguishable from the low-priced blocks put up, as part of the postwar reconstruction, at Châtillon-sur-Seine or Givors, except that in Dacca the rooms were made of bare cement (as was the wash-room, with its single tap), and as scantily furnished as a little girl's bedroom. Squatting on the concrete floor, in the dim light of a single bulb hanging by its flex from the ceiling, I once—oh, Arabian Nights! —ate a dinner full of succulent ancestral savours, picking up the food with my fingers: first, *Khichuri,* rice and the small lentils which are called pulses in English, and the multicoloured varieties of which can be seen standing in sackfuls in the markets. Then *nimkorma,* broiled chicken; *chingri cari,* an oily fruity stew of giant shrimps, and another stew with hard-boiled eggs called *dimer tak,* accompanied by cucumber sauce, *shosha;* finally the dessert, *firni,* made of rice and milk.

I was the guest of a young teacher; also present were his brother-in-law, who acted as butler, a maid, a baby, and lastly my host's wife who was in process of being emancipated from purdah. She was like a silent, frightened doe, but, in order to underline her recent liberation, her husband showered sarcastic remarks on her, with a tactlessness which embarrassed me as much as it did her. Since I was an anthropologist, he made her bring out her personal underwear from a modest little chest-of-drawers, so that I could note the different items. With a little encouragement he would have made her undress in front of me, so anxious was he to prove his esteem for Western ways, of which he knew nothing.

I could thus see, taking shape before my very eyes, an Asia characterized by workers' dwellings and cheap blocks of flats. This Asia of the future, which rejects all forms of exoticism, may link up again, after an eclipse of five thousand years, with that dreary yet efficient style of life which the Asiatics perhaps invented in 3000 B.C. It subsequently moved across the earth's surface, making a temporary halt in the New World, so that we tend to think of it as being specifically American; but then, as early as 1850, it resumed its advance westwards, reaching first Japan and now at last its place of origin, after going right round the world.

In the valley of the Indus, I wandered among the austere remains of the oldest Oriental culture, which have managed to withstand the passing of the centuries, sand, floods, saltpetre and Aryan invasions: Mohenjo-Daro and Harappa, hardened outcrops of bricks and shards. These ancient settlements present a disconcerting spectacle. The streets are all perfectly straight and intersect each other at right-angles;

there are workers' districts, in which all the dwellings are identical, industrial workshops for the grinding of grain, the casting and engraving of metals and the manufacture of clay goblets, fragments of which lie strewn on the ground; municipal granaries which occupy several blocks (as we might be tempted to say, making a transposition in time and space); public baths, water-pipes and sewers; and solid but unattractive residential districts. No monuments or large pieces of sculpture, but, at a depth of between ten and twenty yards, flimsy trinkets and precious jewels, indicative of an art devoid of mystery and uninspired by any deep faith, and intended merely to satisfy the ostentatiousness and sensuality of the rich. The complex as a whole reminds the visitor of the advantages and defects of a large modern city; it foreshadows those more advanced forms of Western civilization, of which the United States of America today provides a model, even for Europe.

It is tempting to imagine that, after four or five thousand years of history, the wheel has come full circle—that the urban, industrial, bourgeois civilization first begun in the towns of the Indus valley was not so very different, in its underlying inspiration, from that which was destined to reach its peak on the other side of the Atlantic, after a prolonged period of involution in the European chrysalis. When the Old World was still young, it was already anticipating the features of the New.

I therefore mistrust superficial contrasts and the apparently picturesque; they may not be lasting. What we call the exotic expresses an inequality of rhythm, which can be significant over a few centuries and temporarily obscure destinies which might well have remained united or parallel, like those of Alexander and the Greek kings on the banks of the Jumna, the Scythian and Parthian empires, the Roman naval expeditions to the coasts of Vietnam and the cosmopolitan courts of the Mogol emperors. When we cross the Mediterranean by plane in the direction of Egypt, we are surprised at first by the sombre symphony of colours formed by the brownish-green of the palm groves, the green of the water—which we finally feel justified in describing as eau-de-Nil—the yellowish-grey sand and the purple mud; and even more than by the landscape, we are surprised by the plan of the villages as seen from the air: they sprawl beyond their boundaries and present that intricate and untidy arrangement of houses and little streets which is the sign of the Orient. Here we seem to have the opposite of the New World which, whether Spanish or Anglo-Saxon, and in the sixteenth century as well as the twentieth, shows a marked preference for geometrical layouts.

After Egypt, the flight over Arabia offers a series of variations on a single theme—the desert. First of all, rocks like ruined, red-brick castles emerge from the opalescent sand; elsewhere intricate designs, like the tracery of tree-branches—or even more like seaweed or crystals—made by the paradoxical behaviour of the wadi which, instead of bringing their waters together in a single stream, branch outwards into tiny rivulets. Further on, the ground seems to have been trampled by some monstrous beast, which has done its best to press it dry with furious stampings.

How delicately coloured are the sands! The desert takes on flesh tints: peach-bloom, mother-of-pearl, the iridescence of raw fish. At Aqaba, the water, although beneficent, reflects the pitilessly hard blue of the sky, while the uninhabitable rocky ranges shade off into soft pearly greys.

Towards the end of the afternoon, the sand gradually merges into the mist, which is itself a kind of celestial sand that has joined forces with the earth against the limpid blue-green of the sky. The desert loses its undulations and eminences; it merges with the evening, in a vast, uniform rosy mass which, as yet, has hardly more substance than the sky. The desert has become a desert even in relationship to itself. Gradually the mist spreads everywhere until there is nothing left but night.

After the touch-down at Karachi, day dawns over the incomprehensible, lunar desert of Thar; then small groups of fields appear, still separated by long stretches of desert. As the light strengthens, the cultivated areas fuse together to form a continuous surface of pink and green tints, like the exquisite and faded colours of some very old tapestry, which has been worn threadbare by long use and tirelessly darned. This is India.

The fields are irregular, yet there is nothing untidy about the collocations of shapes and colours. However they are grouped, they present a balanced pattern, as if a great deal of thought had been given to the drawing of their individual outlines in relationship to the whole. They might be geographical musings by Paul Klee. The whole scene has a rarified quality, an extreme and arbitrary preciosity, in spite of the recurrence of the triple theme: village, network of fields, pond surrounded by trees.

As the plane lands at, and takes off from, Delhi, one gets a brief glimpse of a romantic India, with ruined temples set in a vivid green undergrowth. Then the floods begin. The water seems so stagnant, so dense and so muddy that it is more like oil floating in streaks across the surface of another form of water constituted by the earth. The plane goes over Bihar with its rocky hills and forests, and then comes the beginning of the delta. The land is cultivated to the last inch, and each field looks like a jewel of green gold, pale and shimmering because of the water with which it is impregnated, and surrounded by the flawless dark rim of its hedges. There are no sharp angles; all the edges are rounded, yet fit against each other like the cells of a living tissue. At the approaches to Calcutta, the small villages increase in number, and their huts appear piled up like ants' eggs in nests of greenery, the vividness of which is still further intensified by the dark red tiles of certain roofs. The plane lands in torrential rain.

Beyond Calcutta lies the delta of the Brahmaputra, a monster of a river, and such a meandering mass that it seems more like a beast than a watercourse. All around, as far as the eye can see, the countryside is obliterated by water, except for the jutefields which, when looked at from above, form mossy squares of a greenness all the sharper through being so cool and fresh. Villages surrounded by trees emerge from the water like bunches of flowers with, all around, a swarm of boats.

Caught as it is, between sand without men and men without earth, India offers a very ambiguous appearance. The impression I was able to form during the eight hours it took me to cross from Karachi to Calcutta, disassociated India definitively from the New World. It has neither the rigid chessboard pattern of the Middle West or Canada, made up of identical units, each with a precise spatter of farm buildings in the same place on the same side; nor, still less so, the deep velvety green of the tropical forest, which is only just being encroached upon here and there by the bold inroads made by the pioneer zones. When the European looks down on this land, divided into minute lots and cultivated to the last acre, he experiences an initial feeling of familiarity. But the way the colours shade into each other, the irregular outlines of the fields and rice-swamps which are constantly rearranged in different patterns, the blurred edges which look as if they had been roughly stitched together, all this is part of the same tapestry, but —compared to the more clearly defined forms and colours of a European landscape—it is like a tapestry with the wrong side showing.

This is no more than a simile, but it corresponds fairly accurately to the respective positions of Europe and Asia in relation to their common civilization (and to the position of Europe itself in relation to its American offshoot). In their material aspects at least. Europe and Asia would seem to represent the reverse sides of each other; one has always been successful, whereas the other has always been a loser; it is as if they were engaged on a common enterprise, but one had drained away all the advantages, leaving the other to glean only poverty and wretchedness. In the one case (but for how much longer?) constant demographic expansion has led to agricultural and industrial progress, since the volume of resources has increased more rapidly than the numbers of consumers. In the other, ever since the eighteenth century, the same revolution has led to a constant decrease in the share available to the individual from a mass of wealth which has remained comparatively static. Europe, India, North America and South America can be said to illustrate the possible range of combinations between geographical setting and density of population. Amazonian America is poor tropical territory but relatively unpopulated (one factor partially compensates for the other), whereas southern Asia is also poor tropical territory, but over-populated (one factor exacerbates the other); and, in the category of temperate countries, North America, with its vast resources and comparatively limited population figures high. But, whichever way one looks at these obvious truths, southern Asia is always the martyred continent.

15. CROWDS

Whether we are considering the mummified towns of the Old World or the foetal cities of the New, we are accustomed to associate our highest values, both material and spiritual, with urban life. But the large towns of India are slum areas. What we are ashamed of as if it were a disgrace, and regard as a kind of leprosy, is, in India, the urban phenomenon, reduced to its ultimate expression: the herding together of individuals whose only reason for living is to herd together in millions, whatever the conditions of life may be. Filth, chaos, promiscuity, congestion; ruins, huts, mud, dirt; dung, urine, pus, humours, secretions and running sores: all the things against which we expect urban life to give us organized protection, all the things we hate and guard against at such great cost, all these by-products of cohabitation do not set any limitation on it in India. They are more like a natural environment which the Indian town needs in order to prosper. To every individual, any street, footpath or alley affords a home, where he can sit, sleep, and even pick up his food straight from the glutinous filth. Far from repelling him, this filth acquires a kind of domestic status through having been exuded, excreted, trampled on and handled by so many men.

Every time I emerged from my hotel in Calcutta, which was besieged by cows and had vultures perched on its windowsills, I became the central figure in a ballet which would have seemed funny to me, had it not been so pathetic. The various accomplished performers made their entries in turn: a shoeblack flung himself at my feet; a small boy rushed up to me; whining 'One anna, papa, one anna!' a cripple displayed his stumps, having bared himself to give a better view; a pander—'British girls, very nice . . .'; a clarinet-seller; a New Market porter begged me to buy everything, not because he himself would get any commission but because the annas he earned by following me would allow him to eat. He listed the items covetously, as if all the goods were presents intended for himself: 'Suit-cases? Shirts? Hose?'

And then there was a whole host of minor players. men who touted for rickshaws, gharries and taxis. There were as many vehicles as one could possibly want, only a yard or two away, waiting in line by the pavement. But how could the drivers tell? I might be too exalted a personage to deign to notice their presence . . . Not to mention the multitude of merchants, shopkeepers and street-hawkers, to whom one's advent brought a promise of Paradise, since one was perhaps going to buy something from them.

Anyone who might be prompted to laughter or irritation should reflect that both would be tantamount to sacrilege. There would be no point in criticizing these grotesque gestures and contorted movements, and it would be criminal to mock them; they should be seen for what they are—clinical symptoms of a life-and-death struggle. A single obsession, hunger, prompts this despairing behaviour; it is the same obsession which drives the country-dwellers into the cities and has caused Calcutta's population to leap from two to five millions in the space of a few years; it crowds refugees into stations, although they cannot afford to board the trains, and, as one passes through at night, one can see them sleeping on the platforms, wrapped in the white cotton fabric which today is their garment but tomorrow will be their shroud; it accounts for the tragic intensity in the beggar's gaze as his eyes meet yours through the metal bars of the first-class compartment, which have been put there—like the armed soldier squatting on the footboard—to protect you from the mute supplication of a single individual, who could easily be transformed into a howling mob if, by allowing your compassion to overcome your prudence, you gave the doomed creatures some hope of charity.

A European living in tropical America is puzzled by certain things. He observes new and strange relations between man and his geographical setting; and the various aspects of human life constantly provide him with food for thought. But interpersonal relations do not take on any novel form; they are recognizably the same as those to which he has always been accustomed. In southern Asia, on the contrary, reality seems to be either far below or far in excess of what man is entitled to demand of the world, and of man.

Daily life appears to be a permanent repudiation of the concept of human relations. You will be offered everything, promised everything; people will lay claim to every kind of skill, while knowing nothing. As a result, one finds oneself, willy-nilly, unable to credit others with that human quality which consists in good faith and the ability to honour agreements and exercise self-discipline. Rickshaw boys will offer to take you anywhere, although they may be even more ignorant of the route to follow than you are. It is difficult, in such circumstances, not to lose one's temper and—whatever moral scruples one may have about using their rickshaws and allowing oneself to be pulled along by them—not to treat them as being less than human, since they oblige you to regard them in this way through such unreasonable behaviour.

The fact that there are beggars everywhere is even more deeply disturbing. You dare not look anyone frankly in the eye for the sheer satisfaction of establishing contact with another human being, since the slightest pause will be interpreted as a weakness, as warranting a plea for alms. The tone of a beggar calling out 'sa-HIB' is astonishingly similar to the one we use in French when rebuking a child with the word 'VO-YONS' (Come, come), increasing the volume and lowering the voice on the last syllable. It is as if he were saying, 'But it is obvious, there is no getting away from it, here I am begging from you and by this fact alone I have a claim on you. So what can you be thinking of? Why don't you do something about it?' The acceptance of the *de facto* situation is so complete that it even manages to cancel out the element of request. All that remains is the recognition of an objective state of affairs, of a natural relationship between him and me, from which alms should flow with the same necessity as links cause and effect in the physical world.

Here again, it is the other person's attitude which compels you to deny him those human qualities you would so much like to acknowledge in him. All the primary situations which establish relationships between people are distorted; the rules of the social game are falsified and one doesn't know where to begin. If one tried to treat these unfortunate wretches as equals, they would protest against the injustice of one's doing so; they do not want to be equal; they beg, they entreat you to crush them with your pride, since it is from the widening of the gap between you and them that they expect their mite,* which will be greater in proportion to the width of the yawning gulf; the higher they place me, the greater will be their hopes that the trifle they are soliciting will turn out to be something substantial. They do not claim any right to live; the mere fact of survival seems to them undeserved alms, barely justified by the homage they render to the mighty.

It never occurs to them, then, to set themselves up as equals. But, even from human beings, it is impossible to tolerate such constant pressure, and the unflagging ingenuity with which they try to deceive you, 'get the better' of you, win something from you by guile, lies or theft. Yet how can one harden one's heart, when—and this is the insuperable point—all these forms of behaviour are modalities of prayer? And it is because the fundamental attitude towards you is one of prayer, even when you are being robbed, that the situation is so completely and absolutely intolerable, and that, in spite of being ashamed at the confusion, I cannot help likening the refugees—whom I can hear from the windows of my luxury hotel moaning and weeping all day long at the Prime Minister's gate, instead of driving us from our rooms which would house several families—to the black, grey-hooded crows cawing ceaselessly in the trees of Karachi.

This debasement of human relationships at first appears incomprehensible to the European mind. We look upon class differences in terms of struggle or tension, as if the initial—or ideal—situation corresponded to the resolution of these antagonisms. But here, the word tension has no meaning. Nothing is tense, since everything that might have been in a state of tension snapped long ago. The break was there at the start, and the non-existence of 'good times', to which people might refer either to discover traces of them or to long nostalgically for their return, leaves you with one conviction only: that all these people you see in the street are doomed. Even if you divested yourself of all your possessions, you could not be sure of delaying that doom for one moment.

And even if we try to think in terms of tension, the view we arrive at is hardly less sombre. Such an approach forces us to admit that everything is in a state of such acute

---

* TRANSLATORS' NOTE: *Bribe*, i.e. shred, fragment. Lévi-Strauss adds in parenthesis here, 'How fitting is the English term *bribery*.'

tension that no kind of equilibrium is possible: in terms of the system itself, unless you start by destroying it, the situation has become irreversible. From the outset, we find ourselves in a state of imbalance with regard to all these supplicants whom we have to repulse, not because we despise them but because they debase us by their veneration, by willing us to be even more impressive and powerful, in the crazy belief that every tiny improvement in their lot can only be the result of a hundredfold improvement in ours. This sheds a great deal of light on the sources of so-called Asiatic cruelty. Perhaps funeral pyres, executions and torture, as well as those surgical weapons intended to inflict incurable wounds, are the result of some appalling fancy to embellish abject relationships, in which the humble reify their superiors by willing their own reification, and vice versa. The gulf separating extreme luxury and extreme poverty destroys the human dimension. The outcome is a society in which those who can achieve nothing survive by hoping for everything (hence the typically Oriental daydream represented by the genii in the Arabian Nights!), and those who demand all offer nothing.

This being so, it is not surprising that human relations which are out of all proportion to those we fondly imagine —often wrongly—to be characteristic of Western civilization, should strike us as being alternately inhuman and sub-human, like those we observe among children. In certain respects at least, these people, although tragic, appear childish to us. First, there is the engaging way in which they look and smile at you; then their indifference to propriety and places, which is forced upon your attention since they sit or lie about in any position; their liking for trinkets and cheap finery; their naïve and indulgent behaviour (men walk about hand in hand, squat down to urinate in public and suck on their chilams as they inhale the sweet fumes); and their belief in the magic power of attestations and certificates, as well as the common conviction that everything is possible, which leads cab-drivers (and, more generally, anyone you happen to employ) to make wildly exaggerated demands, which are quickly satisfied by a quarter or a tenth of what had been asked for. Once, the governor of eastern Bengal, visiting the natives of the Chittagong hills who were suffering acutely from disease, malnutrition and poverty and were also being maliciously persecuted by the Moslems, asked, through his interpreter, 'Have they anything to complain about?' After considerable reflection, they replied, 'The cold . . .'

Every European in India finds himself surrounded, whether he likes it or not, by a fair number of general men-servants, called bearers. I cannot say whether their eager-ness to serve is to be explained by the caste system, the tradition of social inequality or the demand for service on the part of the colonizers. However, their obsequiousness very quickly has the effect of making the atmosphere in-tolerable. If necessary, they would lie down on the ground to let you walk over them, and they suggest a bath ten times a day—if you blow your nose, eat fruit or dirty your fingers. Each time, they are there at once, begging for orders. There is something sexual in this anguished sub-mission. And if your behaviour does not correspond to their expectations, if you do not behave on all occasions like their former British masters, their universe collapses: What, no pudding? A bath after dinner and not before? The world must be coming to an end . . . Dismay is written all over their faces. I would have quickly to countermand my original instructions, abandon my usual habits and forgo rare opportunities. I would eat a pear as hard as a stone or swallow slimy custard, since to ask for a pineapple would have caused the moral collapse of a fellow human being.

I spent a few days at the 'Circuit House' in Chittagong. It is a wooden palace, built in Swiss-chalet style, and I was given a room nine metres by five, and six metres high. There were no less than twelve electric switches—for the ceiling light, the wall lights, the indirect lighting, the bath-room, the dressing-room, the mirror, the electric fans, etc. There could be no doubt about it; this was the Bengal of the Bengal lights. Some maharajah or other had had this wealth of electric equipment installed for the daily enjoy-ment of private illuminations.

On one occasion, I stopped the chauffeur-driven car, put at my disposal by the district commissioner, in front of a respectable-looking shop in the lower part of the town—'Royal Hair Dresser, High class cutting, etc.'—and was about to enter it. The driver looked at me with horror: How can you sit there? What indeed would have been the effect on his prestige among his own people, if the master had lost caste, and at the same time had made him lose caste, by sitting down side by side with members of his race? Disheartened, I left him to arrange the ritual of the

haircut for a being of a superior nature. As a result, I had
to wait for an hour in the car until the hairdresser had
finished with his clients and gathered his equipment together. Then we all returned to Circuit House in our
Chevrolet. I was no sooner back in the room with the
twelve switches than the bearer started running a bath so
that, once the cutting was completed, I could wash away
the contamination caused by the touch of menial hands on
my hair.

Such attitudes are deeply rooted in a country where the
cultural tradition encourages every individual to behave
like a king in relation to someone else, if only he can succeed in finding or inventing some inferior being. The bearer
would have liked me to treat him as he would have treated
a common labourer belonging to the 'scheduled' castes:
that is the lowest castes, which the English administration
'scheduled' as being entitled to its protection, since custom
almost denied them the right to be considered as human
beings. And indeed one may wonder if they are human,
these sweepers and close-stool emptiers, whose dual function obliges them to remain in a squatting position all day
long, either because they are collecting the dust from the
steps leading up to the bedrooms, using their hands and a
small brush, or because they are banging on the lower part
of the privy doors at the back of the building to urge the
occupants to finish quickly with the monstrous contraptions
known as 'commodes': as if, by being always bent double
and scuttling like crabs across the courtyard to snatch the
master's substance from him, they too had discovered a
means of asserting a prerogative and acquiring a status.

Much more than independence and the passage of time
will be needed to wipe out this habit of slavery. The point
was brought home to me one night in Calcutta, as I was
leaving the Star Theatre after a performance of a Bengali
play on a mythological theme, entitled *Urboshi*. I felt
rather lost in an outlying district of a town where I had
arrived only the day before, and the single, cruising taxi
had already been hailed by a local middle-class family. But
the driver would not accept their custom: there was an
animated conversation in the course of which the word
'sahib' occurred repeatedly, and he seemed to be emphasiz-
ing that it was a breach of manners on their part to compete with a white man. After a discreet display of irritation, the family set off into the night on foot, and the taxi

took me back to my lodging. Perhaps the driver was counting on a more substantial tip, but as far as I could understand from my limited command of Bengali, the discussion had centred around something quite different: a traditional order of things which had to be respected.

I was all the more distressed, since I had had the illusion that evening of overcoming certain barriers. In the vast dilapidated hall, which was as much like a barn as a theatre, the fact that I was the only foreigner present had not prevented me mixing with the local community of very dignified shopkeepers, tradesmen, employees and civil servants, in many cases accompanied by their wives, whose grave charm seemed to show that they were not used to going out. The indifference they showed towards me was rather soothing, after the events of the day; however negative their attitude was, or perhaps precisely because it was negative, it established a kind of unobtrusive brotherhood between us.

The play, which I understood only in snatches, was a mixture of Broadway spectacle, musical comedy and Offenbach. There were comic scenes and scenes with soubrettes, sentimental love scenes, the Himalayas, a disappointed lover who lived there as a hermit, a god armed with a trident and whose baleful glare protected him from a heavily moustachioed general; and lastly a troop of chorus girls, half like prostitutes from a garrison town, and half like precious Tibetan idols. During the interval, tea and lemonade were served in disposable earthenware goblets—as was the practice four thousand years ago at Harappa, since the fragments are still there to be picked up—while loudspeakers broadcast jolly, vulgar music, a sort of cross between Chinese melodies and a *paso doble*.

As I watched the contortions of the *jeune premier*, whose scanty costume showed to advantage his curls, his double chin and his ample proportions, I remembered a sentence I had read a few days before on the literary page of a local paper, and which I transcribe textually because of the characteristic Anglo-Indian flavour: '. . . and the young girls who sigh as they gaze into the vast blueness of the sky, of what are they thinking? Of fat, prosperous suitors . . .' The reference to fat suitors had surprised me, but as I watched the stage where the self-satisfied hero was causing the folds of his stomach to undulate, and remembered the starving beggars I would see as I left the theatre,

I gained a better understanding of the poetic value of repletion for a society living in such close and painful familiarity
with famine. The English, incidentally, realized that the
surest way to give the impression of being supermen was to
convince the natives that they need a much greater quantity
of food than is required by an ordinary man.

During a journey among the Chittagong hills along the
Burmese frontier that I undertook with the civil-servant
brother of a local rajah, I was soon astonished at the care
with which he saw to it that his servants stuffed me with
food. At dawn, I had *palancha,* that is 'tea in bed' (if the
term 'bed' can be applied to the springy floors of woven
bamboo of the native huts in which we slept); two hours
later, a substantial breakfast; the midday meal; a copious
tea at five o'clock, and lastly dinner. And this in hamlets
where the people ate only two meals a day, consisting of
rice and boiled pumpkins with, in the richest families, a
little fermented fish sauce as flavouring. I was soon unable
to stand my diet, for physiological as well as moral reasons.
My companion, a Buddhist aristocrat brought up in an
Anglo-Indian school and proud of his family tree which
went back forty-six generations (he referred to his very
modest bungalow as his 'palace', because he had learned at
school that that was the term for a prince's abode), was
flabbergasted and vaguely shocked by my abstemiousness:
'Don't you take five times a day?' No, I did not 'take' five
times a day, especially when I was surrounded by people
dying of hunger. A stream of questions followed, because
he had never before been in contact with a white man who
was not English. What did people eat in France? What was
the composition of a French meal? How long were the intervals between meals? I did my best to tell him, like a conscientious native replying to an anthropologist's inquiries,
and with each word I uttered I could gauge the upheaval
which was taking place in his mind. His whole conception
of the world was changing: a white man could, after all, be
just a man.

Yet, in India, how very little is needed to create a human
community. A craftsman will sit all alone on the pavement
where he has laid out a few scraps of metal and his tools.
He devotes himself to some very humble task which supplies him with food for himself and his family. What kind
of food? In open-air kitchens, meat hash pressed on to
sticks is grilled over wood embers; curds drip into cone-

shaped pans; rounds of leaves arranged in spirals are used to wrap betel quids; golden grain seeds are roasted in hot sand. A child is carrying a few chick-peas in a bowl; a man buys the equivalent of a large spoonful of them and at once squats down to eat, with the same indifference to passers-by as when he later urinates in the same position. In wayside tea-houses made of wooden planks, idlers spend hours drinking milky tea.

Very little is needed in order to exist: little space, little food, little joy, few utensils or tools; it is life on a pocket-handkerchief scale. But, on the other hand, there seems to be no lack of soul; one is aware of it in the bustle of the streets, the intensity of the look in people's eyes, the passion which marks the most trifling discussion, and the courteous smiles with which passing strangers are greeted, and—in Moslem territory—the accompanying 'salaam', a low bow in which the palm of the right hand is placed on the forehead. Only quality of soul can explain the ease with which these people fit into the cosmos. Theirs is indeed a civilization in which a prayer rug represents the world, or a square drawn on the ground marks out a place of worship. They live in the open streets, each within the universe of his tiny display of goods and placidly occupied with his particular trade, among the flies, the passers-by and the hubbub made by barbers, copyists, hairdressers and craftsmen. In order to survive, each must have a very strong and personal link with the supernatural, and this, perhaps, is one of the secrets of Mohammedanism and of the other religions in this part of the world: each believer feels that he is constantly in the presence of his God.

I remember a walk along Clifton Beach, which is on the Indian Ocean near Karachi. After two miles of dunes and marshes, you come to a long beach of dark sand. On that particular day it was deserted, but on feast days crowds make their way there in carriages drawn by camels even more garishly bedecked than their masters. The ocean was a greenish white, and the sun was setting; all illumination seemed to be rising from the sand and the sea, while the sky above appeared to be set against the light. An old man, in a turban, had fashioned a small mosque for himself with the help of two iron chairs borrowed from a neighbouring eating-house, where kebabs were roasting. He was all alone on the beach, and he was praying.

16. MARKETS

Without deliberate intention on my part, a kind of mental 'tracking shot' has led me from central Brazil to southern Asia; from the most recently discovered lands to those in which civilization first made its appearance; and from the most thinly, to the most heavily, populated—if it is true that the density in Bengal is three thousand times what it is in the Mato Grosso or Goyaz. On reading over what I have written, I realize that the difference goes even deeper. In America, I was, first and foremost, looking at natural or urban landscapes, and in both cases these are objects defined by their shapes, colours and peculiar structures, which confer on them an existence independent of the living beings who occupy them. In India, these large objects have disappeared, having been destroyed by history and reduced to a physical or human dust which has become the only reality. In America, what I saw in the first place was the physical universe, whereas in India I saw only human beings. A sociological order worn away over hundreds of centuries was collapsing, and it was replaced by a multiplicity of interpersonal relationships, so completely did the human density interpose itself between the observer and the disintegrating object. In the light of this, the term 'subcontinent', which is often applied to India in India itself, takes on a new meaning. Instead of simply signifying a part of the Asiatic continent, it seems to imply a world hardly deserving of the name of continent, since disintegration, carried to the extreme limit of its cycle, has destroyed the structure which in the past maintained a few hundred million human particles within organized frameworks; they have now been set loose in a void created by history, and are being driven in all directions by the most elementary motivations of fear, suffering and hunger.

In tropical America, men are concealed, in the first place, by their rarity, but even in those areas where they have grouped together in more dense communities, individuals remain set, as it were, in the still strongly marked pattern

146

of their newly formed association. However low the standard of living may be in the interior or even in the towns, only exceptionally does it sink to a level at which human beings cry out in pain, since so very little is needed for survival in territory which man began to pillage—and even then in certain specific places—only 450 years ago. But in India, which has been an agricultural and manufacturing country for five or ten thousand years, the basic conditions of life are no longer available. The forests have disappeared; in the absence of wood, manure has to be used as fuel for the cooking of food and is therefore withheld from the fields; the arable land, eroded by the rains, is carried seawards; the starving cattle breed less rapidly than the people and owe their survival to the taboo on the eating of their flesh.

There could be no more vivid illustration of the basic contrast between the empty and the overpopulated tropics than a comparison between their fairs and markets. In Brazil, as in Bolivia or Paraguay, these important occasions in the social calendar emphasize that production still remains an individual matter; each stall reflects the peculiarity of the person behind it: as in Africa, the female stall-holder offers the customer the tiny surplus of her domestic activities. A couple of eggs, a handful of peppers, a bunch of vegetables or flowers, two or three rows of beads made from wild seeds—'goats' eyes', red with black speckles, or 'Our Lady's tears', grey and glistening—which have been gathered and threaded in leisure moments; a homemade basket or piece of pottery, or some antique talisman continuing to change hands in a complex cycle of transactions. These miniature displays, each of them a modest work of art, express a great variety of tastes and activities, as well as an equilibrium specific to each, and both these features are arguments in favour of the freedom which is still generally enjoyed. And if the passerby hears a voice hailing him, the intention is not to shock him with the spectacle of a maimed or skeleton-like body, or to beg him to save someone from death, but to ask him to *tomar a borboleta*, 'take the butterfly'— or some other creature in the lottery known as the *bicho*, an animal game, in which numbers are combined with the figures of a charming bestiary.

We know everything about our Oriental bazaar before visiting one, except that we are not acquainted with two things—the human density and the filth. It is impossible to imagine either, until one has actually experienced them. Impact immediately allows one to realize a fundamental dimension of reality. In this atmosphere black with flies and in the swarming masses of people we recognize a natural human setting, the setting in which what we call civilization was slowly secreted, from the time of Ur of the Chaldees to the Paris of Philippe le Bel, by way of Imperial Rome.

I have visited all kinds of markets; in Calcutta, the new one and the old ones; the Bombay Bazaar at Karachi; the markets in Delhi and the Sadar and Kunari in Agra; Dacca, which is a series of soukhs, with families living huddled in the nooks and crannies between the stalls and craftsmen's workshops; Riazuddin Bazaar and Khatunganj at Chittagong; all those at the gates of Lahore: Anarkali Bazaar, Delhi, Shah, Almi and Akbari; and Sadr, Dabgari, Sirki, Bajori, Ganj and Kalan at Peshawar. At country fairs in the Khyber Pass along the Afghan frontier, and at Rangamati near the Burmese frontier, I have visited fruit and vegetable markets, with their piles of egg-plants, pink onions and burst pomegranates releasing a heady, guava-like smell; flower markets where florists intertwined roses and jasmine with tinsel and angel hair; the displays of dried-fruit merchants, brown, tawny heaps on a background of silver paper; I have seen and smelt spices and curries, pyramids of red, orange and yellow powder; mountains of peppers, emitting a pungent odour of dried apricots and lavender which was enough to make the senses reel. I have seen meat-roasters, the boilers of milk-curds, the pancake-makers—*nân* or *chapati;* tea and lemonade sellers, wholesale date merchants with their produce piled up in sticky mounds of pulp and stones suggesting the excreta of some dinosaur; pastry-cooks, who might have been mistaken for vendors of flies, presenting their wares on a base of cake; tinkers who could be heard a hundred yards away because of the loud rumble of their hammers; basket-makers and rope-makers, with their yellow and green straw; hat-makers who had arranged the gilded cones of *kallas,* resembling the mitres of the Sassanid kings, in rows interspersed with turban cloths; textile shops, hung with lengths of freshly dyed blue or yellow material, as well as with saffron and pink artificial silk scarves in the Bokhara style; cabinet-makers, wood-carvers and lacquerers of bedsteads; knife-grinders pulling on the cords of their grinding-wheels;

scrap-iron fairs, separate from the rest, and cheerless; tobacco vendors with their heaps of golden leaves, alternating with russet masses of *tombak,* alongside bundles of chilam tubes; vendors of sandals, stacked in hundreds like bottles in a wine store; sellers of bracelets or bangles, like pink and blue glass intestines lying higgledy-piggledy as if they were the product of a recent disembowelling; potters' shops, with oblong, varnished, chilam water-vases arranged in rows; jars fashioned out of micaceous clay, and others painted brown, white and red on a background of tawny earthenware, with vermicular ornamental markings; and chilam bowls strung together like rosaries; flour vendors sieving flour all day long; gold- and silversmiths weighing tiny fragments of precious braid in shopfronts which were less brilliant than those of the nearby tinsmiths; calico-printers striking the white cotton fabric with a deft, monotonous movement which left a delicate coloured pattern; and blacksmiths working in the open air. All this formed a swarming and ordered world above which rose a forest of multicoloured children's windmills, mounted on sticks and fluttering like leaves stirring in the breeze.

Even country districts can provide equally striking spectacles. Once when I was making a trip by motor-boat along the Bengal rivers, we landed on an island in the middle of the Buliganga, a river lined with banana plants and palm trees, sheltering white-tiled mosques which seem to float on the surface of the water. A thousand or more boats and sampans moored in the vicinity indicated that a *hat,* or country market, was in progress. Although no permanent building was visible, a veritable town had sprung up for one day only, and the crowd of inhabitants had set up their stalls in the mud, with a clearly defined area for each particular kind of trade: paddy, livestock, boats, bamboo poles, wooden planks, pottery, fabrics, fruit, betel nuts and fishing-nets. The river traffic was so dense in the channels around the island that they were like liquid streets. Newly bought cows were being taken away without any fuss, each one standing up in its boat and sailing blankly past the landscape, which watched it go by.

The whole countryside in this area is extraordinarily soft and mild. There is something soothing and soporific in the greenery, tinged with the blue of water-lilies, and in the swamps and rivers with their gliding sampans; one is tempted to let oneself rot away like the old red-brick walls, which have been pushed out of shape by banyan trees.

Yet, at the same time, there is something disturbing about this gentleness. The landscape is not a normal one; it contains too much water for that. The annual floods create exceptional living conditions, since they cause a drop in vegetable production and in fish-catching. High-water time is a season of famine. Even the livestock is reduced to skin and bone and tends to waste away, through being unable to find adequate nourishment in the spongy water-lilies. The inhabitants are a strange people who seem to live more in water than in air, and their children learn to use their little dinghies almost as soon as they can walk. This is a place where, during the floods, through lack of any other fuel, the dried residue of processed jute is sold to people who earn less than the equivalent of three thousand francs (old francs) a month at the rate of 250 francs per 200 stalks.

However, one has to go into the villages to understand the tragic situation of these people, who are close to the most primitive communities in their customs, forms of habitation and way of life, yet who hold markets as elaborately laid out as a modern department store. Barely a hundred years ago, their bones littered the countryside. They were mainly weavers and had been reduced to starvation and death through being forbidden by the colonial authorities to practise their traditional trade, so as to leave the market open for cotton goods from Manchester. Now, every inch of cultivatable land, even though it may be flooded for six months of the year, is given over to the production of jute which, after processing, is sent off to the factories at Narrayanganj and Calcutta, or even straight to Europe and America; so that these illiterate and half-naked peasants still depend for their daily sustenance, in a different but no less arbitrary way, on the fluctuations of the world market. Although they can, and do, catch fish, the rice which forms their staple diet is almost entirely imported; and to eke out the meagre income from crops—since only a minority are landowners—they spend their days in pathetic occupations.

Demra is almost a village of lake dwellings, so precarious is the network of mounds emerging from the water and on which the huts are clustered together among clumps of trees. Here I saw the entire community, even quite tiny children, busy from dawn onwards weaving by hand the muslin veils for which Dacca used to be so famous. A little further on, at Langalbund, an entire region is engaged in the making of pearl buttons of the kind used in the Western world for men's shirts and nightwear. A caste of boatmen, the Bidyaya or Badia, who live permanently in the straw cabins of their sampans, gather and sell the river mussels which provide the mother-of-pearl; the heaps of muddy shells make the hamlets look like *placers*. After being passed through an acid bath, the shells are hammered to pieces and the fragments then made into rounds on a hand-operated grinding-wheel. Next, each disc is placed on a stand, to be fashioned into shape with the help of a piece of broken file that revolves at the tip of a wooden spindle operated by means of a bow. A similar instrument with a sharp point is used to pierce the four holes. Children sew the finished buttons, a dozen at a time, on to foil-covered cards, such as can be seen in Europe in provincial drapers' shops.

Before the major political changes brought about by the granting of independence to the Asiatic countries, this modest industry which supplied the Indian market and the Pacific islands provided the workers with a livelihood, in spite of the fact that they were, and continue to be, exploited by the *mahajans*, a class of money-lenders and middlemen who supply *t*he raw materials and the products needed for processing. The price of the latter increased five or six times, while production in the area dropped from sixty thousand gross per week to less than fifty thousand per month because of the closing of the market; at the same time, the price paid to the producer fell by 75 per cent. Almost overnight, fifty thousand people discovered that an already pathetically low income had been reduced to a mere fraction of what it had been before. Yet in spite of primitive modes of life, the fact is that the size of the population, the quantity of goods produced and the appearance of the finished articles make it impossible to consider these people as true craftsmen. In tropical America— in Brazil, Bolivia and Mexico—the term craftsmanship can still be applied to work done with metals, glass, wool, cotton or straw. The raw materials are of local origin, the skills are traditional and the work is carried out in domestic conditions; the purposes and forms of the products depend on the tastes, habits and requirements of the makers.

In Bengal, medieval communities have been plunged headlong into the industrial era and exposed to the vagaries of the world market. From start to finish they are victims of alienation. The raw material is foreign to them, totally so in the case of the Demra weavers, who depend on thread imported from England and Italy, and partially so in the case of the Langalbund button-makers, who use local shells but also need chemicals, cardboard and sheets of foil. And, throughout the area, production is planned 'according to foreign standards', the unfortunate workers themselves being hardly in a position to buy clothes, let alone put buttons on them. Behind the verdant landscapes and peaceful canals lined with cottages can be glimpsed the ugly outlines of an abstract factory, as if history and economics had managed to establish, indeed superimpose, their most tragic phases of development on these wretched victims: the shortages and epidemics of medieval times, frenzied exploitation as in the early years of the industrial revolution, and the unemployment and speculation of modern capitalism. The fourteenth, eighteenth and twentieth centuries come together to make a mockery of the idyll implicit in the setting provided by tropical nature.

It was in this part of the world, where the density of the population sometimes exceeds a thousand people per square kilometre, that I fully grasped the historical privilege that tropical America (and to some extent the whole of the American continent) still enjoys through remaining completely, or relatively, unpeopled. Freedom is neither a legal invention nor a philosophical conquest, the cherished possession of civilizations more valid than others because they alone have been able to create or preserve it. It is the outcome of an objective relationship between the individual and the space he occupies, between the consumer and the resources at his disposal. And it is far from certain that abundance of resources can make up for a lack of space, and that a rich but overpopulated society is not in danger of being poisoned by its own density, like those flour parasites which manage to kill each other at a distance by their toxins, even before their food supply runs out.

One has to be very naïve or dishonest to imagine that men choose their beliefs independently of their situation. Far from the forms of social existence being determined by political systems, it is they which give meaning to the ideologies by which they are expressed. Ideologies are signs which only constitute a language in the presence of the objects to which they relate. At the moment, the misunderstanding between East and West is primarily semantic: the concepts or 'signifiers' that we try to propagate in the East refer to 'signifieds' which are different there or non-existent. On the other hand, if it were possible for circumstances to change, it would matter very little to their victims if this occurred within a framework that we Westerners would deem intolerable. They would not be conscious of being enslaved but, on the contrary, would feel that they had been liberated, if they graduated to forced labour, food rationing and regimented thought, since this would be the historical development by virtue of which they would obtain work, food and some measure of intellectual life. Modalities, which appear to us to be forms of deprivation, would be cancelled out by the plausibility of a proffered reality, which we had denied them on the grounds of its appearance.

Over and above the political and economic remedies that might be found for it, the problem posed by the confrontation between tropical Asia and tropical America remains the problem of the multiplication of the human species within a limited space. We are bound to reflect that, in this connection, Europe occupies an intermediary position between these two continents. India tried to solve the population problem some three thousand years ago by endeavouring, by means of the caste system, to change quantity into quality, that is, to differentiate between human groups so as to enable them to live side by side. She even conceived of the problem in still broader terms, extending it beyond man, to all forms of life. The vegetarian rule, like the caste system, was intended to prevent social groups and animal species from *encroaching* on each other, and to guarantee each group its own particular freedom. It is tragic for mankind that this great experiment failed; I mean that, in the course of history, the various castes did not succeed in reaching a state in which they could remain equal because they were different—equal in the sense that there would have been no common measure between them—and that a harmful element of homogeneity was introduced which made comparison possible, and consequently led to the creation of a hierarchy. Men can coexist on condition that they recognize each other as being all *equally*, though *differently*, human, but they can also coexist by denying each other a comparable degree of humanity, and thus establishing a system of subordination.

India's great failure can teach us a lesson. When a community becomes too numerous, however great the genius of its thinkers, it can only endure by secreting enslavement. Once men begin to feel cramped in their geographical, social and mental habitat, they are in danger of being tempted by the simple solution of denying one section of the species the right to be considered as human. This allows the rest a little elbow-room for a few more decades. Then it becomes necessary to extend the process of expulsion. When looked at in this light, the events which have occurred in Europe during the past twenty years, at the culmination of a century during which the population figures have doubled, can no longer appear as being simply the result of an aberration on the part of one nation, one doctrine, or one group of men. I see them rather as a premonitory sign of our moving into a finite world, such as southern Asia had to face a thousand or two thousand years ahead of us, and I cannot see us avoiding the experience unless some major decisions are taken. The systematic devaluation of man by man is gaining ground, and we would be guilty of hypocrisy and blindness if we dismissed the problem by arguing that recent events represented only a temporary contamination.

What frightens me in Asia is the vision of our own future which it is already experiencing. In the America of the Indians, I cherish the reflection, however fleeting it may have now become, of an era when the human species was in proportion to the world it occupied, and when there was still a valid relationship between the enjoyment of freedom and the symbols denoting it.

PART FIVE

Caduveo

---

17. PARANA

Campers, camp in Parana. But no, on second thoughts, don't. Keep your greasy papers, indestructible bottles and gaping tins for the last beauty spots of Europe! Cover European landscapes with the blight of your camping sites. But, during the short interval before their final destruction, respect the torrents plumed with virgin foam which cascade down the steplike sides of purple basalt rocks beyond the pioneer fringe. Do not trample the acid green of the volcanic moss; take care not to tread beyond the threshold of the uninhabited prairies and the great damp forest of conifers bursting up through the tangle of lianas and ferns to thrust skyward shapes that are an inversion of those of our fir trees; instead of having the form of tapering cones, they spread the hexagonal planes of their branches around their trunks in ever-widening circles—with a vegetable regularity by which Baudelaire would have been pleasantly surprised—until the last is a giant umbel. This is a virgin and solemn landscape which seems to have preserved the aspect of the carboniferous era intact over millions of centuries and which, because of its altitude and its distance from the Tropic, is spared the Amazonian luxuriance and has an orderliness and a majesty which are inexplicable, unless we attribute them to the effect of some immemorial custom instituted by a wiser and more powerful race than our own, and whose disappearance allows us to make our way into this sublime parkland, now given over to silence and neglect.

It was in this territory overlooking the two banks of the Rio Tibagy at about one thousand metres above sea-level, that I made my first contact with the natives, while accompanying a district commissioner belonging to the Department for the Protection of Indians, who was making his rounds.

When it was first discovered, the entire southern zone of Brazil was inhabited by communities which were closely related, both in language and culture, and which used to be

known collectively as the Ge group. They had most probably been pushed westwards by recent Tupi-speaking invaders, with whom they were in conflict and who already
occupied the whole coastal strip. Having withdrawn into
regions which were difficult of access, the Ge of southern
Brazil survived the Tupi by several centuries, since the
latter were quickly killed off by the colonizers. In the
forests of the southern states of Parana and Santa Catarina,
small bands of savages managed to exist right up until the
twentieth century; a few, perhaps, still survived in 1935, but
they had been so fiercely persecuted during the previous
hundred years that they had gone into hiding; most of
them, however, had been rounded up by the Brazilian government and, about 1914, established in several reserves.
At first, some attempt was made to integrate them into
modern life. At the village of São Jeronymo, which I used
as a base, there had been a smithy for ironwork, a sawmill,
a school and a chemist's shop. Tools, such as axes, knives
and nails, arrived regularly at the outpost. There were dis-
tributions of clothing and blankets. Twenty years later,
these attempts had been abandoned. In leaving the Indians
to their own resources, the Protection Service reflected the
indifference with which it itself had come to be regarded
by the public authorities (it has since recovered a certain
degree of importance); so, willy-nilly, it was obliged to try
a different method, which meant encouraging the natives to
recover some initiative, and forcing them to take control of
their own affairs.

From their brief contact with civilization, the natives had
retained only Brazilian clothes, the axe, the knife and the
sewing-needle. In all other respects, the experiment had
been a failure. Houses had been built for them, and they
continued to live in the open. An attempt had been made
to settle them in villages, and they remained nomadic. They
had broken up their beds for firewood, and slept on the
ground. The herds of cows sent by the government were
allowed to roam at large, since the natives found both beef
and milk repugnant. The wooden pestles which were operated mechanically by an oscillating receptacle which auto-
matically filled and emptied as a beam went up and down
(a device frequently found in Brazil, where it is known as a
monjolo, and which may have been imported by the Portuguese from the East) rotted unused, and pounding by hand
continued to be the general practice.

So, to my great disappointment, the Tibagy Indians were neither completely 'true Indians', nor, what was more important, 'savages'. But, by removing the poetry from my naïve vision of what experiences lay ahead, they taught me, as a beginner in anthropology, a lesson in prudence and objectivity. Although I found them to be less unspoiled than I had hoped, I was to discover that they were more mysterious than their external appearance might lead one to believe. They were a perfect illustration of that sociological situation which tends to be the only one available to the observer in the second half of the twentieth century; they were 'primitives' who had had civilization brutally thrust upon them, but once the danger they were supposed to represent had been overcome no further interest had been taken in them. Their culture was an individual mixture, made up on the one hand of ancient traditions which had withstood the influence of the whites (such as the practice, still frequent among them, of filing and incrusting the teeth) and on the other of borrowings from modern civilization, and its study, however deficient in the element of the picturesque, was to prove no less instructive than that of the pure Indians whom I was subsequently to encounter.

But the most important point was that since these Indians had been thrown back on their own resources, there had been a strange reversal of the superficial balance between modern culture and primitive culture. Ancient modes of life and traditional techniques re-emerged from a past, the still-living proximity of which it would have been a mistake to overlook. I wondered about the provenance of the beautifully polished stone pestles which I found in native houses, mixed up with enamelled tin plates, cheap spoons and even —occasionally—the skeletal remains of a sewing-machine. Perhaps they had been obtained through bartering, in the silence of the forest, with savage communities belonging to the same racial group, whose aggressive behaviour still kept the settlers out of certain areas of Parana. It might have been possible to answer these questions, if I had got to know the life-story of an old Indian *bravo,* who was then living in retirement in the government settlement.

The implements which arouse such speculations survive among the tribes as evidence of a time when the Indians had neither houses, nor clothes, nor metal utensils. And the old techniques, too, are preserved as half-conscious memories. The Indians are quite familiar with matches, although these are dear and difficult to obtain, but they always prefer to make fire by the rotation or rubbing together of two soft pieces of palmwood. And the antiquated guns and pistols once distributed by the government can often be seen hanging in the deserted houses, while the man is hunting in the forest with a bow and arrows as technically reliable as those of communities which have never seen a firearm. In this way, ancient forms of life, after being hastily covered up by official initiative, forge ahead again slowly and surely, like the files of Indians I would meet travelling along the narrow forest paths, after leaving the roofs to collapse in their deserted villages.

For about a fortnight we travelled on horseback along barely visible tracks through stretches of forest so vast that we often had to keep going until very late at night in order to reach the hut where we were to break our journey. How the horses managed to pick their way in spite of the darkness, which was made even more impenetrable by the vegetable canopy thirty metres above our heads, I do not know. All I remember is being jolted for hours by the ambling pace of our mounts. Sometimes, when descending a steep hillock, the horse would throw its rider forward, and one had to be ready to clutch the high pommel of the peasant-type saddle; the cool freshness rising from below and a noisy splashing would indicate that we were fording a stream. Then, tipping the other way, the horse would stumble up the opposite bank and would seem, from its uncontrolled movements, which were difficult to interpret in the dark, to be doing its best to throw off both saddle and rider. Once you regained your balance, all you had to do was to remain on the alert so as not to lose the benefit of that curious foresight which made it possible, although one was advancing blindly, to duck one's head, more often than not just in time to avoid being struck by some low branch.

It would not be long before an unmistakable sound could be heard in the distance; this time it would be not the roar of the jaguar, which had been audible for a while at nightfall, but the barking of a dog, indicating the proximity of our stopping-place. A few minutes later our guide would change course and we would follow him into a small clearing which was fenced off with split trunks so as to serve as a cattle-pen. Two figures clad in thin white cotton fabric would be moving about in front of a straw-roofed hut made of loosely assembled palm-stems. These were our hosts; most often the husband was of Portuguese origin and had an Indian wife. By the light of a wick dipped in paraffin, one could quickly take stock of the inside of the hut: a floor of beaten earth, a table, a sleeping-bench made of planks, a few wooden boxes which did duty as chairs, and on the clay hearth kitchen utensils consisting of old petrol drums and salvaged tins. Soon we would have slung our hammocks by threading the ropes through chinks in the walls, or we would go outside to sleep in the *païol,* a kind of porch intended to protect the maize harvest from rain. Surprising as it may seem, a heap of dry corn cobs with the leaves still on them makes a comfortable bed; the oblong shapes slide one against another and the mass adapts itself to the sleeper's body. The delicate, sweet, grassy scent of dried maize is wonderfully soporific. But at dawn one is awakened by the cold and damp; milk-white mist rises above the clearing and one hurries back into the hut where the hearth is glowing in the perpetual twilight of the windowless abode, with walls that are little more than open-work partitions. The hostess prepares the coffee, the beans of which have been roasted to a shiny black on a bed of sugar, as well as a *pipoca,* puffed corn with pieces of bacon. We round up the horses, saddle them and set off again. A few moments later, the dripping forest has closed around the hut, now consigned to oblivion.

The São Jeronymo reserve covered an area of about 300,000 acres, and was inhabited by 450 natives, grouped together in five or six hamlets. Before we set out, I had been able to appreciate, from the statistics kept at the station, the devastation caused by malaria, tuberculosis and alcoholism. During the previous ten years the total number of births had not exceeded 170, while infant mortality alone accounted for 140 deaths.

We visited wooden houses built by the federal government and grouped in villages of five or ten dwellings on the banks of streams. We also saw the more isolated houses that the Indians sometimes build; these consist of a square palisade of palm-trunks, held together by creepers and supporting a roof of leaves, which is fixed to the walls only by its four corners. Lastly, we looked under the awnings made of branches, where a family sometimes chooses to live, next to an unused house.

The inhabitants gather round a fire which burns day and

night. The men are usually dressed in a ragged shirt and an old pair of trousers; the women wear a cotton dress next to the skin, or sometimes just a blanket tucked under their armpits; the children go completely naked. All wear, as we did during the journey, the broad straw hats which constitute their only handicraft and their only source of revenue. Both sexes, at all ages, are obviously Mongolian in type: they have short, broad, flat faces, prominent cheekbones, slanting eyes, yellow skins and straight black hair—which the women may wear either long or short—and little or no body hair. Only one room is inhabited. Here, at all hours, they eat sweet potatoes, which roast in the hot ash and which they pull out with long bamboo tongs. Here too they sleep on a thin layer of ferns, or on mats made from maize straw, each person with his or her feet towards the fire. In the middle of the night, the few remaining embers and the wall of loosely assembled trunks offer very little protection against the freezing cold at a thousand feet above sea-level.

The houses that the Indians make themselves consist only of this one room, and only one room is used in the houses built by the government. All the Indians' possessions are strewn on the floor in an untidy mess which shocked our guides, *caboclos* from the neighbouring *sertão*, and which was composed of an almost inextricable mixture of objects of Brazilian origin and products of local craftsmanship. The former usually include axes, knives, enamel plates and metal receptacles, rags, sewing-needles and -thread, sometimes a few bottles and even an umbrella. The furniture is just as rudimentary: a few low wooden stools of Guarani origin, such as are also used by the *caboclos;* baskets of all sizes and for all purposes illustrating the 'twilled' technique, so often found in South America; flour sieves, wooden mortars, wood or stone pestles, a few pieces of pottery; and lastly, a vast quantity of differently shaped receptacles with various purposes, made with the *abobra,* a gourd which is hollowed out and dried. It was extremely difficult to obtain possession of one or other of these modest objects. A preliminary distribution of rings, necklaces and cheap brooches to all members of the family was sometimes not enough to establish the necessary friendly relationship. Even the offer of a quantity of milreis out of all proportion to the paltry worth of the utensil might leave the owner indifferent. He would say that he couldn't part with it. If he had made the object himself, he would willingly have handed it over, but

Fig 4. Caingang pottery

he had obtained it a long time before from an old woman who was the only person who knew how to make that kind of object. If he let us have it, how could he replace it? Of course the old woman was never there. But where was she? He didn't know—and he would make a vague gesture in the direction of the forest. In any case, of what use would all our milreis be to an old Indian shaking with a fever a hundred kilometres from the nearest shop run by whites? One felt ashamed to deprive people who have so little of a small tool the loss of which would be an irreparable loss . . .

But often it was a different story. I might ask an Indian woman if she would sell me one of her pots, and she would say yes. Unfortunately, it did not belong to her. To whom did it belong?—Silence—To her husband? No—To her brother? No, not to her brother either.—To her son? Not to her son.—It belonged to her granddaughter. The granddaughter inevitably owned all the objects we wanted to buy. We looked at her; she was three or four years old and was squatting near the fire, totally engrossed in the ring I had slipped on to her finger a little while before. And so we had to embark on lengthy negotiations with the young lady, in which her parents did not take part. She was unmoved by the offer of a ring and five hundred reis, but let herself be persuaded by a brooch and four hundred reis.

The Caingang grow a few crops, but their main occupations are fishing, hunting and gathering wild fruit. Their fishing techniques, being clumsy imitations of the white man's methods, cannot be very productive: they use a flexible branch, a Brazilian fish-hook fixed to the end of a line with a piece of resin, or sometimes a piece of rag as a net. Hunting and gathering regulate their nomadic life in the forest; whole families disappear for weeks on end and no one has ever followed them along their complicated routes to their secret hide-outs. Occasionally we would encounter a small group which had come out into the open on to a track, but it would at once disappear again into the forest. The men would be in front, armed with the *bodoque,* a bow used for shooting pellets at birds, and carrying the dried-clay ammunition in wickerwork quivers slung across their back. The women followed, carrying all the family possessions in baskets supported by cloth scarves or wide strips of bark passed round their foreheads. Both children and domestic objects are transported in this way. We would pull in our reins, they would barely slacken their pace, and a few words would be exchanged before silence settled again over the forest. But we knew that the next house—like so many others—would be empty. But for how long?

Their nomadic existence may last for days or weeks. The hunting season and fruit-gathering—*jaboticaba,* orange and *lima*—entail movement involving the entire population. But we do not know what kind of shelters they live in in the depths of the forest, nor where they hide their bows and arrows—only occasional specimens of which have been found by chance through being forgotten in a corner of some house—nor what traditions, rites and beliefs they return to at these times.

Gardening is the most neglected skill in their primitive economy. Sometimes in the heart of the forest, one comes across a patch of ground that has been cleared by the natives. Between the high walls of the trees, there will be a few square yards of meagre green vegetation—banana trees, sweet potatoes, manioc and maize. The corn is first of all dried at the fire, then pounded with a mortar by the women, who either work singly or in pairs. The flour may be eaten as it is, or mixed with fat to make a solid cake. An additional element in their diet is black beans, while game and semi-domesticated pigs provide them with meat.

The flesh is always skewered on to a branch and roasted over the fire.

Mention must also be made of the *koro,* pale-coloured grubs which are to be found in abundance in certain rotting tree-trunks. Having been jeered at by the whites for eating these creatures, the Indians deny the charge and will not admit to liking them. But you only have to go through the forest to see on the ground the traces of some *pinheiro,* twenty or thirty metres long, that has been torn down by a storm, then later hacked to pieces and reduced to a mere ghost of its former self. The hunters of *koro* have dealt with it. And if you arrive unexpectedly at an Indian house, you may catch a glimpse of a bowl swarming with the treasured delicacy, before it is hastily whisked out of sight.

This being so, it is no easy matter arranging to be present at a search for *koro.* Like conspirators, we had to work out a plan at some length. A fever-stricken Indian, the only person left in a deserted village, seemed an easy prey. We put an axe into his hands, shook him and pushed him. But to no purpose; he did not seem to grasp what we wanted of him. Thinking we were about to fail once more, we used our last argument: we would like to eat some *koro.* We succeeded in dragging our victim to a tree-trunk. One blow with the axe revealed thousands of hollow little chambers, deep inside the tree. In each was a fat, cream-coloured creature, rather like a silkworm. I had to keep my word. While the Indian looked on impassively I decapitated my catch; from the body spurted a whitish, fatty substance which I managed to taste after some hesitation; it had the consistency and delicacy of butter, and the flavour of coconut milk.

18. PANTANAL

After this initiation, I was ready for real adventures. An opportunity was to occur during the university vacation, which, in Brazil, takes place between November and March, that is, during the rainy season. In spite of this drawback, I planned to establish contact with two native communities: the Caduveo, along the Paraguayan frontier —on whom very little research had been done and whose numbers had probably dwindled to a quarter of what they had formerly been—and the better-known but still promising Bororo, in the central Mato Grosso. In addition, the National Museum of Rio de Janeiro suggested that I should reconnoitre an archaeological site which was on my route and which no one had yet had a chance to investigate, although it had been known about for a long time.

Since then, I have frequently made the journey between São Paulo and the Mato Grosso, sometimes by plane, sometimes in a lorry and sometimes by train and boat. In 1935–6, I went by rail and river, as the site I have just referred to lay near the railway terminus at Porto Esperança, on the left bank of the Rio Paraguay.

There is little to be said about this wearisome journey. The first lap was by the Noroeste Railway to Bauru, in the heart of the pioneer zone; there you changed to the Mato Grosso night-train, which crossed the southern part of the State. Altogether the journey lasted three days and was made at a leisurely speed. The engines were stoked with wood, and this involved long and frequent stops for re-fuelling. The carriages, too, were made of wood and pretty roughly put together, so that when you woke up, your face was covered with a film of hardened clay formed by the fine red dust of the *sertão* which had settled in every fold of flesh and every pore. The dining-car menu was already typical of the culinary pattern of the interior: meat, fresh or dried as the case might be, rice and black beans, and *farinha* to soak up the gravy. *Farinha* is made from maize pulp or fresh manioc pulp which has been dehydrated

166

through heating and then ground to a coarse powder; lastly the eternal Brazilian dessert, consisting of a slice of quince or guava curd accompanied by cheese. At each station, in exchange for a few coppers, urchins offered juicy yellow-fleshed pineapples which provided cool and timely refreshment.

You enter the State of Mato Grosso just before the station of Tres-Lagoas, when you cross the Rio Parana, which is so broad that, although the rains had already started when I made the journey, the bottom was visible in many places. Beyond lay the landscape which was to become at once familiar, intolerable and necessary to me during my years of wandering through the interior, since it is the typical landscape of central Brazil between the Parana and the Amazonian basin: it consists of flat or slightly undulating plateaux, sweeping vistas and scrub-type vegetation, with an occasional herd of zebus which scatter as the train goes past. Many travellers mistakenly translate Mato Grosso as 'great forest'; the feminine *mata* corresponds to 'forest', whereas the masculine form refers to the complementary feature of the South American landscape, that is, Mato Grosso means literally 'great bush'. No term could more appropriately describe this wild and desolate land, although there is something grandiose and exciting in its very monotony.

It is true that I have also translated *sertão* as *brousse* or bush, although it has slightly different connotations. *Mato* refers to an objective feature of the landscape: bush as opposed to forest. *Sertão*, on the other hand, refers to a subjective aspect: bush in relation to man, and in opposition to inhabited and cultivated areas; there are no permanent settlements in the *sertão*. French colonial slang has perhaps an exact equivalent in the term *bled*.

Sometimes the plateau is intersected by a green and wooded valley, which appears almost welcoming beneath the clear sky. Between Campo Grande and Aquidauana, a deeper fault reveals the dazzling cliffs of the Serra de Maracaju, in the gorges of which, at Corrientes, there is a *garimpo*, that is a diamond-mining centre. Then suddenly the whole aspect of the landscape changes. Once you get beyond Aquidauana, you enter the Pantanal, the largest swamp in the world, which fills the central basin of the Rio Paraguay.

Seen from the air, this region of rivers winding their

way through flat country presents a pattern of arcs and meanderings of stagnant water. The river-bed itself seems to be edged wtih pale curves, as if nature had hesitated before giving the river its present, temporary course. At ground level, the Pantanal becomes a dream landscape, where herds of zebus take refuge on the tops of hillocks which look like floating arks, while in the flooded swamps flocks of large birds, such as flamingoes, egrets and herons, form dense white-and-pink islands, less feathery however than the fan-like foliage of the carandá palms, the leaves of which secrete a precious wax, and whose scattered clumps offer the only interruption in the deceptively smiling vistas of this aquatic desert.

Dismal Porto Esperança, so wrongly named, remains in my memory as the weirdest spot one could hope to find on the face of the earth, with the possible exception of Fire Island in New York State. The two are now associated in my mind, since they are analogous in offering combinations of the most contradictory features, although each in a different key. Both express the same kind of geographical and human absurdity, comic in the one instance and sinister in the other. Fire Island might have been invented by Swift. It is a narrow strip of sand, devoid of vegetation, off the coast of Long Island. It is literally a strip, eighty kilometres long, but only two or three hundred metres wide. On the Atlantic side, the open sea is too rough for bathing. On the landward side, the sea is always calm but the water is too shallow for swimming. The only pastime is catching non-edible fish; at regular intervals along the beaches, there are notices stating that the fish should not be left to rot but should be at once buried in the sand. The dunes on Fire Island are so shifting, and their hold on the sea so precarious, that further notices warn the public to keep off in case they should collapse into the water below. The place is like an inverted Venice, since it is the land which is fluid and the canals solid: in Cherry Grove, the village occupying the central part of the island, the inhabitants must obligatorily use a network of wooden footbridges forming a road system on stilts.

To complete the picture, I must add that Cherry Grove is chiefly inhabited by male couples, attracted no doubt by the general pattern of inversion. Since nothing grows in the sand, apart from broad patches of poisonous ivy, provisions are collected once a day from the one and only shop, at the end of the landing-stage. In the tiny streets, on higher ground more stable than the dunes, the sterile couples can be seen returning to their chalets pushing prams (the only vehicles suitable for the narrow paths) containing little but the weekend bottles of milk that no baby will consume.

Fire Island gives an impression of gay farcicality, whereas Porto Esperança offers a corresponding scene adapted to a community which is even more hopelessly damned. There is no reason for its existence, except that this happens to be where the railway line comes to an end at the river, after crossing 1,500 kilometres of largely uninhabited country. Beyond Porto Esperança, the only communication with the interior is by boat, and the railway stops just above a muddy bank, only loosely shored up by the planks which serve as a landing-stage for the little river-steamers.

The only inhabitants were the railway employees, and there were no houses apart from theirs—wooden shanties built right in the middle of the swamp, and reached by shaky planks which formed a crisscross pattern in the inhabited area. We were housed in a chalet put at our disposal by the company. It was a cube-shaped box, one small room perched high on piles and reached by a ladder. The door opened on to the void above a siding; at dawn we would be awakened by the whistle of the locomotive which served as our private runabout. The nights were unpleasant: the humid heat, the large swamp mosquitoes which attacked our refuge, and the inefficiency of our mosquito nets which we had designed too ingeniously before the start of the expedition—all these things combined to make sleep impossible. At five o'clock in the morning, when the engine sent its steam up through our thin floorboards, the heat of the previous day was still present. There was no mist, in spite of the humidity, but a leaden sky, and an atmosphere as oppressive as if an extra element had been added to the air and was making it unbreathable. Fortunately the engine travelled fast and, sitting in the breeze with our legs dangling over the guard-rail, we would manage to shake off the heaviness of the night.

The single track, which was used by only two trains a week, was laid precariously over the swamp, and was no more than a flimsy bridge that the engine seemed liable to part company with at any moment. On either side, a musty stench rose from the muddy, repulsive water of the swamp.

Yet it was this water that we were to drink for several weeks.

To right and left were shrubs, spaced out as if in an orchard, but merging in the distance to form dark masses, while, beneath their branches, the reflection of the sky in the water made glistening patches. The whole landscape seemed to be simmering in a warmth which must encourage slow processes of ripening. Were it possible to remain for thousands of years in this prehistoric landscape to follow its development, one would no doubt be able to witness the transformation of organic matter into peat, coal or oil. I even imagined I could see oil rising to the surface and colouring the water with delicate iridescent patterns; the workers helping us refused to believe that we were taking so much trouble and inflicting so much on them merely for the sake of a few potsherds. Since they attached a symbolic value to our sun-helmets, the sun-helmet being the emblem of 'the engineer', they concluded that archaeology was just a pretext for more important kinds of prospecting.

Occasionally the silence was broken by animals not intimidated by man: a *veado,* a surprised roebuck with a white tail; groups of emu—small ostriches—or white flocks of egrets skimming the surface of the water.

On the way, workers would join the engine and climb up beside us. Our destination was Kilometre 12, the point of termination of the secondary line, and thereafter we had to reach the site on foot. We could see it in the distance with its typical *capão*-like look.

Contrary to appearances, the water of the Pantanal does flow to some extent, carrying with it shells and silt which accumulate at certain points, allowing vegetation to take root. As a result, the area is dotted with clumps of greenery called *capões,* where the Indians of old used to set up camp and where traces of their life can still be found.

Every morning, we walked to our *capão* along a track which we had made with the help of the wooden sleepers stacked near the railway line. On the site, we spent utterly exhausting days because it was almost impossible to breathe and we had to drink the sun-warmed marsh water. At dusk, the engine would come for us, or sometimes it would be replaced by one of those vehicles called in French a *diable* (a trolley), which was punted along by workmen standing at each of the four corners and vigorously thrusting their poles against the ballast, like gondoliers. Weary and thirsty

we would return to sleepless nights in the emptiness of
Porto Esperança.

About a hundred kilometres short of Porto Esperança
was a *fazenda,* or ranch, which we had chosen as the base
from which we would set out to find the Caduveo. The
'Fazenda Francesa', as it was called along the railway line,
covered an area of about 125,000 acres, and some 120
kilometres of the railway line ran through it. Over this
region of brushwood and coarse grass roamed a herd of
seven thousand beasts (in tropical countries, each animal
needs between twelve and twenty-five acres), which were
periodically exported to São Paulo by rail from the two or
three stops on the estate. The halt next to the settlement
was called Guaycurus, thus perpetuating the name of the
great warlike tribes who formerly controlled the area and
of whom the Caduveo are the last survivors in Brazilian
territory.

The ranch was run by two Frenchmen, with the help of
a few families of cowherds. I cannot remember the name
of the younger of the two, but the other, who was approaching forty, was called Félix R.—and, more familiarly,
Don Félix. He was murdered a few years ago by an Indian.

Our hosts had grown up, or served, during the First
World War, and their temperaments and abilities would
have fitted them to be French colonists in Morocco. But
some kind of speculative venture originating in Nantes had
led them to chance their arm in this remote and desolate
area of Brazil. However, ten years after its foundation, the
Fazenda Francesa was declining, because most of the initial
capital had had to be used for the initial buying of the
land, so that no margin was left for improving the livestock
and equipment. The two men led an austere life in a huge
English-style bungalow, acting half as cattle-breeders and
half as grocers. The ranch shop was almost the only supply
centre within a radius of a hundred kilometres or so. The
empregados—that is, the employees, whether workers or
peons—came there to spend with one hand what they had
earned with the other. A system of book-keeping allowed
them to change their credit into debts, and so the whole
undertaking could function practically without money ever
changing hands. Since, as was customary, the prices of the
goods were fixed at two or three times the normal rate, the
ranch might have been a paying concern, had the shop-
keeping side not been such a subsidiary aspect. There was

something heart-breaking about seeing the workers, every Saturday, return to the fazenda with a few bundles of sugar-cane, which they immediately pressed in the *engenho* —a machine, made from roughly hewn tree-trunks, which crushes the canes by means of three rotating wooden cylinders. The resulting juice was then thickened by evaporation in huge steel pans, before being poured into moulds, where it set in buff-coloured, granulous blocks. This product, known as *rapadura,* was then stored in the adjoining shop, where that same evening, the workers would buy it back at a high price, in order to provide their children with the only sweetmeat available on the *sertão*.

Our hosts accepted their role as exploiters quite philosophically. Having no contact with their employees outside working hours, and being without neighbours of their own class (since the Indian Reserve lay between them and the nearest plantations along the Paraguayan frontier), they kept to an austere routine which was probably the best defence against discouragement. Their only concessions to the South American way of life were in dress and drink. In that frontier region, with its mixture of Brazilian, Paraguayan, Bolivian and Argentinian traditions, they had adopted the typical pampa dress. This consisted of a Bolivian hat of brownish-grey, finely woven straw, with a high crown and a wide upturned brim, and the *chiripá,* a kind of swaddling-cloth for adults made of striped cotton fabric in pastel shades of lilac, pink or blue, which left the legs and thighs exposed above calf-high boots of coarse white canvas. In colder weather the *chiripá* was replaced by the *bombacha*—baggy, Zouave-style trousers, elaborately embroidered down the sides.

Their days were spent almost entirely in the corral 'working' the beasts, that is inspecting them after the periodic round-ups and selecting those to be sold. Driven by the guttural cries of the *capataz* and in swirling clouds of dust, the animals filed past the owners and were allotted to various different pens. Long-horned zebus, fat cows and terrified calves all clambered on top of each other in the wooden gangways, which a bull sometimes refused to enter. Forty metres of finely woven lash would whirl round the *lassoeiro's* head, and at the same moment, or so it seemed, the beast would sink to the ground, while the *lassoeiro's* horse reared triumphantly.

But twice a day—at eleven thirty in the morning and

seven in the evening—everybody would assemble under the pergola surrounding the living quarters for the ritual of the *chimarrão*, the imbibing of maté through a pipe. It is well known that the maté is a shrub of the same family as our holly-oak; the twigs are lightly roasted in the smoke of an underground fire, then reduced to a coarse greenish powder which keeps for a long time in casks. I am referring to the genuine maté; the product sold under this name in Europe has usually undergone such noxious transformations that it bears no resemblance whatever to the real thing.

There are several ways of drinking maté. If, in the course of an expedition, we were so exhausted that we longed for the immediate comfort it could provide, we would simply throw a large handful into cold water, which was then quickly brought to the boil but removed from the heat—this was an essential point—at the first sign of bubbling; otherwise the maté would lose all its flavour. This method, the reverse process to making an infusion, produces what is called *cha de maté*, a dark green liquid, almost oily like a cup of strong coffee. When we were short of time, we made do with *téréré*: cold water is poured on to a handful of power and then sucked up through a pipette. Those who dislike the bitter taste can, like Paraguayan ladies, choose *maté doce*: the powder is mixed with sugar and caramelized over a hot fire; boiling water is then poured on to it and the liquid is passed through a sieve. But I know of no maté lover who does not infinitely prefer the method of the *chimarrão*, as it was practised at the fazenda; it is at once a social rite and a private vice.

The company sits in a circle around a little girl, the *china*, who is equipped with a kettle, a stove and the *cuia*. The latter may be a gourd, the orifice of which has been edged with silver, or sometimes, as at Guaycurus, a zebu's horn carved by a peon. The receptacle is two-thirds full of powder, which the little girl gently soaks with boiling water. Once the mixture forms a paste, she takes the silver tube, the lower end of which is bulb-shaped and pierced with holes, and carefully makes a cavity for it. This allows the pipette to rest at the bottom, in a tiny space where the liquid can collect, while the tube has just enough play not to break up the paste, but not so much that the water does not mix in properly. The *chimarrão* is now ready and has only to be filled with liquid before being offered to the master of the house; after sucking two or three times on

the pipette, he hands back the receptacle and the same
operation is performed for all participants, the men first,
and then the women, if there are any present. The instrument goes the rounds until there is no more water left in
the kettle.

The first mouthfuls produce a delightful sensation—for
the regular maté drinker at least, since the beginner is likely to scald himself—made up of the somewhat viscous contact with the hot silver, and the foaming water enhanced
with a thick froth: it is at once bitter and fragrant, like a
whole forest concentrated in a few drops. Maté contains an
alkaloid similar to those in coffee, tea and chocolate, and
its soothing and invigorating effect is perhaps to be explained by the amount and the semi-raw state of the medium. After a few rounds, the maté loses its flavour, but
careful prodding with the pipette can reveal still-unex-
plored nooks and crannies which prolong the pleasure with
tiny explosions of bitterness.

There can be no doubt maté is far superior to the Amazonian *guaraná* that I shall refer to later, and infinitely
superior to the dreary coca of the Bolivian plateau, an in-
sipid mastication of dried leaves which rapidly turn into a
slightly herbal, fibrous mush which anaesthetizes the mu-
cous membranes and transforms the chewer's tongue into a
foreign body. The only worthy comparison I can think of is
a betel stuffed with spices, although this assails the unsuspecting palate with a terrifying salvo of savours and perfumes.

The Caduveo Indians lived in the lowlands on the left
bank of the Rio Paraguay, which were separated from the
Fazenda Francesa by the heights of the Serra Bodoquena.
Our hosts looked upon them as lazy, degenerate thieves and
drunks who had to be vigorously expulsed from the grazing
lands, whenever they ventured there. They also considered
the failure of our expedition a foregone conclusion, and
in spite of giving us generous help, without which we
could never have carried out our plan, they disapproved
of it. They were quite astonished when, a few weeks later,
we returned with our oxen as laden as those of any caravan; we brought back huge, painted and engraved pottery
jars, deerskins illuminated with arabesques, and wood-carv-
ings representing the pantheon of a forgotten religion . . .
This was a revelation to them and it brought about a
curious change in their way of life. When Don Félix paid

me a return visit in São Paulo two or three years later, I
gathered that he and his companion, after previously treating the local community with contempt, had, as the English say, 'gone native'; the small bourgeois parlour at the
fazenda was now hung with painted skins, and there were
pieces of native pottery in every corner; the two men had
developed an interest in the local crafts, as they would
have done if they had followed their true bent and become
colonial administrators in the Sudan or Morocco. Now that
the Indians had become their regular suppliers, whole families of them were welcomed and housed at the fazenda, in
exchange for their objects. I do not know how far this new
intimacy went. It is unlikely that two bachelors were able to
resist the charms of the young Indian girls, when they saw
them half-naked on feast days, their bodies patiently decorated with delicate black or blue scrolls which seemed to
fit their skin like a sheath of precious lace. Be that as it
may, Don Félix was killed, in 1944 or 1945 I think, by one
of his new-found friends, and he was perhaps not so much
a victim of the Indians as a victim of the mental confusion into which he had been plunged ten years previously
by the visit of a party of young anthropologists.

The fazenda shop supplied us with provisions: dried
meat, rice, black beans, manioc flour, maté, coffee and
rapadura. We were also lent means of transport—horses for
the men, and oxen for our baggage—since we were taking
goods to exchange for the native objects we hoped to collect; we had children's toys, glass-bead necklaces, mirrors,
bracelets, rings, scent, pieces of material, blankets, clothing
and tools. Fazenda workers were to act as our guides, much
against their will, as it happened, because we were taking
them from their families at the time of the Christmas festivities.

The natives were expecting us in the villages. As soon as
we arrived at the fazenda, Indian *vaqueiros* had gone off to
announce the advent of strangers bringing presents. The
prospect filled the natives with various forms of anxiety,
uppermost being the fear that we had come to *tomar conta*
—take possession of their lands.

19. NALIKE

Nalike, the capital of the Caduveo country, is about 150 kilometres from Guaycurus, that is, three days' ride on horseback. The oxen carrying our baggage had been sent on ahead, being more slow-moving. During the first day, we proposed to climb the slopes of the Serra Bodoquena and then to spend the night on the plateau, in the last outpost belonging to the fazenda. We soon found ourselves in narrow valleys, overgrown with tall grasses through which the horses had difficulty in forcing their way. Progress was made more difficult by the swamp mud underfoot. The horses would slip and scramble back on to solid ground as best they could, and where they could, and we might find ourselves completely surrounded by vegetation; one had to keep a sharp look-out then in case the underside of some innocent-looking leaf released the seething egg-shaped cluster formed by a swarm of *carrapatos*. The myriad orange-coloured creatures crawl under one's clothes, cover the body with a moving layer and cling to the flesh; the only remedy is for the victim to race them to it, by dismounting, taking off all his clothes and beating them vigorously, while a companion carefully examines his skin. Less disastrous are the large, solitary, grey-coloured parasites, which fasten painlessly on to the flesh; a few hours or a few days later, they are visible only as swellings, and have to be extirpated with a knife.

Eventually, the bush thinned out and we followed a rocky path which sloped gently upwards to a dry forest, where trees and cacti intermingled. The storm which had been brewing since the morning burst just as we were going round a peak bristling with tall cacti. We dismounted and looked for shelter in a rock-fissure, which proved to be the entrance to a damp but protective cave. No sooner had we got inside than the air was filled with the booming sound made by *morcegos*, swarms of bats that we had disturbed as they hung sleeping on the walls.

As soon as the rain stopped, we resumed our journey in

a dark, leafy forest full of fresh scents and wild fruits—
genipapo, heavy-fleshed and sharp in taste, *guavira,* which
grows in clearings and is well known as a thirst-quencher
because of its always cold pulp, or *caju,* a sign of some
former Indian plantation.

On the plateau, we found ourselves again in the typical
Mato-Grosso landscape—tall grass, with trees dotted here
and there. As we neared our first halting-place, we had to
cross a marshy area, with wind-wrinkled mud and lots of
small wader birds; then a corral and a hut, the outpost of
Largon, where we found a family absorbed in the task of
slaughtering and cutting up a *bezerro,* or young bull. Inside
the bleeding carcass, which they were treating as if it were
a boat, two or three naked children were sprawling and
rocking with shouts of pleasure. The *churrasco* was roasting and dripping with fat, over an outdoor fire which
glowed in the twilight, while the urubus, or griffon-vul-
tures, which had alighted on the scene in their hundreds,
were fighting with the dogs for the blood and the scraps.

From Largon onwards, we were to follow 'the Indian
road'; the slope of the serra was very steep and we had to
go down on foot, guiding the nervous horses over the difficult surface. The track ran above a torrent, which we
could hear bouncing and cascading over the rocks, although we could not see it; we slithered over wet stones or
through muddy pools left by a recent fall of rain. Finally,
at the foot of the serra, we reached a circular open space,
the *campo dos Indios,* where we rested for a while with
our horses before setting off again across the marsh.

As early as four o'clock in the afternoon, we had to
start thinking about where we would make our next halt.
We found a few trees between which hammocks and
mosquito nets could be slung; the guides lit a fire and
prepared the meal of rice and dried meat. We were so
thirsty that we had no hesitation in gulping down pints of
the mixture of earth, water and permanganate which was
the only liquid available. Night began to fall, and from
behind the coarse, dirty muslin of the mosquito nets, we
gazed for a while at the fiery sky. We had hardly got to
sleep when it was time to set off once more. The guides
woke us at midnight, with the horses already saddled. In
the hot season one has to take advantage of the cool night
air in order to spare the animals. Barely awake, numb and
shivering, we began following the track again in the moon-

light; as the hours went by, we watched for signs of dawn, while the horses stumbled forward. About four o'clock in the morning, we arrived at Pitoko where the Department for the Protection of Indians once had an important station. All that was left was three ruined houses, between which there was only just enough room to sling the hammocks. The Rio Pitoko flowed silently by; it rises in the Pantanal, into which it is reabsorbed a few kilometres further on. This wadi of the marshes, which has neither source nor outlet, is inhabited by *piranhas,* which are a menace for the unwary, although they do not prevent the prudent Indian from bathing and drawing water. There are still a few Indian families scattered about the marshes.

From then on, we were in the heart of the Pantanal, which consists, in places, of waterlogged hollows between wooded crests, and elsewhere of vast, muddy, treeless stretches. Saddle-oxen would have been preferable to horses; although the heavier animals, which are guided by means of a rope passed through a nasal ring, advance slowly, they are better able to withstand the exhausting journeys through the marshes where the water is often breast high.

We were on a plain which stretched perhaps as far as the Rio Paraguay and was so flat that the water could not drain away, when there occurred the most violent storm I have ever experienced. There was no possibility of shelter, not a tree visible anywhere. We had no choice but to forge ahead, soaked and dripping like our horses, while the lightning struck to right and left like shells from an artillery barrage. After the ordeal had lasted for two hours, the downpour stopped and we could see the rain squalls moving slowly across the horizon as if we were out at sea. And already, at the far end of the plain, we could distinguish the outline of a clayey terrace, a few metres high, and on it the silhouettes of a dozen huts standing out against the sky. This was Engenho, near Nalike; we had chosen to stay there rather than in the old capital which, in 1935, boasted no more than five huts.

To the unobservant eye, these hamlets might seem little different from those belonging to the nearest Brazilian peasants. The natives were like the Brazilians in dress, and often similar in physical type, because of the high proportion of cross-breeding. In language, however, there was no resemblance. Guaycuru speech is pleasant to listen to; the natives' rapid utterance and polysyllabic words, largely made up of clear vowels alternating with dentals, gutturals and an abundance of palatalized or liquid phonemes, give the impression of a stream leaping over pebbles. Their present name, Caduveo (pronounced not as it is written, but 'cadiueu'), is a corruption of Cadiguegodi, which was the natives' own name for themselves. But there could be no question of learning the language during such a short stay, although the natives' Portuguese was very rudimentary.

The framework of the houses consisted of trunks which had been stripped of their bark and planted in the ground so as to support the crossbeams in the crutch of the first fork, specially left for this purpose by the woodcutter. A covering of faded palms provided the double-sided roof, but unlike the Brazilian huts, these houses had no walls. They thus represented a kind of compromise between the white men's dwellings (from which the shape of the roof had been copied), and the old native open shelters with flat matting roofs.

The size of these rudimentary dwellings was a more significant aspect: few huts housed only one family; some, like elongated barns, might contain up to six, each of which had its allotted area between two roof-posts, with a wooden shelf—one per family—on which the occupants spent their time sitting, lying or squatting, among deerskins, cotton

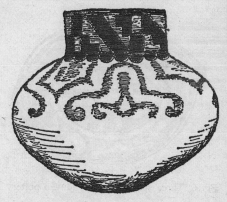

FIG 5. A water-jar with a bright red decoration, varnished with black resin

FIG 6. Three specimens of Caduveo pottery

fabrics, gourds, nets and straw receptacles, all of which were scattered, stacked or hanging anywhere and everywhere. In the corners were the large ornamented waterjars, resting on stands consisting of three-branched treeforks, fixed in the ground and occasionally carved.

In former times, these dwellings had been 'long houses', in the Iroquois style; from their appearance, some could still be described as such, but the reasons for incorporating several families into a single working community had ceased to be compelling; it was not a case as formerly, of matrilocal residence, with the sons-in-law coming to live with their wives in their parents-in-law's home.

Indeed, one felt very far removed from the past in this wretched hamlet, where there seemed to be hardly even a memory of the prosperity that Guido Boggiani had found there forty years before. He stayed in the area on two occasions, in 1892 and again in 1897, and left important anthropological documents relating to his journeys, as well as a charming travel diary. The population in the three centres consisted of hardly more than two hundred people, who depended for their livelihood on hunting, the gathering of wild fruits, the rearing of a few oxen and farmyard animals and the cultivation of patches of manioc, which could be seen on the far side of the single stream which flowed at the foot of the terrace. We visited it either to wash among the mosquitoes or to draw water, which was opalescent and slightly sweet.

Apart from the plaiting of straw, the weaving of the cotton belts worn by the men and the hammering of coins —nickel more often than silver—to turn them into discs and tubes to be threaded for necklaces, pottery-making was the main activity. The women mixed the clay from the Rio Pitoko with ground shards, rolled the resulting strands of paste into spirals and then patted them together until the pot reached the desired shape; while still soft, it was decorated with indentations made by pressing with a cord, and painted with an iron oxide found in the serra. Then it was baked in the open air, after which the process of decoration was continued, while the pottery was still warm, with the help of two varnishes of liquid resin; black made from *pau santo*, and a translucid yellow made from *angico*. Once the pot had cooled, it was rubbed with white powder —either chalk or ash—to emphasize the design.

FIG 7. Two wooden statuettes: *(left)* the Little Old Man, *(right)* the Mother of the Twins

FIG 8. A piece of Caduveo jewellery made of hammered coins and thimbles

As playthings for the children, the women made figures representing characters or animals with anything that came to hand—clay or wax, or dried husks, which they simply adapted to the required shape by the addition of modelling.

We also saw the children playing with little, carved wooden statues, usually dressed in cheap finery, which served them as dolls, while other statuettes of similar type were carefully preserved by a few old women at the bottoms of their baskets. It was impossible to say whether they were dolls, statues of gods, or figures representing ancestors, since they served contradictory purposes, and especially since the same statuette might have first one function, then the other. Some, which are now in the Musée de l'Homme in Paris, have an undeniably religious significance, since one can be recognized as the Mother of the Twins, and another as the Little Old Man, a god who came down from Heaven and was ill-treated by mankind, whom he punished except for one family which had given him shelter. On the other hand, it would be too facile to interpret the handing over of the *santos* to the children as a symptom of the collapse of a religion; this situation, which seems so unstable to us, had been described in exactly the same terms by Boggiani forty years before, and by Fritch ten years after him; it is also mentioned in observations made ten years after mine. Circumstances which remain unchanged for fifty years must, in some sense, be normal. There has certainly been a decline in religious values, but the explanation is to be sought not so much in this as in a

FIG 9. Two statuettes representing mythological figures: the one on the left is stone, the other wood

way of dealing with the relationships between the sacred
and the profane which is commoner than we are inclined
to think. The opposition between the two terms is neither
as absolute nor as continuous as has sometimes been as-
serted.

In the hut next to mine was a medicine-man whose
equipment comprised a round stool, a straw crown, a gourd
rattle covered with a beaded net, and an ostrich-feather
fan for capturing 'animals', *bichos*—that is, evil spirits
which cause diseases. The cure consisted in expelling them
by means of the opposing power of the medicine-man's
own *bicho*, his guardian spirit, and furthermore a conser-
vative, for it was the spirit who forbade him to let me have
the precious utensils 'to which'—so ran the message—'he
was accustomed'.

During our stay there was a feast to celebrate the puberty
of a girl living in another hut. First, she was dressed in the
old manner: her cotton dress was replaced by a square
piece of material which was wrapped around her body
under the armpits. Her shoulders, arms and face were
painted with elaborate patterns, and all the available necklaces were hung round her neck. This, incidentally, may
have been prompted less by ancient custom than by a
desire to impress us. Young anthropologists are taught that
natives are afraid of having their image caught in a photograph, and that it is proper to overcome this fear and
compensate them for the risk they think they are taking by
making them a present in money or in kind. The Caduveo
had perfected the system: not only did they insist on being
paid before allowing themselves to be photographed; they
forced me to photograph them so that I should have to pay.
Hardly a day went by but a woman came to me in some
extraordinary get-up and obliged me, whether I wanted
to or not, to pay her photographic homage, accompanied
by a few milreis. Being anxious not to waste my film, I
often just went through the motions and handed over the
money.

However, it would have been bad anthropological practice to resist this behaviour, or even to consider it as a
proof of decadence or money-mindedness. It represented
the re-emergence, in a transposed form, of certain specific
features of Indian society: the independence and authority
of women of high birth, ostentatious behaviour in front of
strangers and the insistence on homage from ordinary mor-

tals. The attire might be freakish and improvised, but the behaviour which prompted it was no less significant because of that; it was my business to see how it fitted into the framework of traditional institutions.

The same was true of the demonstrations which followed the affixing of the girl's loincloth. The drinking of *pinga*, or cane-sugar alcohol, began in the afternoon, with the men sitting in a circle and loudly boasting of various titles taken from the lower ranks of the military hierarchy (the only one they were acquainted with), such as corporal, adjutant, lieutenant or captain. It was undoubtedly one of those 'solemn drinking sessions' described by eighteenth-century writers, at which the chiefs were seated according to their rank and served by their squires, while the heralds enumerated the drinker's qualifications and recounted his doughty deeds. Alcohol had a curious effect on the Caduveo: after a period of excitement, they would fall into a gloomy silence, then begin sobbing. Two of the less intoxicated men would take the weeping individual by the arms and walk him up and down, whispering words of consolation and affection, until he decided to vomit. Then all three would return to their places and the drinking bout would continue.

Meanwhile, the women chanted a short, three-note tune, which was repeated over and over again. A few old women, who were drinking apart, would from time to time rush out into the open, gesticulating and holding forth in an apparently incoherent manner, amid laughter and jeers. Here again, it would be wrong to consider their behaviour simply as lack of self-control on the part of drunken old women. The old writers mention that feast days, particularly those marking the most important stages in the growth of a girl of noble birth, were characterized by displays in which women dressed as men simulated processions of warriors, dances and tournaments. These ragged peasants, in their remote, marshy setting, were a sorry sight, but their very degradation made it all the more striking that they should have tenaciously preserved certain features of the past.

20. A NATIVE COMMUNITY
AND ITS LIFE-STYLE

The customs of a community, taken as a whole, always have a particular style and are reducible to systems. I am of the opinion that the number of such systems is not unlimited and that—in their games, dreams or wild imaginings—human societies, like individuals, never create absolutely, but merely choose certain combinations from an ideal repertoire that it should be possible to define. By making an inventory of all recorded customs, of all those imagined in myths or suggested in children's games or adult games, or in the dreams of healthy or sick individuals or in psycho-pathological behaviour, one could arrive at a sort of table, like that of the chemical elements, in which all actual or hypothetical customs would be grouped in families, so that one could see at a glance which customs a particular society had in fact adopted.

These remarks are particularly relevant in the case of the Mbaya-Guaycuru, of whom, along with the Toba and Pilaga of Paraguay, the Caduveo of Brazil are the last living representatives. Their civilization is undeniably reminiscent of one that European society playfully invented in a traditional pastime, and the model of which was imaginatively defined with such success by Lewis Carroll: these knightly Indians looked like the court figures in a pack of cards. The resemblance was noticeable first of all in their attire: leather tunics and cloaks that broadened the shoulders fell in stiff folds and were decorated in black and red patterns which the old writers compared to Turkish carpets and which had recurrent motifs in the shape of spades, hearts, diamonds and clubs.

These Indians had kings and queens, and like Alice's queen, the latter liked nothing better than to play with the severed heads brought back by their warriors. Noble lords and ladies disported themselves at tournaments; menial tasks were carried out by the Guana, who were different

186

both in language and culture and had settled earlier in the
territory. The last living representatives of the Guana, the
Tereno, live in a government reserve, not far from the
little town of Miranda, where I went to visit them. The
Guana cultivated the land and handed over part of their
produce to the Mbaya lords in return for their protection
against the pillaging and depredation practised by bands of
armed horsemen. A sixteenth-century German who ventured into these regions compares the relationships between
the two populations with those existing in his day in Central Europe between the feudal lords and their serfs.

The Mbaya were organized into castes; at the top of
the social scale were the nobles, divided into two categories,
great hereditary nobles and individual new creations; usually the latter had been promoted because of their birth
coinciding with that of a child of high rank. Furthermore,
the great noble families had senior and junior branches.
Next came the warriors, the best of whom, after an initiation ceremony, were admitted into a brotherhood and
entitled to adopt special names and to use an artificial
language formed by the addition of a suffix to each word,
as in certain kinds of slang. The lower orders were made
up of Chamacoco slaves, or slaves of other origins, and
Guana serfs, although the latter, imitating their masters,
had in turn adopted a division into three castes.

The nobles displayed their rank by stencilled body paintings, or tattooed designs which were the equivalent of
coats of arms. They removed all facial hair, including eyebrows and eyelashes, and referred in disgust to bushy-eye-
browed Europeans as 'ostrich brothers'. Men and women
appeared in public accompanied by a retinue of slaves and
clients, who danced attendance on them and anticipated
their every want. Even in 1935, the painted old hags laden
with pendants, who were the best designers, were still
apologizing for having been forced to abandon their artistic accomplishments because they had been deprived of
the *cativas*—slaves—formerly assigned to them. At Nalike
there were still a few former Chamacoco slaves who had
been integrated into the group but were treated conde-
scendingly.

Even the Spanish and Portuguese conquerors were intimidated by the arrogance of these aristocrats, and used
the titles Don and Doña in referring to them. It was said
that a white woman had nothing to fear if captured by the

FIG 10–11. Caduveo patterns

FIG 12–13. Motifs used in body painting

Mbaya, since no warrior would think of polluting his blood by union with her. Some Mbaya ladies refused to meet the viceroy's wife, because they considered that only the Queen of Portugal would have been worthy of their company. Another, known as Doña Caterina, while still only a girl, refused an invitation from the governor of the Mato Grosso to go to Cuiaba; as she was of marriageable age, she supposed that he would ask for her hand in marriage, and she could neither accept a *mésalliance* nor offend him by her refusal.

These Indians were monogamous, but adolescent girls sometimes chose to follow the warriors on their campaigns and acted as squires, pages and mistresses. A noble lady might have a *cavaliere servante,* who was also her lover, without her husband deigning to display jealousy, because that would have made them both lose face. It was a society remarkably adverse to feelings that we consider as being natural. For instance, there was a strong dislike for procreation. Abortion and infanticide were almost the normal practice, so much so that perpetuation of the group was ensured by adoption rather than by breeding, and one of the chief aims of the warriors' expeditions was the obtaining of children. It was estimated at the beginning of the nineteenth century that barely 10 per cent of the members of a certain Guaycuru group belonged to the original stock.

When children were born and survived, they were not brought up by their parents but entrusted to another family, and visited only at rare intervals. Up to the age of fourteen, they were kept ritually smeared from head to foot with black paint, and called by the name the natives applied later to Negroes when they first saw them; then, they were initiated and washed, and one of the two concentric rings of hair which had so far adorned their heads was shaved off.

However, the birth of a child of high rank was made the occasion of celebrations which were repeated at each stage of the child's growth—weaning, the first steps, the first participation in the games, etc. Heralds proclaimed the family's titles and forecast a glorious future for the newly born child. Another baby, who had been born at the same moment, was appointed his brother-in-arms. There were drinking sessions, during which mead was served in vessels made from horns or skulls. The women would borrow the warriors' equipment and engage in mock combats. The nobles were seated in order of rank and served by slaves, who were not allowed to drink, so that they could help their masters to vomit should the need arise, and take care of them until they fell asleep to experience the delightful visions produced by intoxication.

The proud confidence of all these Davids, Alexanders, Caesars and Charlemagnes, Rachels, Judiths, Pallases and Argines, Hectors, Ogiers, Lancelots and Lahires was based on the belief that they were predestined to govern mankind. A myth assured them of this; it has survived only in fragmentary form but, as it has come down to us refined by succeeding centuries, it has a splendid simplicity, and presents in the most concise form the obvious truth I was to grasp later during my travels in the East, namely that the degree of slavery is a function of the finished character of the given society. Here is the myth: when Gonoenhodi, the Supreme Being, decided to create men, he first drew forth the Guana from the earth, then the other tribes: to the former he allotted agriculture, to the latter hunting. The Trickster, who was the other divinity in the native pantheon, then noticed that the Mbaya had been forgotten at the bottom of the hole and brought them out; but since there was nothing left for them, they were granted the one remaining function, which was to oppress and exploit the others. It is difficult to imagine a more profound social contract than that.

These Indians, who were like characters in some romance of chivalry, absorbed in their cruel game of prestige and domination in a society which might be said to be doubly 'clear-cut',* created a graphic art which is quite unlike almost everything that has come down to us from pre-Columbian America, although it does have some similarity to the figures and patterns on our playing cards. I have already made some reference to it, but I would now like to describe this extraordinary feature of Caduveo culture.

In the tribe we visited, the men were sculptors and the women painters. The men fashioned the statuettes I men-

---

* Translators' Note: A *l'emporte-pièce*, literally, tooled or punched out; metaphorically, clear-cut, trenchant. The author appears to be referring to the sharply defined social relations and to the clear-cut decorative motifs.

FIG 14–17. Motifs used in body painting

FIG 18. Drawings made by a Caduveo boy

tioned earlier from the hard, bluish wood of the gum tree. They also embossed figures of men, ostriches and horses on the zebu horns they used as cups. Occasionally they made drawings, but only of foliage, human beings or animals. The women's speciality was decorating pottery and leather, and doing body paintings, at which some were undeniably expert.

Their faces, and sometimes even their whole bodies, were covered with a network of asymmetrical arabesques, alternating with delicate geometrical patterns. The first person to describe this feature was the Jesuit missionary, Sanchez Labrador, who lived among them from 1760 to 1770, but exact reproductions were only made a century later by Boggiani. In 1935, I myself collected several hundred designs in the following manner. My first intention was to photograph the faces, but the financial demands of the ladies of the tribe would soon have exhausted my resources. I next tried to draw faces on sheets of paper and suggested to the women that they should paint them, as they would have painted their own countenances; the result was so successful that I abandoned my clumsy sketches. The women were not put off by the blank sheets, and this showed that their art in no way depended on the natural contours of the human face.

FIG 19. Another drawing made by the same small boy

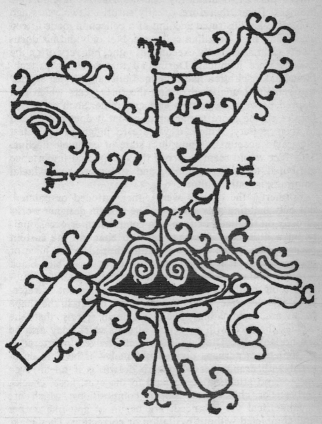

FIG 20. Two face-paintings; note the motif consisting of two opposed spirals which represent—and are applied on—the upper lip

Only a few very old women seemed to have preserved the ancient skills; and for a long time I remained convinced that I had made my collection at the last possible moment. I was, therefore, greatly surprised two years ago to receive an illustrated account of a collection made fifteen years later by a Brazilian colleague. Not only did his documents seem as expertly executed as mine, but very often the designs were identical. During all that time, style, technique and inspiration had remained unchanged, just as they had remained unaltered during the forty years which had elapsed between Boggiani's visit and mine. Such conservatism is all the more remarkable in that it does not extend to their pottery, which, if we are to judge by the latest illustrated accounts, is now in a state of complete decline. This fact would seem to prove the exceptional importance attributed to body paintings, and still more so to facial paintings, in native culture.

Formerly, the designs were either tattooed or painted, but only painting now survives. The woman designer works directly on the body or face of a companion, or occasionally on a little boy. The men tend to abandon the custom earlier. With a fine bamboo spatula dipped in the juice of the *genipapo*—it is colourless at first but turns blue-black through oxidation—the artist improvises on the living subject, using neither pattern, nor sketch, nor point of reference. She decorates the upper lip with a design in the shape of an arc, terminating on either side in spirals; then she divides the face with a vertical stroke, which may also be cut horizontally. The face, after being halved, quartered— or sometimes perhaps divided obliquely—is lavishly decorated with arabesques which are drawn as if on an even surface, no attention being paid to the eyes, nose, cheeks, forhead or chin. These skilful compositions, which are asymmetrical yet balanced, are begun at any one corner and completed without hesitation or correction. They make use of relatively simple motifs, such as spirals, S-shapes, crosses, mascles, Greek key-patterns and scrolls, but combined in such a way that each pattern has an original character; among the four hundred designs I collected in 1935, I did not notice two alike, but since I made the opposite observation when I compared my collection and the one assembled later, we must conclude that the artists' extraordinarily varied repertoire corresponds nevertheless to a fixed tradition. Unfortunately, neither I myself nor my successors were able to discover the theory underlying these Indian patterns: the informants mentioned certain terms corresponding to the basic motifs, but claimed not to know, or to have forgotten, all the details concerning the more complex designs. Either they were practising an empirical skill which had been handed down from generation to generation, or they were determined not to reveal the secret of their art.

Nowadays, the Caduveo only paint themselves for pleasure, but in former times the custom had a much deeper significance. According to Sanchez Labrador, the noble castes wore paint only on the forehead, while the common people decorated the whole face. Also, at that period, only young women followed the fashion. 'It is rare', he wrote, 'to find old women wasting their time on these patterns: they make do with those that time has engraved on their faces.' The missionary was alarmed by the lack of respect for the Creator's handiwork, and wondered why the natives should thus spoil the appearance of the human face. He tried to suggest explanations: was it to soothe the pangs of hunger that they spent long hours drawing their arabesques? Or to prevent their enemies recognizing them? Whatever reasons he imagined, they always involved deception, and he asked himself why. In spite of his distaste for the practice, even he was aware that these paintings were of prime importance to the natives and, in a sense, an end in themselves.

He condemned Indian men who, forgetful of hunting, fishing and their families, wasted whole days in having themselves painted. But they would ask the missionaries, 'Why are you so stupid?' 'In what way are we stupid?' the latter would reply. 'Because you do not paint yourselves like the Eyiguayeguis.' To be a man it was necessary to be painted; to remain in the natural state was to be no different from the beasts.

It is fairly certain that the continuance of the custom among the women at the present time is to be explained by erotic motives. The reputation of Caduveo women is firmly established along both banks of the Rio Paraguay. Many half-castes and Indians belonging to other tribes have come to settle and marry at Nalike. Perhaps the facial and body paintings explain the attraction; at all events, they strengthen and symbolize it. The delicate and subtle markings, which are as sensitive as the lines of the face, and sometimes accentuate them, sometimes run counter to them, make the women delightfully alluring. They constitute a kind of pictorial surgery grafting art on to the human body. And when Sanchez Labrador anxiously protests that they are 'adding artificial ugliness to natural graces' he is not being consistent because, a few lines further on, he maintains that the finest tapestries could not compare with these paintings. No doubt the erotic effect of facial make-up has never been more systematically and consciously exploited.

In these facial paintings, as well as in their practice of abortion and infanticide, the Mbaya were expressing the same abhorrence of nature. Native art regarded human clay with supreme contempt, and in this sense it is almost sinful. Looking at it from the point of view of a Jesuit and missionary, Sanchez Labrador was acute enough to see that it was the work of the devil. He himself stresses the Promethean aspect of this savage art, in describing the technique used by the natives to cover their bodies with star-shaped motifs: 'Thus each Eyiguayegui looks upon himself as another Atlas who uses not only his shoulders and his hands but his whole body to support a clumsy representation of the universe.' The secret of the exceptional quality of Caduveo art could be that man, through its medium, refuses to be a reflection of the divine image.

As we look at the motifs in the shape of stripes, spirals and whorls, which are particularly prevalent in Caduveo art, we cannot help being reminded of Spanish baroque, with its wrought-iron work and stuccoes. Might this not be a case of a primitive imitation of a style brought by the Spanish conquerors? It is certain that the natives appropriated certain themes, and we know of precise instances. After the Indians saw a European warship for the first time, when the *Maracanha* sailed up the Paraguay in 1857, the sailors noticed the next day that their bodies were covered with anchor-shaped motifs; one Indian even had an officer's uniform painted in great detail all over his torso —with buttons and stripes, and the sword-belt over the coat-tails. All that this proves is that the Mbaya were already in the habit of painting themselves, and that they had become extremely skilful at the practice. Moreover, although their curvilinear style is rare in pre-Columbian America, it shows certain resemblances to archaeological finds that have come to light at various points on the continent, some of them dating back to a time several cen-

Fig 21. A pattern painted on leather

turies before Columbus's voyage: Hopewell, in the Ohio valley, and the recent Caddo pottery in the Mississippi valley; Santarem and Marajo at the mouth of the Amazon, and Chavin in Peru. The very fact that they are so widely dispersed is a sign of antiquity.

The real problem lies elsewhere. When we study the Caduveo patterns, one point is obvious: their originality is not in the primary motifs, which are simple enough to have been invented independently rather than borrowed (and probably invention and borrowing took place simultaneously), but lies in the way in which the motifs are combined: it is evident in the final achievement, the finished work. The methods of composition are so subtle and systematic that they go far beyond the corresponding suggestions that these Indians could have borrowed from European art at the time of the Renaissance. Whatever the starting-point, such an unusual development can only be explained by reasons peculiar to itself.

I once tried to elucidate some of these reasons by a comparison between Caduveo art and art forms found elsewhere which show similarities to it: for instance, archaic China, the north-west coast of Canada and Alaska, and New Zealand.* The hypothesis I am about to put forward now is somewhat different, but it completes, rather than contradicts, my earlier interpretation.

As I observed in my earlier study, Caduveo art is characterized by a male/female dualism—the men are sculptors, the women painters; the art of the former is figurative and naturalistic, in spite of its stylizations, whereas the latter practise a non-figurative art. Restricting myself now to the consideration of this feminine art, I would like to emphasize that it exhibits a continuation of the dualism on several levels.

The women employ two styles, both prompted by a sense of decoration and abstraction. One is angular and geometrical, the other, curvilinear and free-flowing. More often than not, the compositions are based on an orderly combination of the two styles. For instance, one is used for the edge or border, the other for the main pattern. In the case of pottery, the division is more striking: the geometrical pattern is usually found on the neck and the curvilinear pattern on the belly, or vice versa. The curvilinear style is more often used for facial paintings, and the geometrical style for body paintings; but sometimes, through an additional division, each area is patterned with a combination of the two styles.

Whatever the mixture, the completed work expresses an urge to find a balance between other principles which also go in pairs: an originally linear pattern may be gone over again in the final phase and partially changed into surfaces (by the filling in of certain sections, as happens with us when we are doodling); most of the designs are based on two alternating themes; and almost always the motif and the background occupy approximately the same amount of surface area, so that it is possible to interpret the design in two ways, by reversing their respective roles—each motif

* 'Le dédoublement de la représentation dans les arts de l'Asie et de l'Amérique', *Renaissance*, Vol. II and III (New York, 1945), pp. 168, 186, 20 illustrations. Reproduced in *Structural Anthropology*, 1958, Ch. XIII.

can be read positively or negatively. Finally, the pattern often obeys a twofold principle of simultaneous symmetry and asymmetry, and this produces contrasting registers which—to use heraldic terms—are seldom parted or couped but more often parted per bend or parted per bend sinister, or even quartered or gyronny. I am using such terms deliberately, for all these rules inevitably remind one of the principles of heraldry.

Let me follow up the analysis with an example: here is a seemingly simple body painting (Fig 17–18). It consists of undulated and accosted pales defining tapering, regular fields filled by a row of small charges, in the proportion of one per field. This description is deceptive; it perhaps gives some idea of the general appearance of the completed pattern, but if we look more closely, we see that the woman who drew it did not begin by drawing her undulated bands and then proceed to decorate each interval with a charge. Her method was quite different and more complicated. She worked like a man laying paving-stones, constructing successive rows by means of identical elements. Each element is composed of one section of ribbon, formed by the concave part of one band and the convex part of the adjacent band, and a tapering field with a charge at the centre of it. These elements interlock with each other through dislocation, and it is only at the end that the pattern achieves a stability which both confirms and belies the dynamic process according to which it has been carried out.

The Caduveo decorative style therefore presents us with a whole series of complexities. There is in the first place a dualism which is projected on to successive planes, as in a hall of mirrors: men and women, painting and sculpture, figurative drawing and abstraction, angle and curve, geometry and arabesque, neck and belly, symmetry and asymmetry, line and surface, border and motif, piece and field, pattern and background. But these oppositions are only perceived retrospectively; they are static in character; the dynamic movement of the art, that is the way in which the motifs are imagined and carried out, intersects the basic duality at all levels: the primary themes are first decomposed, then reconstituted as secondary themes which use fragments taken from the first as elements of a provisional unity, and then these secondary themes are juxtaposed in such a way that the original unity re-emerges as if it had been conjured back into existence. Finally, the complex

FIG 22–23. Body painting: *(left)* as recorded by Boggiani (1895); *(right)* as recorded by the author (1935)

FIG 24-25. Two motifs used in face- and body-painting

patterns obtained by this method are themselves redivided and juxtaposed by means of quarterings like those in heraldy, when two patterns are divided between four cantons arranged in contrasting pairs, and simply repeated or coloured from one to the other.

It is now possible to explain why this style is reminiscent of that of European playing cards, although more delicate. Each figure on a playing card fulfils two needs. It must first of all assume a twofold function: it has to be an object which can be used in the dialogue—or duel—between two partners who are facing each other; and it must also play the part which devolves upon each card as an object in a collection—the pack. Certain obligations flow from this complex nature: there must be symmetry relating to the function, and asymmetry corresponding to the part played. The problem is solved by the adoption of a composition that is symmetrical but set along an oblique axis, thus avoiding the completely asymmetrical formula, which would have met the demands of the role but run counter to those of the function, and the reverse and completely symmetrical formula, which would have had the opposite effect. Here again we are faced with a complex situation corresponding to two contradictory forms of duality and ending in a compromise, achieved by a secondary opposition between the ideal axis of the object and that of the figure it represents. But, in order to reach this conclusion, we have been obliged to go beyond the level of stylistic analysis. In order to understand the style of playing cards, we must do more than merely study their design; we must also ask ourselves what purpose they serve. What, therefore, is the purpose of Caduveo art?

I have already given a partial reply to this question, or rather the natives have done so for me. In the first place, facial paintings confer human dignity on the individual; they ensure the transition from nature to culture, from 'stupid' beast to civilized man. Next, since they vary in style and pattern according to caste, they express differences in status within a complex society. This means that they have a sociological function.

However important this observation may be, it cannot account for the original characteristics of this native art; at most it can explain its existence. The analysis of the social structure must be carried further. The Mbaya were divided into three castes, each of which was predominantly con-

FIG 26. A facial painting

cerned with questions of etiquette. For the nobles, and to a certain extent for the warriors too, the main problem was one of prestige. The early accounts show that they were paralysed by the fear of losing face, of not living up to their rank and, most important of all, of marrying below their station. The danger present in a society of this kind was therefore segregation. Either through choice or necessity, each caste tended to shut itself in upon itself, thus impairing the cohesion of the social body as a whole. In particular, the inbreeding practised by the castes and the ever-increasing gradations in the hierarchy must have made it more difficult to have marriages that corresponded to the concrete necessities of collective life. This alone can explain the paradox of a society being opposed to procreation and, in order to safeguard itself against the dangers of improper alliances within the group, having recourse to a form of inverted racialism through the systematic adoption of enemies or foreigners.

This being so, it is significant that, at the opposite extremes of the vast area once controlled by the Mbaya, to the north-east and south-west respectively, we should find forms of social organization which are practically identical, in spite of the geographical distance between them. The Guana of Paraguay and the Bororo of the central Mato Grosso used to have (and, in the case of the latter, still have) a hierarchical social structure, similar to that of the Mbaya; they were, or are, divided into three classes which, in the past at least, seem to have corresponded to differing statuses, and were hereditary and endogamous. However, the danger I referred to above in connection with Mbaya society was to some extent offset both among the Guana and the Bororo by a division into two moieties which, as we know in the case of the Bororo at least, cut across the class system. Although members of the different classes could not intermarry, the reverse obligation was imposed on the moieties: a man from one moiety had to marry a woman from the other, and vice versa. It is fair to say, then, that the asymmetry of the classes was, in a sense, counterbalanced by the symmetry of the moieties.

We may wonder whether this complex structure of three hierarchical classes plus two equally balanced moieties is to be considered as a single system or not. Perhaps it is, or perhaps we ought to separate the two aspects and regard one as being older than the other. If so, there would be no lack of arguments in favour of the seniority of one or the other.

The question with which I am concerned at this point is quite different in nature. Although I have given only a brief description of the Guana and Bororo system (it will be amplified later when I describe my experiences with the Bororo), it is clear that, on the sociological level, it presents a structure analogous to the one I worked out, on the stylistic level, in connection with Caduveo art. We are dealing with a double opposition in both cases. In the first instance, it consists primarily in this opposition between a

ternary and a binary organization, one asymmetrical, the
other symmetrical; and in the second instance, in the opposition between social mechanisms, some of which are
based on reciprocity, others on hierarchy. In its effort to
remain faithful to these contradictory principles, the social
group divides and subdivides into related and opposing
sub-groups. Just as a coat of arms unites within its field
prerogatives deriving from several lines, this society could
be said to be parted, parted per bend, parted per bend
sinister and couped. We need only study a plan of a
Bororo village (as I shall do later) to see that it is organized in the same way as a Caduveo pattern.

It would seem, then, that the Guana and the Bororo,
having been faced with a contradiction in their social structure, had succeeded in resolving (or concealing) it by
essentially sociological methods. Perhaps they were divided
into moieties before being incorporated into the Mbaya
sphere of influence, so that the means was already to hand;
or they may have invented moieties at a later date—or
borrowed them from others—because artistocratic arrogance was less pronounced among provincial communities;
it would also be possible to suggest other hypotheses. This
solution never existed among the Mbaya: either they did
not know of it (which is unlikely), or, more probably, it
was incompatible with their fanaticism. They therefore
never had the opportunity of resolving their contradictions
or of at least concealing them by means of artful institutions. But the remedy they failed to use on the social level,
or which they refused to consider, could not elude them
completely; it continued to haunt them in an insidious way.
And since they could not become conscious of it and live it
out in reality, they began to dream about it. Not in a direct
form, which would have clashed with their prejudices, but
in a transposed, and seemingly innocuous, form: in their
art. If my analysis is correct, in the last resort the graphic
art of the Caduveo women is to be interpreted, and its
mysterious appeal and seemingly gratuitous complexity to
be explained, as the phantasm of a society ardently and in-
satiably seeking a means of expressing symbolically the
institutions it might have, if its interests and superstitions
did not stand in the way. In this charming civilization,
the female beauties trace the outlines of the collective
dream with their make-up; their patterns are hieroglyphics

describing an inaccessible golden age, which they extol in their ornamentation, since they have no code in which to express it, and whose mysteries they disclose as they reveal their nudity.

PART SIX

Bororo

---

21. GOLD AND DIAMONDS

Corumba, the gateway to Bolivia, situated opposite Porto Esperança on the right bank of the Rio Paraguay, seems to have been imagined for a novel by Jules Verne. The town is perched at the top of a limestone cliff overlooking the river. Surrounded by a mass of canoes, one or two small paddle-boats, with low hulls and two layers of cabins surmounted by a slender funnel, are moored at the quayside, from where the road climbs up. Along its first stretch are a few buildings—the customs house, the arsenal, etc.—out of proportion with the rest and a reminder of the time when the Rio Paraguay provided a precarious frontier between recently independent states seething with new ambitions, and when the river carried the heavy traffic plying between the Rio de la Plata and the interior.

After reaching the top of the cliff, the road runs along the edge for about two hundred metres; then it makes a right-angled turn and enters the town in the form of a long street lined with low, flat-roofed houses, distempered in white or beige. The street terminates in a square, where there are acid-coloured orange and green coral trees with grass growing between them. Beyond lies the stony country-side stretching as far as the hills which line the horizon.

There is only one hotel and it is always full. A few rooms are let off in private houses, which at ground level are filled with the damp from the swamps, and where the sleeping visitor experiences nightmares true to reality, which change him into a new kind of Christian martyr, who has been thrown into a stifling pit to be devoured by bugs. The food is abominable, because the countryside, being unproductive or undeveloped, cannot provide for the needs of the two to three thousand people who are resident in, or passing through, Corumba. Everything is exorbitant in price, and the apparent activity, contrasting as it does with the flat desert-like landscape—a brown, spongy mass stretching beyond the river—gives an impression of bustle and gaiety such as must have characterized the pioneer town in Cali-

fornia or the Far West a century ago. In the evenings, the
entire population gathers along the cliff road. The girls,
whispering to each other, parade in groups of three or four
in front of the boys, who sit in silence with their legs
dangling over the balustrade. The observer might think
himself present at a ceremony; nothing could be more
curious than this solemn prenuptial parade which takes
place in flickering electric light on the edge of five hundred
kilometres of marshland, with ostriches and boas venturing
into the vicinity of the town.

As the crow flies, Corumba is barely four hundred kilometres from Cuiaba. I saw the various stages in the development of air transport between the two towns, from the
small four-seater planes which covered the distance in a
bumpy flight lasting two or three hours to the twelve-seater
Junkers which came into service in 1938–9. In 1935, however Cuiaba could only be reached by boat, and the four
hundred kilometres were made twice as long by the bends
in the river. During the rainy season, it took a week to
reach the State capital, and sometimes three weeks in the
dry season, when the boat, in spite of its shallow draught,
would run aground on the sandbanks: days were lost trying
to refloat it with the help of a cable tied to some sturdy
tree-trunk along the bank, on which the engine pulled
furiously. In the company's offices a temptingly worded
notice was prominently displayed. A literal rendering, which
respects both the style and layout, is to be found on the
opposite page. Needless to say, the reality did not correspond very closely to the description.

And yet what a delightful voyage it was! There were very
few passengers: cattle-breeders and their families going
back to their herds, travelling Lebanese salesmen, soldiers
posted to some garrison town, or provincial civil servants.
No sooner did they go on board than this motley company
donned the beach attire habitual in the interior—striped
pyjamas (silk in the case of the more fastidious), which
were a flimsy covering for hairy bodies, and slippers; twice
a day we sat down to an unchanging menu, consisting of a
dish of rice, another of black beans and a third of dried
manioc flour, all of which accompanied fresh or preserved
beef. This is what is called *feijoada*, from *feijão*, meaning
bean. The robustness of my travelling companions' appe-
tites was equalled only by the discernment with which
they pronounced judgment on the fare. The *feijoada* was

DOES YOUR EXCELLENCY PROPOSE TO TRAVEL?

If so, absolutely insist on taking the splendid

N/M CIDADE DE CORUMBA

belonging to the River Transport Company of Messrs —— and Co., a steamship which has superior fittings, excellent bathrooms, electric light, running water in all cabins and a perfect garçonière* service.

The fastest and most comfortable ship of the Cuiaba–Corumba–Porto-Esperança line.

By taking N/M CIDADE DE CORUMBA here in Corumba, or at Porto-Esperança, Your Excellency will arrive **3 days or more earlier** than with any other ship and as the **time** problem is an important factor on the field of action, preference must be given to the most rapid and the one which offers the highest degree of comfort.

THE STEAMSHIP GUAPORE

The better to serve its passengers, the Company has recently renovated the splendid steamship GUAPORE, putting the dining-room on the upper deck, an idea which provides the ship with a magnificent **Dining-Room** and a large area for locomotion of our distinguished passengers.

You must therefore prefer the rapid steamships **N/M CIDADE DE CORUMBA and GUAPORE**

---

* In French in the original, and with this spelling.

variously declared *muito boa* or *muito ruim,* that is, 'first-rate' or 'foul'; similarly, they had only one expression to describe the dessert, which consisted of cheese and fruit paste, speared up with the tip of the knife: the thick fruit jelly was either *bem doce,* very sweet, or not sweet enough.

About every thirty kilometres, the boat stopped to refuel at a depot; and when necessary, we would wait two or three hours while the man in charge of the depot went off into the prairie to lassoo a cow, which was slaughtered and skinned with the help of the crew, who then hauled the carcass on board, to give us a supply of fresh meat for the next few days.

The rest of the time the steamboat glided gently along the narrow arms of the river. This was called 'negotiating' the *estirões*—those stretches of the river bounded by bends sharp enough to prevent one seeing round the corner. Because of the meanderings of the river, these *estirões* sometimes come so close together that, in the evening, we would find ourselves only a few metres from the point we had started from in the morning. Often the boat brushed against the dripping forest trees lining the river-bank. The noise of the engine disturbed countless birds: macaws with plumage that flashed like red, blue and gold enamel; diving cormorants with necks so sinuous that they looked like winged serpents; parakeets and parrots that filled the air with cries sufficiently like the human voice to be described as inhuman. This wild life was so close and so monotonous that it held the attention and induced a kind of torpor. From time to time the passengers would be aroused by some more unusual incident: it might be a couple of deer or tapirs swimming across the river, or a *cascavel*—rattlesnake—or a *giboya*—python—writhing on the surface as light as a piece of straw; or a swarming herd of *jacarés*—harmless crocodiles which one soon wearied of shooting in the eye with a rifle bullet. Fishing for *piranhas* was more exciting. At one point along the river was a huge *saladeiro,* a gibbet-like construction for drying meat: the ground was strewn with bones, and purplish sides of meat were hanging along parallel bars, above which vultures were darkly wheeling. Over a distance of several hundred metres. the river ran red with the blood of slaughtered cattle. Here, if a fishing-line was cast into the water, several blood-drunk *piranhas* would leap at it, even before the bare hook was below the surface, and one would remain hanging like a golden lozenge. But care was needed when unhooking the catch. One bite by the fish could remove a finger.

Once we had passed the junction with the São Lourenço —along the upper reaches of which I would later travel by land to meet up with the Bororo—the Pantanal disappeared; on both sides of the river the landscape was predominantly *campo*, grass savannahs with more frequent homesteads and herds of cattle.

Cuiaba offers few features of note to the traveller approaching it by water: a paved ramp at river level, and at the top of its slope the outlines of the old arsenal. From there a road, two kilometres long and lined with rustic houses, leads to the cathedral square where the white-and-pink edifice stands between two avenues of imperial palms. To the left is the bishop's palace; to the right, that of the governor; and on the corner of the main street, the inn. It was the only one at the time of my visit and was run by a portly Lebanese.

I have already described Goyaz and I would be repeating myself if I dwelt at any length on Cuiaba. The setting is less beautiful, but the town, with its austere houses, half palaces half cottages, has the same charm. Since it is built on hilly ground, one can always see some vista or other from an upper storey: white houses with roofs of orange tile, the same colour as the earth, enclosing the greenery of the gardens, the *quintaes*. Around the L-shaped central space, there remains a network of alleyways, a characteristic feature of eighteenth-century colonial towns; they end in stretches of waste ground used as camping-sites, or in ill-defined avenues edged with mango trees and banana plants, sheltering a few adobe huts. Immediately beyond is the open country where teams of oxen can be seen grazing before they leave for the *sertão* or on arriving from it.

The founding of Cuiaba goes back to the middle of the eighteenth century. About 1720, explorers from São Paulo called *bandeirantes* penetrated into the region for the first time. They established a small post with a few settlers not far from the present site of the town. The country was inhabited by Cuxipo Indians, some of whom agreed to work on the cleared land. One day, a settler—appropriately called Miguel Sutil—sent a few natives to look for wild honey. They came back that same evening with handfuls of gold nuggets that they had simply picked up from the ground. Sutil and a companion called Barbudo—the

Bearded One—at once followed the natives to the spot where they had made their find. There was gold lying about everywhere, and in one month they gathered five tons of nuggets.

This being so, it is not surprising that the countryside around Cuiaba should in places look like a battlefield; mounds covered with grass and shrubs bear witness to the gold fever. Even today a Cuiabano may find a nugget in his vegetable patch. And there are grains of gold dust everywhere. In Cuiaba, beggars are gold-seekers: they can be seen at work in the bed of the river running through the lower part of the town. A day's search may yield enough to buy food, and several shopkeepers still use the fine scales which make it possible to accept a pinch of gold dust in exchange for meat or rice. Whenever there has been heavy rain and water is streaming through the gullies, children rush out with balls of clean wax and hold them in the current, so as to catch the tiny brilliant particles. Moreover, the Cuiabanos maintain that a vein of gold runs below their town at a depth of several metres. Rumour has it that it passes under the modest premises of the Bank of Brazil, which is richer through this hidden treasure than because of the sums contained in its out-of-date safe.

An echo of Cuiaba's past glory is to be found in its slow and ceremonious way of life. The newcomer spends his first day crossing and re-crossing the square between the inn and the governor's palace. On arrival, I left my visiting card; then, an hour later, the aide-de-camp, a gendarme with a heavy moustache, returned the compliment. After the siesta, which kills the town stone-dead every day between noon and four o'clock, I went to pay my respects to the governor (or 'interventor', as he was then called) who greeted me with bored politeness. He would, of course, have been happier had there been no Indians for an anthropologist to bother about; as far as he was concerned, they could only be an irritating reminder of political disfavour and evidence of his banishment to a backward area. The bishop's attitude was very much the same: the Indians, he was careful to explain to me, were neither as fierce nor as stupid as one might believe. Just think: a Bororo Indian woman had become a nun! And the Brothers at Diamantino, by dint of great effort, had succeeded in turning three Paressi into decent joiners. As far as research was concerned, the missionaries had really collected all the material worthy of preservation. I might find it hard to believe, but the ignorant Service of Protection wrote Bororo with the tonic accent on the final vowel, whereas Father So-and-So had established, twenty years previously, that it should fall on the middle vowel. As far as legends were concerned, the Indians were acquainted with the story of the Flood, which was proof of the fact that Our Lord did not intend them to be damned for ever. He had no objection to my going among them. But I should at all costs avoid undoing the work accomplished by the Fathers: no frivolous gifts, such as mirrors or necklaces. Only axes; the Indians were lazy and must be reminded of the sanctity of labour.

Once these formalities were over, it was possible to move on to serious matters. Days were spent in the back-premises of Lebanese shopkeepers, known as *turcos*. They are part wholesale-dealers, part money-lenders, who supply hardware, fabrics and medicine to dozens of relatives, clients or protégés, each of whom goes off with his unpaid-for load and a few oxen or a canoe to scour the depths of the bush or the river-banks for the last available milreis (after twenty or thirty years of this existence, which is as hard for him as for the people he exploits, he eventually settles down with the millions he has accumulated). Also, at the baker's, to arrange for the sacks of *bolachas,* round loaves of unleavened bread bound with fat: these are as hard as bricks, but turn soft when heated, and what with the jolting of the beasts and the sweat from the oxen, they become a crumbly, indefinable kind of food, as rancid as the dried meat we ordered from the butcher. The Cuiaba butcher was a dissatisfied man; he had one ambition and very little hope of it ever being fulfilled. He longed for a circus to come to Cuiaba, because he would have loved to see an elephant: 'All that meat! . . .'

Lastly, there were the B—— brothers; they were Frenchmen of Corsican origin who had settled in Cuiaba a long time before, but for what reason they did not say. They spoke their mother tongue with a remote and hesitant lilt. Before becoming garage proprietors, they had hunted egrets, and they described their technique, which consisted in placing cornets of white paper on the ground in such a way that when the tall birds, fascinated by the immaculate whiteness similar to their own, thrust their beaks into them, they became hoods which blinded the birds and made them easy to capture. The finest feathers were plucked from

living birds during the mating season. There were, in
Cuiaba, cupboards full of egret feathers, for which there
was no sale since they were no longer in fashion. The B——
brothers next became diamond prospectors. Now they were
specializing in equipping lorries which they sent out, as
boats were dispatched in the old days across unknown seas,
along tracks where both cargo and vehicle were in danger
of falling into ravines or rivers. But should they reach their
destination safely, a 400 per cent profit made up for
previous losses.

I often travelled through the country around Cuiaba by
lorry. The day before starting out would be spent loading
up with petrol drums, which were particularly numerous
since we had to allow not only for the return trip but also
for the fact that we would be travelling almost all the time
in second and first gear. The supplies and camping equipment were packed in such a way as to allow the passengers
to sit down and also to take shelter in case of rain. Jacks
and other tools were hung along the sides, together with a
supply of ropes and planks for crossing streams where the
bridges had been destroyed. The following day at dawn, we
would climb on top of the load as if we were mounting a
camel, and the lorry would lurch off on its journey. Trouble
would begin before the day was half over: the track might
be flooded or marshy and require strengthening with wood.
I once spent three days moving a carpet of logs twice the
length of the lorry from the back to the front until we were
safely over a difficult stretch. Or the track might be sandy,
and we had to dig under the wheels and fill in the gaps with
leaves. When the bridges were standing, we still had to unload completely in order to keep the weight down, and then
reload once we had crossed the rickety planks. If we discovered that they had been destroyed in a bush fire, we
would set up camp in order to rebuild them, and then dismantle them again because we might need the planks on a
later occasion. Finally, there were the major rivers which
could only be crossed by means of ferries consisting of three
canoes linked together with slats which, under the weight of
the lorry alone without its load, settled into the water up to
the rim. And they would sometimes carry the lorry to a
bank which was either too steep or too muddy to be
climbed; then we had to improvise tracks over a distance
of several hundred metres until we found a better landing-
place or a ford.

The men whose job it was to drive these lorries were accustomed to journeys lasting weeks or sometimes months. They worked in pairs—the driver and his assistant, one at the wheel and the other perched on the footboard to watch for obstacles and make sure that the way was clear ahead, like a sailor standing on the prow to help the pilot to negotiate a narrow strait. They always kept their rifles within reach, since it was not unusual for a buck or a tapir to stop in front of the lorry, more out of curiosity than fear. One or other of the men would take a pot-shot and the result would determine whether or not we halted at that place: a slaughtered animal had to be skinned and gutted and the meaty parts turned into slices by cutting in a spiral, as if a potato were being pared to the centre. The slices of meat were immediately rubbed with a mixture of salt, pepper and crushed garlic which was always kept ready. They were spread out in the sun for several hours, and so would keep until the operation was continued the next day and completed during the following days. The *carne de sol* thus obtained is less tasty than *carne de vento*, which is dried by being fixed to the top of a pole and exposed to the wind rather than the sun, but which keeps less well.

These expert lorry-drivers lead a very strange existence. They have to be ready to carry out the most intricate repair jobs; they remake and dismantle the road as they go along, and they are liable to be stranded for several weeks deep in the bush at the spot where their lorry has broken down, until a rival lorry comes along and gives the alarm at Cuiaba, from where a request goes to São Paulo or Rio for the necessary spare part. Meanwhile the lorry men camp, hunt, do their washing, sleep and possess their souls in patience. My best driver was a fugitive from justice because of a crime to which he never referred. The people in Cuiaba knew about it but said nothing, since there was no one else to carry out the impossible journeys he accomplished. It was generally thought that, by risking his life daily, he was making ample restitution for the life he had taken.

When we left Cuiaba at about four in the morning it was still dark. We could just make out a few churches decorated with stucco from base to belfry. The lorry jolted over the last streets paved with stones from the river and lined with mango trees clipped into rounded shapes. The characteristically orchard-like appearance of the savannah—because of the natural spacing of the trees—gave the illusion of a

man-made landscape, whereas we had already reached the
bush; the track soon became difficult enough to convince
us of this fact: it climbed away from the river in stony
curves intersected by ravines and muddy fords, overgrown
with *capoeira*. As soon as we had reached a certain height,
we could see a faint rosy line, too stationary to be confused
with the first glint of dawn. Yet for a long time we were
uncertain about its nature and its reality. But after travelling for a further three or four hours, we arrived at the
top of a rocky slope, from where we could scan a wider
horizon, and there, undeniably, before us we saw a red
wall-face, running from north to south and rising some two
or three hundred metres above the green hills. To the north
it sloped gently down until it merged with the plateau, but
to the south, the direction in which we were approaching,
we began to distinguish certain features. The wall-face,
which a short while before had appeared to be without a
fault, was now seen to be broken up into narrow chimneys,
a preliminary range of peaks, and terraces and platforms.
In this stone fortification system, there were bastions and
gorges. It took the lorry several hours to climb the slope,
only slightly improved by human effort, leading to the
upper edge of the *chapada* of the Mato Grosso, which gives
access to a plateau sloping gently downwards to the north,
over a distance of a thousand kilometres, as far as the
Amazonian basin: the *chapadão*.

It is like entering another world. The coarse grass, milky-
green in colour, barely conceals the white, pink or ochre-
coloured sand produced by the surface breaking-up of the
sandstone floor. The vegetation consists of only a few
gnarled and scattered trees with thick bark, glossy leaves
and thorns to protect them against the drought which
prevails for seven months in the year. But it only has to rain
for a few days and this desert-like savannah is transformed
into a garden: the grass becomes green and the trees are
covered with white and mauve flowers. However, the major
impression is always one of vastness. The ground is so level
and the incline so gradual that there is an unbroken vista
to the horizon dozens of kilometres away: it takes half a
day to cross a landscape that one has been looking at since
morning, and which is an exact replica of the one traversed
the day before, so that perception and memory are fused in
a kind of obsessive immobility. However far the land may
stretch, it is so uniform and so featureless that one can

mistake the distant horizon for clouds in the sky. The land-scape is too weird to be monotonous. From time to time the lorry fords bankless streams which flood, rather than cross, the plateau, as if this territory—one of the oldest in the world and a still-intact fragment of the continent of Gondwana, which linked Brazil and Africa in the secondary era—were still too new for the rivers to have had time to hollow out their beds.

In a European landscape, you find clearly defined shapes bathed in diffused light. Here what we consider as the tradi-tional roles of the sky and the earth are reversed. Above the milky expanse of the *campo,* the clouds build the most extravagant constructions. The sky is the region of shapes and volumes, while the earth retains a primeval softness.

One evening we stopped not far from a *garimpo,* a colony of diamond-seekers. It was not long before human shapes loomed up around our fire; they were *garimpeiros,* and from their bags or the pockets of their tattered clothes they produced small bamboo tubes, the contents of which —uncut diamonds—they tipped into our hands, hoping to sell them to us. But the B—— brothers had told me enough about the habits of the *garimpo* for me to know that none of the stones could have any particular value. The *garimpo* has its own laws, which may be unwritten but are none the less strictly adhered to.

The *garimpeiros* can be divided into two categories: ad-venturers and fugitives. Since the latter outnumber the former, it is understandable that most of the men find it difficult to leave the *garimpo,* once they have joined it. The little river-courses, in the sand of which the diamonds are found, are under the control of the men who first arrived there. Their resources are inadequate to allow them to wait for a really big find, which does not occur very often. So they are organized in bands, each financed by a leader who is referred to as 'captain' or 'engineer'; he has to have capital to arm his men and provide them with the necessary equipment—galvanized iron pails to haul up the gravel, sieves, wash-troughs and sometimes also divers' helmets and air-pumps so that they can explore potholes—and, most important of all, to ensure a regular food supply. In ex-change, the member of the band undertakes to sell his finds only to recognized buyers (who are connected with the famous Dutch or English firms of diamond-cutters) and to share the profits with his chief.

The fact that the men are armed is not to be explained simply by the frequent clashes between rival bands. It has in the past made it possible, and indeed still does, to deny the police access to the *garimpo*. The diamond-producing zone formed a State within the State, the former sometimes engaged in open warfare with the latter. In 1935, people were still talking about the minor war that the *engenheiro* Morbek and his men, the *valentões,* had waged for several years against the police of the State of Mato Grosso and which ended in a compromise. It should be said in defence of the outlaws that any man who had the misfortune to be captured by the police in the vicinity of a *garimpo* rarely reached Cuiaba. A famous chief, *capitão* Arnaldo, was caught along with his lieutenant. They were left in a tree with ropes around their necks and with their feet resting on a small plank; when they lost their balance through fatigue, they fell off and were hanged.

The group law is so strictly observed that, at Lageado or at Poxoreu, which are the centres of the *garimpo*, it is not uncommon to see a table in an inn that has been temporarily vacated and has been left covered with diamonds. No sooner has a stone been found than it is classified in terms of shape, size and colour. These details remain so clear and so charged with emotion that years later the discoverer can still recall the appearance of each stone. A man, talking to me about a particular diamond, said: 'When I looked at it, it was as if the Holy Virgin had let fall a tear into the hollow of my hand . . .' But the stones are not always as pure as this: often they are still concealed in the gangue, and it is impossible to assess their value right away. The recognized buyer announces his price (this is called 'weighing' the diamond), and just as the sale must be made to him, so his offer has to be accepted. The assistant thereupon breaks the gangue against the grindstone, and the assembled company sees the result of the buyer's speculative guess.

I asked if there were no cases of cheating; sometimes no doubt, but they come to nothing. A diamond offered to another buyer, or behind the chief's back, would be immediately *queimado* ('done for'): that is, the buyer would offer a paltry price, and systematically lower it at each subsequent attempt to sell. This explains how some dishonest *garimpeiros* have died of hunger, with their hands full of diamonds.

In the later stages, it is quite a different matter. Fozzi, the

Syrian, apparently grew rich by acquiring impure diamonds at a low price, heating them on a Primus stove and then dipping them in a dye solution; this process gives a yellow diamond a more attractive surface colour, so that it is called *pintado,* painted.

Another type of fraud was also practised, but at a much higher level, in order to avoid paying duty on exported diamonds to the State of Brazil. At Cuiaba and Campo Grande, I met professional smugglers, called *capangueiros,* which means 'strong-arm men'. They too were full of stories; for instance, they would conceal diamonds in fake cigarette packets and if they were stopped by the police would casually throw the packets into a bush as if they were empty. One can imagine how anxiously they went to look for them, as soon as they were free again.

But on that particular evening, the conversation round our camp fire dealt with the everyday incidents our visitors had to face. Thus I learned the picturesque language of the *sertão,* which makes use of an extraordinarily varied collection of terms to convey the meaning of the pronoun 'one': *o homem,* the man; *o camarada,* the comrade, or *o collega,* the colleague; *o negro,* the Negro, *o tal,* so and so, *o fulano,* the fellow, etc. . . . 'One' had been unlucky enough to find gold in the wash troughs; this is an unfortunate omen for a diamond-seeker, and the only thing to do is to throw the gold back immediately into the river; anyone who kept it would be faced with weeks of unsuccessful effort. One man, while dredging up the gravel with his hands, had been struck by the spiked tail of a sting-ray. Injuries thus caused are difficult to heal. You have to find a woman willing to strip and urinate into the wound. As there are hardly any women in the *garimpo* except peasant prostitutes, this simple cure, more often than not, leads to a particularly virulent kind of syphilis.

These women are attracted by stories of lucky finds. A diamond-seeker may become rich from one day to the next, but if he cannot move because of his police record, he has to spend all his money on the spot. This explains the coming and going of lorries laden with superfluous goods. Providing they manage to reach the *garimpo* with their load, it will be bought up at any price, and less through need than because of a desire for ostentation. At dawn, before resuming my journey, I went as far as the hut belonging to a *camarada,* on the bank of the river which is infested with mosquitoes and other insects. With his old-fashioned diver's helmet on his head, he was already busy scratching the river-bed. The inside of the hut was as wretched and depressing as the surrounding countryside; but in a corner, his woman proudly showed me her man's twelve suits and her own silk dresses which were being eaten by termites.

The night had been spent in singing and chatting. Each guest was invited to 'do a turn', which was usually a memory of an item from the programme of some *café-concert* attended long ago. I was to find a similar time-lag in the Indian frontier districts at banquets attended by minor civil servants. In Brazil, as in India, people recited monologues, or did what in India were called 'caricatures', that is imitations: the clicking of a typewriter, the back-firing of a motorcycle in difficulties, followed—in an extraordinary contrast—by a noise suggesting a 'fairy-dance', then by a vocal representation of a galloping horse. And to end, 'funny faces', called 'grimaces', as in French.

In the notes I made on my evening with the *garimpeiros*, I find a fragment of a lament based on a traditional form. It tells of a soldier who, being dissatisfied with the army food, writes a complaint to his corporal; the latter transmits the message to the sergeant, and the operation is repeated at every level—lieutenant, captain, major, colonel, general and emperor. The latter can only address himself to Jesus Christ who, instead of passing on the complaint to the Eternal Father, 'takes up his pen and sends everybody to hell'. Here is this brief specimen of *sertão* poetry:

> O Soldado . . .
> O Oferece . . .
> O Sargento que era um homem pertinente
> Pegô na penna, escreveu pro seu Tenente.

> O Tenente que era homem muito bão
> Pegô na penna, escreveu pro Capitão.

> O Capitão que era homem dos melhor'
> Pegô na penna, escreveu pro Major.

> O Major que era homem como é
> Pegô na penna, escreveu pro Coroné.

O Coroné que era homem sem igual
Pegô na penna, escreveu pro General.

O General que era homem superior
Pegô na penna, escreveu pro Imperador.

O Imperador . . .
Pegô na penna, escreveu pro Jesu' Christo.

Jesu' Christo que é filho do Padre Eterno
Pegô na penna e mandô tudos pelo inferno.

Yet there was no real jollity. The diamond-yielding gravel
was becoming exhausted, and the region was infested with
malaria, leshmaniosis and hookworm. A few years before,
yellow fever had made its appearance. Two or three lorries
at most now journeyed along the track every month, as
against four per week in the old days.

The track we were now proposing to follow had been
abandoned since the bridges had been destroyed by bush
fires, and no lorry had used it during the last three years.
Nothing was known about the condition it was in, but if
we got as far as São Lourenço, we would be over the worst.
There was a large *garimpo* on the river-bank, where we
would find everything we needed—provisions, men and
canoes to take us to the Bororo villages along the Rio
Vermelho, which is a tributary of the São Lourenço.

How we got through I do not know; the journey remains
in my memory as a confused nightmare: pitching camp
interminably in order to overcome a few yards of arduous
terrain, loading and unloading, halts where we were so exhausted through shifting the logs to the front of the lorry
every time it managed to move a length forward that we
fell asleep on the ground, only to be awakened in the
middle of the night by a rumbling which came from the
bowels of the earth: the termites were rising to the surface
to attack our clothes and were already swarming over the
outsides of the rubber capes we used as mackintoshes and
ground-sheets. Finally, one morning our lorry moved down
towards the São Lourenço, which could be located by the
dense valley mist. Feeling that we had accomplished a great
feat, we announced our approach with much blowing of the
horn. Yet not a child came to meet us. We emerged on to
the bank among four or five silent huts. There was no one,

not a sign of life anywhere, and a quick look round convinced us that the hamlet had been abandoned.

Somewhat frayed after the previous days' efforts, we began to lose heart, and wondered whether we should not give up. Before going back, we decided to make one last attempt. Each of us would set off in a given direction and explore the surrounding area. Towards evening we returned, only to report failure, except for the driver who had discovered a fisherman and his family and had brought the man back with him. The latter, bearded and with an unhealthily white skin, as if he had spent too much time in the river, explained that yellow fever had struck six months before, and that the survivors had scattered. But upstream we would still find one or two people and an extra canoe. He would be pleased to accompany us, because for months he and his family had lived entirely on fish caught in the river. He would obtain manioc and tobacco plants from the Indians, and we would give him a little money. On these terms he could also guarantee the co-operation of the other canoeist, whom we would pick up on the way.

I shall have occasion to describe other canoe trips which have remained more vividly in my memory than this particular one. I shall therefore pass quickly over the week we spent sailing upstream against a current swollen by the daily rain. On one occasion, we were eating our midday meal on a tiny stretch of sand when we heard a rustling sound: it was a boa, seven metres long, which had been awakened from its sleep by our voices. It took a lot of shooting, since these animals are impervious to body wounds and have to be hit in the head. While skinning it—the operation took half a day—we discovered inside it a dozen live little snakes, which were just about to be born, but died as soon as they were exposed to the sun. Then, one day, just after successfully shooting an *irara*, which is a kind of badger, we caught a glimpse of two nude forms moving on the bank: our first Bororo. We drew in to the bank and tried to get into conversation; they knew practically only one Portuguese word: *fumo*—tobacco—which they pronounced *sumo* (the old missionaries used to say that the Indians had neither faith, law nor king, since the initial sounds of these words in Portuguese, *f, l* and *r,* were missing from their phonetic system). Although they themselves grew tobacco, their product was not concentrated like the fermented rolled variety, of which we offered them liberal supplies.

We explained by means of gestures that we were going in
the direction of their village; they indicated that we would
reach it that evening. They would go on ahead to announce
our arrival; whereupon they vanished into the forest.

A few hours later, we moored alongside a clayey bank,
above which we could see the huts. Half a dozen naked
men, painted red with urucu from the tips of their toes to
the roots of their hair, greeted us with bursts of laughter, as
they helped us to disembark and carried our belongings. We
found ourselves in a large hut which housed several families; the village chief had cleared a corner for our use;
during our stay he himself would live on the other side of
the river.

22. VIRTUOUS SAVAGES

In what order should one describe those profound and confused impressions which assail the traveller when he first arrives in a village where the native culture has remained comparatively untouched? In visiting the Caingang and the Caduveo, whose hamlets are similar to those of the neighbouring peasants, and notable for their extreme wretchedness, the initial reaction is one of weariness and discouragement. When one is faced with a society which is still alive and faithful to its traditions, the impact is so powerful that one is quite taken aback: which strand in the multicoloured skein should one first try to unwind and disentangle? In thinking back to the Bororo, with whom I had my first experience of this kind, I rediscover feelings which assailed me again during the most recent such experience, in a Kuki village on the Burmese frontier, when I reached the summit of a high hill, after hours spent scrambling on all fours up slopes which had been transformed into slippery mud by the unceasing monsoon rains: physical exhaustion, hunger, thirst and mental confusion, certainly; but the organic giddiness was shot through with perceptions of forms and colours: the houses were majestic in size in spite of their fragility, and were the result of the utilization of materials and techniques which we in the West are acquainted with in small-scale forms: they were not so much built as knotted together, plaited, woven, embroidered and mellowed by use; instead of crushing the occupants under an indifferent mass of stones, they adapted to their presence and their movements; they were the opposite of our houses in that they remained always subordinate to man. The village rose round its occupants like a light, flexible suit of armour, closer to Western women's hats than to Western towns; it was a monumental adornment retaining something of the living bowers and foliage whose natural gracefulness the builders had skilfully reconciled with the rigorous demands of their plan.

The nakedness of the inhabitants seemed to be protected

by the grassy velvetiness of the outside walls and the fringe of palm trees: when the natives slipped out of their huts, it was as if they were divesting themselves of giant ostrich-feather wraps. Their bodies, the jewels in these downy caskets, were delicately modelled, and the flesh tones were heightened by the brillance of their make-up and paint, which in turn semed to be intended as a background to set off even more splendid ornaments: the rich, bright glint of the teeth and fangs of wild animals among feathers and flowers. It was as if an entire civilization were conspiring in a single, passionate affection for the shapes, substances and colours of life and, in order to preserve its richest essence around the human body, were appealing to those of its manifestations which are either the most lasting or the most fleeting but which, through a curious coincidence, are its privileged repositories.

As I proceeded to settle into our corner of a large hut, I was soaking up these images rather than grasping them intellectually. One or two details began to fall into place. Although these native dwellings still retained their traditional dimensions and layout, architecturally they betrayed some neo-Brazilian influence: they were rectangular in shape, instead of oval, and although the materials used for the roofs and the walls were the same—branches supporting a covering of palms—the two parts were separate and the roof had a double slope, instead of being rounded and reaching almost to the ground. Nevertheless, the village of Kejara, where we had just arrived, was, with the two others of the Rio Vermelho group, Pobori and Jarudori, one of the last not to have been much affected by the activities of the Salesian Fathers. These missionaries who, along with the Protection Service, succeeded in bringing the strife between Indians and colonists to an end, had both carried out excellent anthropological research (it is our best source of information about the Bororo, after the earlier studies of Karl von den Steinen) and at the same time pursued the systematic obliteration of native culture. Two facts clearly showed that Kejara was one of the last strongholds of independence. First, it was the place of residence of the chief of all the villages of the Rio Vermelho, a haughty and enigmatic character who knew no Portuguese or pretended not to; he saw to our needs and speculated on our presence; but for reasons of prestige as much as for linguistic reasons, he avoided communicating with me except through the members of his council, in conjunction with whom he took all his decisions.

Secondly, there lived in Kejara a native who was to be my interpreter and chief informant. This man, who was about thirty-five years old, spoke Portuguese fairly well. He said that he had once been able to read and write the language (although he could no longer do so), having been a pupil at the mission. The Fathers, proud of their success, had sent him to Rome, where he had been received by the Holy Father. On his return, there had apparently been an attempt to make him go through a Christian marriage ceremony, without regard for the traditional native rules. This had brought on a spiritual crisis during which he was reconverted to the old Bororo ideal: he then settled in Kejara where, for the last ten or fifteen years, he had been living an exemplary savage life. This papal Indian, who was now stark naked, befeathered, smeared with red paint and wearing the pin and the lip-plug in his nose and lower lip, was to prove a wonderful guide to Bororo sociology.

For the time being, we were surrounded by a dozen or so natives who were talking among themselves with great guffaws of laughter accompanied by mutual pummellings. The Bororo are the tallest and sturdiest of the Brazilian

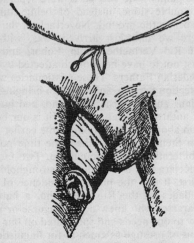

Fig 27. The penis sheath

Indians. Their round heads, their oval faces with strong, regular features and their burly athletic figures are reminiscent of certain Patagonian types, with whom they may have some racial link. A comparable physical harmony is not often found among the women, who are, generally speaking, smaller and less robust, and have irregular features. From the very first, there was a remarkable contrast between the joviality of the men and the off-putting attitude of the opposite sex. Although there were epidemics in the area, the villagers gave an impression of physical health; however, there was one leper among them.

The men were quite naked except for the little straw cornet covering the tip of the penis and kept in place by the foreskin, which is stretched through the opening to form a little roll of flesh on the outside. The majority were smeared from head to foot with red pigment made by pounding urucu seeds in fat. Even their hair, which was worn either shoulder-length or cut in a round mop at ear level, was covered with this paste and so took on the appearance of a helmet. Other paintings were superimposed on this base: a horseshoe pattern in shiny black resin, covering the forehead and terminating on both cheeks near the sides of the mouth; bands of white down stuck on the shoulders or the arms; or a dusting of pounded mother-of-pearl on the shoulders and chest. The women wore a cotton loincloth dyed with urucu around a stiff bark belt supporting a softer strip of beaten white bark which passed between the thighs. Across the chest they had a double row of finely plaited cotton straps. Little bands of cotton, tied tightly round their ankles, upper arms and wrists, completed their attire.

Gradually, all these people went away; we were sharing the hut, which measured approximately twelve metres by five, with the silent and unfriendly family of a medicine-man, and an elderly widow who subsisted on the charity of a few relatives who lived in neighbouring huts. But they often forgot about her, and she would sing for hours about the loss of her five successive husbands and of the happy time when she lacked neither manioc, maize, game nor fish.

Already singing was beginning outside in a low-pitched, resonant, guttural tongue, with clearly enunciated sounds. Only the men sang; and their combined voices, the simple and constantly repeated melodies, the contrast between solos and choruses and the tragic virile style recalled the marital choruses of some Germanic *Männerbund*. When I

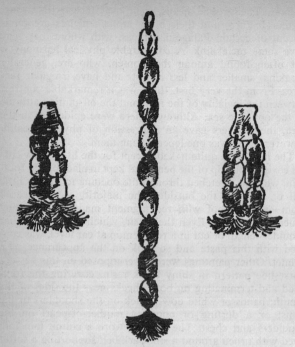

FIG 28. A lip ornament and earrings made of mother-of-
pearl and feathers

asked why they were singing, I was told it was because of
the *irara*, which we had brought with us. Before it could be
eaten, a complicated ritual had to be performed to pacify
its spirit and consecrate the hunt. Being too exhausted to
behave as a conscientious anthropologist, at dusk I fell into
a sleep which was troubled by fatigue and the singing which
went on until dawn. This, incidentally, was to be the pattern
throughout our entire visit: the nights were given over to
religious ceremonies, and the natives slept from dawn until
midday.

Apart from a few wind instruments which were brought
out at certain prescribed moments in the ritual, the only
accompaniment to the voices was provided by gourd rattles
filled with gravel and shaken by the principal players, who
were wonderful to listen to: sometimes unleashing or stop-

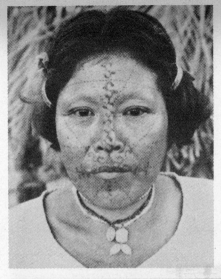

A Caduveo woman
with a painted face

TRISTES TROPIQUES

A Caduveo belle in
1895 (taken from
Boggiani)

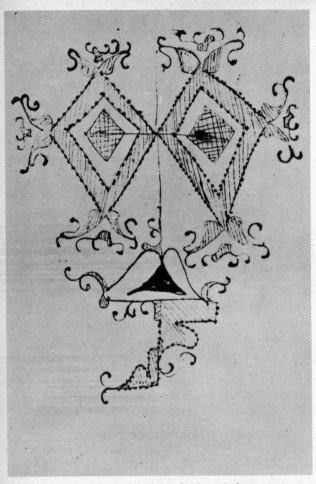

Facial painting: an original drawing by a Caduveo woman

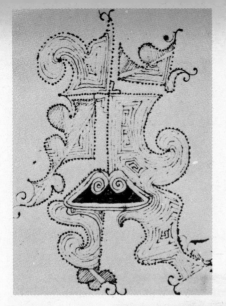

Two further facial
paintings drawn by
natives

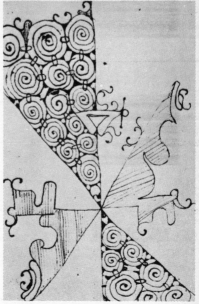

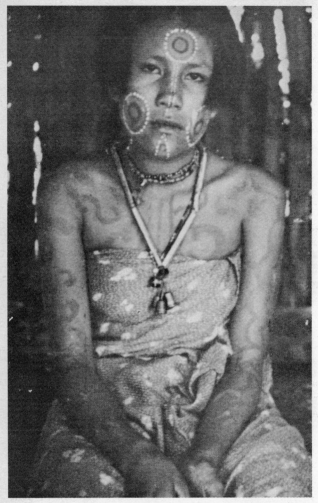

A Caduveo girl made ready for her puberty rites

The author's best informant, in ceremonial dress

A meal in the Men's House

Bringing out the *mariddo*

A funeral ceremony (photograph by M. René Silz)

The Nambikwara group on the move

Sabané, the sorcerer

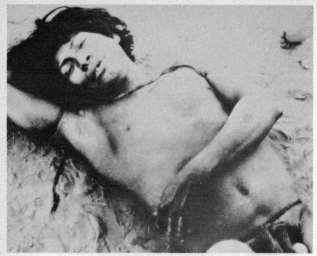

The chief of the Wakletoçu

A Nambikwara woman piercing mother-of-pearl
from river shells to make ear-rings

The siesta

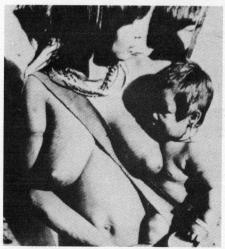

The native method of carrying a baby

Day-dreaming

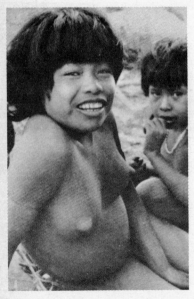

A Nambikwara smile

The Mundé village square

A Mundé woman with her child (its eyebrows are coated with wax in preparation for plucking)

A Tupi-Kawahib man (Potien) skinning a monkey (note the belt, a recent gift, and the penis sheath)

Taperahi, the Tupi-Kawahib chief

Kunhatsin, Taperahi's chief wife, carrying her child

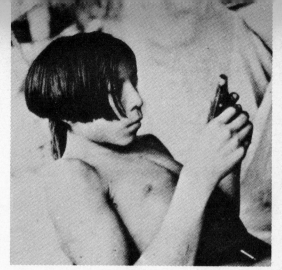

Pwereza, Taperahi's son

Penhana, the young wife shared by the two brothers

Maruabai, the co-wife (with her daughter, Kunhatsin) of Chief Taperahi

ping the voices with a short sharp crack; sometimes filling in the silences with the rattling of their instruments in long-drawn-out crescendos or diminuendos; and sometimes directing the dancers with alternations of silence and noise, so varied in their duration, intensity and quality that no conductor of a large European orchestra could have surpassed them in indicating his intentions. It is not surprising that, in former times, natives of different tribes, and even missionaries, should have thought they could hear the demons speaking through the medium of the rattles. Besides, it is a well-known fact that although old illusions about the so-called 'drum languages' have now been dispelled, very probably—among certain peoples at least—such languages are based on a genuine coding of speech, which has been reduced to a few significant symbolically expressed outlines.

At dawn, I got up to go out and visit the village; at the door I tripped over some pathetic-looking birds: these were the domesticated macaws which the Indians kept in the village so as to be able to pluck them alive and thus obtain the feathers needed for head-dresses. Stripped of their plumage and unable to fly, the birds looked like chickens ready for the spit and afflicted with particularly enormous beaks since plucking had reduced their body size by half. Other macaws, whose feathers had regrown, were solemnly perched on the roofs like heraldic emblems, enamelled gules and azur.

I found myself in the middle of an open space, bordered on one side by the river and on all the others by patches of forest which concealed gardens and through which could be glimpsed in the distance steep-sided hills of red sandstone. Around the periphery ran a single row of huts—exactly twenty-six in number—similar to mine and laid out in a circle. In the centre stood another hut, about twenty metres long and eight metres wide, and consequently much bigger than the others. This was the *baitemannageo*, the men's house, where the bachelors slept and where the male members of the population spent their days when they were not busy fishing or hunting, or involved in some public ceremony on the dance area, an oval space situated to the west of the men's house and marked off with stakes. Women were strictly forbidden to enter the men's house: they occupied the circular row of houses and their husbands went backwards and forwards several times a day between their

club and their conjugal abodes, following the paths running through the low bushes in the clearing. Seen from a
treetop or a roof, a Bororo village looks like a cartwheel,
the rim being the family huts, the spokes the paths and the
men's house the hub.

This remarkable plan was formerly common to all the
villages, but the population figures were much higher than
the present average (about 150 people in Kejara); instead
of one circle, there would be several concentric circles. The
Bororo are not the only people to build circular villages;
with certain variations in detail, they seem to be typical of
all the tribes of the Ge linguistic group who occupy the central Brazilian plateau, between the Araguaya and São Fran-
cisco rivers, and of whom the Bororo may be the most
southerly representatives. But we know that their nearest
neighbors to the north, the Cayapo, who live on the right
bank of the Rio dos Mortes and who were visited for the
first time only ten years ago, build their villages in a similar
manner, as do also the Apinayé, the Sherenté and the
Canella.

The circular arrangement of the huts around the men's
house is so important a factor in their social and religious
life that the Salesian missionaries in the Rio das Garças
region were quick to realize that the surest way to convert
the Bororo was to make them abandon their village in
favour of one with the houses set out in parallel rows. Once
they had been deprived of their bearings and were without
the plan which acted as a confirmation of their native lore,
the Indians soon lost any feeling for tradition; it was as if
their social and religious systems (we shall see that one
cannot be dissociated from the other) were too complex to
exist without the pattern which was embodied in the plan
of the village and of which their awareness was constantly
being refreshed by their everyday activities.

It must be said in defence of the Salesian Fathers that
they went to a great deal of trouble to understand, and preserve the memory of, this complex pattern. Anyone visiting
the Bororo must begin by studying their researches. Yet, at
the same time, it was imperative that I should examine their
conclusions in the light of others that I might arrive at in
an area into which they had not penetrated and where the
system still retained its vitality. Starting from the previously
published documents, I therefore set about obtaining from
my informants an analysis of the plan of their village. We

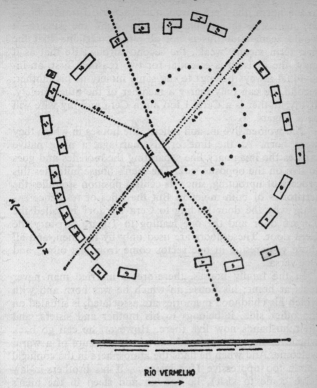

RIO VERMELHO
→

FIG 29. The plan of Kejara village

spent our days going from house to house, taking a census of the inhabitants, determining their position in the community and marking out on the ground by means of sticks the imaginary lines of demarcation between sectors associated with an intricate network of privileges, traditions, hierarchical grades, rights and obligations. In order to simplify my account, I shall modify the statements concerning direction, since the natives' conception of the cardinal points never corresponds exactly to the compass readings.

The circular village of Kejara lies close to the left bank of the Rio Vermelho, which flows more or less in an east-west direction. One diameter of the village, theoretically parallel to the river, divides the population into two groups:

to the north, the Cera (pronounced *tchéra;* I transcribe all
the names in the singular), to the south, the Tugaré. It
would seem—but this is not absolutely certain—that the
first term means 'weak', the second 'strong'. Be that as it
may, the division is essential for two reasons: first, an individual always belongs to the same moiety as his mother;
second, he can only marry a member of the other moiety.
If my mother is a Cera, I too am a Cera and my wife will
be a Tugaré.

The women live in, and inherit, the houses in which they
were born. At the time of his marriage, a male native
crosses the imaginary line separating the moieties and goes
to live on the opposite side. The men's house mitigates this
process of uprooting, since its central position straddles the
territories of both moieties. But the rules of residence explain why the door leading to Cera territory is called the
Tugaré door and the one leading to Tugaré territory the
Cera door. These doors are used only by the men, and all
those who reside in one sector come from the other, and
vice versa.

In the family houses, therefore, a married man never
feels at home; his house, in which he was born and with
which his childhood memories are associated, is situated on
the other side; it belongs to his mother and sisters, and
their husbands now live there. However, he can go back
whenever he wants to, and can always be sure of a warm
welcome. And when he finds the atmosphere in the conjugal
abode too oppressive (for instance, if his brothers-in-law
have come to visit), he can go and sleep in the men's
house, with its memories of adolescence, its male companionship, and its religious atmosphere which by no means
excludes flirtations with unmarried girls.

The moieties govern not only the marriage pattern, but
also other aspects of social life. Each time a member of
one moiety is entitled to a right or subject to a duty, it is
to the advantage of, or with the assistance of, the other
moiety. Thus a Cera's funeral is conducted by the Tugaré,
and vice versa. The two moieties of the village are therefore in partnership, and every social or religious act involves the help of the opposite number who plays a part
complementary to that of the person primarily concerned.
Such collaboration does not exclude rivalry: each moiety
has its pride and there may be mutual jealousy. We should
try to imagine their social life as being like the interaction

FIG 30. A wooden club
for killing fish

of two football teams which, instead of trying to thwart
each other's strategical moves, are doing their best to help
each other, and which judge their relative superiority by the
degree of perfection and generosity they manage to attain.

Let us move on now to a new aspect:- another diameter,
perpendicular to the first, cuts through the moieties along
a north-south axis. All the people born to the east of this
axis are known as upstream dwellers, those born to the
west as downstream dwellers. So instead of two moieties,
we have four sections, since the Cera and the Tugaré are
both partly on the one side and partly on the other. Unfortunately, no observer has managed to understand the precise function of this second division.

In addition, the population is divided into clans. These
are family groups which believe themselves to be akin
through descent, on the female side, from a common
ancestor, a mythological character whose identity in some
cases has been forgotten. It can be said at least that clan
members are recognizable by the fact that they all bear the
same name. In the past, there were probably eight clans in
all: four in the Cera moiety and four in the Tugaré. But
with the passage of time some have disappeared, and others
have been subdivided, with the result that the empirical
situation is not at all clear. However, the fact remains that
the members of a given clan—with the exception of the
married men—all live in the same hut, or in adjacent huts.
Each clan, therefore, has its particular place in the circle
of huts: it is Cera or Tugaré, upstream or downstream, or
it is split up into two sub-groups by this last-mentioned
division which, on both sides, may run through the huts of
a given clan.

As if these complications were not enough, each clan
comprises hereditary sub-groups, also descended through
the female line. Thus, in each clan there are 'red' families
and 'black' families. Furthermore, it would appear that formerly each clan was divided into three grades—upper,
middle and lower—a reflection perhaps, or a transposition,
of the graded castes of the Mbaya-Caduveo. I shall come
back to this point later. The possibility of the link is made
more plausible by the fact that these grades appear to have
been endogamous: a member of the upper grade could
only marry an upper-grade person (belonging to the other
moiety); a middle grade a middle-grade, and a lower grade
a lower-grade. Because of the demographic collapse of the
Bororo villages, we can do no more than make conjectures.
Now that they have only between one and two hundred inhabitants instead of a thousand or more, there are not
enough families left to fill all the categories. Only the rule
concerning the moieties is strictly respected (although certain high-born clans are perhaps exempt from it); for the
rest, the natives improvise makeshift solutions according to
the possibilities of the situation.

The distribution of the population into clans no doubt
constitutes the most important of those various ways of
'dealing out the cards', of which Bororo society seems so
fond. Within the framework of the general system of marriages between moieties, the clans were once linked by

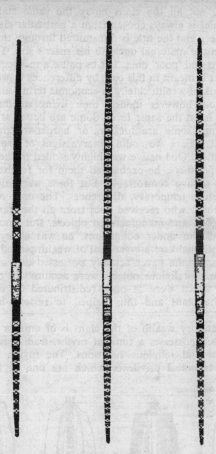

FIG 31. Bows decorated with bark rings arranged in patterns
indicating the owners' clans

special affinities: a Cera clan would intermarry preferably with one, two or three Tugaré clans, and vice versa. Furthermore, not all the clans enjoy the same status. The village chief is always chosen from a particular clan in the Cera moiety and the title is transmitted through the female line, from the maternal uncle to his sister's son. There are 'rich' clans and 'poor' ones. Let us pause a moment to consider what is meant in this case by differences in wealth.

We think of wealth chiefly in economic terms; among the Bororo too, however modest their living standards, not everyone is on the same level. Some are better at hunting and fishing; some are luckier, or harder-working, than others. At Kejara we could observe signs of professional specialization. One native was highly skilled in the making of stone polishers; he exchanged them for foodstuffs and appeared to live comfortably. But these were individual, and therefore temporary, differences. The only exception was the chief, who received dues from all the clans in the form of food and manufactured objects. But since acceptance laid him under obligations, he was always in the position of a banker: a great deal of wealth passed through his hands, but he never actually possessed any of it. My collections of religious objects were acquired in exchange for gifts which were at once redistributed by the chief among the clans and thus helped to restore his trade balance.

The statutory wealth of the clans is of quite a different order. Each possesses a fund of myths, traditions, dances and social and religious functions. The myths, in turn, establish technical privileges which are one of the most

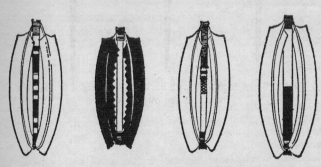

FIG 32. Arrow-ends with clan decorations

curious features of Bororo culture. Almost all objects are
decorated with emblems indicating the clan and sub-clan
of the owner. The privileges consist in the use of certain
feathers, or certain colours of feather; in the way they are
cut or notched; in the arrangement of feathers of different
species and colours; in the carrying out of certain decorative work—the plaiting of fibres or feather mosaics; and in
the use of special themes, etc. Thus, ceremonial bows are
decorated with feathers or bark rings according to rules
laid down for each clan; the arrow shafts have a specific
decorative pattern at their base between the feathers; the
mother-of-pearl elements of the hinged lip-plugs are cut in
various patterns—oval, fish-shaped, rectangular—according to the clan; the colour of the fringes varies; the feather
crowns worn in the dances have an emblem (usually a
small wooden plate covered with a stuck-on feather mosaic) relating to the owner's clan. On feast days, even the
penial sheaths are topped by a ribbon of stiff straw, which
is decorated or carved in the colours and shapes of the
clan; we may think this a strange place in which to carry
a standard.

All these privileges (which are, incidentally, negotiable)
are jealously and fiercely guarded. It is said to be inconceivable for one clan to usurp the prerogatives of another:
a fratricidal struggle would ensue. Yet, from this point of
view, the differences between the clans are enormous:
some enjoy luxury, others are deprived; one has only to
inspect the objects in the huts to realize this. The difference
should be expressed not so much as one between rich and
poor as one between the crude and the refined.

The material possessions of the Bororo are characterized
by simplicity combined with an unusual perfection of finish.
Their tools have remained archaic, in spite of the axes and
knives which used to be distributed by the Protection Service. Although the natives have recourse to metal instruments for heavy work, they continue to finish off the clubs
used in fishing, as well as their bows and their arrows made
from finely barbed hard wood, with a tool which is a cross
between an adze and a chisel and which they use for everything as we might use a pocket-knife: it consists of the
bent incisor of a *capyvara* (a rodent found along the river-
banks), bound to the end of a handle. Apart from the
wicker-work mats and baskets, the weapons and tools—
made from bone or wood—used by the men, and the

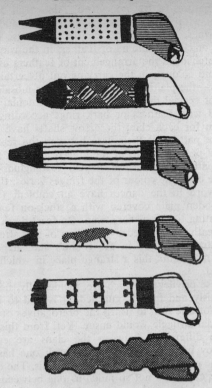

FIG 33. Emblazoned penis sheaths

digging stick employed by the women who are responsible for agricultural tasks, the equipment in a hut amounts to very little indeed: receptacles made from gourds or black clay; hemispherical basins and shallower bowls with a handle projecting from the side, like our soup ladles. These objects have a great purity of line, which is emphasized by the plainness of the material. One curious thing is that Bororo pottery seems formerly to have been decorated, but that a religious prohibition put an end to the practice in comparatively recent times. Perhaps the same taboo also accounts for the fact that the natives no longer execute rock-paintings, such as can still be found in the cave shelters of the *chapada*, where, however, many themes of their culture are recognizable. To confirm the point, on one occasion I asked an Indian to decorate a large sheet of paper for me. He set to with urucu paste and resin; and although the Bororo have preserved no memory of the time when their tribe painted cave walls, and hardly ever visit the steep slopes where the rock-shelters are found, the picture I was handed seemed like a small-scale version of a rock-painting.

In contrast to the plainness of their objects of everyday use, the Bororo put all their riches and imagination into their dress, or rather—since they wear so few clothes—into its accessories. The women possess collections of jewels which are handed down from mother to daughter: these consist of bracelets and necklaces made from monkey's teeth or jaguar's fangs, mounted on wood and held in place by delicate binding. While they thus make use of the remnants of the hunt, they allow their own temples to be plucked by the men, who make long braids out of their wives' hair to wind round their own heads in the manner of a turban. On feast days the men also wear crescent-shaped pendants made from a pair of claws taken from the large tatu—the burrowing animal which stands more than a metre high and has hardly changed since the tertiary era —decorated with mother-of-pearl inlays and feather or cotton fringes. Toucans' beaks fixed on plumed sticks, sprays of egrets' tufts, and long macaw tail-feathers set in fretted bamboo tubes stuck with white down, are inserted in their real or artificial *chignons*, like hairpins counter-balancing the feather crowns which encircle their foreheads. Sometimes these adornments are combined in a composite head-dress which can only be arranged on the dancer's head by dint of several hours' work. I acquired one of these head-dresses for the Musée de l'Homme in exchange for a gun and after negotiations lasting a week. It was essential for the ritual, and the natives could only part with it after hunting expeditions had yielded the required assortment of feathers with which to make a new one. It consists of a fan-shaped diadem; a feather visor covering the upper part of the face; a high cylindrical crown surrounding the head, and made of rods surmounted by harpy-eagle feathers; and a wickerwork disc set with a bristling mass of stalks stuck with feathers and down. The whole head-dress is almost two metres high.

Even when they are not in ceremonial garb, the men have

FIG 34. A black pottery bowl

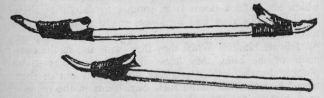

FIG 35. Two specimens (single and double) of the Bororo 'pocket-knife'

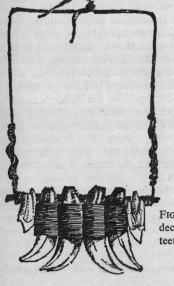

FIG 36. A pendant decorated with jaguars' teeth

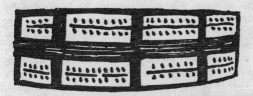

Fig 37. Crowns of dried and painted straw used
as ephemeral adornments

such a passion for ornamentation that they are constantly improvising adornments. Many wear crowns: fur head-bands decorated with feathers, wickerwork rings also covered with feathers and coronets made from jaguars' claws mounted on wooden rings. But they may be delighted with something much less elaborate: a strip of dried straw, which has been picked up from the ground and rapidly shaped into a circle and painted, can provide a fragile head-dress which the bearer will flaunt until another lucky find inspires him to some new whimsical concoction; sometimes this desire for ornamentation will lead to a tree being stripped of its flowers. A piece of bark and a few feathers will provide these indefatigable designers with a pretext for creating a striking set of ear-pendants. You have to go inside the men's house to realize how much energy these great strapping fellows devote to titivating themselves: in every corner someone is busy cutting, shaping, carving or sticking; river shells are being broken up into fragments and vigorously polished on grindstones to be made into necklaces and lip-plugs; fantastic constructions of bamboo and feathers are gradually taking shape. With the meticulous care of theatrical dressers, burly stalwarts are transforming each other into fluffy chickens, by means of down stuck straight on to the skin.

The men's house may be a workshop but it is something more besides. The adolescents sleep there; during periods of inactivity, the married men come there to take a siesta, or to chat and smoke their thick cigarettes rolled in dried maize leaves. They also eat certain meals there, since the clans are obliged to provide food for the *baitemannageo,* according to a carefully drawn-up rota system. About every two hours, a man goes off to his family hut to fetch a pan full of the maize gruel called *mingau,* which is prepared by the women. When he returns, he is greeted by loud cries of joy, 'au, au,' which break the silence of the day. According to a fixed ritual, the bringer of the food invites six or eight men and leads them up to the gruel, which they dip into with pottery or shell bowls. I have already explained that women are not allowed into the men's house. This rule relates to married women; unmarried girls, of their own accord, avoid going near, knowing full well what might happen if, through accident or design, they came too close; they would be in danger of being caught and raped. However, each has to go in voluntarily on one occasion in her life to present her proposal of marriage to her future husband.

23. THE LIVING AND THE DEAD

The *baitemannageo* is not only workshop, club, dormitory and occasional brothel, it is also a temple. It is there that the religious dancers get ready and that certain ceremonies from which women are excluded, such as the making and whirling of bull-roarers, are carried out. The bull-roarers are elaborately painted wooden musical instruments, not unlike flat fish in shape, and varying in length between some thirty centimetres and one and a half metres. If they are made to spin on the end of a cord, a dull roar is produced, and this is attributed to the spirits which visit the village and which the women are supposed to be afraid of. Woe betide any woman who happens to see a bull-roarer; even today there is a strong possibility that she will be clubbed to death. The first time I was present at the making of bull-roarers, the natives tried to persuade me that they were culinary objects. Their extreme reluctance to let me have a set of them was due not so much to the fact that they would have to make new ones as to the fear that I might betray the secret. I had to take a chest to the men's house at dead of night. The bull-roarers were wrapped up and placed in the chest, which was then locked; I was made to promise that I would not open it again before reaching Cuiaba.

For the European observer, the apparently incompatible activities carried out in the men's house seem to harmonize in an almost shocking way. Few peoples are as deeply religious as the Bororo, and few have such a complex metaphysical system. But spiritual beliefs and everyday habits are closely intermingled, and the natives do not appear to be conscious of moving from one system to another. I found the same easy-going religiosity in Buddhist temples along the Burmese frontier, where the priests live and sleep in the same hall as is used for worship, arrange their jars of ointment and personal collections of medicines on the ground in front of the altar and are not averse to

253

caressing their pupils in the interval between two reading lessons.

This casual attitude to the supernatural was all the more surprising for me in that my only contact with religion dated back to childhood when, already a non-believer, I lived during the First World War with my grandfather, who was Rabbi of Versailles. The house was attached to the synagogue by a long inner passage, along which it was difficult to venture without a feeling of anguish, and which in itself formed an impassable frontier between the profane world and that other which was lacking precisely in the human warmth that was a necessary pre-condition to its being experienced as sacred. Except when services were in progress the synagogue remained empty and its temporary

Fig 38. A bull-roarer

occupation was never sustained or fervent enough to remedy the state of desolation which seemed natural to it and in which the services were only an incongruous interruption. Worship within the family circle was no less arid. Apart from my grandfather's silent prayer at the beginning of each meal, we children had no means of knowing that we were living under the aegis of a superior order, but for the fact that a scroll of printed paper fixed to the dining-room wall proclaimed the motto: 'Chew your food well for the good of your digestion.'

Not that religion was treated with greater reverence among the Bororo; on the contrary, it was taken for granted. In the men's house, ritualistic gestures were performed with the same casualness as all others, as if they were utilitarian actions intended to achieve a particular result and did not require that respectful attitude which even the non-believer feels compelled to adopt on entering a place of worship. On a particular afternoon there would be singing in the men's house in preparation for the evening's public ritual. In one corner, boys would be snoring or chatting; two or three men would be humming and shaking rattles, but if one of them wanted to light a cigarette, or if it were his turn to dip into the maize gruel, he would hand the instrument to a neighbour who carried on; or sometimes he would continue with one hand, while scratching himself with the other. When a dancer paraded up and down to allow his latest creation to be admired, everybody would stop and comment upon it; the service might seem to be forgotten until, in some other corner, the incantation was resumed at the point where it had been interrupted.

Yet the significance of the men's house goes beyond the function that I have tried to describe, of being the centre of social and religious life. Not only does the structure of the village allow subtle interplay between institutions: it summarizes and ensures relations between man and the universe, between society and the supernatural world, and between the living and the dead.

Before broaching this further aspect of Bororo culture, I must digress for a moment on the subject of the relations between the dead and the living; otherwise it would be difficult to understand the particular way in which Bororo thought has solved this universal problem. The solution is extraordinarily similar to one found at the other extremity of the Western hemisphere, among the Indians of the for-

ests and prairies of the north-eastern area of North America, such as the Ojibwa, the Menomini and the Winnebago.

There is probably no society which does not treat its
dead with respect. Even Neanderthal man, that borderline
case of *Homo sapiens,* buried his dead in roughly prepared
tombs. No doubt funeral practices vary from group to
group. We may think that the diversity is negligible, given
the unanimity of the feeling behind it. But even if we
evolve the most extremely simplified statement of the attitudes towards the dead observed in human societies, we
are obliged to recognize a major division, between the opposite poles of which all sorts of intermediary positions are
to be found.

Some societies let their dead rest; provided homage is
paid to them periodically, the departed refrain from trou-
bling the living. If they come back, they do so only at intervals and on specified occasions. And their return is
salutary, since through their influence the dead ensure the
regular return of the seasons, and the fertility of gardens
and women. It is as if a contract had been concluded between the dead and the living: in return for being treated
with a reasonable degree of respect, the dead remain in
their own abode, and the temporary meetings between the
two groups are always governed by concern for the interests
of the living. There is a universal theme in folklore which
expresses this formula very clearly: the theme of the *grate-
ful corpse.* A rich hero buys a corpse from creditors who
were objecting to its being buried, and has it interred. The
dead man appears to his benefactor in a dream and promises him success, on condition that the advantages gained
are shared fairly between the two of them. The hero soon
wins the love of a princess, whom he rescues from many
dangers with the help of his supernatural protector. The
question now arises: must the princess be shared? She, as it
happens, is bewitched, half woman, half dragon or snake.
The dead man claims his share; the hero agrees and his
partner, pleased by his fairness, takes only the diabolical
part, leaving the hero a humanized wife.

Contrasting with this conception is another, also illustrated by a theme found in folklore, and which I will call
the theme of *the enterprising knight.* The hero is poor, instead of rich. His only possession is a grain of wheat which
he manages, through guile, to exchange for a cock, then for
a pig, an ox and a corpse, which he finally barters for a

living princess. In this instance, the dead man is clearly object, not subject. Instead of being a partner with whom the hero negotiates, he is an instrument manipulated for purposes of speculation in which lying and deceit play a part. Some societies display this kind of attitude towards their dead. They allow them no rest, but press them into service: sometimes literally, as is the case in cannibalism and necrophagy when the intention is to absorb the virtues and powers of the deceased; symbolically too, in societies which are engaged in competitive prestige relationships so that their members must, as it were, be constantly appealing to the dead to *come to their aid,* and trying to justify their prerogatives by reference to their ancestors and by genealogical fraud. These societies, more than others, are worried by the dead, whom they exploit. They believe that the dead pay them back in kind, and are all the more demanding and importunate towards the living, since the latter are making use of them. But whether it is a question of fair division, as in the first case, or of unrestrained speculation, as in the second, the idea governing the relationships between the dead and the living is that some form of sharing cannot be avoided.

Between the two extreme attitudes, there are intermediary modes of behaviour: the Indians living on the west coast of Canada and the Melanesians summon all their ancestors to their ceremonies and force them to testify in favour of their descendants; in certain forms of Chinese or African ancestor worship, the dead retain their personal identity, but only for a few generations; among the Pueblo in the southwest of the United States, they cease immediately to have any identity as deceased persons, but they share a number of special functions. Even in Europe, where the dead have become apathetic and anonymous, traces of the other possibility persist in folklore through the belief in the existence of two kinds of dead: those who succumbed through natural causes and who form a body of protective ancestors; and suicides, murder victims and victims of spells who change into evil and jealous spirits.

In the history of the development of Western civilization, there can be no doubt that the speculatory attitude has gradually been replaced by the contractual conception of the relationship between the dead and living, while the latter is now being ousted by the kind of indifference forecast perhaps in the Gospel saying, 'Let the dead bury their dead.' But there is no reason to suppose that this development corresponds to a universal model. It would seem rather that all cultures are vaguely aware of both formulas and, while opting mainly for one, try to insure themselves with regard to the other by means of various superstitious practices (just as we ourselves continue to do, whether we claim to be believers or non-believers). The originality of the Bororo, and of the other communities I have quoted, lies in the fact that they formulated both possibilities clearly, evolved a system of beliefs and rites corresponding to each and invented mechanisms for moving from one to the other, in the hope of effecting a reconciliation between the two.

It would not be quite accurate to say that, for the Bororo, there is no such thing as natural death: for them, a man is not an individual, but a person. He is part of a sociological universe: the village which has existed from the beginning of time, side by side with the physical universe, which is itself composed of other animate beings—celestial bodies and meteorological phenomena. Such is the belief, in spite of the temporary nature of the actual villages, which (because of the exhaustion of the land used for crop-growing) rarely remain in the same spot for more than thirty years. So what constitutes the village is neither the site nor the huts, but a certain structural pattern such as has been described above and which is reproduced in every village. It is therefore easy to understand why the missionaries, by interfering with the traditional layout of the villages, destroy everything.

Animals, especially fish and birds, belong partly to the world of men, whereas certain terrestrial animals belong to the physical universe. Thus the Bororo believe that their human form is a transitional state: between that of a fish (whose name they have taken as their own) and that of the macaw (in the guise of which they will finish their cycle of transmigrations).

Since the Bororo way of thinking is governed by a fundamental opposition between nature and culture (and in this they resemble anthropologists), it follows that, being even more sociologically minded than Durkheim and Comte, they regard human life as belonging to culture. To say that death is natural or anti-natural becomes meaningless. In fact and in theory, death is at once *natural* and *anti-cultural*. That is, every time a native dies, this is a loss not only for his nearest relatives, but for the community as a whole. The harm that nature has done to society puts nature in *debt*, a term which conveys fairly accurately an essential Bororo notion, that of *mori*. When a native dies, the village organizes a collective hunt which is carried out by the moiety to which the deceased did not belong. It is an expedition against nature, and the aim is to kill a large animal, preferably a jaguar, whose skin, claws and fangs will constitute the dead man's *mori*.

When I arrived at Kejara, a bereavement had just occurred; unfortunately, the deceased had died a long way away in another village, so I was not to see the two stages of the interment, which involves, first, placing the corpse in a grave covered with branches in the centre of the village until the flesh has rotted, and second, washing the bones in the river, painting them and decorating them with mosaics of stuck-on feathers, and then placing them in a basket at the bottom of a lake or stream. All the other ceremonies, at which I was present, were enacted in accordance with tradition, including the ritual scarifications of the female relatives at the spot where the provisional tomb should have been dug. Through another stroke of ill-luck, the collective hunt had taken place during the evening or the afternoon previous to my arrival, I don't know which; what was certain was that no animal had been killed. An old jaguar skin was used in the funeral dances. I even suspect that our *irara* was promptly appropriated to replace the missing animal. The natives would not admit that this was so, which was a pity: if it were the case, I could have claimed to be the *uiaddo,* the leader of the hunt representing the dead man's soul. I would have received from his family the armband made of human hair and the *poari,* a mystical clarinet consisting of a small feathered gourd acting as an amplifier for a bamboo reed which is sounded over the captured animal, before being attached to its dead body. According to the prescribed rules, I would have shared out the flesh, hide, teeth and claws among the dead man's relatives, who would have given me in exchange a ceremonial bow with arrows, another clarinet in commemoration of my duties and a necklace made of shell discs. I would also no doubt have had to paint myself black, so as not to be recognized by the maleficent soul responsible for the death, which would be obliged by the law of the *mori* to enter into the body of the dead animal—and thus offer itself as compensation for the harm done—but would still be full of vindictive hatred towards the person who had constrained it to do so. In a sense, nature in this destructive form is seen as being human. It operates through a special category of souls, which depend directly on it and not on society.

I mentioned earlier that I was sharing a hut with a shaman. These *bari* form a special category of human beings who belong neither to the physical universe nor to society, but whose function it is to act as mediators between the two worlds. It is possible, but not certain, that they all originate from the Tugaré moiety; this was the case with mine, because our hut was in the Cera moiety and, as was the custom, he was living in his wife's house. The function of *bari* is a vocation, often discovered through a revelation,

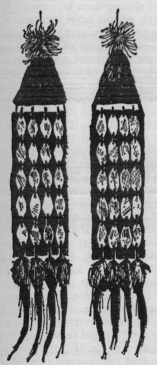

FIG 39. Ceremonial earrings made of mother-of-pearl mounted on bark and decorated with feathers and hair

the central theme of which is the conclusion of a pact with certain members of a very complex community of evil, or simply awesome, spirits, partly celestial (and therefore regulators of astronomical and meteorological phenomena), partly animal and partly subterranean. These beings, whose numbers are regularly increased by the souls of deceased medicine-men, are responsible for the movement of the stars, for wind, rain, sickness and death. They are described as having various terrifying appearances: hairy, with holes in their heads through which tobacco fumes escape when they are smoking; aerial monsters, sending forth rain through their eyes or their nostrils, or with excessively long nails and hair; one-legged creatures with swollen bellies and downy bodies like bats.

The *bari* is an asocial character. The personal link uniting him with one or more spirits gives him certain privileges: supernatural help when he goes off on a solitary hunting expedition, the power to change into an animal and knowledge of diseases as well as prophetic gifts. Game killed during a hunting expedition and the first garden produce are unfit for consumption until the *bari* has been given his share, which constitutes the *mori* owed by the living to the spirits of the dead. In the native system, this share therefore plays a part which is both symmetrical to, and the reverse of, the role played by the funeral hunt referred to earlier.

But the *bari* is also governed by his guardian spirit or spirits. They use him as a means of assuming bodily form, and when he is thus acting as a medium, he falls into trances and convulsions. In exchange for his protection, the spirit keeps a constant watch on the *bari;* he is the real owner not only of the shaman's possessions but even of his body. The *bari* has to account to the spirit for his broken arrows, his damaged crockery and his nail and hair clippings. Nothing may be destroyed or thrown away; the *bari* has to drag with him the debris of his past life. The old legal saying, 'Le mort saisit le vif', thus takes on a sinister and unexpected significance.* The shaman and the spirit are so jealously interlinked that it is impossible in the last resort to know

* TRANSLATORS' NOTE: 'The dead man seizes the living.' This technical formula means, in legal parlance, that the heir is immediately invested with the possessions and prerogatives of the dead man.

which of the two partners is the master and which the servant.

It is obvious then that, for the Bororo, the physical universe consists of a complex hierarchy of individualized powers. Although the personal nature of these powers is clearly affirmed, the same cannot be said of their other attributes: they are at once beings and things, living and dead. In native society, the shamans form, on the one hand, the connecting link between humans, and, on the other, the ambiguous universe of maleficent souls who are at once people and objects.

In contrast to the physical universe, the sociological world presents very different characteristics. The souls of ordinary men (I mean those who are not witch-doctors), instead of being identified with natural forces continue to exist as a society; but conversely, they lose their personal identity to merge into a collective being, the *aroe,* which like the *anaon* of the ancient Bretons, should no doubt be translated as 'the society of souls'. It is a two-part society since, after the funeral ceremonies, the souls are divided between two villages, one of which lies to the east, the other to the west, and over which preside the two great divinized heroes of the Bororo pantheon: Bakororo, the elder, in the west and Ituboré, the younger, in the east. It will be noted that the east-west axis corresponds to the course of the Rio Vermelho. There is very probably, then, a relationship, as yet obscure, between the duality of the villages occupied by the dead and the subsidiary division of the village into the upstream part and the downstream part.

Just as the *bari* is in an intermediary position between human society and maleficent, individual and cosmological souls (we have seen that the souls of the dead *bari* have all three characteristics at once), there exists another mediatory agent who presides over relations between the society of the living and the beneficent, collective and anthropomorphic society of the dead. He is the 'master of the way of the souls', or *aroettowaraare.* He can be distinguished from the *bari* by his opposite characteristics. Moreover, they fear and hate each other. The master of the way is not entitled to receive offerings, but he is required to observe certain rules very strictly: some foods are taboo for him, and he has to dress very soberly; he is not allowed to wear ornaments or bright colours. On the other hand, there is no pact between him and the souls; the latter are always pres-

Fig 40. A Bororo painting representing religious objects

ent to him and, as it were, immanent within him. Instead of taking possession of him in hypnotic trances, they appear to him in his dreams; when, from time to time, he invokes them, he does so only for the benefit of others.

While the *bari* foresees sickness and death, the master of the way takes care of people and cures them. It is said, incidentally, that the *bari*, who is an expression of physical necessity, is not averse to confirming his forecasts by killing off the sick who are slow in conforming to his baleful predictions. But it should be noted that the Bororo do not have exactly the same conception of the relationship between life and death as we do. On one occasion, when a woman was lying in a corner of her hut with a very high temperature, she was described to me as being dead, which no doubt meant that they had given her up for lost. After all, this way of looking at things is not unlike that of European armies which use the same word 'losses' to refer to both dead and wounded. From the point of view of immediate effectiveness, to be dead or wounded comes to the same thing, although from the point of view of the wounded, it is clearly an advantage not to be counted among the dead.

Lastly, although the master can, like the *bari*, change into an animal, he never assumes the form of the jaguar, which is man-eating and therefore the creature which—before it is killed—exacts the *mori* for the dead from the living. He limits himself to food-providing animals: the macaw which gathers fruit, the harpy-eagle which catches fish or the tapir whose flesh provides a feast for the tribe. The *bari* is pos-

sessed by the spirits, the *aroettowaraare* sacrifices himself
for the salvation of men. Even the revelation by which he
is summoned to accomplish his mission is painful: he first
becomes aware of the fact that he has been chosen by the
stench which pursues him, a stench no doubt reminiscent
of the foul smell which pervades the village during the
weeks when the corpse is superficially and provisionally
interred in the centre of the dancing area, but which is associated with a mythical being called the *aije*. This is a
repulsive, foul-smelling and affectionate aquatic monster
which appears to the initiate and whose caresses he is

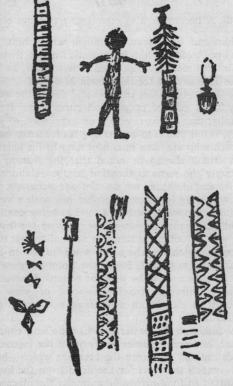

FIG 41. A Bororo painting representing an offi-
ciant, trumpets, a rattle and various ornaments

forced to endure. The scene is mimed during the funeral ceremonies by young men smeared with mud who embrace the personage dressed up to represent the young soul. The natives have a clear-enough mental image of the *aije* to depict it in paintings; and they use the same name for the bull-roarers, the booming sound of which heralds the emergence of the animal and imitates its cry.

It is not surprising that the subsequent funeral ceremonies should extend over several weeks, since their functions are extremely varied. First, they take place on the two levels I have just indicated. Considered from the individual point of view, each death is the occasion of a kind of arbitration between the physical universe and society. The hostile forces which constitute the first have inflicted harm on the second, and reparation must be made: this is the function of the funeral hunt. After being avenged and redeemed by the community of hunters, the dead person has to be received into the society of souls. This is the function of the *roiakuriluo*, a great funeral lament at which I was to have the good fortune to be present.

In a Bororo village, there is one event in the day of special importance: this is the evening assembly. At dusk, a big fire is lit on the dancing area, and the clan chiefs come together there; in a loud voice, a herald calls each group: *Badedjeba*, 'the chiefs'; *O Cera*, 'those of the ibis'; *Ki*, 'those of the tapir'; *Bokodori*, 'those of the great tatu'; *Bakoro* (from the name of the hero Bakororo); *Boro*, 'those of the lip-plug'; *Ew a guddy*, 'those of the buriti palm'; *Arore*, 'those of the caterpillar'; *Paiwe*, 'those of the porcupine'; *Apibore* (whose meaning is doubtful) . . .* As they appear in turn, orders for the following day are communicated to the people concerned, and always in a high-pitched voice which is intended to carry to the outermost huts. However, by this time, most of the huts are empty or nearly so, because at dusk, when the mosquitoes disappear, all the men who had gone there about six o'clock begin coming out again. Each carries under his arm a mat that he spreads out on the beaten earth of the large circular area to the west side of the men's house. He lies down and wraps himself in a cotton blanket which is stained an orange colour through long contact with urucu-painted bodies and which the Protection Service

---

* Specialists in the Bororo language might well dispute or clarify some of these translations; I am only going by what the natives told me.

would now hardly recognize as being one of its gifts. Five or six men may share one of the larger mats, but very few words are exchanged. One or two individuals lie apart from the rest, and there is frequent coming and going among the prostrate bodies. As the roll-call continues, the heads of families, who rise one after the other at the mention of their names, receive their orders and then go back to stretch out again, looking up at the stars. The women too leave the huts and gather in groups at the doors. The sound of conversation dies away and gradually one begins to hear, from inside the men's house, then from the dancing area itself—led first by two or three officiants, then increasing in volume as more and more men arrive—the chants, recitatives and choruses which are to last throughout the night.

The dead man belonged to the Cera moiety, so it was the Tugaré who were officiating. At the centre of the dancing area, a scattering of leaves marked the absent tomb, and to the right and left of it were bundles of arrows with bowls of food standing in front of them. There were a dozen priests and singers, most of whom wore on their heads a large crown of brilliantly coloured feathers (others had it dangling over their buttocks) above a rectangular wicker-work fan covering their shoulders and kept in place by a piece of string tied round their necks. Some were completely naked and painted either red or black all over, or with bands of red, or covered with bands of white down; others wore long straw skirts. The chief character, who represented the young soul, appeared in two different costumes according to the stages of the ceremony: sometimes he was clad in green foliage and was crowned with the enormous head-dress I have already described, and wore the jaguar skin like a court train borne up behind him by a page; sometimes he was naked and painted black, his only adornment being a straw object round his eyes, like huge empty spectacle frames. This is a particularly interesting detail, because a similar symbol is characteristic of Tlaloc, the rain god of ancient Mexico. The Pueblo of Arizona and New Mexico may provide the key to the enigma, since the souls of their dead change into gods of rain, and they have, moreover, various beliefs relating to magical objects which protect the eyes and allow the possessor to become invisible. I have often noticed that spectacles have a strong fascination for South American Indians; so much so, indeed, that on my last expedition I took with me a supply of empty frames which were extremely popular with the Nambik-wara, as if certain traditional beliefs predisposed the Indians to appreciate such unlikely objects. No previous reference had ever been made to straw spectacles among the Bororo, but since the purpose of the black paint is to make the person wearing it invisible, it seems probable that the spectacles have the same function—and in fact they are known to fulfil this function in Pueblo mythology.* Also, the *butarico,* the spirits responsible for rain in the Bororo system, are depicted as having the same terrifying appearance —fangs and clawlike hands—as the water goddess of the Maya.

During the first few nights, we watched dances performed by various Tugaré clans: *ewoddo,* the dance of the palm clan; *paiwe,* the dance of the porcupine clan. In both cases, the dancers were covered in foliage from head to foot and, as their faces were invisible, it was natural to imagine them as being on a level with the feather crowns, the predominating feature of their attire, and this meant that the dancers gave the impression of being enormously tall. In their hands, they carried palm stems or sticks decorated with leaves. There were two kinds of dances. In the first, the male dancers came forward alone, in two sets of four, facing each other at each end of the dancing floor, then ran towards each other shouting 'ho! ho!' and whirling round until they had exchanged their initial positions. Later, women cut in between the male dancers and the dance developed into an interminable farandole which came forward or marked time, according to the indications of the naked leaders who walked backwards shaking their rattles, while other men sang in a squatting position.

Three days later, the ceremonies were interrupted to allow for the preparation of the second act: the dance of the *mariddo.* Groups of men went into the forest to fetch armfuls of green palms, which were stripped of their leaves and then divided up into sections about thirty centimetres long. These were crudely tied together by the natives with dried grass, in bundles of two or three, like the rungs of a rope ladder several metres long. Two ladders of unequal length were made in this way, and then rolled up to form two solid discs, standing edgewise and respectively about

---

* After the publication of this book, the Salesians disputed my interpretation. According to their informants, the straw circles were meant to represent the eyes of a nocturnal bird of prey.

FIG 42. A diadem of yellow and blue macaw
feathers, with the clan sign

1.50 metres and 1.30 metres high. The sides were decorated with leaves held in place by a network of fine string
made of plaited hair. These discs were the male and female
mariddo, and the making of them devolved upon the
Ewaguddu clan.

Towards evening two groups, each consisting of five or
six men, set out, one to the west, the other to the east. I
followed the first group, and saw them making their preparations about fifty metres from the village, behind a screen
of trees which concealed them from the other villagers.
They covered themselves with leaves, like the dancers, and
fixed their crowns in position. But this time, the secrecy of
their preparations could be explained by the part they were
playing: like the other group, they represented the souls
of the dead which had come from their villages in the east
and the west to welcome the deceased. When all was
ready, they moved towards the dancing area, whistling as
they went. The eastern group had already preceded them
there (one group was, symbolically, going upstream, the
other downstream, and the latter therefore moved faster).
Their timid and hesitant gait admirably conveyed their

ghostly nature; I was reminded of Homer—of Ulysses struggling to prevent the flight of the ghosts conjured up by blood. But all at once, the ceremony burst into life: men seized one or other of the two *mariddo* (which were all the heavier through having been made with fresh vegetation), lifted it high in the air and, thus encumbered, danced until they were exhausted and had to allow a rival to take it from them. The scene no longer had any mystic character; it had turned into a fair, where the young men were showing off their physical prowess in an atmosphere characterized by sweat, thumping and gibes. And yet this sport, which exists in secular forms among neighbouring communities—for instance, in the log races practised by the Ge tribes of the Brazilian plateau—retains its full religious significance with the Bororo: in the mood of gay abandon, the natives feel they are playing with the dead and wresting from them the right to remain alive.

The major contrast between the dead and the living is expressed in the first instance by the division of the villagers, during the ceremonies, into actors and spectators. But the chief factors are men, who are protected by the secret of their communal house. It has to be recognized, then, that the plan of the village has a still deeper significance than the one I attributed to it on the sociological level. On the occasion of a death, each moiety takes it in turn to play the part of the living or the dead, one in relation to the other. However, this alternation reflects another, in which the roles are permanently assigned: the men who live together in the brotherhood of the *baitemannageo* symbolize the society of souls, whereas the huts on the periphery belonging to the women, who are excluded from the most sacred rites and are thus in a sense inevitably spectators, constitute the audience of the living and the abode reserved for them.

We have already seen that the supernatural world itself is twofold, since it includes the domains of the priest and the medicine-man. The latter is the master of the celestial and telluric powers, from the tenth heaven (the Bororo believe that there are several heavens one above the other) to the depths of the earth; the forces he controls—and on which he is dependent—are therefore arranged along a vertical axis, whereas the priest, who is master of the way of souls, presides over the horizontal axis linking east and west and on which the two villages of the dead are situated. The many indications suggesting that the *bari* is always of

Tugaré origin, and the *aroettowaraare* Cera, lead one to
believe that the division into moieties is a further expression
of this duality. It is significant that all the Bororo myths
present Tugaré heroes as creators and demiurges, and Cera
heroes as pacifiers and organizers. The former are responsible for the existence of things—water, rivers, fish, vegetation and manufactured objects; the latter organized
creation, delivered mankind from monsters and assigned a
specific food to each animal. There is even a myth which
relates that supreme power once belonged to the Tugaré,
who relinquished it in favour of the Cera, as if, by the opposition between the moieties, native thought was trying to
express the transition from unrestrained nature to civilized
society.

This makes it possible to understand the apparent paradox whereby the Cera, who exercise political and religious
power, are called 'weak' and the Tugaré 'strong'. The
Tugaré are closer to the physical world, the Cera to the
human world, and after all the latter is not the more powerful of the two. The social order cannot altogether cheat the
cosmic hierarchy. Even among the Bororo, nature can only
be conquered by acknowledging its supremacy and by making allowances for its imperatives. In a sociological system
such as theirs, there is, moreover, no freedom of choice: a
man cannot belong to the same moiety as his father and his
son (since he belongs to his mother's moiety); he is related
by moiety only with his grandfather and his grandson.
Although the Cera try to justify their authority by their
exclusive affinity with the founder heroes, they agree at the
same time to be separated from them by a further gap
of one generation. In relation to their ancestors, they are
'grandsons', whereas the Tugaré are 'sons'.

The natives are deluded by the logic of their system, but
are they not also deluded in another way too? When all is
said and done, I cannot help feeling that the dazzling metaphysical dance I witnessed is little more than a rather
sinister farce. The brotherhood of male villagers claims to
represent the dead, in order that the living should have the
illusion of being visited by the souls; the women are excluded from the rites and deceived as to their real nature,
no doubt in order to ratify the division according to which
they are granted priority in matters of status and residence,
and the mysteries of religion are reserved for the men. Yet
their real or supposed credulity also has a psychological

function: namely, to give, for the benefit of both sexes, an emotional and intellectual content to puppets whose strings the men might otherwise manipulate with less earnest intent. It is not only to deceive our children that we keep up their belief in Father Christmas: their enthusiasm warms the cockles of our hearts, helps us to delude ourselves and to believe, since they believe it, that a world of one-way generosity is not absolutely incompatible with reality. However, men die and do not come back; and every social order has a similarity with death in that it takes something away and gives nothing in return for it.

Bororo society offers a lesson to the student of human nature. If he listens to his native informants they will describe for him, as they did for me, this ballet in which two village moieties strive to live and breathe each through and for the other; exchanging women, possessions and services in fervent reciprocity; intermarrying their children, burying each other's dead, each providing the other with a guarantee that life is eternal, the world full of help and society just. To provide evidence of these truths and to foster these beliefs, their wise men have worked out an impressive cosmology and embodied it in the plan of the villages and the layout of the dwellings. They arranged and rearranged the contradictions they encountered, never accepting any opposition without repudiating it in favour of another, cutting up and dividing the groups, joining them and setting them one against the other, and turning their whole social and spiritual life into a coat of arms in which symmetry and asymmetry are equally balanced, like the subtle patterns with which a Caduveo beauty, tormented by the same anxiety, at some less conscious level, scars her face. But what remains of it all? What is left of the moieties, counter-moieties, clans and sub-clans, when observed in the light of the conclusion which recent observations seem to force upon us? In this society, which appears to have delighted in complexity, each clan is divided into three groups —upper, middle and lower—and over all other rules and regulations hangs the obligation for an upper-grade person from one moiety to marry an upper-grade person from the other, a member of the middle grade to marry a middle-grade person and a member of the lower grade to marry a lower-grade person; in other words, under the disguise of fraternal institutions, the Bororo village can be seen in the last resort as consisting of three groups each of which inter-

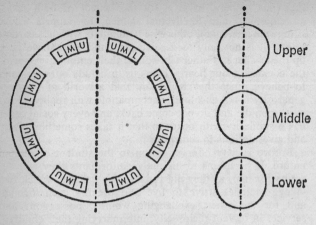

FIG 43. A diagram illustrating the apparent and real structure of the Bororo village

marries within itself. Three societies which, without realizing it, will remain for ever separate and isolated, each
imprisoned in a kind of pride which is concealed even from
itself by a smokescreen of institutions, so that each is the
unconscious victim of devices, the purpose of which it can
no longer discover. It is in vain that the Bororo crown their
system with a fallacious impersonation of the dead: they
have been no more successful than other societies in denying the truth that the image of a society evolves of the
relationship between the living and the dead is, in the final
analysis, an attempt, on the level of religious thought, to
conceal, embellish or justify the actual relationships which
prevail among the living.

PART SEVEN

Nambikwara

---

24. THE LOST WORLD

An anthropological expedition into central Brazil begins at the Carrefour Réaumur-Sébastopol. This is where the wholesale firms specializing in sewing requisites and fancy goods are concentrated, and where one can expect to discover the sort of products likely to satisfy the fastidious taste of the Indians.

One year after my visit to the Bororo, all the required conditions for turning me into a fully fledged anthropologist had been fulfilled. Lévy-Bruhl, Mauss and Rivet had given me their retrospective blessing; my collections had been exhibited in a gallery in the Faubourg Saint-Honoré; I had delivered lectures and written articles. Thanks to Henri Laugier, who was in charge of the department of scientific research, then in its early stages, I obtained an adequate subsidy for a more ambitious undertaking. The first task was to assemble my equipment; the three months I had spent in close contact with the natives had made me familiar with their requirements, which are astonishingly similar throughout the South American continent.

So, in an area of Paris which was as unknown to me as the Amazon, I found myself engaging in strange practices under the watchful eye of Czech importers. Knowing nothing of their trade, I lacked the technical terms with which to specify my needs, and could only apply native criteria. I set about choosing the smallest of the embroidery beads known in French as *rocaille,* which were piled up in the trays in heavy hanks. I tried to bite through them to test their toughness; I sucked them in order to make sure that they were made of tinted glass and that the colour would not run at the first contact with river water; I varied the amounts purchased in accordance with the basic Indian colour scheme: first, black and white in equal quantities; next red; then a much smaller quantity of yellow; and, for form's sake, a few blue and green which would no doubt be spurned.

The reasons for these preferences are easy to understand.

Since they make their own beads by hand, the Indians look upon the smallest as having the greatest value, that is, as requiring more work and skill; their raw material is the black shell of palm nuts and the milky mother-of-pearl of river shells, and they seek to achieve effects by alternating the two colours. Like everybody else, they appreciate most what they know best, and so I was to have great success with the black and the white beads. Yellow and red are often considered by them as belonging to a single linguistic category, because of the variations in shade of the urucu dye, which ranges between scarlet and a yellowy orange, according to the quality and ripeness of the seeds; however, red remains the dominant colour of the two, because of its intensity, with which the Bororo are familiar through certain seeds and feathers. As for blue and green, these are cold colours which, in the natural state, are chiefly represented in perishable plants: a twofold reason for the natives' indifference and the vagueness of their vocabulary relating to these hues: blue is assimilated to black in some languages and to green in others.

The needles had to be thick enough to take strong thread, but not too thick, because of the smallness of the beads they were meant to go through. The thread I was looking for had to be fast-coloured, preferably red (the Indians dye theirs with urucu), and had to have a thick twist so as to retain a handmade appearance. Generally speaking, I had learned to be wary of shoddy goods: the example of the Bororo had given me a profound respect for native techniques. The Indian way of living puts objects to severe tests; however paradoxical it may appear, so as not to be discredited in the eyes of these primitive people, I had to have the hardest steel, coloured beads dyed right through and thread that would not have been disdained by Her Britannic Majesty's court saddler.

Sometimes I came across tradesmen whose imaginations were fired by exotic orders corresponding to their particular expertise. A maker of fish-hooks in the Canal Saint-Martin area let me have all his oddments very cheaply. For a whole year, I carried with me through the bush several kilos of fish-hooks which nobody wanted, because they were too small for fish worthy of Amazonian fishermen. I finally managed to get rid of the lot at the Bolivian frontier. All this merchandise had to serve a double purpose: as presents and bartering material in dealing with the Indians, and as a means of obtaining food and services in remote regions rarely frequented by tradesmen. When I ran out of money towards the end of the expedition, I managed to prolong my stay for a few more weeks by opening up shop in a hamlet of rubber gatherers. The local prostitutes would give me two eggs in exchange for a necklace, although not without haggling.

My intention was to spend a whole year in the bush, and it took me a long time to make up my mind what exactly my objective should be. Having no suspicion that the result would run counter to my plans, and being more anxious to understand America than to study human nature by basing my research on one particular instance, I finally decided to take a sort of cross-section through Brazilian anthropology—and geography—by travelling across the western part of the plateau, from Cuiaba to the Rio Madeira. Until recent times, this region had remained one of the least known in all Brazil. The Paulist explorers of the eighteenth century, discouraged by the desolate nature of the country and the savagery of the Indians, had hardly ventured beyond Cuiaba. At the beginning of the twentieth century, the 1,500 kilometres stretching between Cuiaba and the Amazon were still forbidden territory, so that to go from Cuiaba to Manaus, or to Belem on the Amazon, the simplest route was by way of Rio de Janeiro and the sea northwards to the river estuary. It was only in 1907 that General (then Colonel) Candido Mariano da Silva Rondon began to explore and open up the territory; he was to be engaged on this task for eight years, during which time he established a strategically important telegraph line linking the federal capital, via Cuiaba, with the north-west frontier posts for the first time.

The reports of the Rondon Commission (which have not yet been published in full), one or two lectures given by the general, the account written by Theodore Roosevelt who accompanied him on one of his expeditions and finally a delightful book by the late Roquette Pinto (then director of the National Museum) entitled *Rondonia* (1912), gave a modicum of information about the primitive communities discovered in the area. But since then, the old curse seemed to have fallen over the plateau again. No professional anthropologist had ever ventured across it. It was tempting to follow the telegraph line, or what was left of it, to try and find out who exactly the Nambikwara were, as well as the mysterious communities further to the north, whom no one had seen since Rondon briefly indicated their existence.

By 1939, interest was beginning to shift from the tribes living along the coast or in the large river towns, the traditional gateways to the interior of Brazil, to the Indians living on the plateau. My stay with the Bororo had convinced me of the exceptional degree of sociological and religious refinement of tribes formerly considered as possessing only an extremely crude culture. The results of the researches carried out by a German, the late Kurt Unkel, who had adopted the Indian name of Nimuendaju, were just beginning to be known; after years spent in the Ge villages of central Brazil, he was able to confirm that the Bororo were not an isolated phenomenon, but rather a variation on a basic theme shared with other communities. This meant that the savannah lands of central Brazil were occupied, over a distance of almost two thousand kilometres, by the survivors of a remarkably homogeneous culture, with a single language diversified into different dialects all belonging to the same family, and with a comparatively low standard of living contrasting with a highly developed social organization and complex religious thought. They should no doubt be recognized as Brazil's first inhabitants, who had been forgotten in their backwater or, shortly before the discovery of America, forced back into the poorest territories by warlike communities who had arrived from some unknown place of origin to conquer the coast and the river valleys.

At various places along the coast, sixteenth-century travellers had encountered representatives of the great Tupi-Guarani culture, who also occupied almost the whole of Paraguay and the course of the Amazon, thus describing a broken circle about three thousand kilometres in diameter and with no more than a slight break at the frontier between Paraguay and Bolivia. The Tupi, who have obscure affinities with the Aztecs, that is, with communities which settled at a late date in the Mexico valley, were themselves newcomers; they continued their penetration into the valleys of the Brazilian interior right up until the nineteenth century. Perhaps they had started off on their wanderings a few hundred years before the discovery, because of the belief that they might, somewhere, find a land free from both death and evil. Such was still their conviction when they finished their migrations and, at the end of the nine-

teenth century, emerged in small groups led by shamans in
the Paulist coastal area, dancing and singing the praises of
the land of eternal life, and fasting for long periods in
order to be worthy of it. In the sixteenth century, at any
rate, they were fiercely contending for the coast with the
previous occupants, about whom we possess little information, but who were perhaps the very Ge we are now concerned with.

To the north-west of Brazil, the Tupi coexisted with
other communities, such as the Carib, who were akin to
them in culture, although different in language, and who
were in the process of conquering the West Indies. There
were also the Arawak, a rather mysterious group, older and
more refined than the other two; they formed the major
part of the West Indian population and had advanced as far
as Florida; although they were different from the Ge
because of their very high level of material culture, especially in ceramics and wood-carving, they seem to have had
a similar type of social organization. The Carib and Arawak
would appear to have penetrated into the interior before
the Tupi: in the sixteenth century they were present in large
numbers in the Guianas, the estuary of the Amazon and
the West Indies. But there are still small colonies in the
interior along certain tributaries on the right bank of the
Amazon, for instance, the Xingu and the Guaporé. The
Arawak even have descendants in Upper Bolivia. It was no
doubt they who taught pottery-making to the Mbaya-Caduveo, since the Guana, who it will be remembered were
enslaved by the Mbaya-Caduveo, speak an Arawak dialect.

By crossing the least-known part of the plateau, I was
hoping to find the most westerly representatives of the Ge
group in the savannah, and then, after reaching the Madeira
basin, to study the as yet unrecorded vestiges of the three
other linguistic families, on the fringe of their main route
into the interior—Amazonia.

My hopes were only partly realized, because of our over-
simplified views on pre-Columbian American history. Today, in the light of recent discoveries and because of the
years I myself have spent studying North American anthropology, I realize that the Western hemisphere must be considered as a single whole. The social organization and religious beliefs of the Ge echo those of tribes living in the
forests and prairies of North America; moreover, analogies
between the Chaco tribes (such as the Guaycuru) and those

living on the plains of the United States and Canada were
noted a very long time ago, without their implications being
followed up. The civilizations of Mexico and Peru must
certainly have come into contact with each other at several
points in their history through boats sailing along the Pacific
coast. All these possibilities have been rather overlooked,
because for a long time American studies were dominated
by the conviction that the continent had been populated
quite recently, around 5000 or 6000 B.C., and solely by
Asiatic communities who had arrived by the Bering Strait.

This meant that we had to explain how, in the few thousands of years at our disposal, these nomads settled down
from end to end of the Western Hemisphere and adapted
to different climates; how they discovered, domesticated and
propagated over such vast areas the wild species which,
thanks to their diligent efforts, were to become tobacco
beans, manioc, sweet potatoes, potatoes proper, peanuts,
cotton and—most important of all—maize; and lastly how
successive civilizations of which the Aztecs, the Mayas and
the Incas were the distant heirs, came into being and developed in Mexico, Central America and the Andes. To succeed, we had to whittle down each development until it
could be contained within the compass of a few centuries:
the pre-Columbian history of America thus became a succession of kaleidoscopic images, the details of which constantly varied according to the whim of the theoretician. It
was as if American specialists were trying to impose on
primitive America that absence of depth characteristic of
the contemporary history of the New World.

This way of looking at things has been completely altered by discoveries which suggest a much earlier date for
man's arrival on the American continent. We know that he
was familiar with, and hunted, varieties of animals which
have now disappeared from America: land sloths, mam-
moths, camels, horses, archaic bison and antelopes, because
his weapons and stone implements have been discovered
alongside their bones. The presence of some of these animals in places such as the Mexico valley indicates very different climatic conditions from those prevailing now, and
the change can only have taken place over several thousands of years. The use of radioactivity to determine the
date of archaeological remains has provided evidence along
the same lines. We must recognize, then, that man was already present in America twenty thousand years ago; in cer-

tain areas, he was growing maize more than three thousand years ago. All over North America, remains have been found which are between ten and twelve thousand years old. At the same time, the dates of the main archaeological strata on the continent, which have been obtained by measuring the residual radioactivity in the carbon, turn out to be between 500 and 1,500 years older than was previously supposed. The pre-Columbian history of America, like those Japanese flowers made of compressed paper which open out when immersed in water, has suddenly acquired the volume it lacked.

But, because of this, we now find ourselves faced with a difficulty which is the reverse of the one encountered by our predecessors: how are we to fill these immense periods? We know that the movements of population I was trying to indicate a little earlier were surface phenomena, and that the great Mexican and Andean civilizations were preceded by something else. In Peru and various regions of North America, traces of the first occupants have already been brought to light: tribes ignorant of agriculture were followed by communities who lived in villages and cultivated gardens, although maize and pottery were as yet unknown. These in turn were followed by populations who carved stone and worked precious metals in a free and more inspired style than anything which came later. The Incas of Peru and the Aztecs of Mexico, whom we had been inclined to consider as representing the peak and epitome of American history, were as far removed from these vital sources as the French Empire style is from Egypt and Rome, from which it borrowed so heavily: all three are instances of totalitarian art, striving for a kind of hugeness in the harsh and the stark, and expressive of a State anxious to assert its power by concentrating its resources on something other than its own refinement, that is, on war or government. Even the Maya monuments seem like the gaudy decadence of an art which had reached its peak a thousand years previously.

Where did the founders come from? The old certainties have now to be replaced by the admission that we do not know. The population movements in the region of the Bering Strait were extremely complex: the Eskimos were recent arrivals; for about a thousand years, they were preceded by Paleo-Eskimos, whose culture was reminiscent of that of archaic China and the Scythians; and during a very

long period, perhaps from 8000 B.C. until just before the
Christian era, there were various populations in America.
Sculptures dating from 1000 B.C. show that the ancient
inhabitants of Mexico were very different in physical type
from present-day Indians: there were plump, smooth-faced,
small-featured Orientals, and bearded individuals with aqui-
line profiles reminiscent of Renaissance portraits. Geneti-
cists, investigating a different area, maintain that at least
forty vegetable species which were gathered wild, or grown
in a cultivated form, in pre-Columbian America have the
same chromosomic composition as the corresponding Asiatic species, or a composition derived from theirs. Has it to
be concluded, then, that maize, which figures on the list,
came from South-East Asia? Yet how could that be possible if Americans were already cultivating it four thousand years ago, at a time when the art of navigation was
certainly in a rudimentary state?

Without accepting Heyerdahl's bold hypothesis that Polynesia was populated by American natives, it must be admitted, after the voyage of the *Kon-Tiki,* that trans-Pacific
contacts may have taken place, and on many occasions.
But at a time when advanced civilizations were already
flourishing in America, that is around 1000 B.C., the Pacific
islands were uninhabited; or at least, nothing dating from
that period has ever been found there.

We should therefore look beyond Polynesia to Melanesia,
which was perhaps already inhabited, and to the Asiatic
coast as a whole. Today we are certain that there was uninterrupted communication between Alaska and the Aleutian
Islands on the one hand, and Siberia on the other. The people of Alaska were using iron tools about the beginning of
the Christian era, and yet they knew nothing of metallurgy;
the same pottery is found from the area around the Great
Lakes of America to central Siberia, and also the same
legends, rites and myths. While Western Europe remained
shut in upon itself, all the northern communities, from
Scandinavia to Labrador by way of Siberia and Canada,
seem to have maintained the closest possible contact with
each other. If the Celts borrowed certain myths from this
sub-Arctic civilization, of which we know practically nothing, it is easy to understand how the Holy Grail cycle happens to be more closely akin to the myths of the forest-
dwelling Indians of North America than to any other

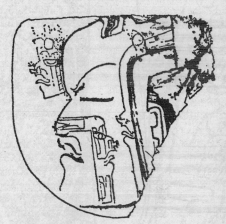

FIG 44–45. Ancient Mexicans: *(left)* south-
eastern Mexico (American Museum of
Natural History); *(right)* the Gulf Coast
(Exhibition of Mexican Art, Paris, 1952)

mythological system. And it is probably no mere chance that the Lapps live in conical tents exactly like those of the Indians.

To the south of the Asiatic continent, other reminiscences of American civilizations can be detected. The communities along the southern frontiers of China, whom the Chinese regarded as barbarians, and, to an even greater extent, the primitive tribes of Indonesia, have extraordinary affinities with the Americans. In the interior of Borneo, myths have been recorded which are indistinguishable from some of the most widespread in North America. Specialists long ago pointed out resemblances between archaeological evidence from South-East Asia and that pertaining to Scandinavian

FIG 46–47. Bas-reliefs known as 'the dancers': *(left)* Chavin, northern Peru (taken from Tello); *(right)* Monte Alban, southern Mexico

proto-history. Thus there are three regions, Indonesia, north-east America and the Scandinavian countries, which in a sense form the trigonometrical points of the pre-Columbian history of the New World.

Is it not conceivable that this major event in the history of mankind—I mean the appearance of neolithic civilization, with the generalization of pottery-making and weaving, the beginning of agriculture and cattle-rearing and the first attempts at metalwork—which was limited in the first instance to the Old World between the Danube and the Indus, may have aroused a kind of excitement among the less advanced communities of Asia and America? It is difficult to understand the origin of the American civilizations, unless we accept the hypothesis that all along the Pacific seaboard—both in Asia and America—intense activity was in progress for several thousands of years, and was spread from one area to another by boats moving along the coasts. Once, we refused to allow pre-Columbian America an historical dimension, simply because post-Columbian America

F

FIG 48. Hopewell, eastern United States (from C. C. Willoughby, *The Turner Group of Earthworks*, Papers of the Peabody Museum, Harvard University, vol. VIII, no. 3, 1922)

FIG 49. Chavin, northern Peru (taken from Tello)

had none. We now perhaps have to correct a second mistake, which consists in assuming that America remained cut off from the world as a whole for twenty thousand years, because it was separated from Western Europe. Everything would seem to suggest rather that the deep silence on the Atlantic side was offset by a buzz of activity all along the Pacific coasts.

Be that as it may, around 1000 B.C., an American hybrid seems already to have produced three shoots firmly grafted on to doubtful varieties resulting from an older evolution: the Hopewell culture, which occupied or contaminated the whole region of the United States to the east of the plains, formed a counterpart in the rustic style to the Chavin culture of northern Peru (echoed by Paracas in the south); at the same time, Chavin resembles the first manifestations of the so-called Olmec civilization, and foreshadows the Maya development. In all three cases, we are dealing with a cursive art, the flexibility and freedom of which, combined with an intellectual passion for double meanings (there are both Hopewell and Chavin motifs which can be interpreted differently according to whether they are looked at rightside or wrong-side up), seem still far removed from the angularity and immobilism which we are accustomed to associate with Pre-Columbian art. I sometimes try to persuade myself that Caduveo patterns are, in their own way, a prolongation of this very early tradition. It was, perhaps, at this period that the American civilizations began to branch out in different directions, Mexico and Peru assuming the initiative and leaping ahead, while the others remained in an intermediary position, or even lagged behind and degenerated into a semi-savage state. We will never know what happened exactly in tropical America, because climatic conditions there are unfavourable for the preservation of archaeological remains; it is significant, however, that the social organization of the Ge, and even the plan of the Bororo villages, should resemble what we have been able to reconstitute of these vanished civilizations through the study of certain pre-Inca deposits, such as the one at Tiahuanaco in Upper Bolivia.

The preceding pages have taken me a long way away from my description of the preparations for an expedition into the western Mato Grosso; the digression was necessary, however, if the reader was to become aware of the highly charged atmosphere in which all American-Indian research,

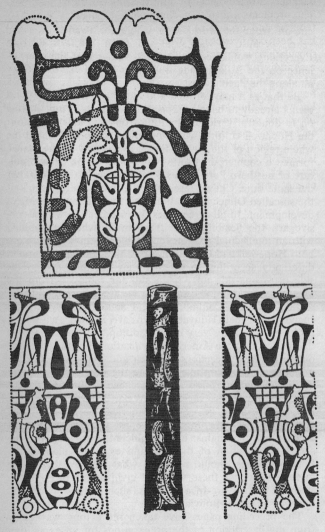

FIG. 50. Hopewell, eastern United States (taken from W. K. Moorehead, *The Hopewell Mound* . . . Field Museum, Chicago, Anthropological Series, Vol. VI, no. 5, 1922)

whether archaeological or anthropological, is carried out. The problems are so vast, the guidelines at our disposal so tenuous and uncertain, the past, over huge tracts of time, has been so irrevocably wiped out, and the basis of our speculations is so precarious, that even the most insignificant reconnoitring of the terrain puts the researcher into a state of uncertainty in which he oscillates between the most humble kind of resignation and the wildest ambition: he knows that the essential evidence has been lost and that all his efforts will amount to no more than a scratching of the surface; yet may he not stumble on some miraculously preserved clue that will shed light? Nothing is possible, so all is possible. The darkness through which we are groping is too thick for us to make any pronouncements about it; we cannot even say that it is doomed to last.

25. IN THE SERTÃO

Back in Cuiaba after an absence of two years, I tried to find out what the situation was really like along the telegraph line, about five or six hundred kilometres to the north.

In Cuiaba, the line was detested for several reasons. Since the founding of the town in the eighteenth century, very occasional contacts with the north had been made by boat in the direction of the middle reaches of the Amazon. In order to obtain *guaraná*, their favourite stimulant, the inhabitants of Cuiaba organized canoe expeditions lasting more than six months along the Tapajoz. *Guaraná* is a hard, brown paste, prepared almost exclusively by the Maué Indians from the crushed fruit of a creeper called *Paulinia sorbilis*. The paste is compressed into a sausage shape and grated on the horny tongue of a *pirarucu* fish, which is kept in a deerskin pouch. These details are significant, because it is believed that the use of a metal grater or of a different kind of leather for the pouch would cause the precious substance to lose its peculiar properties. Similarly, the Cuiabanos maintain that twist tobacco should be broken and crumbled by hand and not cut with a knife, since this causes it to go stale. Powdered *guaraná* is dropped into sweetened water where it remains in suspension instead of dissolving: the faintly chocolate-flavoured beverage is then drunk. Personally, I never felt it had the slightest effect on me, but in the lives of the inhabitants of the central and northern areas of the Mato Grosso it occupies a place similar to that of maté in the south.

The virtues of *guaraná* were felt to justify much trouble and effort. Before going beyond the rapids, the expedition would leave a few men behind to clear a patch of forest along the river-bank and grow maize and manioc, so that fresh food would be available on the return journey. But once steamboats came in, the *guaraná* could reach Cuiaba more quickly and in greater quantities by way of Rio de Janeiro, where it was brought by sea from Manaus and

Belem. Eventually the expeditions along the Tapajoz came to belong to an heroic, half-forgotten past.

However, when Rondon announced his intention of opening up the north-west region to civilization, these memories were revived. The approaches to the plateau were known to some extent, since two little old towns, Rosario and Diamantino, situated respectively 100 and 170 kilometres to the north of Cuiaba, still maintained a drowsy existence, although their gold-seams and gravel beds had become exhausted. Beyond, it would be necessary to continue by land, cutting across the succession of streams feeding the tributaries of the Amazon, instead of travelling down them by canoe: a formidable undertaking over such a vast distance. As late as 1900, the northern plateau still remained a mythic region, and was even supposed to contain a mountain range called Serra do Norte, which most maps still continue to mention.

This ignorance, combined with stories about the recent opening up of the American Far West and the gold rush, aroused wild hopes among the inhabitants of the Mato Grosso and even among those of the coast. In the wake of Rondon's men as they established the telegraph line, a flood of immigrants was expected to invade the area and use its hitherto unsuspected resources to build some Brazilian Chicago. The illusion was short-lived; like the north-east of Brazil, with its inhospitable wastes which have been described by Euclides da Cunha in *Os Sertões*, the Serra do Norte turned out to be desert-like savannah and one of the most barren areas of the South American continent. Moreover, the invention of radio-telegraphy, which coincided more or less with the completion of the telegraph line around 1922, meant that the latter was completely superseded, and was no sooner finished than it became an archaeological relic of a previous technological age. It had an hour of glory in 1924, when the federal government was cut off from the interior by the São Paulo rebellion. Thanks to the telegraph line, Rio continued to remain in contact with Cuiaba, via Belem and Manaus. Then the decline set in: the handful of enthusiasts who had sought employment on the line either went back home or were forgotten about. At the time when I went out there, they had received no food supplies for several years. No one dared to close down the line but everyone had lost interest in it. The poles were allowed to collapse and the wires to rust; the last survivors manning the posts lacked the courage to leave and indeed could not afford to do so; they were slowly dying out because of sickness, famine and loneliness.

The situation weighed all the more heavily on the consciences of the Cuiabanos in that the disappointed hopes had at least produced a modest but tangible result which consisted in the exploitation of the staff manning the line. Before taking up their posts, the employees had each to choose a *procurador* in Cuiaba, that is, a representative who could draw their salaries and use the money according to their instructions. These were usually confined to orders for rifle bullets, oil, salt, sewing-needles and cloth. All these goods were sold at the highest prices as a result of collusion between the *procuradores,* the Lebanese traders and the organizers of the transport caravans. Consequently, the unfortunate wretches living at the back of beyond could not even hope to return since, after a few years, they found themselves involved in debts that they would never be able to pay off. It was obvious that I would do better to forget all about the line, especially since my plan to use it as a base met with little encouragement. I tried to locate retired non-commissioned officers who had been Rondon's companions, but all I could get out of them was the dismal lament: 'Um pais ruim, muito ruim, mais ruim que qualquer outro' ('vile country, absolutely vile, viler than any other'). I should, at all costs, avoid going there.

Then there was the question of the Indians. In 1931, the telegraph station at Parecis, lying three hundred kilometres north of Cuiaba, in a not completely uninhabited region only eighty kilometres from Diamantino, had been attacked and destroyed by unknown Indians who had come from the valley of the Rio de Sangue, hitherto believed to be uninhabited. These savages had been nicknamed *beiços de pau,* wooden snouts, because of the discs they wore in their lower lips and the lobes of their ears. Since then, they had repeated their attacks at regular intervals with the result that the track had had to be moved about eighty kilometres to the south. As for the Nambikwara, nomads who had been coming to the posts from time to time since 1909, they had had varying relationships with the whites—good at first, but gradually deteriorating until, in 1925, seven workers were invited by the natives to their villages and were never seen again. From that time onwards, the Nambikwara and the telegraph workers avoided each other. In 1933, a Prot-

estant mission came to settle not far from the post at
Juruena; it would seem that relations soon became embit-
tered, the natives having been dissatisfied with the gifts—
inadequate, apparently—that the missionaries had given
them in return for their help in building the house and
planting the garden. A few months later, an Indian with a
high temperature presented himself at the mission and was
publicly given two aspirin tablets, which he swallowed;
afterwards he bathed in the river, developed congestion of
the lungs and died. As the Nambikwara are expert poi-
soners, they concluded that their fellow-tribesman had been
murdered; they launched a retaliatory attack, during which
six members of the mission were massacred, including a
two-year-old child. Only one woman was found alive by a
search party sent out from Cuiaba. Her story, as it was
retold to me, coincides exactly with that of the authors of
the attack, who for several weeks acted as my companions
and informants.

Ever since this incident, and one or two other subsequent
ones, the atmosphere had remained extremely tense all
along the line. As soon as I was able to establish contact
with the main stations from the main Cuiaba post office
(each operation took several days), we heard the most depressing news: at one place, the Indians had made a threatening move; at another they had not been seen for three
months, which was also a bad sign; at yet another, where
they had been in the habit of working, they had gone back
to being *bravos*, savages, etc. The one and only encouraging, or seemingly encouraging, sign was that, for the past
few weeks, three Jesuit Fathers had been trying to re-establish a mission at Juruena, on the edge of Nambikwara territory, six hundred kilometres to the north of Cuiaba. I
could always go there, get information from them and
make definite plans later.

So I spent a month at Cuiaba organizing the expedition;
since no attempt was made to prevent me leaving, I resolved
to go through with my intention: six months of travelling,
during the dry season, across a plateau where, I was told,
desert conditions prevailed, with neither grazing land nor
game to be caught; food therefore had to be taken, not only
for the men but also for the mules which would carry us as
far as the Madeira basin, where we would be able to continue our journey by canoe (a mule which is deprived of
maize is not strong enough to travel). In order to transport

provisions, we would need oxen, which are tougher and which can make do with whatever they find in the way of rough grass and foliage. Nevertheless, since I could expect a proportion of them to die of hunger and fatigue, I should take an adequate number with me. And since I had to have drovers to lead them, and to load and unload them at each stage, my company would be increased accordingly, and so at the same time would the quantity of mules and provisions, which in turn would call for extra oxen . . . It was a vicious circle. Finally, after discussions with experts such as former employees of the line and members of the transport caravans, I settled for fifteen men, as many mules and thirty or so oxen. As regards the mules, I had no choice: within a radius of fifty kilometres of Cuiaba, there were only about fifteen mules for sale and I bought them all, at prices varying between 150 and 1,000 francs each (at the 1938 exchange rate), according to their physical condition. As leader of the expedition, I kept the most majestic animal for myself: a huge white mule which I bought from the already mentioned butcher with the longing to see an elephant.

The real problem began with the choosing of men: there were four of us in the expedition, and we knew full well that our success, our safety and even our lives would depend on the trustworthiness and capabilities of the team I was about to take on. I spent days on end rejecting rogues and adventurers, the dregs of the population of Cuiaba. Finally, an old 'colonel' who lived on the outskirts of the town told me to try one of his former drovers who had settled in an out-of-the-way hamlet and whom he described to me as being poor, wise and virtuous. I went to see this man and was at once won over by his natural dignity, a feature not uncommon among the inland peasants. Instead of begging me, as the others had done, to grant him the unheard-of privilege of a year's wages, he stated certain conditions: he alone would choose the men and the oxen, and he would have the right to take along a few horses that he could sell at a profit in the north. I had already bought a team of oxen from a caravaneer in Cuiaba, because I had been attracted by their height and even more so by their somewhat antique tapir-hide pack-saddles and harness. Furthermore, the Bishop of Cuiaba had insisted that I take one of his protégés as cook: after a few days' travelling, he was discovered to be a *veado branco*, a white roebuck, in other words a homosexual, who suffered so badly from piles

that he could not sit on a horse. He was only too glad to
part company with us. As for the splendid oxen (which,
unknown to me, had already done a journey to five hundred
kilometres), they had not an ounce of fat on their bodies.
One after the other they began to develop sores through the
friction of the pack-saddles against their skin. In spite of the
skill of the *arrieiros*, they began to lose the hide over their
spines: great bloodstained gashes appeared, swarming with
maggots, and their backbones became visible. These fester-
ing skeletons were our first casualties.

Fortunately, the leader of the team, Fulgencio (pronounced 'Frugencio'), had managed to make up the numbers with quite ordinary-looking beasts, most of which,
however, completed the journey. The men he chose were
youths from his own village or the surrounding district,
whom he had known since birth and who respected his
knowledge. Most of them belonged to old Portuguese
families which had been established in the Mato Grosso for
a hundred or two hundred years and among which certain
austere traditions were still preserved. Poor they might be,
but each man had an embroidered, lace-trimmed towel,
given him by his mother, his sister or his betrothed, and at
no point in the journey would he have consented to wipe his
face with anything else. But the first time I offered them
sugar to put in their coffee, they proudly replied that they
were not *viciados*, perverts. I had some trouble with them,
because on all questions their ideas were as definite as my
own. I only just managed to avoid a rebellion over the food
supplies for the journey, since the men were convinced
they would die of hunger if I did not devote all the carrying
capacity to rice and beans. At a pinch, they could tolerate
the idea of dried meat, in spite of their conviction that there
would always be plenty of game. But they were horrified at
the thought of sugar, dried fruit and preserved foods. Although they would have risked their lives for us, they
treated us with gruff familiarity and would not have agreed
to wash a handkerchief that did not belong to them, since
washing was women's work. Our contract was based on the
following terms: for the duration of the expedition, each
man would be lent a mule and a gun; and in addition to receiving food he would be paid the equivalent of five francs
a day, at the 1938 exchange rate. The 1,500 or 2,000 francs
saved by the end of the expedition (they refused to be paid
until the end) would provide capital allowing some to get

married, others to buy cattle for breeding . . . It was also
agreed that Fulgencio would recruit a few young, half-
civilized Paressi Indians, when we crossed the former territory of the tribe which today supplies most of the maintenance personnel employed on the telegraph line along the
border of the Nambikwara territory.

So the organization of the expedition proceeded slowly,
as men and beasts, in groups of two or three, were recruited
from the hamlets around Cuiaba. They were all to assemble
one day in June 1938, just outside the town and, under
Fulgencio's leadership, oxen and riders set off with part of
the baggage. Each ox carries between 60 and 120 kilos,
according to its strength; the load is divided into two equal
parts which hang on either side on a straw-stuffed pack-
saddle, and a dried hide is stretched over as a cover. The
rate of travelling is about twenty-five kilometres a day, but
after a week's march, the beasts need a few days' rest.
We therefore decided to let the animals go on ahead, with
as small a load as possible; I myself was to follow in a
large lorry as far as the track allowed, that is to Utiarity,
five hundred kilometres north of Cuiaba. This is a telegraph
post in Nambikwara territory on the Rio Papagaio, which
the lorry would not be able to cross because of the inadequacy of the ferryboat. The real adventure would begin
beyond the river.

A week later than the 'troop' of oxen—a caravan of oxen
is called a *tropa*—our lorry set off with its load. We had
covered less than fifty kilometres when we caught up with
our men and beasts, serenely encamped in the savannah,
whereas I expected them to be at Utiarity, or nearly there.
I lost my temper for the first, and not the last, time. But
further disappointments would have to be endured before I
realized that the sense of time did not exist in the world I
was now entering. The expedition was being led neither by
me nor by Fulgencio, but by the oxen. These ponderous
beasts were like duchesses, whose vapours, whims and fits
of weariness had to be carefully studied. An ox cannot warn
you that it is tired, or that its load is too heavy: it keeps
going until it suddenly collapses, and either dies or is so
exhausted that six months' rest is needed for recovery, in
which case the only solution is to leave it behind. It follows
that the drovers are ruled by their oxen. Each animal had a
name corresponding to its colour, its bearing or its temperament. Mine were called *Piano* (the musical instrument),

Maça-Barro (mud-crusher), *Salino* (salt-taster), *Chicolate* (my men, who had never eaten chocolate, applied the word to a mixture of hot sweetened milk and egg-yolk), *Taruma* (a palm tree), *Galão* (big cock), *Lavrado* (red ochre), *Ramalhete* (posy), *Rochedo* (reddish), *Lambari* (a fish), *Açanhaço* (a blue bird), *Carbonate* (faulty diamond), *Galalá* (?), *Mourinho* (half-caste), *Mansinho* (small and gentle), *Correto* (correct), *Duque* (duke), *Motor* (motor, because, as his drover explained, 'he walks very well'), *Paulista*, *Navegante* (navigator), *Moreno* (brown), *Figurino* (model), *Brioso* (lively), *Barroso* (earthy), *Pai de Mel* (bee), *Araça* (a wild fruit), *Bonito* (pretty), *Brinquedo* (toy) and *Pretinho* (swarthy).

As soon as the drovers deem it necessary, the whole troop stops. The beasts are unloaded one by one, and camp is set up. If the area is safe, the oxen are allowed to scatter; if not, they are put to *pastorear,* that is to graze, while a watch is kept on them. Each morning, a few men reconnoitre the countryside over a radius of several kilometres until every animal has been located. This is called *campear.* The *vaqueiros* believe that their beasts are not without a certain perversity: they often deliberately run away and hide, and may remain undiscovered for days on end. I was once stuck for a whole week, because one of our mules, or so I was assured, had set off into the *campo,* first walking sideways, then backwards, to make sure that its *rastos* (tracks) could not be followed by its pursuers.

When the animals have been assembled, their sores have to be inspected and smeared with ointment, and the pack-saddles reorganized so that the load does not rest on the sore places. Finally the beasts have to be harnessed and loaded. This may be the start of fresh trouble: four or five days' rest are enough to make the oxen lose the habit of work; some no sooner feel the saddle than they kick and rear, scattering the painstakingly balanced load, so that everything has to be begun all over again. And one can consider oneself lucky if an ox, which has broken free, does not trot off into the countryside. If it does, one has to pitch camp again, unload, *pastorear, campear,* etc., until the whole troop has been reassembled and loaded, a process which sometimes has to be repeated five or six times until—for reasons unknown—general docility is obtained.

Being still less patient than the oxen, it took me weeks to resign myself to our erratic progress. Leaving the troop behind, we went on to Rosario Oeste, a village of about a thousand inhabitants, mostly black, stunted and goitrous, who lived in *casebres,* brilliantly red adobe shanties with roofs made of light-coloured palms, set along straight avenues overgrown with grass.

I remember my host's little garden, which was so meticulously laid out that it looked like a room in a house. The ground had been beaten and swept and the plants arranged as carefully as the furniture in a drawing-room: two orange trees, a lemon tree, a patch of pimentoes, a dozen or so manioc plants, two or three *chiabos* (edible hibiscus), the same number of vegetable silk plants, two rose trees, a clump of banana trees and another of sugar-cane; lastly, a parakeet in a cage and three hens each tethered by one leg to the same tree.

At Rosario Oeste, the food served on ceremonial occasions followed the 'half-and-half' principle: we were given half a chicken roasted, then the other half cold, with a sharp sauce; half a fish fried and the other half boiled. The meal ended with *cachaça,* a sugar-cane spirit, which one has to accept with the ritual formula, 'cemitério, cadeia, cachaça não é feito para uma só pessoa' ('the cemetery, prison and sugar spirit [the three Cs] are not intended for the same person'). Rosario is in the heart of the bush; its population consisted at the time largely of former rubber-collectors or gold- and diamond-seekers, who might be able to give me useful information about the route I was to follow. So, in the hope of picking up hints from one or the other, I listened while my visitors related their adventures, which were an inextricable mixture of legend and experience.

I could not bring myself to believe in the existence, in the north, of *gatos valentes,* 'valiant cats', the result of cross-breeding between domestic cats and jaguars. But I was told another story which is perhaps significant, at least as an indication of the style and spirit of the *sertão.*

At Barra dos Bugres, a village in the western part of the Mato Grosso, on the upper reaches of the Rio Paraguay, there lived a *curandeiro,* a healer who cured snakebites; he would begin by pricking the sick man's forearm with the teeth of a boa (a *sucuri*). Next, he would make the shape of a cross on the ground with gunpowder, and set it alight so that the sick man could put his arm into the smoke. Lastly, he would take some burnt cotton from an *artificio* (a flint-lighter in which the tinder consists of cotton waste packed into a horn receptacle) and soak it in *cachaça,* which the patient drank. This completed the operation.

One day, the leader of a *turma de poaieros* (gatherers of the medicinal plant, ipecacuanha), after witnessing the treatment, asked the healer to wait until the arrival of his men the following Sunday, since they would certainly all want to be vaccinated (for a fee of five milreis each, or five francs at the 1938 rate of exchange). The *curandeiro* agreed. On the Saturday morning a dog was heard howling outside the *barracão,* or collective hut. The leader of the *turma* sent a *camarada* to investigate: it was an angry *cascavel,* a rattlesnake. He ordered the healer to capture the reptile, but the latter refused. The leader became angry and declared that unless the snake were captured, there would be no vaccination. The healer had to comply; he stretched out his hand towards the snake, was bitten and died.

The man who told me this story explained that he had been vaccinated by the *curandeiro* and had subsequently allowed himself to be bitten by a snake in order to check the effectiveness of the treatment. It proved to be a complete success. He admitted, however, that he had chosen a non-poisonous snake.

I have transcribed this story because it illustrates so well the mixture of shrewdness and ingenuousness—in respect of tragic incidents that are treated as trivial events of everyday life—which is characteristic of the popular mentality in the inland districts of Brazil. One should not be misled by the conclusion, which is not as absurd as it appears. The narrator's reasoning was similar to the argument I was later to hear put forward by the leader of the neo-Moslem sect of the Ahmadi, during a dinner to which he had invited me at Lahore. The Ahmadi are unorthodox chiefly because of their assertion that all those individuals who throughout history have proclaimed themselves to be messiahs (and among whom they include Socrates and Buddha) really were messiahs: otherwise God would have punished them for their effrontery. Similarly, my informant in Rosario no doubt believed that, had the magic not been real, the supernatural powers set in motion by the healer would most certainly have proved him to be wrong by turning a normally harmless snake into a poisonous one. Since the treatment was looked upon as a form of magic, he had at least

checked its effectiveness experimentally, on a similarly
magic level.

I had been assured that the track leading to Utiarity held
no surprises in store for us—at least, nothing comparable to
the adventures we had met with two years previously on the
São Lourenço track. Yet, on reaching the summit of the
Serra do Tombador, at a place called Caixa Furada, 'holed
chest', a chain-wheel of the driving shaft broke. We were
about thirty kilometres from Diamantino; our drivers set off
to walk there in order to cable Cuiaba so that the new part
could be dispatched by plane from Rio and then brought to
us by lorry as soon as it had been received. If all went well,
the operation would take a week; the oxen would have
time to overtake us.

So we found ourselves camping on top of the Tombador,
a rocky spur terminating the *chapada* and overlooking the
Paraguay basin from a height of three hundred metres; on
the other side, the streams flow into the tributaries of the
Amazon. Once we had found the odd trees between which
we could sling our hammocks and mosquito nets, there was
nothing else to do in that thorny savannah but sleep, dream
and hunt. The dry season had started a month before; it
was June, and apart from a few slight showers in August,
the *chuvas de caju* (which that year failed to materialize),
there would not be a drop of rain before September. The
savannah had already taken on its winter aspect: the plants
had dried up and withered, and in places had been entirely
destroyed by bush fires, revealing broad patches of sand
under their scorched stems. This is the time when the few
animals which roam across the plateau congregate in the
capões, impenetrable thickets of trees with rounded domes
marking the presence of springs near which a few patches
of grazing land are still to be found.

During the rainy season, from October to March, when it
pours nearly every day, the temperature rises, reaching 42
or 44 degrees C. during the day; it is cooler at night and
there is a short sharp drop at dawn. On the other hand, the
dry season is characterized by extreme variations in temperature: it is not unusual to go from a maximum daily temperature of 40 degrees to a minimum night temperature of
between 8 and 10 degrees.

As we drank maté round our camp fire, we would listen
to the two brothers in our team and the drivers telling tales
of the *sertão*. They explained why the great ant-eater,

tamandua, is harmless in the *campo,* where he cannot maintain his balance in an upright position; but in the forest he
props himself against a tree with his tail and uses his fore-
paws to suffocate anyone who comes near him. Moreover
the ant-eater does not fear nocturnal attacks, 'for he sleeps
with his head tucked along his body, and even the jaguar
cannot tell where his head is'. During the rainy season, you
must always listen for the wild pigs which roam in herds of
fifty or more .The grating sound made by their jaws can be
heard several kilometres away (hence the name given to
these animals: *quiexada,* from *queixo,* 'chin'). On hearing
this sound, the hunter must take flight, because if one beast
is killed or wounded, all the others attack. He must climb
into a tree or on to a *cupim,* an ant-hill.

One man related how one night when he was travelling
with his brother, he heard someone calling. They hesitated
to give help through fear of Indians, so they waited for daylight. Meanwhile, the cries continued. When dawn came,
they found a hunter who had dropped his gun and had been
up a tree since the previous evening, surrounded by pigs.

His fate was less tragic than that of another hunter who
heard a *queixada* in the distance and took refuge on an ant-
hill. The pigs surrounded him. He fired at them until his
ammunition ran out, then defended himself with a hacking-
tool called a *facão.* The next day a search party set out to
look for him, and soon spotted his position because of the
urubus (vultures) flying overhead. On the ground, there
remained only his skull and the carcasses of the pigs.

Next came funny stories, like the one about the *seringueiro,* or rubber-hunter, who met a starving jaguar. They
chased each other round and round a clump of trees until,
through a wrong reaction on the man's part, they suddenly
found themselves face to face. Neither dared move, and the
man was even afraid to call out. 'And it was only half an
hour later that, seized with cramp, he made an involuntary
movement, bumped against the butt of his rifle, and realized
he was armed.'

Unfortunately, the place was infested with the usual insects: *maribondo,* wasps, mosquitoes, and *piums* and *bor-
rachudos,* minute bloodsucking midges which fly about in
swarms; there were also *pais-de-mel,* fathers of honey, that
is, bees. The South American species do not sting, but are
troublesome in other ways; in order to satisfy their thirst for
human sweat, they vie with each other for the most favour-

able spots, such as the corners of the lips and eyes and
inside the nostrils, where they become drunk with the secretions of their victim and will allow themselves to be crushed
rather than fly away, so that their squashed bodies act as a
lure for still more bees. This explains their nickname,
lambe-olhos, 'lick-eyes'. They are the real pest in the tropical bush, and are more bother than the infection caused by
mosquitoes and midges, to which the human body becomes
inured after a week or two.

But where there are bees there is honey, and this can be
harvested without danger, either by breaking open the holes
in which the ground species live, or by discovering honey-
combs full of spherical cells the size of eggs in some hollow
tree. All species produce honeys of different flavours—I
counted up to thirteen—but all so strong that, like the
Nambikwara, we soon learnt to dilute them with water. The
complex aromas can be broken down into their successive
effects, rather like the bouquets of Burgundies, and are
disturbingly strange; I found something comparable in a
condiment used in South-East Asia, which is extracted from
the glands of the cockroach and worth its weight in gold.
A trace is enough to flavour a dish. Very similar, too, is the
odour emitted by a certain very dark-coloured French
beetle known as *procruste chagriné.*

Eventually, the relief lorry arrived with the new part and
a mechanic to fix it. We set off once more, through Diamantino, lying half in ruins in its valley which opens in the
direction of the Rio Paraguay. Then we climbed back on to
the plateau—this time without mishap—keeping close to
the Rio Ariños which runs into the Tapajoz, a tributary of
the Amazon, and turning off in a westerly direction towards
the hilly valleys of the Sacre and the Papagaio, which also
run into the Tapajoz, over waterfalls sixty metres high. At
Paressi, we stopped to examine the weapons abandoned by
the *Beiços de Pau,* who were said to be again active in the
neighbourhood. A little further on, we spent a sleepless
night in a marshy area, because we were made uneasy by
the smoke we could see rising straight into the clear dry-
season sky from native camp fires only a few kilometres
away. We spent one more day visiting the falls and collecting information in a village of Paressi Indians. Then we
reached the Rio Papagaio, which was about a hundred
metres wide and so clear that, in spite of the depth of the
water, the rocky bed was visible. On the other side were a

dozen straw huts and adobe shacks: Utiarity telegraph station. We unloaded the lorry and carried the food and baggage across on the ferry. We took leave of the lorry-drivers. Already on the far bank we could see two naked figures: they were Nambikwara.

26. ON THE LINE

Anyone living on the Rondon line might well believe he was on the moon. Imagine an area as big as France, three-quarters of it unexplored, frequented only by small groups of native nomads who are among the most primitive to be found anywhere in the world, and traversed, from one end to the other, by a telegraph line. The roughly cleared track which runs alongside—the *picada*—provides the only land-mark over a distance of seven hundred kilometres, since, apart from some reconnoitring to the north and the south carried out by the Rondon Commission, the unknown be-gins on either side of the *picada*, that is, in those places where the track itself has not become indistinguishable from the bush. Admittedly, there is the telegraph wire, but since it became useless as soon as it was set up, it sags between posts which are not replaced when they collapse, through having been either eaten away by termites or de-stroyed by Indians, who mistake the characteristic hum of the telegraph wire for the buzzing of a hive of wild bees at work. In places the line either trails on the ground or has been carelessly hooked on to nearby shrubs. Surprisingly enough, the line adds to, rather than detracts from, the sur-rounding desolation.

Completely virgin landscapes have a monotony which de-prives their wildness of any significant value. They with-hold themselves from man; instead of challenging him, they disintegrate under his gaze. But in this scrubland, which stretches endlessly into the distance, the incision of the *picada*, the contorted silhouettes of the poles and the arcs of wire linking them one to another seem like incongruous objects floating in space, such as can be seen in Yves Tanguy's paintings. Being evidence of man's former pres-ence and of the futility of his efforts, they mark the extreme limit he has tried to exceed, making it more obvious than it would have been without them. The erratic nature of his enterprise and the failure by which it has been punished confirm the authenticity of the surrounding wilderness.

The community living along the line consisted of about a hundred people: partly Paressi Indians who had been recruited on the spot by the telegraph commission and trained by the army to maintain the line and work the apparatus (although they still continued to hunt with bows and arrows), and partly Brazilians who had been attracted to these unexplored areas by the hope of finding there an Eldorado or a new Far West. Their expectations had been disappointed: the further one travels across the plateau, the more difficult it becomes to find diamond 'forms'.

'Forms' are small stones of an unusual colour or shape which indicate the presence of diamonds, in the same way as tracks reveal the presence of animals: 'When you find them, you know there are diamonds around.' They may be *emburradas,* 'rough stones'; *pretinhas,* 'little negresses'; *amarellinhas,* 'little yellow ones'; *figados-de-gallinha,* 'chicken livers'; *sangues-de-boi,* 'ox blood'; *feijões-reluzentes,* 'shiny beans'; *dentes-de-cão,* 'dog's teeth'; *ferragens,* 'tools'; or *carbonates, lacres, friscas-de-ouro, faceiras, chiconas,* etc.

In the absence of diamonds, there is nothing to be found on these sandy wastes, which are lashed by rain for one half of the year and without a drop during the other half, except spiky, twisted shrubs; nor is there any game. The unfortunate inhabitants—left behind by one of those waves of colonization, so frequent in the history of central Brazil, and which sweep groups of adventurers or restless, poverty-stricken individuals on a great surge of enthusiasm into the interior and then immediately leave them stranded there, cut off from all contact with the civilized world—developed different forms of madness so as to adapt to their solitary existence in tiny stations, each consisting of a few straw huts and separated from each other by distances of eighty to a hundred kilometres, which can only be covered on foot.

Every morning, the line comes briefly to life: news is exchanged; such and such a station has spotted the camp fires of a group of hostile Indians who are preparing to wipe it out; at another station, two Paressi have been missing for several days, and the Nambikwara, who have a firmly established reputation all along the line, have no doubt dispatched them *na invernada do ceu,* 'to the celestial winter quarters' . . . Someone may recall with grim humour how the missionaries were murdered in 1933, or how a certain telegraph operator was found buried up to the waist, with his chest riddled with arrows and his morse-key on his head. The Indians have a kind of morbid fascination for the telegraph workers: they represent a daily hazard, exaggerated by local legend; yet at the same time visits by their small nomadic bands provide the only distraction and, what is more important, the only opportunity for human contact. When these visits occur, once or twice a year, the usual jokes are exchanged between the potential slaughterers and their possible victims, in the incredible jargon used along the line, which comprises in all some forty words, partly Nambikwara and partly Portuguese.

In the intervals of these jolly occasions, which provide a little thrill of excitement on either side, each station leader evolves his own particular style of living. There was the hot-head, whose wife and children were dying of hunger, because every time he undressed to bathe in the river, he could not resist firing five shots with his Winchester to scare off the natives he imagined to be lying in ambush along both banks all ready to slit his throat. He thus used up ammunition, which it was impossible to replace: this is called *quebrar bala,* 'breaking bullets'. Then there was the man-about-town, who had been a student in pharmacy at the time he left Rio, and still imagined himself to be engaged in supercilious back-chat along the Largo do Ouvidor: but as he no longer had anything to say, his conversation had been reduced to dumb-show, clickings of the tongue or fingers, and glances heavy with innuendo: on the silent screen he would still have been recognizable as a true son of Rio. Lastly, mention must be made of the wise man, who managed to keep his family in a state of biological balance with a herd of deer which came to drink at a nearby stream: every week he would go off and kill one animal, never more; the herd continued to survive, the station too, but for the past eight years (the lapse of time since the ox-caravans which formerly brought supplies once a year had been gradually discontinued) they had eaten nothing but venison.

The Jesuit Fathers, who had arrived a week or two before us and had just finished settling in near the Juruena station about fifty kilometres from Utiarity, added a picturesque note of a quite different nature. There were three of them: a Dutchman who prayed to God, a Brazilian who was preparing to civilize the Indians and a Hungarian, a former nobleman and an expert hunter, whose function it was to keep the mission supplied with game. Shortly after their arrival, they received a visit from the Provincial, an elderly Frenchman who rolled his 'r's and seemed to have stepped straight out of the age of Louis XIV; from the solemn way in which he talked about the 'savages'—this was the term he invariably used in referring to the Indians—he sounded as if he had just landed in Canada, along with Cartier or Champlain.

No sooner had he arrived than the Hungarian—who had apparently entered the priesthood to do penance for a wild and stormy youth—had an attack of the kind French colonials call *le coup de bambou* (tropical madness). Through the walls of the mission, he could be heard insulting his superior who, behaving more characteristically than ever, exorcized him with a great many signs of the cross and cries of 'Vade retro, Satanas!' When the devil had been finally cast out, the Hungarian was put on bread and water for a fortnight—symbolically, at least, since there was no bread at Juruena.

For different reasons, the Caduveo and the Bororo constitute what might be called, without any play on words, learned societies; with the Nambikwara, the observer is taken back to what he might easily, but wrongly, consider to be the infancy of the human species. We had set up our camp, on the outskirts of the hamlet, under a partly dismantled straw hangar which had been used for the storing of equipment when the line was being built. We were only a few yards from the native encampment, which comprised about twenty people divided into six families. This small band had arrived a few days before us, in the course of one of the expeditions of their nomadic period.

The Nambikwara year is divided into two distinct periods. During the rainy season, from October to March, each group lives on a hillock above a stream, where they build crude huts with branches or palm-fronds. They burn clearings in the gallery-forest growing in the damp valleys, and plant and cultivate gardens. They grow mainly manioc (sweet and bitter), several varieties of maize, tobacco, occasionally beans, cotton, ground-nuts and gourds. The women grate the manioc on boards into which the spikes of certain palm trees have been fitted, and, if they are dealing with the poisonous species, they squeeze out the juice by pressing the fresh pulp in a piece of twisted bark. Gardening provides enough food to last during part of their sedentary life. The Nambikwara even preserve cakes of manioc by

burying them in the ground; they dig them up, half rotten,
a few weeks or months later.

At the beginning of the dry season, they leave the village
and each group breaks up into several nomadic bands. For
seven months, these bands wander through the savannah
looking for game, especially small creatures such as larvae,
spiders, crickets, rodents, snakes and lizards, as well as
fruit, seeds, roots or wild honey; in short, anything which
will prevent them dying of hunger. Their encampments,
which they set up for one or several days, or sometimes
even for a few weeks, consist of crudely constructed shelters—one per family—made from palm-fronds or branches
stuck in the sand in a semicircle and tied together at the
top. As the day wears on, the palm-fronds are pulled out
on one side and stuck in on the other, so that the protective
screen is always angled in such a way as to keep out the
sun or, as the case may be, the wind or the rain. During
this period, the search for food is an all-absorbing activity.
The women are equipped with digging sticks, which they
use to extract roots or club small animals; the men hunt
with large palm-wood bows, and arrows of various types:
those intended for birds have blunted points to prevent
them sticking into branches; fishing arrows are longer, are
not feathered and have three or five divergent points at the
end; poisoned arrows, the tips of which are smeared with
curare and encased in bamboo sheaths, are kept for medium
game, whereas those intended for big game, such as jaguars
and tapirs, have a spear-shaped tip made from a thick piece
of bamboo—this is to cause bleeding, since the amount of
poison carried by an arrow would not be enough to kill.

After the splendour of the Bororo palaces, the bareness
of the lives led by the Nambikwara is hardly credible.
Neither sex wears any clothes, and they are different from
neighbouring tribes both in physical type and in their
rudimentary culture. The Nambikwara are small: the men
are about 1.60 metres tall and the women 1.50 metres, and
although the latter, like so many South American Indian
women, do not have a well-defined waist, their limbs are
more slender, their hands and feet tinier and their joints
smaller than is generally the case. Their skin is also darker.
Many have skin diseases which cover their bodies with
round, purplish-blue patches but, in the case of the healthy
ones, the sand in which they love to roll powders the body,
giving it a beige-coloured bloom which, on the young wom-

en especially, is extremely attractive. They have oval-shaped heads, often delicate and finely chiselled features and bright eyes. They have more body hair than most peoples of Mongolian stock; their slightly wavy hair is rarely quite black. The first visitors were struck by their physical type to the point of suggesting that it might be the result of cross-breeding with Negroes who escaped from the plantations to take refuge in the *quilombos,* or colonies of rebel slaves. But if the Nambikwara had received a dose of Negro blood at a recent period in their history, it seems impossible that they should all belong to the 'O' blood group, as I verified was the case, since this group implies, if not purely Indian origins, at least prolonged demographic isolation during several centuries. Today we are less puzzled by the physical type of the Nambikwara; it is similar to that of an ancient race with whose bone structure we are familiar and whose remains have been found in Brazil in the Lagoa Santa caves, in the State of Minas Gerais. I was astonished to see that some had the almost Caucasian faces of certain statues and bas-reliefs of the Veracruz region, which are now attributed to the most ancient civilizations of Mexico.

The similarity was all the more surprising in that the very low level of material culture of the Nambikwara, far from indicating a link with the highest forms of culture in Central or North America, made them appear rather as survivors from the Stone Age. The women's only attire was a thin string of shell beads tied round the waist, and a few others worn as necklaces or slung across one shoulder; they had ear-pendants made of mother-of-pearl or feathers, bracelets carved from the shell of the great tatu, and sometimes narrow bands made of cotton (woven by the men) or straw, tied tightly round the upper arm or ankles. Male attire was even scantier, being often no more than a straw tassel hanging from a belt above the sexual organs.

In addition to bow and arrows, their weapons included a flattened spike which seemed to be employed for magical, as well as warlike, purposes. I only saw it used to make movements intended to ward off hurricanes, or thrown in a certain direction to kill the *atasu,* the evil spirits of the bush. The natives have the same word for stars and for oxen, of which they have a great fear (whereas they are quite prepared to kill and eat mules, with which they became acquainted at the same time). My wristwatch was also an *atasu.*

All the possessions of the Nambikwara fit easily into the baskets carried by the women during the nomadic period. These baskets are made from split bamboo canes, loosely plaited in six strands (two pairs perpendicular to each other and one pair running across) forming an open, star-shaped mesh: they are slightly wider at the top and taper off at the bottom like a finger-stall. They are sometimes as much as 1.50 metres high, that is, as tall as the women who carry them on their backs. A few manioc cakes are put at the bottom and covered with leaves; on top are laid chattels and tools—gourd receptacles, knives made from sharp splinters of bamboo or from crudely carved stones or pieces of iron—obtained through barter—and fixed by means of wax and string between two wooden slats which form a handle, and drills consisting of an iron or stone borer, fitted to the end of a shaft which is rotated between the palms. The natives have metal axes and hatchets given them by the Rondon Commission, and their own stone axes are hardly used at all except as anvils for the shaping of shell or bone objects, although they continue to use grindstones and stone polishers. Pottery is unknown among the eastern groups (among whom I started my inquiry), and in other areas it exists only in crude forms. The Nambikwara are without canoes and are in the habit of swimming across rivers, sometimes using bundles of sticks as floats.

Such primitive pieces of equipment hardly deserve to be called manufactured objects. The Nambikwara hod chiefly contains raw materials, with which objects can be made as need arises: these materials comprise various kinds of wood, particularly those used for kindling fire by friction, lumps of wax or resin, skeins of vegetable fibre, animal bones, teeth and claws, scraps of fur, feathers, porcupine quills, the husks of nuts and the empty shells of freshwater crustacea, stones, cotton and seeds. When such a miscellaneous load is laid out, it discourages the collector, who feels he is dealing less with the products of human industry than with the activities of a giant race of ants, that he is observing through a magnifying-glass. And the fact is that, as they walk in single file through the high grass, with each woman weighted down by her light-coloured, wickerwork hod, as ants often are by their eggs, the Nambikwara look exactly like a column of ants.

Among the Indians of tropical America, to whom we owe

the invention of the hammock, poverty is symbolized by the non-possession of this device, or of any other form of bed or bedding. The Nambikwara sleep naked on the ground. As the nights are cold during the dry season, they keep warm by huddling together or coming close to the dying embers of the camp fires, so that when they wake up at dawn, they are sprawling in the still-warm ashes. This is why the Paressi have nicknamed them *uaikoakoré*, 'those who sleep on the bare earth'.

As I have already mentioned, the group who were our neighbours at Utiarity, then at Juruena, consisted of six families: the chief's family, which comprised his three wives and adolescent daughter; and five others, each of which consisted of a married couple and one or two children. All were interrelated, since the Nambikwara prefer to marry a niece, the daughter of a sister, or a cousin of the kind that anthropologists refer to as 'cross-cousins', that is, a daughter of the father's sister or of the mother's brother. Such cousins are called from birth by a name signifying spouse, whereas the other cousins (who are the respective offspring of two brothers or two sisters and are therefore referred to by anthropologists as 'parallel cousins') regard each other as brother and sister and cannot marry. All the natives seemed to be on very cordial terms, yet even in a small group such as this—twenty-three individuals including the children—there were difficulties. A young widower had just married a rather vain young girl, who refused to take any interest in the children he had had by his first wife, two little girls, one aged about six and the other about two or three. In spite of the kindness of the elder girl, who tried to mother her little sister, the baby was very neglected. The families took turns in looking after her, but this was a cause of irritation. The adults were keen for me to adopt her, while the children favoured another solution, which they thought tremendously funny: the little girl had only just learned to walk, so they brought her to me and, with unequivocal gesture, invited me to take her as my wife.

Another family consisted of somewhat elderly parents, who had been rejoined by their pregnant daughter after she had been deserted by her (now absent) husband. Lastly, a young married couple, whose child was still being breast fed, were subject to the taboos connected with recent parenthood: they were extremely dirty, because they were not allowed to bathe in the river, emaciated because of the prohibitions affecting most foods, and condemned to idleness, since the parents of an unweaned child cannot participate in the life of the community. Sometimes the man would go off to hunt or gather wild produce alone; the wife received her food from her husband or her parents.

Although the Nambikwara were easy-going, and unperturbed by the presence of the anthropologist with his notebook and camera, the work was complicated by linguistic difficulties. In the first place, the use of proper names is taboo; in order to identify individuals, we had to follow the custom adopted by the telegraph workers, that is, come to an agreement with the natives about arbitrary appellations such as Portuguese names—Julio, José-Maria, Luiza, etc.— or nicknames like *Lebre* (hare) or *Assucar* (sugar). There was one Indian who had been christened Cavaignac by Rondon, or one of his companions, because he had a goatee, a very rare feature among Indians, who are usually beardless.

One day, when I was playing with a group of children, a little girl who had been struck by one of her playmates took refuge by my side and, with a very mysterious air, began to whisper something in my ear. As I did not understand and was obliged to ask her to repeat it several times, her enemy realized what was going on and, obviously very angry, also came over to confide what seemed to be a solemn secret. After some hesitation and questioning, the meaning of the incident became clear. Out of revenge, the first little girl had come to tell me the name of her enemy, and the latter, on becoming aware of this, had retaliated by confiding to me the other's name. From then on, it was very easy, although rather unscrupulous, to incite the children against each other and get to know all their names. After which, having created a certain atmosphere of complicity, I had little difficulty in getting them to tell me the names of the adults. When the latter understood what our confabulations were about, the children were scolded and no more information was forthcoming.

In the second place, the Nambikwara language comprises several dialects, none of which have been studied. They are characterized by their peculiar word-endings and the use of certain verb forms. Along the line, the language of communication was a kind of pidgin, which was only useful as an introduction. So, helped by the willingness and quick-wittedness of the natives, I learned a rudimentary kind of Nambikwara. Fortunately, the language includes magic words—*kititu* in the eastern dialect, *dige, dage* or *tchore* elsewhere—which, when added to nouns, turn them into verbs that can be completed when necessary with a negative particle. This method made it possible to say everything that had to be said, although such 'basic' Nambikwara did not allow for the expression of very subtle ideas. The natives are well aware of the method, since they reverse the process when they try to speak Portuguese; 'ear' and 'eye' mean respectively to hear—or understand—and to see, and they convey the opposite ideas by saying, *orelha acabô* or *ôlho acabô*, 'ear or eye I finish . . .'

The sound of Nambikwara speech tends to be muted, as if the language were aspirated or whispered. The women like to emphasize this characteristic by distorting certain words (thus *kititu* is prononced by them *kediutsu*); by articulating indistinctly, they produce a kind of mumbling reminiscent of children's speech. Their pronunciation is marked by an affectation and preciosity of which they are perfectly aware; when I failed to understand them and asked them to repeat what they had said, they would deliberately exaggerate their manner of speaking. If I became disheartened and gave up, they would all laugh and joke together: they had got the better of me.

I was soon to realize that, in addition to the verbal suffix, Nambikwara uses a dozen others, which divide beings and things into as many categories: human hair, animal hair and feathers; pointed objects and orifices; elongated objects, either rigid or pliable; fruit, seeds and rounded objects; things which hang or quiver; swollen shapes, or shapes full of liquid; tree-barks, skins and other coverings, etc. This feature suggests a comparison with a linguistic family found in Central America and the north-west part of South America, Chibcha, the language of a great civilization which once flourished in what is now Columbia and which was an intermediate form between the civilizations of Mexico and Peru; Nambikwara could perhaps be a southern offshoot of Chibcha.* This is a further reason for mistrusting appearances. In spite of the bareness of their lives, it is unlikely that natives who resemble the earliest Mexicans in physical type and whose language structure is

---

* But, in fact, this kind of division of beings and things exists in many other American languages, and the link with Chibcha seems less convincing to me now than it did in the past.

reminiscent of that of the Chibcha kingdom should be true primitives. Their past history, of which we know nothing as yet, and the harshness of their present geographical environment, may perhaps one day make it possible to explain their lot as that of prodigal sons to whom history has so far denied the fatted calf.

27. FAMILY LIFE

The Nambikwara wake up at dawn, stir the fire, warm themselves as best they can after the long cold night, then eat a light meal of food left over from the previous evening. A little later, the men go off hunting, either in groups or singly. The women remain in the camp to attend to the cooking. They take their first bath when the sun has begun to rise in the sky. The women and children often like to frolic together in the water, and sometimes they light a fire and crouch in front of it afterwards to get warm, humorously exaggerating the natural tendency to shiver. Bathing also takes place at other times during the day. The usual occupations vary very little. The preparation of food is the activity requiring most time and care: manioc has to be grated and pressed, then the pulp dried and cooked; or *cumaru* nuts, which are used to give a bitter almond flavour to most dishes, have to be hulled and boiled. When the need arises, the women and children go off to pick or gather wild produce. When food supplies are ample, the women engage in spinning, either in a squatting position or kneeling with their buttocks resting on their heels. Or they may carve, polish and thread beads made from nut shells or empty fish shells, or they may make ear-pendants and other adornments. And if they become bored with work, they delouse each other, laze about or sleep.

During the hottest part of the day, the camp is quiet; the inhabitants, asleep or silent, enjoy the precarious shade afforded by their shelters. The rest of the time they chat together as they pursue their tasks. Almost always merry and gay, they make jokes or sometimes obscene or scatological remarks, which are greeted by great guffaws of laughter. Work is often interrupted by visits or questions; should two dogs or pet birds begin to copulate, everyone stops to gaze at the operation with rapt attention. Then work is resumed after the important event has been commented on.

The children laze about for most of the day; occasionally the little girls help the older women with certain tasks, while

the small boys remain idle or fish along the banks of
streams. The men who have stayed behind in the encampment spend their time doing basketwork, or making arrows
and musical instruments, and sometimes helping with the
domestic chores. Harmony usually reigns within each family
group. At about three or four o'clock, the other men return
from hunting, the atmosphere becomes more lively, the conversations grow more animated and groups other than family units are formed. Manioc cakes or any other foodstuffs
that have been found during the day are consumed. At
nightfall, one or two women, whose turn it is to undertake
this duty go off into the nearby scrub to gather or fell a
supply of wood for the night. They can just be made out
as they return in the waning light, stumbling under their
burdens which strain the headbands supporting the baskets.
In order to unload, they crouch down and lean back slightly
so that the bamboo basket rests on the ground in such a
way that they can slip the band from their forehead.

The branches are piled up in one corner of the camp and
everybody helps himself according to his needs. Family
groups gather round their respective fires, which are beginning to glow. The evening is spent in talking, or in singing
and dancing. Sometimes these entertainments go on until
the early hours, but usually, after a certain amount of
mutual caressing and friendly sparring, the married couples
draw more closely together, mothers clasp their sleeping
children to them, everything becomes quiet, and the chilly
stillness of the night is broken only by the crackling of a
log, the light step of someone replenishing a fire, the barking of a dog or the crying of a child.

The Nambikwara do not have many children: as I was
to observe subsequently, childless couples are not infre-
quent; one or two children seem to be the normal number
and it is rare to find more than three in one family. Sexual
intercourse is forbidden between parents until the youngest
child is weaned, that is until about its third year. The mother carries her child astride her thigh and supported by a
broad strap made of bark or cotton; it would be impossible
for her to carry a second child in addition to her basket.
The demands of their nomadic existence and the meagre
resources of their environment force the natives to be extremely careful; if necessary, the women do not hesitate to
use mechanical means or medicinal plants to cause abortion.

Nevertheless, the natives feel, and show, very great affection towards their children, and the affection is reciprocated. Yet these feelings are sometimes concealed by fits of irritability and moodiness to which they are also prone. A little boy was suffering from indigestion; he had a headache and was sick and spent his time either moaning or sleeping. No one paid the slightest attention to him and he was left alone for a whole day. When evening came, his mother went up to him, deloused him gently while he was still asleep, signed to the others to keep back and made him a sort of cradle in her arms.

On another occasion, a young mother was playing with her baby by giving him gentle slaps on the back; the baby started to laugh and the mother became so caught up in the game that she struck him harder and harder until he began to cry. Whereupon she stopped and consoled him.

I once saw the little orphan I have already referred to literally trampled underfoot during a dance; in the general excitement she had fallen down without anyone noticing.

When thwarted, children often hit their mothers and the latter do not protest. Children are never punished, and I never saw anyone beat a child or even make as if to do so, except in fun. Sometimes a child cries because it has hurt itself, because it has had a quarrel or is hungry, or because it does not want to be deloused. But the last instance is unusual; delousing seems to delight the patient as much as it amuses the operator. Also, it is taken as an indication of interest or affection. When a child or a husband wants to be deloused, he lays his head on the woman's knees, turning it first to one side then to the other. The operation is conducted by making several partings, or by holding the strands of hair up to the light. The louse is no sooner caught than it is gobbled up. A child who cries is consoled by a member of his family or by an older child.

So, mother and child together provide a gay and charming picture. The mother will hand the child an object through the straw wall of their shelter, then take it back just when the child thinks he is about to catch it: 'Take it from the front! Take it from behind!' Or she picks up the child, and with shrieks of laughter pretends she is about to throw him to the ground: 'Amdam nom tebu!' ('I am going to throw you down!'). 'Nihui!' replies the baby in a shrill voice: 'Don't!'

The children respond by surrounding their mother with

an anxious and demanding affection; they see to it that she
receives her share of the outcome of the hunt. The child
lives close to his mother during his early years. When they
are on the move, she carries him until he can walk; later he
walks along beside her. He stays with her in the camp or
village while the father is away hunting. After a few years,
however, a distinction has to be made between the sexes. A
father shows more interest in his son than in his daughter,
since he must teach him masculine skills; and the same is
true of the relationship between mother and daughter. But
in his dealings with his children, the father shows the same
tender concern that I have already mentioned. The father
carries his child on his shoulders and makes him weapons
suitable for his tiny arms.

It is the father, too, who tells his children about the traditional myths, transposing the stories as he goes along into
a style that the little ones can understand: 'Everybody was
dead! Nobody was left! Not a single man! Nothing!' Such
is the beginning of the children's version of the South
American story of the Flood which destroyed the first race
of men.

In the case of a polygamous marriage, special relationships exist between the children of the first wife and their
young stepmothers. The latter live with all the little girls in
a spirit of comradeship, so that the group, however limited,
can be defined as a society of little girls and young women
who bathe in the river together, go off collectively into the
bushes in order to relieve nature, smoke and joke together,
and indulge in pastimes in doubtful taste, such as spitting
great jets of saliva in turn into each other's faces. Such
relationships, being close-knit, and much prized, although
not distinguished by politeness, are similar to those which
may exist in our society between young boys. Although they
rarely involve reciprocal help and care, they have the rather
curious effect of making the little girls become independent
more quickly than the boys. The girls follow the young
women and take part in their activities, whereas the boys
are left to their own devices and tentatively try to form
similar groups, but without much success; during their early
years at least, they tend to stay at their mother's side.

Games are unknown to Nambikwara children. Sometimes they make objects from rolled or plaited straw, but
their only form of amusement consists in wrestling matches,
or playing tricks on each other, and their life is an imitation

of adult behaviour. The little girls learn to spin, laze about, laugh and sleep; the little boys begin later (between eight and ten) to shoot with small bows and to be introduced to men's work. But both boys and girls very quickly become aware of the fundamental, and at times tragic, problem of the Nambikwara, which is the search for food, and of the active part that they are expected to play. They help enthusiastically in picking-and-gathering expeditions. In times of scarcity, it is a not uncommon sight to see them looking for their food around the encampment, struggling to dig up roots, or tiptoeing through the grass holding large branches —stripped of their leaves—with which to kill grasshoppers. The little girls know the part that women have to play in the economic life of the tribe and are eager to prove themselves worthy of it.

I once met a little girl tenderly carrying a puppy in the bark carrying-strap that her mother used for her little sister. 'Are you stroking your baby dog?' I asked her. She solemnly replied, 'When I am big, I will kill wild pigs and monkeys; I will club them all to death when he barks!'

Incidentally, she made a grammatical mistake, which her father laughingly pointed out: she should have said *tilondage,* the feminine form of 'when I am big', whereas she used the masculine form, *ihondage.* The mistake is interesting, in that it shows a feminine desire to raise the economic occupations peculiar to women to the same level as those activities which are a masculine prerogative. Since the precise meaning of the verb used by the little girl is 'to kill by felling with a club or stick' (in this case, a digging stick), she seemed to be trying unconsciously to identify female picking and gathering (which includes the catching of small animals) with the male hunt, in which bows and arrows are the weapons used.

Special mention must be made of the relationships between children belonging to the category of cousins required to address each other as 'spouse'. Sometimes they behave like real married couples, and leave the family fire in the evening to take half-burned logs off into some corner of the encampment, where they light their own fire. After which, they settle down for the night and, in so far as their capacities allow, indulge in the same amorous play as their elders, who look on with amusement.

While I am on the subject of children, I must say a word or two about the domestic animals which live in close as-

sociation with them and which are themselves treated like
children: they share the family meals and are shown the
same marks of affection or concern—delousing, games, conversation and caresses—as humans. The Nambikwara have
many kinds of domestic animals: dogs, in the first place,
then cocks and hens, which are descended from those introduced into the area by the Rondon Commission; monkeys, parrots, birds of various species, and occasionally pigs
and wild cats or coati. Only dogs seem to have a utilitarian
function, since they accompany the women when the latter
go hunting with sticks; men never use them when hunting
with bows and arrows. The other animals are reared purely
as pets. They are not eaten, nor incidentally are the hens'
eggs which, in any case, are laid in the scrub. But if a young
bird dies while the natives are attempting to tame it, they
will devour it without compunction.

When they are on the move, the entire menagerie, apart
from the animals capable of walking, is carried along with
the rest of the belongings. The monkeys cling to the wom-
en's hair and crown them with a charming live helmet,
terminating in the tail which is wound round the bearer's
neck. Parrots and hens perch along the top of the baskets,
and other animals are carried. None are given a copious
supply of food, but each gets its share, even in times of
scarcity. In turn, they provide the group with a source of
entertainment and amusement.

Let us now turn to the adults. The Nambikwara's attitude towards love can be summed up in their expression,
tamindige mondage, the literal, though not very elegant,
translation of which is, 'Making love is nice.' I have already
noted the erotic atmosphere which pervades their daily life.
In all matters concerning love the natives show the highest
degree of interest and curiosity; they are eager to talk about
such subjects and their conversation in the encampment is
full of allusions and innuendoes. Sexual intercourse usually
takes place at night, sometimes near the camp fires, but
more often than not the couple concerned withdraws a
hundred yards or so into the nearby scrub. Their absence is
noticed at once and arouses general merriment; comments
and jokes are exchanged and even the young children share
in the excitement, being fully acquainted with its cause.
Sometimes a small group of men, young women and children follow the couple and watch the various stages of the
operation through the undergrowth, whispering to each

other and trying to stifle their laughter. The two persons concerned take a poor view of this behaviour, but their best course is to resign themselves to it, as well as to all the teasing and jeers which are in store for them on their return to the camp. Sometimes, a second couple follows the example of the first and seeks the solitude of the bush.

However, such occurrences are rare and the restrictive taboos which make them so afford only a partial explanation of the fact. The real cause would seem rather to lie in the native temperament. During the amorous fondling in which couples indulge so freely and so publicly, and which is often quite uninhibited, I never once noticed even an incipient erection. The pleasure aimed at would seem to relate less to physical satisfaction than to love-play and demonstrations of affection. This perhaps explains why the Nambikwara do not wear the penis sheath, which is common to almost all the communities of central Brazil. Indeed, the purpose of this accessory may be, if not to prevent an erection, at least to indicate that the wearer is not sexually aggressive. People who live in a state of complete nudity are not unaware of what we call modesty: they define it differently. Among the Indians of Brazil, as in certain regions of Melanesia, the distinction between modesty and immodesty does not depend on different degrees of bodily exposure but on the difference between quiescence and excitement.

However, these fine gradations could lead to misunderstandings between the Indians and ourselves, for which neither we nor they were to blame. It was difficult, for instance, to remain indifferent to the sight of one or more pretty girls sprawling stark naked in the sand and laughing mockingly as they wriggled at my feet. When I went bathing in the river, I was often embarrassed by a concerted attack on the part of half-a-dozen or so females—young or old—whose one idea was to appropriate my soap, of which they were extremely fond. They would take liberties of this kind in all the circumstances of daily life; not infrequently I had to make do with a hammock stained red by a native girl who had taken her siesta in it, after painting herself with urucu; and when I was sitting on the ground working, surrounded by a circle of informants, I would sometimes feel a hand tugging at my shirt-tails: some woman had decided that it was easier to blow her nose on my garment than to go and pick up a small branch and fold it pincer-wise for this purpose, as was the usual practice.

In order fully to understand the attitude of the two sexes towards each other, it is essential to bear in mind the fundamental nature of the husband-and-wife relationship in Nambikwara society: the married couple is the essential economic and psychological unit. Among these nomadic groups, which are constantly banding together and disbanding, it is the married couple which appears (in theory at least) to be the stable reality, and which ensures subsistence. Nambikwara economy has two aspects: hunting and gardening, which is done by the men, and collecting and gathering, which is the concern of the women. While the male group is away hunting all day with bows and arrows, or is busy gardening during the rainy season, the women, armed with their digging sticks, wander across the savannah with the children, gathering, uprooting, clubbing, capturing or seizing anything they come across that can be used as food: seeds, fruit, berries, roots, tubers, eggs and small animals of every kind. At the end of the day, husband and wife come together again around the fire. When the manioc is ripe and while there is still a supply, the man brings back a load of roots, which the woman grates and kneads into flat cakes, and if the hunt has been successful, the pieces of game are quickly cooked under the red-hot ashes of the family fire. But during seven months of the year, manioc is scarce; as for hunting, it is largely a matter of luck in these sandy wastes, where animals are few and far between and hardly ever leave the thickets and grazing grounds near streams or water-holes, which are scattered over vast tracts of semi-desert scrub. It follows that the family has to rely mainly on female gathering and collecting.

I have often shared these appallingly frugal meals which, during half the year, represent the Nambikwara's only hope of survival. When the man returns to the encampment silent and tired and throws down beside him the bow and arrows he has been unable to use, the woman produces a touching collection of odds and ends from her basket: a few orange-coloured *buriti* fruits, two fat poisonous spiders, tiny lizards' eggs, one or two lizards, a bat, small *bacaiuva* or *uaguassu* palm nuts and a handful of grasshoppers. The soft fruit is crushed by hand in a gourd filled with water, the nuts are broken with stones and the animals and larvae are thrust under the hot ash; then they cheerfully gobble up a meal which would hardly allay the hunger of one white man but in their case provides sustenance for a whole family.

The Nambikwara have only one word for 'pretty' and 'young', and another for 'ugly' and 'old'. Their aesthetic judgments are thus based essentially on human, and especially sexual, values. But the interest the two sexes show in each other is complex in character. The men see the women as a whole as being slightly different from themselves; they display desire, admiration or tenderness towards them, as the case may be; the very ambiguity of the terms I have just mentioned is in itself a kind of homage. Yet, although the sexual division of labour assigns an essential role to the women (since the family's food supply to a very large extent depends on female gathering and collecting), their occupations are looked upon as an inferior form of activity; the ideal form of life is considered to be agriculture or hunting: the thought of an ample supply of manioc and large pieces of meat is a dream which is constantly cherished but seldom realized. Provender haphazardly collected is looked upon as the normal wretched fare—and wretched it is. In Nambikwara folklore, the expression 'to eat grasshoppers', insects which are gathered by women and children, is the equivalent of the French expression *'manger de la vache enragée'* (to starve). Similarly, a woman is regarded as a dear, precious but second-class possession. Among the men it is the done thing to talk about women with kindly commiseration and to address them with slightly mocking forbearance. The men can often be heard making remarks such as, 'The children do not know, but I know, the women do not know,' and they refer to the group of *doçu* (women) and their typical jokes and conversations with affectionate condescension. But that is only a social attitude. Once the man is alone again with his wife by the camp fire, he will listen to her complaints, note her requests and ask for her help in any number of different tasks; masculine boastfulness is replaced by co-operation between two partners who realize how vitally important they are to each other.

This ambiguity in the attitude of the men towards the women has an exact counterpart in the equally ambivalent behaviour of the women as a group. They think of themselves as a collective entity and show this in various ways; we have already seen that they speak differently from the men. This is chiefly true of young women who have not yet had children, and of concubines. In the case of mothers and old women the difference is much less marked, although they too at times may show it. Also, the young women enjoy the company of children and adolescents, and play and joke with them; and it is the women who look after the animals in that very humane way typical of certain South American Indians. All this helps to ensure that, within the group, the women live in a special atmosphere, which is at once child-like, gay, affected and flirtatious; the men share in this atmosphere when they come back from hunting or gardening.

But the women display quite a different attitude when they have to cope with their own particular forms of activity. Seated back to back in a circle in the silent encampment, they work at their arts and crafts with skill and patience. When they move from place to place, they march sturdily along under the heavy basket holding the provisions and belongings of the whole family as well as the bundle of arrows, while the husband strides on ahead with a bow and one or two arrows, the wooden spear or the digging stick, and keeps a look-out for any animal on the run, or for fruit-bearing trees. The women will walk for miles, with their backs entirely covered by the narrow, inverted bell of the basket and with the bark carrying-strap passed around their foreheads; they have a characteristic gait: thighs pressed close together, knees touching, ankles well apart and feet turned inwards; they rest their weight on the outside edge of the foot and shake their hips as they forge ahead, active, strong-minded and gay.

The contrast between psychological attitudes and economic tasks is transposed on to the philosophical and religious plane. For the Nambikwara the relationships between men and women are connected with the two poles around which their existence is organized: the sedentary agricultural life based on the twofold male activity of hut-building and gardening, and the nomadic period during which food is chiefly supplied by female gathering and collecting—the first representing security and gastronomic well-being, the second uncertainty and famine. The Nambikwara react very differently to these two seasonal modes of existence. They speak of the summer period with the melancholy that normally goes with the conscious and uncomplaining acceptance of the human lot and the dreary repetition of identical actions, whereas they describe the winter period with the excitement and enthusiasm of a new discovery.

Yet, their metaphysical conceptions reverse these relationships. After death, the souls of men are embodied in jaguars; but those of women and children are carried up into the air where they vanish for ever. This distinction explains why women are excluded from the most sacred ceremonies; these occur at the beginning of the agricultural period and consist in the making of bamboo pipes, which are 'fed' with offerings and played by the men far enough away from the shelters to be out of the women's sight.

Although it was not the season for these ceremonies, I was very anxious to hear the flutes and to acquire one or two specimens. In response to my request, a group of men set off on an expedition to the distant forest where the large bamboo canes are to be found. Three or four days later, I was awakened in the middle of the night; the travellers had waited until the women were asleep. They took me to a hiding-place in the bushes a hundred yards or so away from the camp, and set about making, then playing, the pipes. Four players performed in unison, but since the instruments did not sound exactly alike, they produced an impression of uncertain harmony. The melody was different from the Nambikwara songs I was used to and which, in their robust structure and their intervals, were reminiscent of French country rounds; it was also different from the shrill calls sounded on the three-holed, nasal ocarinas made of two pieces of gourd joined together with wax. The tunes played on the pipes, which comprised only a few notes, were characterized by chromatic effects and rhythmic variations which seemed to me to have a striking similarity with certain passages of the *Sacre,* especially the woodwind modulations in the section entitled 'Action rituelle des ancêtres' (Ritual action of the ancestors). Had any curious or imprudent woman ventured into our midst, she would have been beaten with clubs. As with the Bororo, a veritable metaphysical curse hangs over the female part of the population: but unlike their Bororo sisters, Nambikwara women do not enjoy a special legal status (although it would seem that among the Nambikwara, too, descent is through the female line). In so loosely organized a society, such tendencies exist only in an implicit form, and the synthesis has to be deduced from vague and subtle patterns of behaviour.

With almost the same tenderness as that with which they caress their wives, the men describe the kind of life characterized by the temporary shelter and the permanent basket, a life during which the most incongruous means of survival are each day avidly dug up, gathered and captured, and in which they are exposed to wind, cold and rain, and which leaves behind no more trace than do the souls of the women on whose activity it essentially depends, once those souls have been dispersed by winds and storms. And they have quite a different conception of their sedentary life (the specific and ancient character of which is nevertheless proved by the original species they cultivate), on which the unchanging sequence of agricultural operations confers the same durable quality as that possessed by the reincarnated masculine souls, the stable rainy season dwelling, and the plantation which will once more spring to life and yield crops 'when the death of the previous cultivator has been forgotten'.

Have we to see a parallel here with the extraordinarily unstable temperaments of the Nambikwara, who can quickly switch from friendliness to hostility? The rare observers who have been in contact with them have all been struck by this feature. The Utiarity group was the one which, five years before, had killed the missionaries. My male informants described the attack with a certain self-satisfaction, and each boasted of having delivered the most efficient blows. To tell the truth, I could not hold this against them. I have known a great many missionaries, and I have admired the human and scientific abilities of several. But the American Protestant missions which were trying to penetrate the central Mato Grosso around 1930 were of a peculiar kind: their members came from Nebraska or Dakota farming families, in which young people were brought up to believe in the reality of Hell with cauldrons of boiling oil. For some, becoming a missionary was like taking out an insurance policy. Once they were certain of their own salvation, they thought there was nothing more they need do to prove themselves worthy of it, so that in the practice of their profession they displayed shocking callousness and lack of feeling.

I wondered how the incident which had sparked off the massacre had occurred. I saw a possible explanation when I myself made a blunder which might have cost me dear. The Nambikwara have a certain knowledge of poisons.

They make curare for their arrows from an infusion of the red outer skin of the root of certain *strychnos,* reducing it over a fire until the mixture reaches a sticky consistency; they also use other vegetable poisons, which each individual carries with him in powder form in quill or bamboo tubes, wound round with cotton thread or bark. These poisons are used as a means of revenge in disputes connected with barter or sex: I shall discuss them again later.

Apart from these scientifically effective poisons, which they prepare openly without any of the magical precautions and complications which surround the making of curare a little further north, the Nambikwara have other, more mysterious poisons. In tubes identical to those containing the true poisons, they keep particles of resin exuded by a tree of the *bombax* species, the trunk of which is swollen in the middle; they believe that by throwing a particle of this resin on to an opponent, they will cause a physical condition similar to that of the tree—in other words, that the victim will swell up and die. The Nambikwara have only one word, *nandé,* which they use both for true poisons and for magical substances. Consequently, the term has a wider range of meanings than our word poison. It denotes any kind of threatening action, as well as products or objects likely to be used in such actions.

These preliminary explanations are necessary for the understanding of the rest of my story. I had brought with me a few of the multi-coloured balloons made of tissue-paper, which are filled with hot air by means of a little torch fixed underneath, and which the Brazilians release in their hundreds on Midsummer's Day. One evening I had the unfortunate idea of showing the Indians how they worked. The first balloon caught fire on the ground, and this caused great hilarity, as if the natives had some idea of what ought to have happened. The second, however, succeeded only too well: it rose quickly into the air, reached such a height that its flame merged with the stars, drifted about above us for a long time and then disappeared. But the initial mirth had given way to other emotions; the men watched intently and angrily, while the women hid their faces in the crook of their arms and huddled against each other in fear. The word *nandé* kept recurring over and over again. The next morning, a delegation of men came to me and asked to inspect the supply of balloons in order to see 'if there were not some *nandé* in them'. They carried out an extremely thorough examination. At the same time, thanks to the fact that the Nambikwara have a remarkably realistic approach (in spite of what I have just said), they understood, or at least accepted, my demonstration—made with the help of little bits of paper released over a fire—of the way hot air rises. As was usual when it was necessary to find an excuse for some incident, they put all the blame on the women, who 'never understand anything', 'took fright' and had foreseen untold calamities.

I was under no illusion; the episode might well have ended in disaster. Yet this particular incident, and others that I shall describe later, in no way impaired the friendship which was an inevitable result of a long and close association with the Nambikwara. I was therefore greatly distressed to read recently, in a book by a foreign colleague, a description of his encounter with the group of natives whose life I had shared at Utiarity, ten years before he visited them. When he went to Utiarity in 1949, two missions were in operation: the Jesuits of whom I have spoken and an American Protestant mission. The native group had been reduced to eighteen individuals, whom he describes as follows:

Of all the Indians which I have visited in Mato Grosso the members of this band of Nambicuara were the most miserable. Of the eight men, one had syphilis, another had some kind of infection in his side, another had an injured foot, another was covered with some kind of scaly disease from head to foot, and another was deaf and dumb. The women and children, however, appeared to be healthy. Owing to the fact that they use no hammocks but sleep on the ground, they are always covered with dirt. On cold nights they remove the fires and sleep in the warm ashes . . . [They] wear clothes only when they are given by the missionaries, who ask that they be worn. Their distaste for bathing permits not only a covering of dust and ashes to accumulate on their skin and hair but also particles of decayed meat and fish, which, combined with stale sweat, makes proximity to them rather distasteful. They also appear to be heavily infected with internal parasites, for their stomachs are distended and they are continually passing wind. On several occasions when a number of them had crowded into the small room we used for working we had to cease work in order to air the room . . .

The Nambicuara . . . are surly and impolite even to rudeness. On many occasions when I went to visit Julio at his camp he was lying down near a fire, and as he saw me approach he turned his back to me saying that he did not wish to talk. The missionaries informed me that a Nambicuara will ask for some object several times and if it is not given to him he will try to take it. In order to keep the Indians out, they would sometimes close the screen door, but if a Nambicuara really wanted to enter he would tear a hole in the screen and walk in . . .

One does not have to remain long among the Nambicuara in order to feel this underlying hatred, mistrust and despair, which create in the observer a feeling of depression not unmixed with sympathy.*

But I, who knew them when they had already been decimated by the diseases introduced by the white man but when no one had tried—at least not since Rondon's humane attempts—to bring them into subjection, I would like to forget this harrowing description and retain only the memory of an experience I recorded one night in my notebook by the light of my pocket-torch:

On the dark savannah, the camp fires sparkle. Near their warmth, which offers the only protection against the growing chill of the night; behind the frail screens of palm-fronds and branches, hurriedly set up on the side from which rain and wind are expected; next to the baskets filled with the pathetic possessions which constitute the community's earthly wealth; lying on the bare ground which stretches away in all directions and is haunted by other equally hostile and apprehensive bands, husbands and wives, closely intertwined, are aware of being each other's support and comfort, and the only help against day-to-day difficulties and that brooding melancholy which settles from time to time on the souls of the Nambikwara. The visitor camping with the Indians in the bush for the first time, is filled

---

* K. Oberg, *Indian Tribes of Northern Mato Grosso, Brazil* (Smithsonian Institution, Institute of Social Anthropology, Publ. No. 15, Washington, 1953), pp. 84–5.

with anguish and pity at the sight of human beings so
totally bereft; some relentless cataclysm seems to have
crushed them against the ground in a hostile land,
leaving them naked and shivering by their flickering
fires. He gropes his way through the scrub, taking
care not to knock against the hands, arms or chests
that he glimpses as warm reflections in the glow of the
flames. But the wretchedness is shot through with
whisperings and chuckles. The couples embrace as if
seeking to recapture a lost unity, and their caresses
continue uninterrupted as he goes by. He can sense in
all of them an immense kindness, a profoundly care-
free attitude, a naïve and charming animal satisfaction
and—binding these various feelings together—something which might be called the most truthful and moving expression of human love.

28. A WRITING LESSON

I was keen to find out, at least indirectly, the approximate size of the Nambikwara population. In 1915, Rondon had suggested a figure of twenty thousand, which was probably too high an estimate; but at that time, each group comprised several hundred members, and, according to information I had picked up along the line, there had since been a rapid decline. Thirty years ago, the known faction of the Sabané group comprised more than a thousand individuals; when the group visited the telegraph station at Campos Novos in 1928, a hundred and twenty-seven men were counted in addition to women and children. However, in 1929 an influenza epidemic broke out when the group was camping in a locality known as Espirro. The illness developed into a form of pulmonary oedema and, within forty-eight hours, three hundred natives had died. The group broke up, leaving the sick and the dying behind. Of the thousand Sabané who were once known to exist, there remained in 1938 only nineteen men with their women and children. These figures are perhaps to be explained, not only by the epidemic, but also by the fact that, a few years before, the Sabané had started a war against some of their eastern neighbours. But a large group, which had settled not far from Tres Buritis, was wiped out by a flu epidemic in 1927, with the exception of six or seven individuals, of whom only three were still alive in 1938. The Tarundé group, which was once one of the largest, numbered only twelve men (plus the women and children) in 1936; of these twelve men four survived in 1939.

Now, there were perhaps no more than two thousand natives scattered across the area. A systematic census was out of the question, because of the permanent hostility shown by certain groups and the fact that all groups were on the move during the nomadic period. But I tried to persuade my Utiarity friends to take me to their village, after organizing some kind of meeting there with other groups to whom they were related either by kinship or marriage;

331

in this way I would be able to gauge the size of a contemporary gathering and compare it in this respect with those previously observed. I promised to bring presents and to engage in barter. The chief of the group was rather reluctant to comply with my request: he was not sure of his guests, and if my companions and myself were to disappear in an area where no white men had set foot since the murder of the seven telegraph employees in 1925, the precarious peace which had prevailed since then might well be endangered for some time to come.

He finally agreed on condition that we reduced the size of our expedition, taking only four oxen to carry the presents. Even so, it would be impossible to follow the usual tracks along the valley bottoms where the vegetation was too dense for the animals to get through. We would have to go across the plateaux following a route specially worked out for the occasion.

In retrospect, this journey, which was an extremely hazardous one, seems to me now to have been like some grotesque interlude. We had hardly left Juruena when my Brazilian companion noticed that the women and children were not with us: we were accompanied only by the men, armed with bows and arrows. In travel books, such circumstances mean that an attack is imminent. So we moved ahead with mixed feelings, checking the position of our Smith-and-Wesson revolvers (our men pronounced the name as "Cemite Vechetone') and our rifles from time to time. Our fears proved groundless: about midday we caught up with the rest of the group, whom the chief had taken the precaution of sending off the previous evening, knowing that our mules would advance more quickly than the basket-carrying women, whose pace was further slowed down by the children.

A little later, however, the Indians lost their way: the new route was not as straightforward as they had imagined. Towards evening we had to stop in the bush; we had been told that there would be game to shoot; the natives were relying on our rifles and had brought nothing with them; we only had emergency provisions, which could not possibly be shared out among everybody. A herd of deer grazing around a water-hole fled at our approach. The next morning, there was widespread discontent, openly directed against the chief who was held responsible for a plan he and I had devised together. Instead of setting out on a hunting or collecting expedition, all the natives decided to lie down under the shelters, leaving the chief to discover the solution to the problem. He disappeared along with one of his wives; towards evening we saw them both return, their heavy baskets full of the grasshoppers they had spent the entire day collecting. Although crushed grasshopper is considered rather poor fare, the natives all ate heartily and recovered their spirits. We set off again the following morning.

At last we reached the appointed meeting-place. It was a sandy terrace overlooking a stream lined with trees, between which lay half-hidden native gardens. Groups arrived intermittently. Towards evening, there were seventy-five persons representing seventeen families, all grouped together under thirteen shelters hardly more substantial than those to be found in native camps. It was explained to me that, during the rainy season, all these people would be housed in five round huts built to last for some months. Several of the natives appeared never to have seen a white man before and their surly attitude and the chief's edginess suggested that he had persuaded them to come rather against their will. We did not feel safe, nor did the Indians. The night promised to be cold, and as there were no trees on the terrace, we had to lie down like the Nambikwara on the bare earth. Nobody slept: the hours were spent keeping a close but polite watch on each other.

It would have been unwise to prolong such a dangerous situation, so I urged the chief to proceed without further delay to the exchange of gifts. It was at this point that there occurred an extraordinary incident that I can only explain by going back a little. It is unnecessary to point out that the Nambikwara have no written language, but they do not know how to draw either, apart from making a few dotted lines or zigzags on their gourds. Nevertheless, as I had done among the Caduveo, I handed out sheets of paper and pencils. At first they did nothing with them, then one day I saw that they were all busy drawing wavy, horizontal lines. I wondered what they were trying to do, then it was suddenly borne upon me that they were writing or, to be more accurate, were trying to use their pencils in the same way as I did mine, which was the only way they could conceive of, because I had not yet tried to amuse them with my drawings. The majority did this and no more, but the chief had further ambitions. No doubt he was the only one who had grasped the purpose of writing. So he asked me for a writing-pad, and when we both had one, and were working together, if I asked for information on a given point, he did not supply it verbally but drew wavy lines on his paper and presented them to me, as if I could read his reply. He was half taken in by his own make-believe; each time he completed a line, he examined it anxiously as if expecting the meaning to leap from the page, and the same look of disappointment came over his face. But he never admitted this, and there was a tacit understanding between us to the effect that his unintelligible scribbling had a meaning which I pretended to decipher; his verbal commentary followed almost at once, relieving me of the need to ask for explanations.

As soon as he had got the company together, he took from a basket a piece of paper covered with wavy lines and made a show of reading it, pretending to hesitate as he checked on it the list of objects I was to give in exchange for the presents offered me: so-and-so was to have a chopper in exchange for a bow and arrows, someone else beads in exchange for his necklaces . . . This farce went on for two hours. Was he perhaps hoping to delude himself? More probably he wanted to astonish his companions, to convince them that he was acting as an intermediary agent for the exchange of the goods, that he was in alliance with the white man and shared his secrets. We were eager to be off, since the most dangerous point would obviously be reached when all the marvels I had brought had been transferred to native hands. So I did not try to explore the matter further, and we began the return journey with the Indians still acting as our guides.

The abortive meeting and the piece of humbug of which I had unwittingly been the cause had created an atmosphere of irritation; to make matters worse, my mule had ulcers in its mouth which were causing it pain. It either rushed impatiently ahead or came to a sudden stop; the two of us fell out. Suddenly, before I realized what was happening, I found myself alone in the bush, with no idea which way to go.

Travel books tell us that the thing to do is attract the attention of the main party by firing a shot. I got down from my mount and fired. No response. At the second shot I seemed to hear a reply. I fired a third, the only effect of which was to frighten the mule; it trotted off and stopped some distance away.

I systematically divested myself of my weapons and photographic equipment and laid them all at the foot of a tree, carefully noting its position. Then I ran off to recapture my mule, which I had glimpsed in the distance, seemingly in docile mood. It waited till I got near, then fled just as I was about to seize the reins, repeating this little game several times and leading me further and further on. In despair I took a leap and hung on to its tail with both hands. Surprised at this unwonted procedure, it made no further attempt to escape from me. I climbed back into the saddle and tried to return to collect my equipment, but we had wandered round so much that I was unable to find it.

Disheartened by the loss, I then decided to try and rejoin the caravan. Neither the mule nor I knew which way it had gone. Either I would decide on one direction which the mule was reluctant to follow, or I would let it have its head, and it would start going round in circles. The sun was sinking towards the horizon, I had lost my weapons and at any moment I expected to be pierced by a shower of arrows. I might not be the first person to have entered that hostile area, but my predecessors had not returned, and, irrespective of myself, my mule would be a most desirable prey for people whose food supplies were scanty. While turning these sombre thoughts over and over in my mind, I waited for the sun to set, my plan being to start a bush fire, since at least I had some matches. Just when I was about to do this, I heard voices: two Nambikwara had turned back as soon as my absence was noticed and had been following my trail since midday; for them, finding my equipment was child's play. They led me back through the darkness to the encampment, where the others were waiting.

Being still perturbed by this stupid incident, I slept badly and whiled away the sleepless hours by thinking over the episode of the exchange of gifts. Writing had, on that occasion, made its appearance among the Nambikwara but not, as one might have imagined, as a result of long and laborious training. It had been borrowed as a symbol, and for a sociological rather than an intellectual purpose, while its reality remained unknown. It had not been a question of acquiring knowledge, of remembering or understanding, but rather of increasing the authority and prestige of one in-

dividual—or function—at the expense of others. A native
still living in the Stone Age had guessed that this great
means towards understanding, even if he was unable to
understand it, could be made to serve other purposes. After
all, for thousands of years, writing has existed as an institution—and such is still the case today in a large part of the
world—in societies the majority of whose members have
never learnt to handle it. The inhabitants of the villages I
stayed in in the Chittagong hills in eastern Pakistan were
illiterate, but each village had its scribe who acted on behalf of individuals or of the community as a whole. All the
villagers know about writing, and make use of it if the need
arises, but they do so from the outside, as if it were a
foreign mediatory agent that they communicate with by
oral methods. The scribe is rarely a functionary or em-
ployee of the group: his knowledge is accompanied by
power, with the result that the same individual is often
both scribe and money-lender; not just because he needs to
be able to read and write to carry on his business, but because he thus happens to be, on two different counts, someone who *has a hold* over others.

Writing is a strange invention. One might suppose that
its emergence could not fail to bring about profound
changes in the conditions of human existence, and that
these transformations must of necessity be of an intellectual
nature. The possession of writing vastly increases man's
ability to preserve knowledge. It can be thought of as an
artificial memory, the development of which ought to lead
to a clearer awareness of the past, and hence to a greater
ability to organize both the present and the future. After
eliminating all other criteria which have been put forward
to distinguish between barbarism and civilization, it is
tempting to retain this one at least: there are peoples with,
or without, writing; the former are able to store up their
past achievements and to move with ever-increasing rapidity
towards the goal they have set themselves, whereas the latter, being incapable of remembering the past beyond the
narrow margin of individual memory, seem bound to remain imprisoned in a fluctuating history which will always
lack both a beginning and any lasting awareness of an aim.

Yet nothing we know about writing and the part it has
played in man's evolution justifies this view. One of the
most creative periods in the history of mankind occurred
during the early stages of the neolithic age, which was re-

sponsible for agriculture, the domestication of animals and various arts and crafts. This stage could only have been reached if, for thousands of years, small communities had been observing, experimenting and handing on their findings. This great development was carried out with an accuracy and a continuity which are proved by its success, although writing was still unknown at the time. If writing was invented between 4000 and 3000 B.C., it must be looked upon as an already remote (and no doubt indirect) result of the neolithic revolution, but certainly not as the necessary precondition for it. If we ask ourselves what great innovation writing was linked to, there is little we can suggest on the technical level, apart from architecture. But Egyptian and Sumerian architecture was not superior to the achievements of certain American peoples who knew nothing of writing in the pre-Columbian period. Conversely, from the invention of writing right up to the birth of modern science, the world lived through some five thousand years when knowledge fluctuated more than it increased. It has often been pointed out that the way of life of a Greek or Roman citizen was not so very different from that of an eighteenth-century middle-class European. During the neolithic age, mankind made gigantic strides without the help of writing; with writing, the historic civilizations of the West stagnated for a long time. It would no doubt be difficult to imagine the expansion of science in the nineteenth and twentieth centuries without writing. But, although a necessary precondition, it is certainly not enough to explain the expansion.

To establish a correlation between the emergence of writing and certain characteristic features of civilization, we must look in a quite different direction. The only phenomenon with which writing has always been concomitant is the creation of cities and empires, that is the integration of large numbers of individuals into a political system, and their grading into castes or classes. Such, at any rate, is the typical pattern of development to be observed from Egypt to China, at the time when writing first emerged: it seems to have favoured the exploitation of human beings rather than their enlightenment. This exploitation, which made it possible to assemble thousands of workers and force them to carry out exhausting tasks, is a much more likely explanation of the birth of architecture than the direct link referred to above. My hypothesis, if correct, would oblige us to recognize the fact that the primary function of written communication is to facilitate slavery. The use of writing for disinterested purposes, and as a souce of intellectual and aesthetic pleasure, is a secondary result, and more often than not it may even be turned into a means of strengthening, justifying or concealing the other.

There are, nevertheless, exceptions to the rule: there were native empires in Africa which grouped together several hundreds of thousands of subjects; millions lived under the Inca empire in pre-Columbian America. But in both continents such attempts at empire building did not produce lasting results. We know that the Inca empire was established around the twelfth century: Pizarro's soldiers would not have conquered it so easily, three centuries later, had they not found it in a state of advanced decay. Although we know little about ancient African history, we can sense that the situation must have been similar: great political groupings came into being and then vanished again within the space of a few decades. It is possible, then, that these examples confirm the hypothesis, instead of contradicting it. Although writing may not have been enough to consolidate knowledge, it was perhaps indispensable for the strengthening of dominion. If we look at the situation nearer home, we see that the systematic development of compulsory education in the European countries goes hand in hand with the extension of military service and proletarianization. The fight against illiteracy is therefore connected with an increase in governmental authority over the citizens. Everyone must be able to read, so that the government can say: Ignorance of the law is no excuse.

The process has moved from the national to the international level, thanks to a kind of complicity that has grown up between newly created states—which find themselves facing problems which we had to cope with a hundred or two hundred years ago—and an international society of privileged countries worried by the possibility of its stability being threatened by the reactions of peoples insufficiently trained in the use of the written word to think in slogans that can be modified at will or to be an easy prey to suggestion. Through gaining access to the knowledge stored in libraries, these peoples have also become vulnerable to the still greater proportion of lies propagated in printed documents. No doubt, there can be no turning back now. But in my Nambikwara village, the insubordinate characters were the most sensible. The villagers who withdrew their allegiance to their chief after he had tried to exploit a feature of civilization (after my visit he was abandoned by most of his people) felt in some obscure way that writing and deceit had penetrated simultaneously into their midst. They went off into a more remote area of the bush to allow themselves a period of respite. Yet at the same time I could not help admiring their chief's genius in instantly recognizing that writing could increase his authority, thus grasping the basis of the institution without knowing how to use it. At the same time, the episode drew my attention to another aspect of Nambikwara life: the political relationships between individuals and groups. I was soon to be able to observe them more directly.

While we were still at Utiarity, an epidemic of putrid ophthalmia had broken out among the natives. The infection, which was gonorrheal in origin, spread to the whole community, causing terrible pain and temporary blindness which could become permanent. For several days the group was completely paralysed. The natives treated the infection with water in which a certain kind of bark had been allowed to soak and which they injected into the eye by means of a leaf rolled into a cornet shape. The disease spread to our group: the first person to catch it was my wife who had taken part in all my expeditions so far, her speciality being the study of material culture and skills; the infection was so serious that she had to be evacuated. Then it affected most of the men, as well as my Brazilian companion. Soon the expedition was brought to a halt; I left the main body to rest, with our doctor to give them such treatment as they needed, and with two men and a few beasts I headed for Campos Novos, near which post several bands of natives had been reported. I spent a fortnight there in semi-idleness, gathering barely ripe fruit in an orchard which had reverted to the wild state: there were guavas, the bitter taste and gritty texture of which always fall far short of their aroma, and caju, as brilliantly coloured as parrots, which contain an acid and strongly flavoured juice in the spongy cells of their coarse pulp. To get meat for our meals we had only to go a few hundred metres from the camp at dawn to a copse regularly visited by woodpigeons, which were easy to shoot. It was at Campos Novos that I met with two groups, whom the expectation of my presents had lured down from the north.

These two groups were as ill-disposed towards each other
as they both were towards me. From the start, they did not
so much ask for my presents as demand to be given them.
During the first few days, only one group was present, as
well as a native from Utiarity who had gone on ahead of
me. I think perhaps he was showing too great an interest in
a young woman belonging to his hosts' group since relations
between the strangers and their visitor became strained almost at once and he started coming to my encampment in
search of a more friendly atmosphere; he also shared my
meals. This fact was noticed and one day while he was out
hunting I received a visit from four natives forming a kind
of delegation. In threatening tones, they urged me to put
poison in my guest's food; they had, in fact, brought the
necessary preparation along with them, a grey powder
packed in four little tubes tied together with thread. It was
a very awkward situation: if I refused outright, I might
well be attacked by the group, whose hostile intentions
called for a prudent response. I therefore thought it better
to exaggerate my ignorance of the language, and I pretended to understand nothing at all. After several attempts,
during which I was told over and over again that my pro-
tégé was *kakoré,* that is, very wicked, and should be got rid
of as soon as possible, the delegation withdrew with many
expressions of displeasure. I warned the interested party,
who at once disappeared; I did not see him again until I
returned to the area several months later.

Fortunately, the second group arrived the next day, thus
providing the first with a different object on which to vent
their animosity. The meeting took place at my encampment which was both neutral territory and the goal of these
various journeyings. Consequently, I had a good view of the
proceedings. The men had come alone, and almost immediately a lengthy conversation began between their respective chiefs. It might be more accurately termed a series of
alternating monologues, uttered in plaintive, nasal tones
which I had never heard before. 'We are extremely annoyed. You are our enemies!' moaned one group, whereupon the others replied more or less, 'We are not annoyed.
We are your brothers. We are friends—friends! We can get
along together! etc'. Once this exchange of provocations and
protestations was over, a communal camp was set up next
to mine. After a few songs and dances, during which each
group ran down its own performance by comparing it with

that of its opponents ('The Taimaindé are good singers! We are poor singers!'), the quarrel was resumed, and before long the tension heightened. The night had only just begun when the mixture of songs and arguments produced a most extraordinary din, the meaning of which I failed to grasp. Threatening gestures were made, and sometimes scuffles broke out, and other natives intervened as peacemakers. All the threatening gestures centred round the sexual organs. A Nambikwara Indian expresses dislike by grasping his penis in both hands and pointing it towards his opponent. This gesture is followed by an assault on that person, the aim being to pull off the tuft of *buriti* straw attached to the front of the belt above the genitals. These 'are hidden by the straw', and 'the object of the fight is to pull off the straw.' The action is purely symbolical, because the genital covering of the male is made of such flimsy material and is so insubstantial that it neither affords protection nor conceals the organs. Attempts are also made to seize the opponent's bow and arrows and to put them beyond his reach. Throughout these actions, the natives remain extremely tense, as if they were in a state of violent and pent-up anger. The scuffles may sometimes degenerate into a free-for-all, but on this occasion the fighting subsided at dawn. Still in the same state of visible irritation and with gestures that were anything but gentle, the two sets of opponents then set about examining each other, fingering their ear-pendants, cotton bracelets and little feather ornaments, and muttering a series of rapid comments, such as 'Give it . . . give it . . . see, that's pretty,' while the owner would protest, 'It's ugly . . . old, . . . damaged!'

This 'reconciliatory inspection' marked the end of the quarrel, and initiated another kind of relationship between the groups: commercial exchanges. Rudimentary the material culture of the Nambikwara may be, but the crafts and produce of each group are highly prized by the others. The eastern Nambikwara need pottery and seeds; those from the north consider that their more southerly neighbours make particularly delicate necklaces. It follows that when a meeting between two groups is conducted peacefully, it leads to a reciprocal exchange of gifts; strife is replaced by barter.

Actually, it was difficult to believe that an exchange of gifts was in progress; the morning after the quarrel, each man went about his usual business and the objects or pro-

duce were passed from one to another without the giver
calling attention to the fact that he was handing over a gift,
and without the receiver paying any heed to his new acquisition. The items thus exchanged included raw cotton
and balls of thread; lumps of wax or resin; urucu paste;
shells, ear-drops, bracelets and necklaces; tobacco, and
seeds, feathers and bamboo laths to be made into arrow
heads; bundles of palm fibres, porcupine quills; whole pots
or fragments of pottery and gourds. This mysterious exchange of goods went on for half a day, after which the
groups took leave of each other and went their separate
ways.

The Nambikwara rely, then, on the generosity of the
other side. It simply does not occur to them to evaluate,
argue, bargain, demand or take back. I offered a native a
machete as payment for taking a message to a neighbouring
group. On his return, I omitted to hand over the agreed reward immediately, thinking that he would come to fetch
it. He did not do so, and the next day I could not find him;
he had departed in a rage, so his companions told me, and
I never saw him again. I had to ask another native to accept the present on his behalf. This being so, it is hardly
surprising that, when the exchanges are over, one group
should go off dissatisfied with its share, and (taking stock
of its acquisitions and remembering its own gifts) should
build up feelings of resentment which become increasingly
aggressive. Very often these feelings are enough to start a
war; of course, there are other causes, such as the need to
commit, or avenge, a murder or the kidnapping of a woman; however, it does not seem that a group feels collectively
bound to exact reprisals for some injury done to one of its
members. Nevertheless, because of the hostility between the
groups, such pretexts are often willingly accepted, especially if a particular group feels itself to be strong. The proposal is presented by a warrior who expounds his grievances
in the same tone and style as is used for the inter-group
speeches: 'Hallo! Come here! Come along! I am angry! very
angry! arrows! his arrows!'

Clad in special finery, consisting of tufts of *buriti* straw
daubed with red and helmets made from jaguar hides, the
men assemble under the leadership of their chief and dance.
A divinatory rite has to be performed: the chief, or the
shaman in those groups which have one, hides an arrow
somewhere in the bush. A search is made for it the follow-

ing day. If it is stained with blood, war is decided upon; if not, the idea is dropped. Many expeditions begun in this way come to an end after a few kilometres' march. The excitement and enthusiasm abate, and the warriors return home. But some expeditions are carried through and may result in bloodshed. The Nambikwara attack at dawn and arrange their ambush by posting themselves at intervals in the bush. The signal for the attack is passed from man to man by means of the whistle which each carries slung around his neck. This consists of two bamboo tubes bound together with thread, and its sound approximates to the cricket's chirp; no doubt this is why its name is the same as that of the insect. The war arrows are identical to those normally used for hunting large animals, except that their spear-shaped tip is given a serrated edge. Arrows dipped in curare poison, which are commonly employed for hunting, are never used, because an opponent hit by one would be able to remove it before the poison had time to spread through his body.

29. MEN, WOMEN AND CHIEFS

In 1938, the post of Vilhena, which lies on the highest point of the plateau beyond Campos Novos, consisted of a few huts in the middle of an open space a few hundred metres square, which had been intended, by the builders of the railway line, as the site of the future Chicago of the Mato Grosso. I understand that it is now a military airfield; in my time, the population was composed of only two families, who had received no supplies for eight years and who, as I have already explained, had managed to maintain themselves in a state of biological balance with a herd of deer, which provided them with a carefully husbanded supply of meat.

At Vilhena, I made the acquaintance of two new native groups, one of which comprised eighteen people, who spoke a dialect akin to those with which I was beginning to be familiar, whereas the other, which had a total of thirty-four members, used an unknown language that I was unable subsequently to identify. Each group was led by a chief; in the first group his function seemed to be purely secular, whereas the leader of the larger group eventually turned out to be some kind of shaman. His group was called Sabané; the others were known as Tarundé.

Apart from the difference of speech, it was impossible to distinguish one group from the other: they were alike both in appearance and culture. That had already been the case with the Campos Novos Indians, but the two Vilhena groups, instead of displaying hostility to each other, were on friendly terms. Although they had separate camp fires, they travelled together, camped side by side and seemed to have thrown in their lot with each other. It was a surprising association, given the fact that the two groups did not speak the same language and the chiefs could only communicate with each other through the one or two individuals in each group who acted as interpreters.

Their coming together must have been quite recent. I have already explained that, between 1907 and 1930, the

epidemics brought in by white men had decimated the Indian population. As a result, several groups were so reduced
in numbers that it was becoming impossible for them to
pursue an independent existence. At Campos Novos, I had
been able to observe the antagonisms within Nambikwara
society and had seen the disruptive forces at work. At Vilhena, on the contrary, I was able to witness an attempt at
reconstruction. There could be no doubt that the natives
with whom I was camping had worked out a plan. All the
adult males in either group addressed the women in the
other group as 'sisters', and the women used the term
'brothers' in speaking to the men in the opposite group.
The men in both groups, in speaking to each other, used a
form of address which, in their respective languages, means
'cross-cousin' and corresponds to the relationship through
marriage that we would translate as 'brother-in-law'. Given
the rules governing marriage among the Nambikwara, the
modes of address meant that all the children in either
group were 'potential spouses' of the children of the other
group. It followed that as a result of inter-marriage, the
two groups could be expected to have merged by the next
generation.

But there were still obstacles in the way of this great
plan. A third group, hostile to the Tarundé, was moving
around in the area; on certain days their camp fires were
visible and the Tarundé were prepared for any eventuality.
As I had a little knowledge of the Tarundé dialect, but not
of the Sabané one, I felt closer to the first group; the other
group, with whom I could not communicate, was also more
suspicious of me. I am therefore not in a position to explain
its point of view. All I can say is that the Tarundé were not
absolutely sure that their friends had agreed without reservations to the principle of union. They were afraid of the
third group, but still more so of the possibility that the
Sabané might suddenly decide to change sides.

It was not long before a curious incident was to show
how well founded were their fears. One day when the men
went hunting, the Sabané chief did not come back at the
usual time. No one had seen him during the day. Night
fell, and at about nine or ten o'clock in the evening the
whole camp was in a state of consternation, particularly the
family of the missing man, whose two wives and child were
huddled together in a close embrace and weeping in advance for the death of their husband and father. At that

point, I decided to take a few natives and make an exploratory tour of the vicinity. Before we had gone even two hundred metres, we discovered the lost chief crouching on the ground and shivering in the darkness; he was completely naked, that is, he had neither necklaces, bracelets, earrings nor belt, and by the light of my torch, we could catch a glimpse of his tragic expression and drawn features. He let himself be helped back to the camp, where he sat down without uttering a word and in a most convincing attitude of dejection.

His account of what had happened was extorted from him by an anxious audience. He explained that he had been carried off by the thunder, which the Nambikwara call *amon* (there had been a storm—heralding the beginning of the rainy season—that same day); the thunder had borne him through the air to a point which he named, twenty-five kilometres away from the encampment (Rio Ananaz), had stripped him of all his adornments, then brought him back in the same way and set him down at the spot where we had found him. The incident was discussed until everybody fell asleep, and the following morning the Sabané chief had recovered not only his usual good humour but also all his adornments too: no one showed any surprise at this, and he offered no explanation. During the next few days, a very different version of the episode began to be repeated among the Tarundé. They maintained that the chief, under pretence of communing with the other world, had begun negotiations with the group of Indians who were camping in the neighbourhood. These insinuations never came to a head, and the official version of the affair was openly accepted. But, in private conversation, the Tarundé chief made no secret of his anxiety. As the two groups left us shortly afterwards, I never heard the end of the story.

This incident, together with my previous observations, prompted me to reflect on the nature of the Nambikwara groups and the political influence that the chiefs were able to exert within them. There can be no more fragile and ephemeral social structure than the Nambikwara group. If the chief appears too demanding, if he claims too many women for himself or if he is incapable of providing a satisfactory solution to the food problem in times of scarcity, discontent becomes manifest. Individuals or whole families will leave the group and go off to join some other with a better reputation. This second group may have a more abundant supply of food through the discovery of new hunting or collecting grounds, or it may have acquired ornaments and instruments by means of commercial exchanges with neighbouring groups, or it may have become more powerful as a result of some victorious expedition. A day will come when the chief finds himself leading a group which is too depleted to cope with the difficulties of everyday life or to protect his women from covetous strangers. This being so, he has no option but to give up his chieftainship and, along with his remaining companions, to amalgamate with some more fortunate community. It is obvious, then, that the social structure of the Nambikwara is quite fluid. The group forms and falls apart, increases or disappears. Within the space of a few months, it can undergo changes in composition, size and distribution which make it unrecognizable. Political intrigues inside the same group and clashes between neighbouring groups superimpose their pattern on these variations, and the ascendancy and downfall of both individuals and groups follow each other in an often surprising way.

What, then, are the principles governing the division into groups? From the economic point of view, the scarcity of natural resources and the large area needed for the feeding of one individual during the nomadic period make the division into small groups almost obligatory. The problem is not why the division occurs, but how. In the initial community, there are men who are recognized as leaders: it is they who form the nuclei around which the groups assemble. The size of the group and its greater or lesser degree of stability during a given period are proportionate to the ability of the particular chief to maintain his rank and improve his position. Political power does not appear to result from the needs of the community; it is the group rather which owes its form, size and even origin to the potential chief who was there before it came into being.

I was well acquainted with two such chiefs: the one at Utiarity, whose group was called Wakletoçu, and the Tarundé chief. The first was remarkably intelligent, conscious of his responsibilities, energetic and ingenious. He anticipated the consequences of any new situation and planned an itinerary specially suited to my needs, explaining it, when necessary, by drawing a map in the sand. When we arrived at his village, we found that, without my having asked him, he had sent a working party on ahead to set up tethering posts for the animals.

He was a most useful informant, since he understood the problems, saw the difficulties and showed an interest in the work. However, his duties took up a good deal of his time; for days on end he would be away hunting, or checking on the state of seed-bearing trees or those with ripe fruit. Frequently too, his wives would invite him to join in amorous play and he would readily respond.

Generally speaking, he displayed a capacity for logical thinking and a continuity of purpose which were quite exceptional in a Nambikwara, since these Indians are often changeable and capricious. In spite of precarious living conditions, and with the pathetically inadequate means at his disposal, he showed himself to be an efficient organizer, capable of assuming sole responsibility for the welfare of his group, whom he led competently, although in a somewhat calculating way.

The Tarundé chief, who was the same age—about thirty —was just as intelligent, but in a different way. The Wakletoçu chief struck me as being a shrewd, very resourceful individual, who was always planning some political move. The Tarundé Indian was not a man of action, but rather a contemplative person with a charming and poetic turn of mind and great sensitivity. He was aware of the decadent state into which his people had fallen, and this realization gave a melancholy tone to his remarks: 'I used to do the same, but now all that is over . . .' he would say, referring to happier days when his group, far from being reduced to a handful of individuals unable to keep up their customs, had comprised several hundred members who were faithful observers of all the traditions of Nambikwara culture. His curiosity about European customs and about those of other tribes I had been able to study was in no way inferior to my own. Anthropological research carried out with him was never one-sided: he looked upon it as an exchange of information and he was always keen to hear anything I had to tell him. Frequently, he would even ask me for drawings of feather ornaments, head-dresses or weapons that I had seen among neighbouring or distant tribes, and these he carefully preserved. Perhaps he hoped to use the information to improve the material equipment and intellectual level of his own group. However, his dreamy temperament was hardly conducive to practical achievement. Yet one day, when I was trying to check the area of distribution of the Pan-pipes and I asked him about them, he replied that he had never seen any but would like to have a drawing. With the help of my sketch, he succeeded in making a crude but playable instrument.

The exceptional qualities shown by these two chiefs were connected with the circumstances in which they had achieved their positions.

In Nambikwara society, political power is not hereditary. When a chief grows old or falls ill and feels that he is no longer capable of carrying out his arduous duties, he himself chooses his successor: 'This man will be chief . . .' However, this autocratic decision is more apparent than real. I shall explain later how weak the chief's authority really is; in this instance, as in all others, the final choice appears to be preceded by a sounding of public opinion: the appointed heir is also the person most favoured by the majority. But the choice of the new chief is limited not only by the positive or negative wishes of the group; the individual concerned must also be prepared to fit in with the arrangement. It is not unusual for the offer of authority to be rejected with a vehement refusal: 'I do not want to be chief.' When this happens, a second choice has to be made. Actually, there does not seem to be any great competition for power, and the chiefs I knew were more inclined to complain about their heavy duties and many responsibilities than to regard them as a source of pride. This being so, we may well ask what privileges the chief enjoys and what are his obligations.

Around 1560, at Rouen, Montaigne met three Brazilian Indians who had been brought back by a navigator, and he asked one of them what privileges the chief (he used the term 'king') enjoyed in his country; the native, who was himself a chief, replied that 'it was to march foremost in any charge of warre'. Montaigne tells the story in a famous chapter of his *Essays,* and expresses astonishment at this proud definition. For me, it was an even greater cause of astonishment and admiration to be given exactly the same reply four centuries later. Such constancy in political philosophy is not displayed by civilized countries! Striking as the definition may be, it is less significant than the Nambikwara word for chief: *Uilikandé* would seem to mean 'he who unites' or 'he who joins together'. The etymology suggests that the native mind is aware of the phenomenon I have already emphasized, namely that the chief is seen as the cause of the group's desire to exist as a group, and not as the result of the need for a central authority felt by some already established group.

Personal prestige and the ability to inspire confidence are the basis of power in Nambikwara society. Both are indispensable for the man who has to act as guide during the hazardous nomadic period of the dry season. For six or seven months, the chief is entirely responsible for the leadership of his group. It is he who organizes the departure, chooses the routes, decides on the camping places and the duration of each camp. He takes the decisions about all hunting, fishing, gathering and collecting expeditions, and he determines the group's policy towards neighbouring communities. When the chief of a group is also a village chief (the term 'village' being taken in the restricted sense of semi-permanent quarters for the rainy season), his obligations extend even further. He fixes the time and place for the sedentary period; he superintends the gardening and decides which plants are to be grown; and, more generally, he relates the group's various activities to its needs and the seasonal possibilities.

It should immediately be noted that the chief, in carrying out these numerous functions, has no clearly defined powers and does not enjoy any publicly recognized authority. Power derives from consent, and it depends on consent to maintain its legitimacy. Any reprehensible behaviour (reprehensible, that is, from the native point of view) or demonstrations of ill-will on the part of one or two malcontents can jeopardize the chief's plans and the well-being of his little community. Should this happen, the chief has no powers of coercion. He can get rid of undesirable elements only if he succeeds in getting everyone else to share his point of view. He must therefore display the skill of a politician trying to maintain an uncertain majority rather than the authority of an all-powerful ruler. Nor is it enough for him to preserve the unity of his group. Although it may live in virtual isolation during the nomadic period, it is not unaware of the existence of other communities. The chief must not only do his job well; he must try—and his group expects this—to do better than the other chiefs.

In fulfilling these obligations, his primary and principal instrument of power lies in his generosity. Generosity is an essential attribute of power among most primitive peoples, particularly in America; it plays a part, even in those rudimentary cultures where the only possessions are crude objects. Although the chief does not seem to be in a privileged position as regards material belongings, he must have at his disposal a surplus of food, tools, weapons and ornaments which, however small, may nevertheless be of considerable value in view of the general poverty. When an individual, a family or the group as a whole feel a desire or a need for something, they turn to the chief. It follows that generosity is the main quality expected of a new chief. This is the note which is constantly struck, and the degree of consent is determined by its harmonious or discordant resonance. There can be no doubt that, in this respect, the chief's capacities are exploited to the utmost. Group chiefs were my best informants and, realizing the difficulties of their position, I was keen to reward them generously. But I rarely saw any of my gifts remain with them for more than a day or two. By the time I took leave of a group, after living with it for a few weeks, its members had become the proud possessors of axes, knives, beads, etc. Yet, as a general rule, the chief remained just as poor as he had been when I arrived. Everything he had been given (and this amounted to considerably more than the average presents made to each individual) had already been extorted from him. This collective greed often drives the chief into a kind of despair. When this happens, his refusal to give is more or less tantamount, in the primitive democracy of the Indians, to the demand for a vote of confidence in a modern parliament. When a chief gets to the point of saying: 'I am not giving anything more! I am not going to be generous any more! Let someone else be generous instead of me!' he must indeed be sure of his power, since his reign is going through the gravest possible kind of crisis.

Ingenuity is the intellectual form of generosity. A good chief displays initiative and skill. It is his business to prepare the poison for the arrows and to make the ball of wild rubber which is used in the games that the Indians sometimes play. The chief must be a good singer and dancer, a jolly person always ready to entertain the group and break the monotony of everyday life. Such functions lead naturally in the direction of shamanism, and some chiefs are also, in fact, healers and medicine-men. However, among the Nambikwara, such mystic preoccupations always remain in

the background, and when magic skills are practised, they
are never more than secondary attributes of chieftainship.
More often than not, temporal power and spiritual power
are shared between two individuals. In this respect, the
Nambikwara differ from their north-westerly neighbours,
the Tupi-Kawahib, whose chiefs are also shamans, given to
premonitory dreams, visions, trances and mediumship.

Although directed towards more positive ends, the skill
and ingenuity of the Nambikwara chief are nonetheless
remarkable. He must have a thorough knowledge of the territory frequented by his group and by neighbouring groups;
he has to be familiar with the hunting grounds and with
the copses where the wild fruit trees grow; he must know,
in each case, which is the best time to go there, and he must
have some idea of the routes taken by neighbouring groups,
whether friendly or hostile. He is always away reconnoitring or exploring and he seems to hover around his
group rather than lead it.

Apart from one or two men who have no real authority,
but are ready to collaborate if suitably rewarded, the group
appears extraordinarily passive in comparison with its dynamic leader. It is as if the group, having yielded certain
advantages to the chief, expects him to take complete
charge of its interests and security.

This attitude is well illustrated by the episode I have already described; when we lost our way and found ourselves
with inadequate provisions, the natives, instead of setting
off on a hunting expedition, settled down to rest, leaving
the chief and his wives to cope with the situation.

I have referred to the chief's wives on several occasions.
Polygamy, which is a privilege practically confined to him,
represents a moral and emotional compensation for his
many obligations, while at the same time affording him a
means of fulfilling them. With few exceptions, only the
chief and the shaman (that is, when the two functions are
shared between different individuals) are allowed several
wives. But the polygamy is of a rather special kind. Instead
of plural marriage, in the exact sense of the term, it has to
be seen rather as monogamous marriage accompanied by
relationships of a different kind. The first wife plays the
same part as the one wife in ordinary marriages. She be-
haves in accordance with the customary division of labour
between the sexes, looks after the children, does the cooking and collects wild produce. Subsequent unions, although

recognized as marriages, are however of a different kind. The secondary wives belong to a younger generation. The first wife addresses them as 'daughters' or 'nieces'. Nor do they obey the rules concerning the sexual division of labour, but take part in both masculine and feminine occupations. At the encampment, they undertake no domestic chores and laze about, either playing with the children—who belong in fact to the same generation as themselves—or caressing their husband, while the first wife busies herself around the fire and attends to the cooking. But when the chief goes off hunting or exploring, or embarks on some other masculine activity, the secondary wives accompany him and give him both moral and physical support. These rather tomboyish girls, who are chosen from among the prettiest and healthiest in the group, behave more like mistresses than wives. Their relationship with the chief is characterized by a kind of amorous comradeship, which is in striking contrast to the conjugal atmosphere of the first union.

Although men and women do not bathe at the same time, a husband and his polygamous wives can sometimes be seen bathing together, an occasion which gives rise to lively sport, pranks and endless jokes. In the evening, he plays with them, either amorously, two, three or four of them rolling closely intertwined with him in the sand, or in a childish manner. For instance, the Wakletoçu chief and his two youngest wives would lie on their backs on the ground so as to form a three-pronged star, and then would lift their legs in the air and rhythmically knock the soles of their feet together.

The polygamous union is, then, a pluralist form of amorous comradeship superimposed on monogamous marriage, and at the same time it is an attribute of authority serving a functional purpose, both psychologically and economically. The women are usually on very good terms with each other, and although the fate of the first wife may seem hard at times—since she carries on working to the sound of laughter coming from her husband and his young mistresses, and may even have to witness more intimate expressions of endearment—she shows no bitterness. The different female roles are not allotted in any permanent or hard-and-fast way, and on occasions the husband and the first wife may have fun together, although more rarely; she is in no sense excluded from the jollities of life. Moreover, her lesser participation in amorous games is counterbalanced by greater respectability and a certain authority over her young companions.

This polygamous system has serious effects on the life of the group. By periodically removing young women from the regular marriage cycle, the chief destroys the balance between the number of boys and girls of marriageable age. The young men are the main victims of this situation, and some of them are doomed either to remain bachelors for several years or to marry widows or old women cast off by their husbands.

The Nambikwara also solve the problem in another way —by homosexual relationships, for which they have the poetic term, *tamindige kihandige*, that is, *l'amour-mensonge*, 'lying love'. Such relationships are frequent between young men and take place far more publicly than normal relationships. The two partners do not withdraw into the bush like adults of opposite sexes. They settle down near the camp fire, while their neighbours look on with amusement. Such incidents are a source of jokes, which generally remain discreet; homosexual relationships are considered to be childish pastimes and little attention is paid to them. It remains an open question whether the partners achieve complete satisfaction or restrict themselves to sentimental demonstrations, accompanied by caresses, similar to the demonstrations and caresses characteristic of conjugal relationships.

Homosexual relationships are only allowed between adolescents who are 'cross-cousins', that is, who would normally marry each other's sisters, so that the brother is acting as a temporary substitute for the girl. When the natives are asked about relationships of this kind, they invariably reply: 'They are cousins [or brothers-in-law] making love.' On reaching adulthood, the brothers-in-law continue to express their feelings quite openly. It is not uncommon to see two or three men, who are both husbands and fathers, walking together in the evening with their arms affectionately around each other.

Whatever the exact truth about these substitute solutions, the privilege of polygamy, which makes them necessary, represents an important concession made by the group to the chief. From his point of view, he has the satisfaction, which (for reasons I have already explained) is not so much physical as sentimental, of enjoying access to young and pretty girls. But the main point is that polygamous marriage with its particular characteristics is the means by which the group helps the chief to fulfil his duties. If he were alone, it would be difficult for him to do more than anyone else. His secondary wives, whose peculiar status relieves them of the obligations of their sex, bring him help and comfort. They are, at one and the same time, the reward of power and its instrument. It may be wondered whether, from the native point of view, the price is worth paying. To answer this question, we must look at the problem from a more general angle and ask ourselves what the Nambikwara group, considered as an elementary social structure, can teach us about the origins and functions of power.

There is a first point that can be rapidly disposed of. The Nambikwara data, taken in conjunction with other evidence, contradicts the old sociological theory, temporarily revived by psychoanalysis, according to which the prototype of the primitive chief was a symbolic father, so that the elementary forms of the state were a development of the family. We have seen that, underlying the most rudimentary forms of power, there is an essential feature which is something new in comparison with biological phenomena: this new element is *consent*. Power both originates in consent and is bounded by it. Apparently unilateral relationships, such as those characteristic of gerontocracy, autocracy or any other form of government, can arise in groups with an already complex structure. They are out of the question in simple forms of social organization, such as the one I have tried to describe here. In such cases, on the contrary, political relationships boil down to a kind of arbitration between, on the one hand, the ability and authority of the chief and, on the other, the size, cohesion and goodwill of the group; these various factors exert a reciprocal influence on each other.

It would be gratifying to be able to show the considerable support given in this respect by contemporary anthropology to the theories put forward by eighteenth-century thinkers. It is true that Rousseau's analysis differs from the quasi-contractual relationships which exist between the chief and his fellow-members of the group. Rousseau was thinking of a quite different phenomenon, namely the renunciation by individuals of their particular independence in the interests of the general will. Nevertheless, it remains

true that Rousseau and his contemporaries displayed profound sociological intuition in grasping the fact that cultural attitudes and features such as the 'contract' and 'consent' are not secondary creations, as they were claimed to
be by the other side, and more particularly, by Hume: they
are the basic material of social life, and it is impossible to
imagine any form of political organization in which they
would not be present.

A second observation follows on from the previous remarks: *consent* is the psychological basis of power, but in
everyday life it is expressed by a process of giving and receiving which goes on between the chief and his companions, and which makes the idea of *reciprocity* another
fundamental attribute of power. The chief has power but
he must be generous. He has duties, but he is allowed
several wives. Between him and the group there exists a
perpetually renewed balance of gifts, privileges, services
and obligations.

But, in the case of marriage, there is something more.
By conceding the privilege of polygamy to the chief, the
group exchanges the *individual elements of security* guaranteed by the rule of monogamy for *collective security*,
which they expect to be ensured by the leader. Each man
receives his wife from another man, but the chief receives
several wives from the group. In return, he provides a
guarantee against want and danger, not for the individuals
whose sisters or daughters he marries, not even for those
men who are deprived of women as a consequence of his
polygamy, but for the group considered as a whole, since
it is the group as a whole which has suspended the common
law for his benefit. Such considerations might be of some
interest for a theoretical study of polygamy; but their chief
importance is as a reminder that the conception of the state
as a system of guarantees, which has been revived in recent
years by discussions about systems of national insurance
(such as the Beveridge Plan and other proposals), is not a
purely modern development. It is a return to the fundamental nature of social and political organization.

Such, then, is the attitude of the group towards authority.
We may go on to ask how the chief sees his function, and
what motives he may have for accepting a not always pleasurable responsibility. The Nambikwara chief has a difficult part to play; he has to exert himself in order to maintain his position. What is more, if he does not constantly

improve it, he runs the risk of losing what it has taken him months or years to achieve. This explains why many individuals are reluctant to accept power. Yet others not only accept it but try to obtain it. It is always difficult to judge psychological motives, and when we are dealing with a culture very different from our own, the task becomes well-nigh impossible. However, it can be said that the privilege of polygamy, whatever attractions it may have from the sexual, sentimental or social points of view, would hardly be enough to inspire a vocation. Polygamous marriage is a technical condition of power; in the providing of any deep satisfaction it can only be of secondary significance. There must be some further reason. When I try to recall the moral and psychological characteristics of the various Nambikwara chiefs and to grasp the elusive aspects of their personalities (which escape scientific analysis but have a certain value, thanks to the intuitive feeling for human communication and the experience of friendship), I am driven to the following conclusion: chiefs exist because, in every human group, there are men who differ from their fellow-beings in that they like prestige for its own sake, are attracted by responsibility and for whom the burden of public affairs brings its own reward. Such individual differences are undoubtedly developed and brought into play to differing degrees by various cultures. But their existence in a society as uncompetitive as Nambikwara society suggests that they are not entirely social in origin, but belong rather to the basic psychological material from which all societies are constructed. Men are not all alike, and even in primitive tribes that sociologists have described as being weighed down by all-powerful traditions, individual differences are as shrewdly perceived and as conscientiously exploited as in our so-called 'individualistic' civilization.

In another form, this was undoubtedly the 'miracle' referred to by Leibnitz in connection with the American savages, whose customs, as recorded by the early travellers, had taught him 'never to accept the hypotheses of political philosophy as proven truths'. As for myself, I had gone to the ends of the earth to look for what Rousseau calls 'the almost imperceptible stages of man's beginnings'. Behind the veil of the over-complicated laws of the Caduveo and Bororo, I had continued my search for a state which —as Rousseau also says—'no longer exists, has perhaps never existed, and probably will never exist, and of which it is nevertheless essential to form a correct notion in order rightly to judge our present state'. I believed that, having been luckier than Rousseau, I had discovered such a state in a moribund society, about which there was no point in wondering whether or not it was vestigial. Whether traditional or degenerate, this society offered one of the most rudimentary forms of social and political organization that could possibly be imagined. I did not need to refer back to the particular sequence of historical events which had kept it in, or more probably had brought it back to, this elementary state. It was enough to observe the sociological experience before me.

But it was precisely that experience which was difficult to grasp. I had been looking for a society reduced to its simplest expression. That of the Nambikwara was so truly simple that all I could find in it was individual human beings.

PART EIGHT

Tupi-Kawahib

30. A CANOE TRIP

I had left Cuiaba in June, and it was now September. For three months, I had been wandering across the plateau, camping with Indians while the beasts rested, or putting together the various stages of the journey in my mind and wondering about the meaning of the whole enterprise, while the jolting movement of my mule confirmed bruises which had become so familiar that they had, as it were, become part of my physical being, so much so that I would have missed them, had I not felt them afresh every morning. Adventure had been watered down into boredom. For weeks now I had seen the same bleak savannah rolling past, so barren that its living plants were hardly distinguishable from the dead vegetable debris which, here and there, marked the site of an abandoned camp. The black traces left by bush fires seemed to be the natural conclusion of a unanimous progress towards calcination.

We had gone from Utiarity to Juruena, then on to Juina, Campos Novos and Vilhena; we were now advancing towards the last outposts on the plateau: Tres Buritis, and Barão de Melgaço, which, in fact, lies at the foot of the plateau. At almost every halt, we had lost one or two oxen: through thirst, exhaustion or *hervado*, that is, killed by grazing on poisonous plants. Several fell into a river with the baggage while crossing a rotten wooden bridge, and only with great difficulty did we manage to salvage our precious anthropological collections. But such incidents were rare; every day, we repeated the same activities; setting up camp, slinging hammocks and mosquito nets, putting the baggage and pack-saddles out of reach of termites and tending the animals, and then the following day we would have to make preparations in reverse order. Or, if a group of natives should happen to appear, there was a different routine to be gone through: taking a census, noting the names of the parts of the body, kinship terms and genealogies, and making inventories. My attempted escapism had turned into bureaucratic routine.

There had been no rain for five months and all game
had vanished. We were lucky if we managed to shoot an
emaciated parrot or capture a large *tupinambis* lizard to
boil in our rice, or managed to roast in their shells a land-
tortoise or an armadillo with black, oily flesh. More often
than not, we had to be content with *xarque*—that same
dried meat prepared months previously by a butcher in
Cuiaba and the thick worm-infested layers of which we
unrolled every morning in the sun, in order to make them
less noxious, although they were usually in the same state
again by the following day. Once, however, someone killed
a wild pig; its lightly cooked flesh seemed to us more in-
toxicating than wine: each of us devoured more than a
pound of it, and at that moment I understood the alleged
gluttony of savages, which is mentioned by so many travellers as a proof of their uncouthness. One only had to
share their diet to experience similar pangs of hunger; to
eat one's fill in such circumstances produces not merely a
feeling of repletion but a positive sensation of bliss.

The landscape was gradually changing. The old crystalline or sedimentary strata which formed the central
plateau were giving way to clayey soils. Beyond the savannah, we began to cross areas of dry forest with chestnut
trees (not the European chestnut, but the one native to
Brazil, the *Bertholletia excelsa*) and copaibas, tall trees
which secrete a kind of balsam. The streams were no longer
clear, but muddy, yellow and tainted. Everywhere we noticed landslides: the hills had been eroded, and below them
swamps had formed, with *sapézals* (high grasses) and
buritizals (palm groves). Along the edges of these swamps,
our mules tramped through fields of wild pineapples: they
were small, yellowy-orange in colour, their flesh was pitted
with big black pips and their taste was halfway between
that of the cultivated species and a very succulent rasp-
berry. From the ground rose a fragrance we had not smelt
for months, an aroma like that of a hot chocolate-flavoured
infusion, which is simply the smell of tropical vegetation
and organic decay. It is a smell which makes you suddenly
understand how this can be the soil which produces cocoa,
just as sometimes in Haute-Provence the scent from a
half-withered lavender-field explains how the same earth
can also produce truffles. One last climb led us to the edge
of a steep grassy slope, running down to the telegraph post
of Barão de Melgaço: before us, as far as the eye could

see, lay the valley of the Machado, which straggles away
into the Amazonian forest; the latter continues without a
break for 1,500 kilometres, as far as the Venezuelan
frontier.

At Barão de Melgaço, there were green fields surrounded
by damp forest, echoing with the vigorous trumpet calls
of the *jacu,* or dog-bird. We had only to spend a couple
of hours in the forest to come back to camp with armfuls
of game. We were seized with a mad desire for food; for
three days we did nothing but cook and eat. From then
on we would lack for nothing. Our carefully husbanded
supply of alcohol and sugar melted away, while we tried
out Amazonian foods: especially *tocari* or Brazil nuts, the
grated pulp of which is used to give sauces a white, unc-
tuous creaminess. Here are details of some of these gas-
tronomical experiments, as I jotted them down in my note-
books:

> —humming-birds (which the Portuguese call *beija-
> flor,* kiss-flower) roasted on skewers and *flambés* with
> whisky;
> —grilled caïman's tail;
> —grilled caïman's tail;
> —roast parrot *flambé* with whisky;
> —*jacu* stewed with the fruit of the *assaï* palm tree;
> —*mutum* (a kind of wild turkey) stewed with palm
> buds, accompanied by a sauce made with Brazil nuts
> and pepper;
> —roast, caramelized *jacu.*

After these excesses, and no less necessary ablutions—
since we had often gone several days without being able
to take off the dungarees which, along with sun-helmet
and knee-boots, constituted our travelling dress—I started
drawing up plans for the second part of the journey. From
now on, the rivers would be preferable to the overgrown
forest *picadas.* Moreover, out of the thirty-one oxen I had
started off with I had only seventeen left, and they were
in such poor condition that it was impossible for them to
carry on even over easy territory. I decided that we would
split up into three groups. My leader, along with one or
two men, would travel overland towards the first rubber-
gathering centres, where we hoped to sell the horses and
some of the mules. Others would stay on at Barão de
Melgaço with the oxen to give them time to recover their

strength in the *capim-gordura* ('fat grass') pastures. Tiburcio, the old cook, was prepared to be in charge of these men, which was easy to arrange since they all liked him; it was said of him—he had a lot of African blood in his veins—that he was *preto na feição, branco na acção,* 'black in hue, white in value', which shows, incidentally, that the Brazilian peasant is not devoid of racial prejudice. In Amazonia, a white girl who is being courted by a black often says, 'Am I such a white carcass that a *urubu* may come and perch on my entrails?' She is referring to the familiar sight of a dead crocodile drifting downstream with a black griffon-vulture floating for days on the corpse and feeding on it.

Once the oxen had recovered, the troop would make the return journey to Utiarity. We assumed there would be no difficulty, since the beasts would be free of their load and the rains, which were now due, would have transformed the desert into a prairie. Lastly, the scientific members of the expedition and the remaining men would take charge of the baggage and transport it by canoe to the inhabited areas, where our party would split up. I myself intended to go on, along the Madeira, into Bolivia, to cross the country by plane, then return to Brazil via Corumba, and from there to make my way back to Cuiaba, then to Utiarity, sometime in December, when I would meet up again with my *comitiva*—my team and beasts—in order to wind up the expedition.

The commander of the Melgaço post lent us two *galiotes* —light boats made from planks—as well as men to paddle them; no more dealings with mules! All we had to do was to follow the Rio Machado downstream. Months of drought had made us careless, and the first evening we did not bother to put our hammocks under shelter, but merely slung them between trees on the river-bank. The storm broke in the middle of the night with a noise like a horse galloping; before we were even fully awake, our hammocks had been transformed into bath-tubs; we fumbled about in the dark trying to unroll a waterproof canvas sheet to serve as a roof, but it was impossible to fix up in the torrential rain. Sleep was out of the question; crouching in the water and supporting the canvas with our heads, we had constantly to keep an eye on the folds which kept filling up with rain, and empty them before it came through.

To pass the time, the men told stories; I remember the one told by Emydio.

Emydio's story

A widower had an only son, who was already an adolescent. One day he called him and explained to him that it was high time he got married. 'What must I do to get married?' asked the son. 'It is very simple,' said his father, 'you only have to visit your neighbours and try to please the daughter.' 'But I do not know how to please a girl!' 'Well, play the guitar, be jolly, laugh and sing!' The son did as he was told, and arrived just when the young girl's father had died; his behaviour was considered offensive, and he was pelted with stones and driven away. He returned to his father's house and complained; the father explained to him how to behave in such circumstances. The son set off once more for the neighbours' house; as it happened, they were killing a pig. But remembering his father's injunctions, he sobbed: 'How sad! He was so good! We were so fond of him! We shall never find anyone better!' The neighbours were furious, and drove him out; he related this fresh misadventure to his father, and was instructed in the appropriate behaviour. On his third visit, the neighbours were busy ridding the garden of caterpillars. Still one lesson behind, the young man exclaimed: 'What marvellous abundance! I hope those animals will multiply in your lands! May you never be without them!' He was driven away.

After the third failure, the father ordered his son to build a hut. He went into the forest to fell the necessary wood. The werewolf passed by the spot during the night and, thinking it a good place to build his abode, he set to work. The next morning the boy returned to the site and found the work well advanced: 'God is helping me.' he thought with satisfaction. So they went on building together, the boy during the day and the werewolf at night, until the hut was finished.

For the house-warming, the boy decided to treat himself to a roebuck and the werewolf opted for a corpse. The former brought the roebuck during the day, the latter the corpse under cover of night. And when the father came next day to take part in the feast, on the table he saw a corpse instead of a roast: 'That settles it, my son, you will never be good at anything . . .'

A day later, it was still raining when we arrived at Pimenta Bueno, and we had to bale the water out of the canoes. This post is situated at the junction of two rivers —the one from which it takes its name and the Rio Machado. Twenty or so people lived there; a few whites from the interior, and Indians of various kinds, who did maintenance work on the line: there were Cabishiana from the valley of the Guaporé, and Tupi-Kawahib from the Rio Machado. They were to provide me with valuable information, some of which concerned the still savage Tupi-Kawahib who, on the strength of earlier reports, were thought to have completely disappeared; I shall return to them later. Other information related to an unknown tribe who, it was said, lived on the Rio Pimenta Bueno, several days' journey away by canoe. I at once planned to make contact with them, but the problem was how.

There happened to be staying at the post a Negro called Bahia, an itinerant merchant who was also partly an adventurer and who every year carried out a fantastic journey. He would go down as far as the Rio Madeira to obtain goods from the river-side trading-posts, come back up the Machado by canoe and go on up the Pimenta Bueno for two days. At that point he knew of a forest track along which it was possible to drag the canoes and the goods for three days as far as a small tributary of the Guaporé, where he could sell his stock at particularly exorbitant prices since the area he finally reached received no other supplies at all. Bahia agreed to go up the Pimenta Bueno further than he normally did, on condition that I paid him in goods rather than money. This was a sound speculation on his part, since wholesale prices in Amazonia are higher than at São Paulo where I had made my purchases. I therefore let him have several bolts of red flannel to which I had taken a dislike ever since, at Vilhena, I had given a bolt to the Nambikwara and next morning found they had covered themselves with red flannel from head to foot, and had even put it on their dogs, monkeys and domesticated peccaries; it is true that the joke had palled within an hour, and scraps of flannel were left strewn about the bush where no one paid any further attention to them.

Our crew consisted of four paddlers and two of our own men, and we borrowed two canoes from the post. We were ready to start on our improvised adventure.

There is no more thrilling prospect for the anthropologist than that of being the first white man to visit a particular native community. Already in 1938, this supreme reward could only be obtained in a few regions of the world—few enough indeed to be counted on the fingers of one hand. Since then, the possibilities have diminished still further. I was about to relive the experience of the early travellers and, through it, that crucial moment in modern thought when, thanks to the great voyages of discovery, a human community which believed itself to be complete and in its final form suddenly learned, as if through the effect of a counter-revelation, that it was not alone, that it was part of a greater whole, and that, in order to achieve self-knowledge, it must first of all contemplate its unrecognizable image in this mirror, of which a fragment, forgotten by the centuries, was now about to cast, for me alone, its first and last reflection.

It may be thought that such enthusiasm was inappropriate in the twentieth century. However little was known about the Indians of the Pimenta Bueno, I could not expect them to make the same impact on me as they had made on the great chroniclers, such as Léry, Staden and Thevet, who set foot on Brazilian territory four hundred years ago. What they saw then, no Western eye will ever see again. Although the civilizations which they were the first to observe had developed along different lines from ours, they had nevertheless reached the full development and perfection of which their natures were capable, whereas the societies we are able to study today—in conditions which it would be illusory to compare with those of four centuries ago—are no more than debilitated communities and mutilated social forms. In spite of the vast distances involved and the operation of all kinds of intermediary agents (the sequence of which is often disconcertingly bizarre when one manages to work it out), they have been shattered by the development of European civilization, that phenomenon which, for a widespread and innocent section of humanity, has amounted to a monstrous and incomprehensible cataclysm. It would be wrong for us Europeans to forget that this cataclysm is a second aspect of our civilization, no less true and irrefutable than the one we know.

The men might be different, but travelling conditions had remained the same. After the dreary ride across the plateau, I savoured the delight of travelling up a pleasant river, the course of which is unmarked on any map but which reminded me, in its smallest details, of the old accounts of which I am so fond.

First of all, it was necessary to revive the knowledge of river lore that had been acquired, three years previously, on the São Lourenço: it involved familiarity with the different kinds and respective merits of canoes—some made from hollowed-out tree-trunks, some from assembled planks —which have various names according to their size and shape: *montaria, canoa, ubá* or *igarité;* getting used to spending hours squatting in the water which comes in through the cracks and has to be constantly baled out with a small gourd; making extremely slow and cautious movements to relieve one's stiffness, since the vessel is always in danger of capsizing *(agua não tem cabellos,* 'water has no hair'; if you fall overboard, there is nothing to catch hold of); lastly, the necessary patience, at every irregularity in the river-bed, to unload the provisions and material which have been packed in with such meticulous care, and to carry them over the rocky bank, along with the canoes, knowing full well that the operation will have to be repeated a few hundred yards farther on.

The irregularities are of various types: *seccos,* where the river-bed is dry; *cachoeiras,* rapids; *saltos,* waterfalls. Each is soon given a picturesque name by the paddlers; this may relate to a feature of the landscape, such as *castanhal* or *palmas;* or to a hunting incident, *veado, queixada* or *araras;* or it may express a more personal relationship to the traveller: *criminosa,* the 'criminal one'; *encrenca,* an untranslatable noun which conveys the fact of being 'cornered'; *apertada hora,* 'the cramped hour' (with an implied etymological meaning of 'anguished'); *vamos ver,* 'we'll see . . .'

There was nothing about our departure that we had not experienced before. We let the oarsmen space out the prescribed rhythms: first, a series of short strokes: plop, plop, plop . . . then, while getting under way, two sharp taps on the edge of the canoe between the oar-strokes: tap-plop, tap; tap-plop, tap . . . —finally, the travelling rhythm, in which the oar dips only at every other stroke, the intervening one barely skimming the surface, but always accompanied by a tap, and separated from the follow-

ing movement by another tap: tap-plop, tap, sh . . . sh,
tap; tap-plop, tap, sh . . . sh, tap . . . In this way, the blue
and orange sides of the oar-blades were revealed alternately, looking as light on the water as the reflections—from
which indeed they seemed indistinguishable—of the great
flocks of aras which crossed the river, displaying in con-
cert, each time they swerved, the brilliance of their golden
underbellies or azure backs. The air had lost the transparency characteristic of the dry season. At dawn everything
merged into the thick roseate haze of the morning mist
rising slowly from the river. We already felt hot, but this
indirect heat would turn into something more precise: what
had previously been a diffused warmth became a direct
attack by the sun on a part of the face or the hands. One
began to realize why one was sweating. The pink haze was
variegated with other shades of colour: blue islands appeared. The mist seemed to be taking on still richer hues
when, in fact, it was breaking up.

Travelling upstream was hard work and the oarsmen
had to rest. The morning was spent angling with a crude
line baited with wild berries to get enough fish for *peixada,*
the Amazonian fish-soup: *pacus,* which are yellow with fat
and are eaten in slices held by the bone, like cutlets; *pira-
canjubas* with silvery scales and red flesh; bright red *doura-
dos; cascudos* encased in shells as hard as a lobster's, but
black in colour; speckled *piaparas; mandi, piava, curimbata,
jatuarama, matrinchão* . . . But one has to beware of poisonous skate and electric fish—*puraké*—which can be
caught without bait but give a shock strong enough to stun
a mule; more dangerous still, according to the men, are
minute fish that can swim up the jet of urine and enter
the bladder of anyone rash enough to relieve himself directly into the river . . . Or, peering through the high wall
of green mould formed by the forest edge along the river-
bank, we would watch for the sudden burst of activity
caused by a band of monkeys, which might be of many
different kinds: the *guariba,* or howler monkey; the *coata,*
with spider-like limbs; the caupchin or 'nail monkey'; the
zog-zog, which arouses the forest with its calls an hour before dawn: because of its huge almond-shaped eyes, its
human carriage and fluffy, silky coat, it looks like a Mongol
prince; and all the various tribes of small monkeys: *saguin,*
or marmoset; *macaco da noite,* 'night monkey', with dark
gelatine eyes; *macaco de cheiro,* 'scented monkey'; *gogo de*

sol, 'sunthroat', etc. A single bullet fired into a leaping band was almost invariably enough to bring down one animal; when roasted, it turned into the mummy of a child with clenched hands, and when stewed it tasted like goose-flesh.

Towards three o'clock in the afternoon, there would be a rumble of thunder, the sky would become overcast and a broad, vertical band of rain would hide half its expanse. While one was wondering whether or not the rain would fall, the band would become streaky and frayed, and then through it would appear a lighter patch, gilded at first and later pale blue. By now only the middle of the horizon would still be occupied by the rain. But the clouds would melt away, their mass would dwindle first on the right then on the left, and finally they would disappear altogether. What was left was a composite sky, made up of bluish-black masses against a blue-and-white background. Now was the time, before the next storm broke, to land on the bank at some point where the forest appeared to be not so dense. We would quickly make a little clearing with the help of our jungle axes, *facão* or *terçado;* we would examine the trees thus disengaged from the undergrowth to see if, among them, there was a *pau de novato,* or 'novice's tree', so called because any inexperienced traveller who slings his hammock from it finds himself covered with a swarm of red ants; or a *pau d'alho,* which smells of garlic, or a *cannela merda,* the name of which speaks for itself. Perhaps, with luck, there might be a *soveira,* which in a few minutes yields more milk than a cow, if a circular incision is made in the trunk. The liquid is frothy and creamy, but when consumed raw, lines the mouth of the unsuspecting drinker with a rubbery film; the *araça,* which has a purplish-blue fruit about as big as a cherry, with a turpentine taste accompanied by a faint acidity which makes the water in which it has been crushed appear fizzy; the *inga,* with pods full of a fine, sugary down; the *bacuri,* which is like a pear stolen from the orchards of Paradise; and lastly, the *assaī,* the supreme delicacy of the forest, which, on being prepared with water, provides a thick raspberry-flavoured syrup for immediate drinking: by next day it has curdled into a fruity, somewhat tart cheese.

While some of our group devoted themselves to these culinary tasks, others would fix up the hammocks under awnings of branches lightly thatched with palm-fronds. This was the time for story-telling round the camp fire, all about apparitions and ghosts: the *lobis-homem* or werewolf; the headless horse or the old woman with a death's head. In any group, there is always a former *garimpeiro* who still yearns for his old, poverty-stricken existence, illumined each day by the hope of wealth: 'I was busy "writing" (that is, sifting the gravel), when I saw a small rice-grain slip into the wash-trough; it glowed like a light. *Que cousa bounita!** I don't think any *cousa mais bounita* [more beautiful thing] could exist. When we looked at it, it was as if electricity were shooting through everyone's body!' Or a discussion would begin. 'Between Rosario and Larenjal, on a hill there is a stone which sparkles. It can be seen for miles, especially at night.—Perhaps it is crystal?—No, crystal doesn't shine at night, only diamonds.—And nobody ever goes to look for it?—Oh, in the case of diamonds like that, the time of their discovery and the name of the person they will belong to have been fixed for a long time!'

Those who did not feel like sleeping would maintain a watch, sometimes until dawn, along the river-bank, where they had observed wild boar, capybara or tapir tracks, and try—unsuccessfully—the *batuque* method of hunting; this consists in striking the ground with a heavy stick at regular intervals: boom, boom, boom. The animals think fruit is dropping from the trees and are said to arrive on the scene always in the same order: the boar first, then the jaguar.

Often, too, we would do no more than build up the fire for the night and then, after commenting on the day's events and passing round the maté, each man would slip into his hammock, enclosed in a mosquito net which had been stretched over it—half cocoon and half kite—by means of an intricate system of sticks and string, and, once inside, he would take care to pull up the slack so that no part of it touched the ground, and form it into a kind of pocket to be held in place by the weight of his revolver, while the weapon remained within reach of his hand. Soon the rain would begin to fall.

---

* I have respected the rustic pronunciation of *coisa bonita*.

31. ROBINSON CRUSOE

We had been travelling upstream for four days; there were
so many rapids that we had to unload, carry and reload up
to five times in the same day. The river flowed between
rock formations which split it up into several arms; the
reefs in the middle had trapped whole trees floating downstream, together with earth and clumps of vegetation. The
vegetation had retaken root so rapidly on the improvised
islands thus created that it remained unaffected by the
chaotic state in which the latest flood had left it. Trees
were growing in all directions, and flowers bloomed across
waterfalls; it was impossible to say whether the river served
to irrigate this fantastic garden, or whether it was about
to be choked by a proliferation of plants and creepers,
which seemed free to develop not only vertically, but
through all spatial dimensions, as a result of the abolition
of the usual distinctions between earth and water. There
was no river any more, nor any river-bank, but instead a
maze of copses watered by the current, while the firm
ground seemed to rise out of the very foam. This sympathy
between the elements extended to living creatures; the native tribes need enormous surfaces in order to survive;
but here a superabundance of animal life bore witness to
the fact that, for decades, man had been powerless to
disturb the natural order of things. The trees were even
more a-quiver with monkeys than with leaves, and it was
as if living fruits were dancing on their branches. One
had only to stretch out one's hand towards the rocks at
water level to brush against the jet-black plumage of the
large amber- or coral-beaked *mutum,* and the *jacamin,*
which were a shimmering blue like Labrador stone. The
birds did not flee at our approach: like live jewels wandering among the dripping creepers and overgrown torrents, they were part of the living reconstitution, before
my astonished eyes, of those pictures by the Brueghels
in which Paradise is marked by a tender intimacy between

plants, beasts and men, and takes us back to the time when there was as yet no division among God's creatures.

On the afternoon of the fifth day, a slim canoe moored to the bank indicated that we had arrived. There was a spinney which seemed a suitable place for us to camp. The Indian village lay one kilometre back from the river: it comprised a garden measuring about a hundred metres over its maximum length, set in an egg-shaped clearing which also held three hemispherical collective huts, the central poles of which stuck out at the top like masts. The two main huts stood facing each other in the broad part of the egg, alongside a dancing floor of beaten earth. The third was situated at the point and was linked to the dancing-area by a path running across the garden.

The population consisted of twenty-five people, plus a boy of about twelve, who spoke a different language and was, so I understood, a prisoner of war, although he was treated in the same way as the children of the tribe. Both men and women were as scantily dressed as the Nambik-wara, except that the men all had a cone-shaped penis sheath, like the one worn by the Bororo; also, the practice of wearing a tuft of straw above the genitals, which exists among the Nambikwara, was more widespread among these Indians. Both sexes wore lip-plugs of hardened resin which looked like amber, and necklaces made of discs or plaques of shiny mother-of-pearl, or even of white polished shells. Their wrists, arms, calves and ankles were bound with strips of cotton. Finally, the women had pierced nasal septa through which were inserted small bars composed of alternate black and white discs tightly threaded on to a stiff fibre.

In physical appearance they were very different from the Nambikwara: they had thick-set bodies, short legs and a very light skin. This last feature, together with their faintly Mongolian cast of countenance, gave some of them a Caucasian look. They remove all body hair very meticulously: the eyelashes are plucked out by hand; the eyebrows are removed by allowing wax to harden on them for several days and then ripping it off. The hair on the front of the head is cut (or, to be more precise, burnt) into a rounded fringe, which leaves the forehead exposed. The temples are denuded by a method which I have never seen used anywhere else. The hair is slipped into a loop made by twisting together the two ends of a cord. One end of the cord is gripped in the clenched teeth, while the loop is held open with one hand and the free end is pulled with the other hand, so that the two strands are wound more closely together and uproot the hair as they tighten.

These Indians, who referred to themselves as Mundé, had never before been mentioned in any anthropological study. They speak a jolly language with words ending in stressed syllables—*zip, zep, pep, zet, tap, kat*—which accentuate their speech like the clashing of cymbals. This language resembles certain dialects of the Lower Xingu which have now disappeared, as well as others recently recorded along the tributaries of the right bank of the Guaporé, the sources of which are close to Mundé territory. As far as I know, no one has seen the Mundé again since my visit, apart from a woman missionary who encountered one or two of them just before 1950 along the Upper Guaporé, where three families had taken refuge. I spent an agreeable week with them, and have rarely known hosts behave with such simplicity, patience and cordiality. They showed me round their gardens; they grew maize, manioc, sweet potatoes, ground-nuts, tobacco, the calabash tree and various species of beans, both large and small. When they clear a patch for planting, they leave the palm-tree stumps to serve as breeding-grounds for fat white grubs which they greatly enjoy eating: their gardens are thus hybrid areas where they raise both plants and livestock.

The round huts let in a diffused light, speckled with the sunshine which came through the cracks. They were carefully constructed by means of poles erected in a circle and bent over into the forks of posts leaning at an angle and acting as internal flying-buttresses; between these posts were slung ten or so hammocks made of knotted cotton. All the poles met at a point about four metres above the ground, and were attached to a central post which jutted through the roof. Horizontal circles of branches completed the frame, over which was placed a dome of palms, the leaves of which had all been flattened in the same direction so as to overlap like tiles. The largest hut was twelve metres in diameter, and contained four families, each occupying the area between two flying-buttresses. There were six buttresses, but the two sectors corresponding to the two opposite doors of the hut were left unoccupied to facil-

itate freedom of movement. I spent my days there, sitting
on one of the small wooden benches that the natives use,
and which consist of sliced, hollowed-out palm logs placed
flat side down. We ate maize kernels that had been grilled
on a pottery plate and drank maize *chicha*—a beverage
halfway between beer and soup—from half-calabashes
coated inside with some black substance and decorated
on the outside with carved or burnt lines, zigzags, circles
and polygons.

Even though I was ignorant of the language and had
no interpreter, I could try to grasp certain aspects of the
Mundé way of thinking and social organization, such as
how the group was made up, the kinship system and vocabulary, the names of the parts of the body, and the colour
vocabulary, according to a chart I always carried with
me. Kinship terms and those used for the parts of the
body, colours and shapes (e.g. the shapes engraved on
the calabashes) often have common characteristics which
put them halfway between vocabulary and grammar: each
group forms a system, and the way in which different languages choose to arrange or confuse the relationships expressed by means of it allows us to make a certain number
of hypotheses, even though they may relate only to the
distinctive features of the particular society.

However, although I had set off on the adventure with
enthusiasm, it left me with a feeling of emptiness.

I had wanted to reach the extreme limits of the savage; it
might be thought that my wish had been granted, now that
I found myself among these charming Indians whom no
other white man had ever seen before and who might never
be seen again. After an enchanting trip up-river, I had certainly found my savages. Alas! they were only too savage.
Since their existence had only been revealed to me at the
last moment, I was unable to devote to them the time that
would have been essential to get to know them. The limited
resources at my disposal, the state of physical exhaustion
in which my companions and I now found ourselves—and
which was to be made still worse by the fevers of the rainy
season—allowed me no more than a short busman's holiday* instead of months of study. There they were, all ready

---

* TRANSLATORS' NOTE: The French expression is *une brève école
buissonnière*, from *faire l'école buissonnière*, to play truant. In the
context, it has the force of a pun: to go to school in the bushes or
bush.

to teach me their customs and beliefs, and I did not know their language. They were as close to me as a reflection in a mirror; I could touch them, but I could not understand them. I had been given, at one and the same time, my reward and my punishment. Was it not my mistake, and the mistake of my profession, to believe that men are not always men? that some are more deserving of interest and attention because they astonish us by the colour of their skin and their customs? I had only to succeed in guessing what they were like for them to be deprived of their strangeness: in which case, I might just as well have stayed in my village. Or if, as was the case here, they retained their strangeness, I could make no use of it, since I was incapable of even grasping what it consisted of. Between these two extremes, what ambiguous instances provide us with the excuses by which we live? Who, in the last resort, is the real dupe of the confusion created in the reader's mind by observations which are carried just far enough to be intelligible and then are stopped in mid-career, because they cause surprise in human beings similar to those who take such customs as a matter of course? Is it the reader who believes in us, or we ourselves who have no right to be satisfied until we have succeeded in dissipating a residue which serves as a pretext for our vanity?

But if the inhabitants were mute, perhaps the earth itself would speak to me. Over and above the marvels which had enchanted me along the river, perhaps it would answer my prayer and let me into the secret of its virginity. Where exactly does that virginity lie, behind the confusion of appearances which are all and yet nothing? I can pick out certain scenes and separate them from the rest; is it this tree, this flower? They might well be elsewhere. Is it also a delusion that the whole should fill me with rapture, while each part of it, taken separately, escapes me? If I have to accept it as being real, I want at least to grasp it in its entirety, down to its last constituent element. I reject the vast landscape, I circumscribe it and reduce it to this clayey beach and this blade of grass: there is nothing to prove that my eye, if it broadened its view of the scene, would not recognize the Bois de Meudon* around this insignificant fragment, which is trodden daily by the most authentic savages

---

* TRANSLATORS' NOTE: i.e. Hampstead Heath or Wimbledon Common.

but from which, however, Man Friday's footprint is missing.

We made the journey downstream with remarkable speed. This time, the oarsmen, still under the spell cast by our hosts, would not hear of portage, and, at every set of rapids, directed the head of the boat towards the seething mass of water. For a few seconds, we would think we had stopped and were being violently shaken, while the landscape was whizzing past. Then, suddenly everything would become calm: we were in still water below the rapids, and only then would we begin to feel dizzy.

Within two days we were back at Pimenta Bueno, where I formed a new plan, which cannot be understood without some explanation. In 1915, towards the end of his expedition, Rondon discovered several Tupi-speaking groups and managed to make contact with three of them, although the others remained resolutely hostile. The largest of these groups had settled along the upper reaches of the Rio Machado, two days' march from the left bank and on a minor tributary, the Igarapé do Leitão (or 'stream of the sucking-pig'). This was the Takwatip ('bamboo') group or clan. It is not certain that the term clan is appropriate, since, generally speaking, the Tupi-Kawahib groups formed a single village, guarded the frontiers of their hunting-ground very jealously, and practised exogamy as a way of entering into alliances with neighbouring groups rather than in observance of some strict rule. The Takwatip were commanded by Chief Abaitara. On the same side of the river, there were: to the north, a group about which nothing was known, apart from the fact that its chief's name was Pitsara; to the south, on the Rio Tamuripa, the Ipotiwat (this is the name of a creeper), whose chief was called Kamandjara; then, between the Rio Tamuripa and the Igarapé do Cacoal, the Jabotifet ('tortoise people'), whose chief was called Maira. On the left bank of the Machado, in the valley of the Rio Muqui, lived the Paranawat ('river people') who are still there but respond with showers of arrows to any attempt at contact, and a little further south, on the Igarapé de Itapici, another unknown group. Such, at least, was the information I managed to glean, in 1938, from the rubber-hunters who had been settled in the area since the time of Rondon's exploration. Rondon himself supplied only fragmentary data in his reports on the Tupi-Kawahib.

Through talking with the civilized Tupi-Kawahib at the Pimenta Bueno post, I managed to bring the list of clan names up to twenty or so. Also, the researches of Curt Nimuendaju, who was a scholar as well as a field-anthropologist, throw some light on the tribe's past. The term Kawahib is reminiscent of the name of a former Tupi tribe, the Cabahiba, often mentioned in eighteenth- and nineteenth-century documents and who at that time lived along the upper and middle reaches of the Rio Tapajoz. It seems that they were gradually driven out by another Tupi tribe, the Mundurucu, and as they moved westward split up into several groups, of which only the Parintintin, on the lower reaches of the Machado, and the more southerly Tupi-Kawahib are known. It is therefore extremely likely that these Indians are the last descendants of the great Tupi communities of the middle and lower reaches of the Amazon, which were related to the coastal groups whom the sixteenth- and seventeenth-century travellers saw in their period of splendour. It was the accounts given by these travellers which began the anthropological awareness of modern times; it was their unintentional influence which set the political and moral philosophy of the Renaissance on the road that was to lead to the French Revolution. To be the first white man, perhaps, to set foot in a still-intact Tupi village would be to bridge a gap of four hundred years and to find oneself on a par with Léry, Staden, Soares de Souza, Thevet and even Montaigne who, in the chapter on cannibals in his *Essays,* reflected on a conversation he had had with Tupi Indians whom he met at Rouen.* It was a strong temptation!

At the time when Rondon made contact with the Tupi-Kawahib, the Takwatip, under the guidance of an ambitious and energetic chief, were extending their authority over several other groups. After months spent in the almost desert-like wastes of the plateau, Rondon's companions were dazzled by the 'miles and miles' (but hyperbole is common in the language of the *sertão*) of plantations opened up by Abaitara's people in the damp forest or along the *igapos,* or floodable river-banks, and thanks to which the Indians were able to supply the explorers with food, after they had been living under constant threat of famine.

Two years after establishing contact with them, Rondon persuaded the Takwatip to move their village to the right bank of the Machado, to the place still marked as *aldeia*

* Cf. above p. 349.

dos Indios on the international map of the world, opposite the mouth of the Rio São-Pedro (11°5′ S and 62°3′ W). This spot was more convenient for surveillance and for obtaining food supplies and the help of Indian canoeists; the rivers are broken up by rapids, narrow channels and waterfalls, and the Indians, with their light bark boats, were expert navigators.

I was able, in addition, to obtain a description of this new village, which has now disappeared. As Rondon had noted at the time of his visit to the forest village, the huts were rectangular, without walls, and consisted only of a palm thatch with a double slope, resting on trunks fixed in the ground. Twenty or so huts (each measuring about four metres by six) were arranged in a circle about twenty metres in diameter, around two more spacious dwellings (eighteen metres by six), one of which was occupied by Abaitara with his wives and young children, and the other by his youngest son who was married. The two eldest sons were bachelors and lived, like the rest of the community, in the outer huts and, like other bachelors, were given their meals in the chief's house. There were poultry-runs in the empty space between the central dwellings and the outer ones.

Such a village was far removed from the vast Tupi dwellings described by the sixteenth-century writers, but the gap is even greater between the five to six hundred inhabitants of Abaitara's village and the present state of affairs. Abaitara was assassinated in 1925. The death of this emperor of the Upper Machado marked the start of a period of violence in a village which had already been reduced to twenty-five men, twenty-two women and twelve children by the 1918–20 influenza epidemic. In the same year, 1925, four people (including Abaitara's murderer) were killed from motives of revenge, mainly connected with love affairs. Shortly afterwards, the survivors decided to abandon the village and to move to the post of Pimenta Bueno, a two-day canoe trip upstream. In 1938, the group consisted of five men, a woman and a little girl, who spoke a Portuguese dialect and seemed to have become part of the local neo-Brazilian community. It looked as if this was the end of the history of the Tupi-Kawahib, at least on the right bank of the Machado, and except for the unapproachable group of Paranawat on the left bank in the valley of the Rio Muqui. However, on arriving at Pimenta Bueno in October 1938,

I learnt that three years previously an unknown group of Tupi-Kawahib had appeared along the river. They had been seen again two years later, and one of the men now at Pimenta Bueno, Abaitara's last surviving son (who bore the same name as his father, and whom I shall call Abaitara in the rest of this account), had gone to their village which was completely isolated in mid-forest, two days' march from the right bank of the Machado and with no path leading to it. The chief of this small group had promised Abaitara that they would pay him a visit the following year, that is, just about the time of our arrival at Pimenta Bueno. This promise was a matter of great importance for the natives at the post, because of their shortage of women (one adult female to five men); they had been particularly interested by Abaitara's observation that there was a surplus of females in the unknown village. He himself had been a widower for several years and was hoping that the establishment of cordial relations with his savage fellow-tribesmen would make it possible for him to obtain a wife. In the circumstances, I persuaded him—although not without difficulty, since he was apprehensive about the outcome—to anticipate the meeting and act as my guide.

The point from which we were to enter the forest in order to reach the Tupi-Kawahib was a three-day canoe trip downstream from the Pimenta Bueno post, at the mouth of the Igarapé do Porquinho, a small stream flowing into the Machado. Not far from the junction of the two rivers, we spotted a small natural clearing, where there was no danger of flooding, since at that point the bank rose several metres above the level of the water. We unloaded our equipment and stores: small cases of gifts for the natives, and supplies of dried meat, beans and rice. We set up a more durable camp than usual, since it would have to last until our return. A day was spent in doing this and in organizing our journey. The situation was rather complicated. As I have already mentioned, I had had to separate from part of my team. Through an additional stroke of ill-luck, Jehan Vellard, the expedition's doctor, was suffering from an attack of malaria and had had to go on ahead to rest at a small centre of rubber-tappers, a three-day canoe trip downstream (on these difficult rivers, journeys upstream take twice or three times as long). Our effectives were thus reduced to Luis de Castro Faria, my Brazilian companion, Abaitara, myself and five men, two of whom would guard the camp, while three went with us into the forest. Since we were so few in number and each of us had to carry a hammock, a mosquito net and a blanket in addition to his weapons and ammunition, there was no question of taking any provisions other than a little coffee, dried meat and *farinha d'agua*. This is made from manioc which has been soaked in the river (whence its name), then fermented: it takes the form of hard, gravel-like lumps which, when appropriately moistened, have a tasty, buttery flavour. For the rest, we relied on finding *tocari*—Brazil nuts—which are plentiful in the area; a single *ouriço* or 'hedgehog' (this hard spherical shell can kill a man if it drops from high branches twenty or thirty metres from the ground) when held between the feet and deftly cracked with a *terçado* yields thirty to forty large, triangular nuts with a milky, bluish pulp—enough for a meal for several people.

We set off before dawn. First we crossed a number of *lageiros,* or almost bare patches where the rocky floor of the plateau had not yet been covered by alluvial soil, then fields of tall spear-shaped grasses called *sapézals;* two hours later we entered the forest.

32. IN THE FOREST

Ever since childhood the sea has inspired me with mixed feelings. The shore and that extra margin periodically ceded by the ebb-tide, which contends with man for dominion over it, attract me because of their challenge to our enterprises, the unexpected universe they conceal and their promise of observations and discoveries stimulating to the imagination. Like Benvenuto Cellini, to whom I feel more akin than I do to the masters of the *quattrocento,* I like to wander along the shore when the tide has receded, following the path forced upon me by a steep coast, gathering pebbles with holes, shells whose geometry has been re-shaped by the wear and tear of the ocean or plant-roots twisted into chimera-like patterns, to make a private museum of all this flotsam and jetsam: for a while at least, it is just as valid as any collection of masterpieces; moreover, the operations which produce the latter although they take place within the human mind and not outside it—may not be fundamentally different from those in which nature delights.

But being neither a sailor nor a fisherman, I feel baulked by all this water which has stolen half my universe and even more so by the fact that its great presence can be felt well inland and often makes the countryside more austere. The diversity customary on land seems to me to be simply destroyed by the sea, which offers vast spaces and additional shades of colouring for our contemplation, but at the cost of an oppressive monotony and a flatness in which no hidden valley holds in store surprises to nourish my imagination.

Moreover, such charms as I find in the sea are denied us in the modern world. Like some ageing animal whose thickening hide has formed an impermeable crust around its body and, by no longer allowing the skin to breathe, is hastening the ageing process, the majority of European countries are letting their coasts become cluttered with villas, hotels and casinos. Instead of the coast providing, as it once did, a symbolical foretaste of oceanic solitude, it is becoming a kind of battlefront where human beings periodically mobilize all their forces for the conquest of freedom, while at the same time denying its value by the conditions in which they agree to deprive each other of it. Beaches, where once the sea offered us the products of its age-old tumult, an astonishing gallery of objects which showed that nature always belonged to the avant-garde, are now trodden by hordes of people and serve only for the arrangement and display of nondescript rubbish.

It follows that I like mountains more than the sea, and for years this fondness took the form of a jealous love. I hated those who shared my preference, since they threatened the solitude by which I set such store; and I was contemptuous of the others for whom mountain were largely synonymous with excessive fatigue and a closed horizon, and who were therefore incapable of experiencing the emotions that mountains aroused in me. I would only have been content if the whole of society had admitted the superiority of mountains while granting me exclusive possession of them. I may add that my passion did not apply to very high mountains; I had been disappointed by the ambiguous, though indisputable, pleasures that they offer; these pleasures can be intensely physical and even organic, in view of the effort required, yet they remain formal and almost abstract in that the attention, being wholly absorbed by very complex tasks, must—in the very heart of nature—concentrate on operations which appertain to mechanics and geometry. I liked the part of the mountain referred to as *la montagne à vaches* (the cow belt), and especially the area between 1,400 and 2,200 metres: here the altitude, while still moderate enough not to impoverish the landscape as it does at the higher levels, discourages crop-growing yet seems to inspire nature with a more spasmodic and more ardent life. On these high terraces, it preserves the spectacle of land less domesticated than that down in the valleys, and close —as we like to imagine, no doubt mistakenly—to land as man must have known it in earliest times.

Whereas the sea offers me a diluted landscape, mountains impress me as being a concentrated world. They are so literally, since their pleats and folds provide a relatively greater surface-area over a given distance. Also, the potentialities of this denser universe are less quickly exhausted; the changeable climate prevailing there and the differences caused by altitude, exposure and the nature of the soil encourage clear-cut contrasts between the various slopes and levels, as well as between the seasons. Unlike so many people, I was never depressed when staying in a narrow valley the sides of which were so close that they seemed like walls, above which only a fragment of sky was visible, to be traversed by the sun in the space of a few hours. On the contrary, I had the feeling that the upright landscape was alive. Instead of offering itself passively to my gaze, like a picture the details of which can be understood from a distance without personal involvement, it invited me to take part in a kind of dialogue in which both of us were required to give of our best. The physical effort I spent in exploring it was something I conceded to it and by which its being was brought home to me. The mountain landscape, at once obstreperous and provocative, always concealing one half of itself from me but only to renew the other half through the complementary vista accompanying ascent or descent, joined with me in a kind of dance that I had the feeling of being able to lead all the more freely the better I had succeeded in understanding the great truths which inspired it.

And yet, at the present time, I am forced to admit that although I am conscious of no change in myself, my love of mountains is ebbing away from me like the tide receding across the sands. My thoughts have remained the same; it is the mountains which are leaving me. The same pleasures are now less keenly felt through my having cultivated them too long and too intensely. Along paths that I have often followed, even surprise has become familiar; I no longer clamber up among ferns and rocks but among the ghosts of my memories. The latter are losing their appeal for two reasons: first, because use has robbed them of their novelty, but mainly because, as the years go by, I have to make a greater effort to achieve a pleasure which each time is rather less keen than before. I am growing old, and the only warning I have of this is the blurring of the once-sharp outlines of my plans and projects. I am still capable of repeating them, but it is no longer in my power to ensure that their realization gives me the satisfaction that they used to bring so often and so faithfully.

It is the forest, now, which attracts me. I find it has the same charms as the mountains, but in a more peaceful and welcoming form. Through having spent so much time crossing the desert-like savannahs of central Brazil, I was able to appreciate afresh that rustic nature so beloved of the ancients: young grass, flowers, and the moist coolness of thickets. It followed that I could no longer continue to feel the same uncompromising love for the rocky Cévennes; I began to realize that my generation's enthusiasm for Provence was a ruse which we had invented but which was now deceiving us. In the interests of discovery—that supreme joy of which our civilization was depriving us—we were sacrificing the object that ought to justify novelty to novelty itself. That kind of nature had been neglected so long as it was possible to get one's fill of another kind. Now that we were deprived of the more valid variety, we had to reduce our ambitions to the scale of the sort of nature that remained available, and glorify dryness and hardness, since from now on these would be the only forms at our disposal.

But, in executing this forced march, we had forgotten about the forest. It was as dense as our towns, and peopled by other creatures forming a society which had held us more securely at arms' length than the deserts through which we had advanced with such frenzy, whether they were high mountain slopes or the sunlit hills of Provence. A community of trees and plants keeps man at a distance and hurriedly covers up his tracks. The forest, being often difficult to penetrate, demands of anyone venturing into it the same concessions that the mountains, more peremptorily, require of the walker. Its horizon, being less extensive than that of the great mountain ranges, soon closes in on a limited world, creating an isolation as complete as that of the desert wastes. There, a population of grasses, flowers, fungi and insects pursues an undisturbed and independent existence, to which we can only be admitted if we show the proper degree of patience and humility. A few dozen square yards of forest are enough to abolish the external world; one universe gives way to another, which is less flattering to the eye but where hearing and smell, faculties closer to the soul than sight, come into their own. Blessings such as silence, coolness and peace, which we thought had vanished, reappear. Intimate communion with the vegetable world grants us what the sea now refuses and what the mountains provide only at too high a price. However, for me to be convinced of this the forest had perhaps first to impose itself upon me in its most virulent form, so that I would grasp its universal features. The fact is that, between the forest into which I was now plunging to meet up with the

Tupi-Kawahib and our European forests, the gap is so great that it is difficult to find words to describe it.

Seen from the outside, the Amazonian forest seems like a mass of congealed bubbles, a vertical accumulation of green swellings; it is as if some pathological disorder had attacked the riverscape over its whole extent. But once you break through the surface-skin and go inside, everything changes: seen from within, the chaotic mass becomes a monumental universe. The forest ceases to be a terrestrial distemper; it could be taken for a new planetary world, as rich as our world, and replacing it.

As soon as the eye becomes accustomed to recognizing the forest's various closely adjacent planes, and the mind has overcome its first impression of being overwhelmed, a complex system can be perceived. It is possible to distinguish superimposed levels which, in spite of some unevennesses in the strata and an occasion blurring of the lines, follow the same pattern: first, the tops of plants and grasses which are no taller than a man; above these, the pale trunks of trees and stems of creepers briefly enjoying a space unencumbered by vegetation; a little higher up, these trunks and stems disappear into the foliage of large shrubs or the scarlet blossoms of the *pacova,* the wild banana trees; they re-emerge momentarily from this vegetable foam, only to vanish once more among the palm-fronds; they then reappear at a still higher point, where their first horizontal branches become visible, leafless, but laden with parasitic plants such as orchids and Bromeliaceae, like a ship's masts with the rigging; and, almost beyond the range of human vision, this plant universe is completed by vast domes, either green or leafless, but in the latter case covered with white, yellow, orange, purple or mauve blossom; the European spectator is astonished to see a freshness like that of springtime in the Old World, but on so disproportionate a scale that the only term of comparison which occurs to him is the broad, majestic glow of European trees in autumn.

Beneath the traveller's feet, there are other levels corresponding to these aerial ones. It would be an illusion to suppose that one was walking on the ground, because it is buried deep under an unstable and inter-grown mass of roots, suckers, tufts and mosses; every time one fails to find a firm foothold, there is a danger of falling, sometimes to alarming depths. And the presence of Lucinda was a still further hindrance to movement.

Lucinda was a small female monkey with a prehensile tail, purple skin and the short grey fur of the Siberian squirrel: she belonged to the *Lagothryx* species, commonly known as *barrigudo* because of the characteristic large belly. I had got her, when she was only a few weeks old, from a Nambikwara woman who fed her from mouth to mouth and carried her night and day in her hair; the little creature clung there as she would have done to her mother's fur and backbone (mother monkeys carry their young on their backs). I saw to it that bottles of condensed milk took the place of mouth-feeding, and when laced with whisky, they would send the poor beast into a deep sleep and so gradually left me free during the night. But during the day Lucinda would only agree to a compromise arrangement: she was willing to give up my hair for my left boot, to which she clung, just above the foot, with all four limbs, from morning till night. This position was tolerable on horseback and perfectly acceptable in a canoe. But travelling on foot was another matter, since every thorn, low branch or swampy patch drew piercing cries from Lucinda. All my efforts to induce her to accept my arm, my shoulder or even my hair were in vain. She would have nothing but my left boot, her only protection and point of security in the forest where she had been born and grown up, but which it had taken only a few months spent in the company of humans to make as strange for her as if she had been brought up among the refinements of civilization. So, limping with my left leg and deafened by shrill reproaches every time I stumbled, I tried not to lose sight of Abaitara's back in the green half-light into which our guide continued to advance with short, rapid steps, sometimes disappearing behind huge trees, hacking a way through bushes and creepers with his machete, and occasionally bearing to the left or the right to follow a route which remained incomprehensible to us but took us even deeper into the forest.

To forget my fatigue I let my mind freewheel. In time to the rhythm of my movements, little poems kept taking shape in my head, where they would go round and round for hours, like a mouthful of food that has been chewed until it has become tasteless, but that one is loath to spit out or swallow because of the atom of companionship provided by its presence. The aquarium-like atmosphere which prevailed in the forest inspired the following quatrain:

> Dans la forêt céphalopode
> gros coquillage chevelu
> de vase, sur des rochers roses qu'érode
> le ventre des poissons-lune d'Honolulu.

> (In the cephalopodic forest,
> A huge sea-shell, hairy
> with slime, on pink rocks eroded
> by the bellies of the Honolulu moon-fish.)

Or, in contrast no doubt, I conjured up bleak memories of suburbia:

> On a nettoyé l'herbe paillasson
> les pavés luisent savonnés
> sur l'avenue les arbres sont
> de grands balais abandonnés.

> (The door-mat lawns have been cleaned
> the pavements gleam with soaping
> along the avenue the trees are
> tall, abandoned besoms.)

Lastly, there was another quatrain, which was appropriate to the circumstances but never seemed to achieve its final form; even today it still nags at me whenever I go for a long walk:

> Amazone, chère Amazone
> vous qui n'avez pas de sein droit
> vous nous en racontez de bonnes
> mais vos chemins sont trop étroits.

> (Amazon, dear Amazon
> you who have no right breast
> you tell us some tall stories
> but your paths are too narrow.)

Towards the end of the morning, on rounding a bush, we suddenly found ourselves face to face with two natives travelling in the opposite direction. The elder, who was about forty, was wearing a pair of torn pyjamas, and had shoulder-length hair; the other had short hair and was completely naked, except for the little straw cornet on his penis; on his back he was carrying a basket made of green palm-fronds tightly fastened around the body of a big harpy-eagle, which was trussed like a chicken and looked a sorry sight, in spite of its grey-and-white striped plumage, its powerful yellow beak and the crown of feathers bristling on its head. Both men had bows and arrows in their hands.

From the conversation between them and Abaitara it transpired that they were respectively the chief of the village we were looking for and his lieutenant; they were in advance of the other villagers, who were wandering somewhere in the forest; all were going towards the Machado in order to visit the post of Pimenta Bueno, according to the promise made the year before; the eagle was a present intended for their hosts. This did not suit our purpose at all, because we were anxious not only to meet the natives but also to visit the village. So, with the promise of the numerous presents awaiting them at the Porquinho camp, we had to persuade the two natives to turn back, go with us to their village and accept us there as guests (which they were extremely reluctant to do); after that, we would all set off for the river together. Once agreement had been reached, the parcelled-up eagle was unceremoniously dumped by the side of a stream, where it seemed doomed to die rapidly of hunger or be eaten by ants. No mention was made of it during the next fortnight, except that its demise was duly, if summarily, noted: 'The eagle is dead.' The two Kawahib disappeared into the forest to announce our arrival to their families, and we continued on our way.

The incident of the eagle provided food for reflection. Several of the early chroniclers say that the Tupi kept eagles and fed them on monkeys, so as to be able to pluck their feathers periodically; Rondon noted the existence of this practice among the Tupi-Kawahib, and other observers mention it in connection with certain tribes along the Xingu and the Araguaya. It was not surprising, then, that it should have survived among a group of Tupi-Kawahib, nor that the eagle, which they looked upon as their most precious possession, should have been brought as a present, if the natives had really decided (as I began to suspect and indeed subsequently confirmed) to leave their village for good and join the civilized world. However, that only made it more difficult to understand why they should have abandoned the eagle to its pitiable fate. Yet the whole history of coloniza-

tion in South America and elsewhere must take into account
this kind of radical renunciation of traditional values, when,
during the break-up of a way of life, the loss of certain
elements leads to the immediate depreciation of all the rest;
what I had just observed was perhaps a characteristic example of this phenomenon.

A scanty meal consisting of a few scraps of *xarque*,
grilled without being de-salted, was embellished with forest
produce: *tocari* nuts; the fruit of the wild cocoa plant with
an acid, and almost frothy, white pulp; berries from the
pama tree, and fruit and seeds of the forest *caju*. It rained
all night on the palm shelter over the hammocks. At dawn,
the forest, which had been silent during the day, resounded
for a few minutes with the cries of monkeys and parrots.
We resumed our forward march, each of us trying not to
lose sight of the back of the man in front, and convinced
that to stray only a few yards off the track would mean
being deprived of all sense of direction and falling immediately out of earshot. One of the most striking characteristics of the forest is that it seems to be immersed in a
medium denser than air; any light that filters through is
green and dim and voices have no carrying power. The extraordinary silence which prevails, and which is perhaps the
result of these conditions, would no doubt also be communicated to the traveller, if he were not already inclined
to keep quiet because of the intense care needed in moving
forward. His mental condition conspires with his physical
state to create an almost unbearable sensation of oppressive-
ness.

From time to time, our guide would bend down towards
the edge of his invisible track and smartly turn back a leaf
to reveal beneath it a spear-shaped splinter of bamboo set
at an angle in the ground so as to pierce the foot of an approaching enemy. These devices, with which the Tupi-
Kawahib protect the paths leading to their villages, are
called *min;* the ancient Tupi used larger ones.

During the afternoon, we reached a *castanhal*, a cluster
of chestnut trees around which the natives (who systematically exploit the resources of the forest) had made a small
clearing so as to be able to harvest the fallen fruit more
easily The entire population of the village was encamped
there; the men were naked, apart from the penis sheath I
had already observed on the chief's companion; the women
too were naked except for a short, tight-fitting skirt of

FIG 51. Bamboo splinters defending the approach
to the village

native cotton; it had originally been dyed red with urucu, but was now a rusty brown through use.

In all there were six women, seven men, one of them only an adolescent, and three little girls who seemed to be one, two and three years of age; it was no doubt one of the smallest groups that could be imagined as managing to survive, cut off from all contact with the outside world for at least thirteen years (that is, since the disappearance of Abaitara's village). Besides, two members of the group were afflicted with paralysis of the lower limbs: a young woman went about on two sticks, and a man, also young, dragged himself along the ground like a legless cripple. His knees stuck out above his emaciated legs, and were swollen on the underside as if full of fluid; the toes of his left foot were paralysed, but he could still move those of his right foot. However, both cripples could move about the forest and even cover long distances with apparent ease. I wondered if poliomyelitis or some other virus had affected them, even before they had had time to establish lasting contact with civilization. Looking at these unfortunate wretches, living on their own in the most hostile natural surrounding that man could ever be called upon to face, it was distressing to recall what Thevet wrote about the coastal Tupi after visiting them in the sixteenth century. He was surprised that a people 'composed of the same elements as ourselves . . . is never afflicted with leprosy, paralysis, the death-trance, cankerous diseases or ulcers, or other blemishes of the body which are to be seem superficially and externally'. Little did he realize that he and his companions were the forerunners of the carriers of these diseases.

33. THE VILLAGE
OF THE CRICKETS

Towards the end of the afternoon we arrived at the village. It stood in an artificial clearing overlooking the narrow valley of a stream that I was later to identify as the Igarapé do Leitão, a tributary of the Machado into which it flows, on the right bank, a few kilometres downstream from the junction with the Muqui.

The village consisted of four more or less square houses placed in a row and parallel to the course of the stream. Two houses—the largest—were used as dwellings, as could be seen from the hammocks made from cords of knotted cotton slung between the posts: the other two (one of which stood between the two larger dwellings) had not been occupied for some time and looked more like barns or shelters. At first glance, one might have thought that these houses were of the same type as the local Brazilian dwellings. Actually, they were quite different in design, since the area enclosed by the posts supporting the high, two-sided palm roof was smaller than the total area of the roof itself, so that the building had the shape of a square mushroom. However, this basic structure was not immediately obvious, because of the existence of false walls in line with the edge of the roof but not reaching up to it. These palings —since that is what they really were—were made of split palm trunks set side by side (and bound together) with the convex surfaces to the outside. In the case of the main dwelling—the one situated between the two barns—the trunks were notched in such a way as to provide pentagonal holes like arrow slits, and the outer wall was covered with paintings roughly daubed in red and black with urucu and a kind of resin. According to the native informant, these paintings represented, respectively, a person, women, a harpy-eagle, children, an object in the shape of an arrow

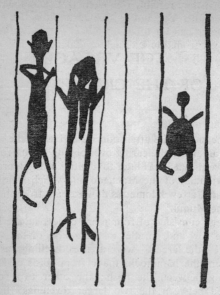

FIG 52. Details of hut wall-paintings

slit, a toad, a dog, a large unidentified quadruped, two bands of zig-zagging lines, two fishes, two quadrupeds, a jaguar and lastly a symmetrical design made up of squares, crescents and hoops.

Although these houses in no way resembled the dwellings of neighbouring Indian tribes, they were probably constructed according to a traditional pattern. When Rondon discovered the Tupi-Kawahib, their houses were already square-shaped or rectangular, and had two-sided roofs. Besides, the mushroom-like structure does not correspond to any neo-Brazilian technique. Such high-roofed dwellings are mentioned, incidentally, in various archaeological documents relating to a number of pre-Columbian cultures.

Another original feature of the Tupi-Kawahib is that, like their Parintintin cousins, they neither cultivate nor consume tobacco. On seeing us unroll our supply of tobacco, the village chief sarcastically exclaimed: 'Ianeapit!' ('This is excrement!'). The reports of the Rondon Commission even mention that when contact was first established with the Tupi-Kawahib, the latter were so irritated by the presence of smokers that they forcibly removed cigars and cigarettes from their mouths. Yet, unlike the Parintintin, the Tupi-Kawahib have a term for tobacco: *tabak*, the same word as ours, borrowed from the old native dialects of the West Indies and most likely of Carib origin. A possible link in the chain of transmission may be provided by the dialects of the tribes along the Guaporé, which have the same term. Either they took it from the Spanish (in Portuguese the word is *fumo*), or (as so much evidence indicates) the cultural traditions along the Guaporé represent the most advanced south-westerly point of an old Guyana–Caribbean civilization, traces of which are also to be found along the lower reaches of the Xingu. It should be added that the Nambikwara are inveterate cigarette-smokers, whereas the other neighbours of the Tupi-Kawahib, the Kepkiriwat and the Mundé, sniff tobacco through hollow tubes. So, the presence in the very heart of Brazil of a group of tribes who do not consume tobacco is something of a mystery, especially if we consider that the ancient Tupi made great use of it.

In the absence of tobacco, we were about to be welcomed in the village with what sixteenth-century travellers called a *cahouin*—the Tupi-Kawahib call it *kaui*—that is, a *chicha*

Fig 53. Details of hut wall-paintings

drinking-session. *Chicha* is made with maize, several varieties of which were grown by the natives on fire-cleared
patches around the village. The early writers described the
pots—as tall as men—in which the liquid was prepared,
and the function of the virgins of the tribe, which was to
spit copious quantities of saliva into them in order to induce fermentation. Either the pots of the Tupi-Kawahib
were too small or there was a shortage of virgins in the
village. The three little girls were brought along and made
to spit into the decoction of pounded corn. As the delicious
drink, at once nutritious and refreshing, was consumed that
very evening, the process of fermentation was not very far
advanced.

On visiting the gardens, we noted—around the huge
wooden cage, previously occupied by the eagle and still
strewn with bones—groundnuts, beans, various kinds of
red peppers, small yams, sweet potatoes, manioc and maize.
The natives supplemented these sources of food by gathering wild produce. For instance, they exploit a kind of forest
grass by tying several stems together at the top, so that the
seeds fall in small heaps. These seeds are heated on a pottery plate until they burst like pop-corn, which they rather
resemble in taste.

While the cahouin was going through its complicated
cycle of mixing and boiling and being stirred by women
armed with ladles made from half-gourds, I took advantage
of the last hours of daylight to study the Indians.

Apart from the cotton skirt, the women wore bands tied
tightly round their wrists and ankles and necklaces made of
tapirs' teeth or flat pieces of deer bone. Their faces were
tattooed with the bluish black juice of the *genipa;* on the
cheeks, a thick oblique line ran from the lobes of the ears
to the corners of the lips, which were marked by four little
vertical strokes, and on the chin were four horizontal lines
one above the other and each adorned with a fringe of
streaks. On the whole, they wore their hair short and
combed it frequently with a rake-comb or a finer instrument
made of small wooden sticks held together by cotton thread.

The only garment worn by the men was the conical penis
sheath to which I have already referred. As it happened, a
native was just busy making himself one. The two sides of a
freshly picked *pacova* leaf were pulled away from the central rib, and the tough outer rim was removed; they were

then folded in two lengthwise. By fitting the two pieces (each about seven by thirty centimetres) together, one into the other, so that the folds meet at a right-angle, a kind of set-square shape is obtained, with two thicknesses of leaf on the sides and four at the top, where the two bands interlock; this part is then folded along the diagonal, and the two arms are cut off and thrown away, so that all the maker is left with is a small isosceles triangle consisting of eight thicknesses; the triangle is then rounded over the thumb, from front to back, the tips of the two lower angles are cut off and the sides sewn together with a wooden needle and vegetable thread. The object is now ready, and only requires to be fixed into position; this is done by stretching the foreskin through the opening so that the sheath cannot fall off and the tension of the skin keeps the penis in an upright position. All the men wore this appurtenance, and if any one of them happened to lose it, he at once stretched the end of his foreskin under the cord he wore as a belt.

The houses were almost empty. All that could be seen in them was: hammocks made of cotton string; a few earthenware pots, and a pan for drying maize or manioc pulp over the fire; gourd vessels; wooden pestles and mortars; manioc graters made from wood set with thorns; basketwork sieves; engraving tools made from rodents' teeth; spindles, and a few bows about 1.70 metres long. The arrows were of several types: some had a single bamboo tip—spear-shaped for hunting, or serrated for war—and some, which were used for fishing, were multipointed. Lastly, there were a few musical instruments—Pan-pipes with thirteen tubes and flageolets with four holes.

At nightfall, the chief ceremoniously brought us the cahouin and a stew of giant beans flavoured with red peppers, which was extremely hot; this was a cheering dish to be given after six months spent among the Nambikwara, who are unacquainted with either salt or spices and whose delicate palates even require that their food should be soused with water to cool it before they eat it. The native salt was presented in a small gourd; it was a brownish fluid so bitter that the chief, who did not partake of the meal but looked on, insisted on tasting it in our presence so as to reassure us, since we might well have thought that it was some kind of poison. This condiment is prepared with the wood ash of the *toari branco*. Although the meal was a modest one, the dignity with which it was served reminded me that the ancient Tupi chiefs must have kept open house, as one early traveller says they did.

Another even more striking detail was that after spending a night in one of the hangars, I noticed that my leather belt had been gnawed by crickets. I had never before had any trouble with these insects, never having encountered any in all the tribes I had been among—Kaingang, Caduveo, Bororo, Paressi, Nambikwara and Mundé. It was among the Tupi that this mishap was fated to occur, as it had been experienced four hundred years earlier by Yves d'Evreux and Jean de Léry: 'And so that, while I am on the subject, I may describe these small creatures . . . being no bigger than our crickets, coming out at night in hordes in the same way near the fire, if they find something, they will not fail to gnaw it. But the chief difference was that they attacked leather collars and shoes in such a way that, eating away the top, the owners found them all white and flayed in the morning . . .' Since crickets (unlike ants and other destructive insects) merely gnaw the surface-skin of leather, my belt was indeed 'all white and flayed', thus testifying to a strange, exclusive and centuries-old association between a species of insect and a human group.

As soon as the sun rose, one of our men went off into the forest to shoot a few of the wood-pigeons which were flying along the edge. Shortly afterwards, we heard the sound of a shot, but no one paid any attention to it. Soon, however, a native, pale with alarm and in a state of intense excitement, came running towards us: he tried to explain something; Abaitara was not at hand to act as interpreter. However, we could hear loud cries approaching from the direction of the forest, and before long the man came running across the cultivated land, holding in his left hand his right forearm, the lower part of which was hanging in shreds: he had leant on his gun, and it had gone off. Luis and I debated about what we should do. Since three fingers had been all but severed and the palm seemed to be shattered it looked as if amputation would be inevitable. But we could not bring ourselves to carry it out, and thus leave our companion maimed for life. We had recruited him along with his brother in a little village on the outskirts of Cuiaba, and felt particularly responsible both because of his extreme youth and because his peasant loyalty and shrewdness had endeared him to us. Since his trade was looking after pack-animals and since the fitting of the loads on to the backs of mules and oxen demands great manual skill, amputation would have been a catastrophe for him. Not without some apprehension, we decided to put his fingers back approximately into place, to bandage him up with the means at our disposal and to begin at once on the return journey. As soon as we got back to the camp, Luis would take the wounded man on to our doctor at Urupa and, if the natives were agreeable, I would stay and camp with them on the river-bank, until the boat came back for me two weeks later (the journey downstream took three days, and the journey upstream about a week). Being terrified by the accident and fearing perhaps that it might change our friendly attitude towards them, the Indians accepted all the proposals we put to them; so, leaving them to make their preparations once again, we went on ahead into the forest.

The journey was accomplished in a nightmarish atmosphere and I can remember very little about it. The wounded man was delirious all the way, and bolted on ahead so quickly that we could hardly follow him; he had taken the lead, leaving even the guide in the rear, and never seemed to hesitate about the way to go, although our previous track seemed to have closed up behind us. At night we managed to get him to sleep with the help of sleeping pills. Fortunately, he was quite unused to drugs, and so they produced their full effect. When, during the afternoon of the following day, we reached the encampment, we found that his hand was crawling with worms, which were the cause of the unbearable pain. But when he was handed over to the doctor three days later, the danger of gangrene had gone, since the worms had gradually eaten away the decayed flesh. There was now no point in amputating, and after a prolonged series of minor surgical operations, which were spread over a month and allowed Vellard to put his skill as a vivisectionist and entomologist to good account, Emydio's hand emerged in not too bad a shape. When we reached the Rio Madeira in December, I dispatched the convalescent to Cuiaba by plane so as to husband his strength. But when I went to visit his parents on returning to the area in January to join the main body of the expedition, they were full of reproaches. It was not their son's sufferings that they held against me—these they considered as an everyday occurrence in the life of the *sertão*—but the fact that I had been so cruel as to send him up into the sky, a diabolical situation which, in their view, it was inconceivable that anyone should ever wish to inflict on a Christian.

34. THE FARCE
OF THE JAPIM BIRD

My new family was made up as follows: first, Taperahi, the village chief, and his four wives: Maruabai, the oldest, and Kunhatsin, her daughter by a previous marriage; Takwame, and Ianopamoko, the young cripple. This polygamous household was bringing up five children: Kamini and Pwereza, two boys who seemed to be respectively seventeen and fifteen years old, and three little girls still in their infancy, Paerai, Topekea and Kupekahi.

Potien, the chief's lieutenant, was about twenty and was Maruabai's son by a previous marriage. There was also an old woman, Wirakaru; her two adolescent sons Takwari and Karamua, the former a bachelor, the latter married to his niece, Penhana, who was barely of marriageable age; and lastly their cousin, a young cripple called Walera.

Unlike the Nambikwara, the Tupi-Kawahib make no secret of their names, which in fact have a meaning, as the sixteenth-century travelers noted was the case among the Tupi. 'As we do with dogs and other beasts,' Léry observes, 'they give at random such names of things as they are familiar with, like Sarigoy, which is a four-footed animal, Arignan, a hen, Arabouten, the tree of Brazil, Pindo, a tall grass, and suchlike.'

This was true in the case of all the natives who offered me explanations of their names. Taperahi is, apparently, a little bird with black-and-white plumage; Kunhatsin means white, or light-skinned, woman; Takwame and Takwari are terms derived from *takwara,* a species of bamboo; Potien means a freshwater shrimp; Wirakaru, a small human parasite (*bicho de pé* in Portuguese); Karamua, a plant; Walera, also a species of bamboo.

Staden, another sixteenth-century traveller, says that women 'normally took the names of birds, fish and fruit'; and he adds that every time the husband kills a prisoner, his wife and he adopt a new name. My companions followed this custom; for instance, Karamua was also called Janaku, because, as was explained to me, 'he had already killed a man.'

The natives also acquire names on passing from childhood into adolescence, and then again when they reach adulthood. So each one had two, three or four names, which they made no attempt to conceal from me. These names were of considerable interest, because each family line tends to use certain groups of terms formed from the same roots and connected with the clan. The village whose inhabitants I was studying belonged, for the most part, to the *mialat* ('wild boar') clan; but it had come into being through inter-marriage with other clans, such as the Paranawat ('river-people'), Takwatip ('bamboo-people'), etc. All the members of this last clan were called by names derived from the eponymous term: Takwame, Takwarumé, Takwari, Walera (which is a large bamboo), Topehi (a fruit of the same family) and Karamua (also a plant, but not identified).

The most striking feature of the social organization of these Indians was that the chief enjoyed a virtual monopoly of the women in the group. Of the six women who had passed the age of puberty, four were his wives. If we remember that, of the two remaining women, one—Penhana—was his sister and therefore taboo, and the other—Wirakaru—an old woman in whom no one any longer took any interest, it would seem that Taperahi had as many wives as was physically possible in the circumstances. The dominant role in his household was played by Kunhatsin who, apart from the lame Ianopamoko, was the youngest woman and—the native view coinciding with that of the anthropologist—extremely beautiful. In the domestic hierarchy, Maruabai was a secondary wife and her daughter took precedence over her.

The principal wife seemed to help her husband in a more direct way than the others, who attended to the domestic chores such as cooking and minding the children, who were all brought up together. As they were suckled by all the women in turn, I could never be sure who their respective mothers were. The principal wife, on the other hand, accompanied her husband wherever he went, helped him to receive strangers, took charge of any presents given them, and directed the household. The situation was exactly the opposite of what I had observed among the Nambikwara, where it was the principal wife who looked after household matters while the young concubines were closely associated with the chief's male role.

The chief's prerogative with regard to the women in the group seemed to be based, primarily, on the belief that he was by nature exceptional. It was said that he had an ungovernable temperament; he would fall into trances, during which he sometimes had to be overpowered in order to be prevented from killing people (I shall quote an instance of this later); he had the gift of prophecy, as well as other talents; lastly, his sexual appetite far exceeded the normal and, in order to satisfy it, he had to have a large number of wives. During the two weeks I spent in the native encampment, I was often struck by the fact that chief Taperahi's behaviour seemed abnormal, in comparison with that of his companions. He appeared to be afflicted with a mania for moving about; three times a day at least he would change the position of his hammock and of the palm awning which protected it from the rain, and would be followed each time by his women, his lieutenant Potien and his babies. Every morning he disappeared into the forest with his wives and children—for purposes of copulation, according to the natives. They would all come back half an hour or an hour later, and set about preparing another removal.

Secondly, the chief's polygamous privilege was offset to some extent by the lending of women to his fellow natives and to strangers. Potien was not just an aide-de-camp; he lived as part of the chief's family, shared their food, occasionally acted as dry-nurse to the babies and enjoyed other favours too. All the sixteenth-century writers dwell on the liberality shown the strangers by the Tupinamba chiefs. The duty of hospitality worked in Abaitara's favour as soon as we arrived in the village, since he was loaned Ianopamoko who, as it happened, was pregnant. All the time I was there, she shared his hammock and received her food from him.

As Abaitara confided in me, this generosity was not entirely disinterested. Taperahi offered to let Abaitara keep Ianopamoko for good, in exchange for his daughter Topehi, who was about eight years old at the time; 'Karijiraen taleko ehi nipoka' ('the chief wants to marry my daughter'). Abaitara was not too enthusiastic, since Ianopamoko, a cripple, could not be much of a helpmate. 'Not even capable', he said, 'of fetching water from the river.' Besides, the exchange of a handicapped adult for a healthy little girl

full of promise did not seem at all fair. Abaitara had other
ambitions: in exchange for Topehi, he wanted Kupekahi,
who was only two, and he stressed the fact that she was
the daughter of Takwame, a member of the Takwatip clan
like himself and over whom he could exercise his privilege
as uterine uncle. He also planned that Takwame herself
should be given to another native at the Pimenta Bueno
post. The matrimonial balance would thus be partially
restored, since Takwari, for his part, was 'engaged' to little
Kupekahi, and once all the transactions were completed,
Taperahi would have lost two of his four wives, while
regaining a third in the person of Topehi.

I do not know what the eventual outcome of these discussions was, but during the two weeks we spent together,
they created considerable tension between the people concerned and at times the situation became rather alarming.
Abaitara was extremely keen on his two-year-old fiancée
who seemed to him to be a wife after his own heart, although he himself was between thirty and thirty-five. He
would give her little presents and, when she was romping
along the river-bank, he never tired of admiring, and asking
me to admire, her sturdy little limbs: what a beautiful girl
she would be in ten or twelve years' time! Although he had
been a widower for years, he was not dismayed by the
prospect of waiting so long: admittedly, he was counting
on Ianopamoko to fill the gap in the meantime. The tender
emotions which the little girl aroused in him were an innocent mixture of erotic daydreams for the future, a quite
paternal feeling of responsibility towards the little person,
and the affectionate comradeship of an elder brother who
had acquired a baby sister rather late in life.

Another factor which compensated for the unfair alloca-
tion of the women was the levirate—the inheriting of widows by their dead husbands' brothers. This was how
Abaitara had entered into his first marriage, against his will.
He had been obliged to marry his elder brother's widow in
obedience to his father's orders and in response to the
woman's insistence; she had 'constantly hung around him'.
As well as the levirate, the Tupi-Kawahib practised fraternal
polyandry, an example of which was provided by Penhana,
a spindly little girl who had barely reached puberty: she
was shared between Karamua, her husband, and her brothers-in-law, Takwari and Walera, the latter being considered

as a classificatory brother of the other two: 'He lends [his wife] to his brother,' because 'brother is not jealous of brother.' Normally, without deliberately avoiding each other, brothers-in-law and sisters-in-law maintained an attitude of reserve. It was possible to tell when a woman had been lent, because on that day she and her brother-in-law would be on more familiar terms. They would laugh and joke together and the brother-in-law would give her food. One day when Takwari had borrowed Penhana, he was having his meal by my side, and just as he was about to begin he asked his brother Karamua to 'go and fetch Penhana so that she can eat'; Penhana was not hungry, having already had her meal with her husband; however she came, accepted a mouthful and then went off again. Similarly, Abaitara would leave my fire and carry off his food to eat it with Ianopamoko.

The problem posed by the chief's prerogatives with regard to marriage was solved, then, by the Tupi-Kawahib through a combination of polygyny and polyandry. Having taken leave of the Nambikwara only a few weeks before, I was struck by the fact that groups which were geographically so close to each other could evolve such different solutions for identical problems. Among the Nambikwara, too, as we saw, the chief enjoys the privilege of polygamy which produces a similar imbalance between the number of young men and the number of available wives. But instead of having recourse to polyandry like the Tupi-Kawahib, the Nambikwara allow their adolescent boys to practise homosexuality. Since the Tupi-Kawahib refer in derisive terms to such practices, they obviously condemn them. But as Léry mischievously observed about their ancestors: 'Since at times when they are quarrelling, they call each other Tyvire [the Tupi-Kawahib use almost the same word: *Teukuruwa*], that is, bugger, it may be conjectured (I make no affirmative statement) that this abominable sin is committed among them.'

Among the Tupi-Kawahib, the chieftainship was marked by a certain complexity of organization to which our village remained symbolically attached, rather in the manner of some small court which has lost its former splendour and where one faithful retainer devotes himself to playing the part of chamberlain to save the dignity of the royal position. This was the way Potien behaved with regard to Taperahi; he served his master so conscientiously and with such re-

spect and he himself was treated with such deference by the
other members of the group that at times one might have
thought that Taperahi, like Abaitara in the past, had several
thousand subjects or liegemen under his command. In
Abaitara's day, the court consisted of at least four grades:
the chief, the bodyguards, the minor officials and the companions. The chief had the right to inflict the death penalty.
As in the sixteenth century, the normal means of execution
was by drowning, the sentence being carried out by the
minor officials. But the chief also looked after his people
and, as I was to discover, conducted negotiations with
strangers in a remarkably astute manner.

I had in my possession a large aluminum pan which we
used for cooking rice. One morning, Taperahi, accompanied
by Abaitara who was acting as interpreter, came to ask me
for this pan, saying that, in exchange, he would keep it filled
with cahouin for us to drink during the whole of our stay.
I tried to explain that the pan was an indispensable cooking-
utensil, but all the time Abaitara was translating, I noticed
with surprise that Taperahi's face remained wreathed in
smiles, as if my answer fulfilled his dearest wishes. And,
indeed, when Abaitara had finished expounding my reasons
for refusing, Taperahi, still smiling broadly, seized the pot
and without further ado added it to his own possessions.
There was no alternative but to accept the situation. Taperahi, for his part, kept his promise and supplied me for a
whole week with a superlative kind of cahouin made from a
mixture of maize and *tocari;* I consumed vast quantities of
it, the only restriction on my thirst being a slight scruple
about overworking the salivary glands of the three tiny tots.
The incident reminded me of a passage from Yves
d'Evreux: 'If one of them wants something which belongs
to one of his fellows, he says so frankly: and the object
must be very dear indeed to the person owning it for him
not to hand it over at once, on the understanding, however,
that if the asker owns some other object which the giver
fancies, he in turn will hand it over whenever it is asked
for.'

The Tupi-Kawahib have quite a different conception from
the Nambikwara of the function of the chief. When pressed
to explain their views, they will reply: 'The chief is always
gay.' The extraordinarily dynamic quality which Taperahi
displayed on all occasions was the best possible commentary
on this definition; however, it is not simply explicable in

terms of his gifts, since the Tupi-Kawahib chieftainship, unlike that of the Nambikwara, is hereditary through the male line: Pwereza would be his father's successor; as a matter of fact, he looked younger than his brother Kamini, and I noted other indications of the fact that the younger son might take precedence over the elder. In the past, one of the duties incumbent upon a chief was that of holding feasts, of which he was said to be the 'master' or 'proprietor'. Men and women covered their bodies with paintings (done chiefly with the purple juice of an unidentified leaf, also used in the painting of pottery), and there were dancing sessions with singing and music; the accompaniment was provided by four or five large clarinets, each made from a piece of bamboo 1.20 metres long, at the top of which a small bamboo pipe, held in place with a wad of fibre, had a single reed cut out along one side. When the 'master of the feast' gave the word, the men would vie with each other in carrying a flute-player on their shoulders, a competitive sport reminiscent of the Bororo game of carrying the *mariddo,* and the Ge tree-trunk races.

Invitations were issued in advance to give the participants time to collect and smoke small animals such as rats, monkeys and squirrels, which they carried threaded round their necks. There was a wheel game, for the purposes of which the village divided up into two camps: the younger people and the older. The teams arranged themselves at the west end of a circular area, while two pitchers or bowlers, one from either camp, took up their respective positions to the north and south. They would roll towards each other a kind of solid hoop, made from a slice of tree-trunk. As this target ran across in front of the marksmen, they had to try to plant an arrow in it. Each successful shot entitled the winner to appropriate one of the other side's arrows. This game is strikingly similar to some that existed in North America.

Another shooting contest, in which the target was a dummy, involved an element of risk. It was believed that anyone whose arrow hit the supporting post was doomed to die from magical causes; the same fate was expected for anyone who dared to carve a wooden dummy in human form, instead of making a straw doll or a dummy representing a monkey.

Thus, as the days went by, I collected scraps of a culture which had once fascinated Europe and was perhaps now

going to disappear altogether from the right bank of the
Upper Machado at the time of my departure: on November
7th, 1938, the very day when I took the boat which had
returned from Urupa, the natives were due to start off in the
direction of Pimenta Bueno to join forces with Abaitara's
companions and family.

And yet, just as the sad liquidation of these last vestiges
of a dying culture was about to be completed, I was to be
given a surprise. It happened in the early hours of darkness,
at a time when everyone was taking advantage of the last
flickerings of the camp fire to settle down for the night.
Chief Taperahi was already stretched out in his hammock;
he began to sing in a halting, faraway voice, which hardly
seemed to belong to him. Immediately two men (Walera
and Kamini) came and crouched at his feet, while a thrill
of excitement ran through the tiny group. Walera uttered
a few calls; the chief's song became clearer, his voice
stronger. And suddenly I realized what it was we were
hearing: Taperahi was performing a play, or to be more
accurate, an operetta in which arias alternated with recita-
tive. All by himself, he was impersonating a dozen or so
characters, each one distinguished by a special tone of voice
—shrill, falsetto, guttural or droning—as well as by a
musical theme tantamount to a *leitmotiv*. The melodies
sounded extraordinarily like a Gregorian chant. The Nambikwara flutes had reminded me of the *Sacre;* I now felt I
was listening to an exotic version of *Noces*.

With the help of Abaitara—who was so interested in the
performance that it was difficult to extract any remarks
from him—I was able to get some vague idea of the subject. The play was a farce, and its hero the *japim* bird
(an oriole with black-and-yellow plumage, whose modulated
song can be mistaken for that of a human voice); among
the other characters were animals: tortoise, jaguar, falcon,
ant-eater, tapir, lizard, etc.; objects: a stick, a pestle and a
bow; and lastly spirits, such as the phantom Maira. Each of
these expressed itself in a style so suited to its nature that I
was very soon able to identify them myself without help.
The plot centred round the adventures of the japim which,
after being at first threatened by the other animals, tricked
them in a variety of ways and eventually got the better of
them. The performance, which was repeated (or continued?) for two consecutive nights, lasted about four hours
on each occasion. At times, Taperahi seemed to be inspired;

words and songs came pouring out of him, causing bursts of laughter on all sides. At other times, he appeared exhausted, his voice would grow weak, and he would try various themes without being able to settle for any one of them. Then one of the narrators, or both together, would come to his aid, either by repeating their calls so as to allow the chief actor a breathing space, or by suggesting some musical theme to him, or again by temporarily taking over one of the roles, so that, for a little while, the performance became a genuine dialogue. After thus being allowed to recover his energy, Taperahi would embark on a new phase of the story.

As the night wore on, it became clear that poetic creation was accompanied by a loss of consciousness and that the performer was being subordinated to his characters. His different voices became foreign to him; each acquired such a distinctive nature that it was hard to believe they were all coming from the same person. At the end of the second session, Taperahi, while still singing, suddenly got out of his hammock and started to stagger wildly about, demanding cahouin; he had been 'seized by the spirit'; suddenly he snatched up a knife and rushed at Kunhatsin, his chief wife, who only just managed to escape from him by running off into the forest, while the other men forcibly held him back and obliged him to return to his hammock, where he immediately fell asleep. By morning everything had returned to normal.

35. AMAZONIA

On arriving at Urupa, from where the river is navigable by
motor-boat, I found my companions installed in a spacious
straw hut standing on pilings and partitioned off into several
rooms. We had nothing to do, except sell what was left of
our equipment to the local community, or exchange it for
chickens, eggs and milk—since there were one or two cows
our equipment to the local community, or exchange it for
the rains to swell the river, and make it possible for the first
boat of the season to get as far. It was expected in about
three weeks. Every morning, we dissolved our remaining
stocks of chocolate in milk, and spent breakfast time watching Vellard extract a few splinters from Emydio's hand, re-
shaping it as he worked. The spectacle, which had something nauseating and yet fascinating about it, was associated
in my mind with a vision of the forest, full of shapes and
threats. Taking my left hand as a model, I began to draw
landscapes made up of hands emerging from bodies as
twisted and tangled as creepers. After making a dozen or
so of these sketches, almost all of which disappeared during
the war and are now no doubt lying forgotten in some German attic, I felt relieved and went back to observing people and things.

From Urupa to Rio Madeira, the posts along the telegraph line coincide with hamlets inhabited by rubber-
tappers, and this gives a degree of logicality to the sporadic
population of the river-banks. The settlements seem less
absurd than those on the plateau, and the kind of life led
there rather less nightmarish. Or at least, the nightmare is
varied and diversified according to the local resources.
There are kitchen-gardens full of water-melons, the flesh of
which is like pink, tepid snow; pens of captive tortoises to
keep the family supplied with the equivalent of the Sunday
chicken. On feast-days, even chicken itself puts in an appearance, in the form of *gallinha em molho pardo* (chicken
in brown sauce), followed by a *bolo podre* (literally, rotten
cake), a *cha de burro* ('donkey's tea'—that is, maize with

milk) and a *baba de moça* ('maid's saliva', sour cream cheese flavoured with honey). Toxic manioc juice, fermented for weeks with red peppers, provides a rich, velvety sauce. It is a land of plenty. 'Aqui só falta o que não tem': here nothing is lacking except what is missing.

All these dishes are 'colossally' delectable, since the Amazonian language has a fondness for superlatives. Generally speaking, a remedy or a dessert are 'devilishly' good or bad; a waterfall is 'vertiginous', a piece of game 'a monster', and a situation 'abysmal'. Conversation provides a rich collection of peasant distortions, such as the inversion of phonemes: *percisa* instead of *precisa; prefeitamente* instead of *perfeitamente; Tribucio* instead of *Tiburcio*. It is also punctuated by long silences broken only by solemn interjections, such as *'Sim Senhor!'* or *'Disparate!'* which are related to all kinds of thoughts as confused and obscure as the forest.

One or two travelling salesmen, *regatão* or *mascate*—for the most part, Syrians or Lebanese who journey by canoe— bring medical supplies and newspapers which, by the time they arrive, are several weeks old and equally spoilt by damp. It was from a newspaper left behind in a rubber-gatherer's hut that I learned, four months after the actual events, of the Munich agreement and mobilization. I may add that the forest-dwellers lead a richer imaginative life than the inhabitants of the savannah. For instance, some have a poetic turn of mind, like the family in which the father and mother, being called respectively Sandoval and Maria, made up names for their children by rearranging the syllables of their own; the girls were called Valma, Valmaria and Valmarisa, and the boys, Sandomar and Marival, and, in the next generation, Valdomar and Valkimar. Pedants call their sons Aristotle and Newton, and are great absorbers of medicines with names like Precious Tincture, Oriental Tonic, Gordona Specific, Bristol Pills, English Water and Celestial Balm, which are very popular in Amazonia. When they do not swallow bichlorhydrate of quinine instead of sodium sulphate, with fatal results, they become so inured to these medicines that they need a whole tube of aspirins in one go to relieve an attack of toothache. There was a small depot on the upper reaches of the Machado which, very symbolically, seemed to dispatch upstream by canoe only two kinds of goods: railing for graves and enema douches.

In addition to this 'learned' medicine, there is another
folk variety, which consists of *resguardos,* taboos, and
orações, orisons or prayers. During pregnancy, a woman is
not subject to any taboos regarding food, but for the first
week after the birth she can only eat chicken and partridge.
Up to the fortieth day, she is allowed, in addition, to eat
deer and some kinds of fish (*pacu, piava* and *sardinha*).
From the forty-first day onwards, she can resume sexual
relations and add boar and so-called 'white' fish to her
diet. For a whole year, she must not touch tapir, land-
tortoise, red deer, *mutum,* or 'leathery' fish (*jatuarama* and
curimata). The comment made by the informants was, 'Isso
é mandamento da lei de Deu, isso é do inicio do mundo, a
mulher só é purificada depois de 40 dias. Si não faz, o fim é
triste.—Depois do tempo da mentruação, a mulher fica im-
munda, o homem que anda com ela fica immundo também,
é a lei de Deu para mulher.' And, as a final explanation: 'E
uma cousa muita fina, a mulher.'*

And here is the 'Oração do sapo secco', The Prayer for
the Dry Toad, which verges on black magic and is to be
found in a chapbook called the *Livro de São Cypriano*. You
must obtain a large toad of the *cururu* or *sapo leiteiro* species and bury it in the ground up to the neck, on a Friday:
then you feed it glowing embers, all of which it swallows. A
week later, when you go to look for it, it has disappeared.
But, in its place, there sprouts 'a tree with three branches',
each branch of a different colour. The white branch is for
love, the red for despair, and the black for mourning. The
name of the prayer derives from the fact that the toad dries
up; even the vulture refrains from eating it. The branch corresponding to the intentions of the celebrant is broken off
and kept hidden from all eyes: 'e cousa muita occulta'. The
prayer is uttered at the time of the burial of the toad:

En te enterro com palma de chão la dentro
En te prende baixo de meus pés até como fôr o possivel
Tens que me livrar de tudo quanto e perigo
So soltarei você quando terminar minha missão

---

* 'It is the commandment of God's law, it goes back to the beginning of the world, woman is only purified on the fortieth day.
If that is not done, the outcome is sad.—After menstruation the
woman is impure, the man who goes with her is impure also; this
is the law God has made for woman.' . . . 'A woman is a very
delicate thing.'

Abaixo de São Amaro será o meu protetor
As undas do mar serão meu livramento
Na polvora do sola sera meu descanso
Anjos da minha guarda sempre me accompanham
E o Satanaz não terá fôrça de me prender
Na hora chegada na pinga de meio dia
Esta oração serà ouvida
São Amaro você e supremes senhores dos animaes crueis
Será o meu protetor Mariterra (?)
Amen*

Two other orisons are the 'Oração da fava' (of the bean)
and the 'Oração do morcego' (of the bat).

In the vicinity of those rivers which are navigable for
small motor-boats, that is, in those areas where civilization,
as represented by Manaus, has not been reduced to an
almost forgotten memory but is still a reality with which
it is possible to re-establish contact twice or perhaps thrice
in a lifetime, wildly eccentric and inventive characters are to
be found. One such was a manager of a post who, although
he lived alone with his wife and two children, had, by his
own efforts, put large areas under cultivation in the very
heart of the forest, at the same time as he made gramo-
phones and distilled casks of brandy. He was also constantly
dogged by fate. Every night his horse was attacked by
vampire bats. He made it a protective covering with tent
canvas, but the horse tore the canvas on branches; he tried
smearing the animal with red pepper, then with copper
sulphate, but the vampires 'wiped everything off with their
wings' and continued to suck the poor creature's blood. The
only effective solution was to dress the horse up to look like
a wild boar, with the help of four skins cut up and then

---

* I bury you under a foot of earth
  I take you under my feet as far as possible
  You must deliver me from all danger
  I will free you only when I have accomplished my mission
  My protector will be in the care of Saint Amaro
  The waves of the sea will be my deliverance
  Peace will come to me in the dust of the earth
  You guardian angels, stay with me always
  And Satan will not have the strength to seize me
  When it is exactly the hour of midday
  This prayer will be heard
  Saint Amaro, you and the supreme lords of the cruel animals
  Will be my protector Mariterra (?)
  Amen.

sewn together. His ever-fertile imagination helped him to
forget a great disappointment: a visit to Manaus, during
which all his savings had disappeared between the doctors
who fleeced him, the hotel which starved him and his children who, aided and abetted by the tradespeople, bought
everything in sight.

One would like to be able to devote more space to these
touching Amazonian characters, so strongly marked by ec-
centricity and desperation. Some, like Rondon and his
companions, were heroes or saints who dotted the map of
the unexplored territories with names from the Positivist
calendar, and in some cases preferred to let themselves be
massacred rather than to retaliate against Indian attacks.
Others were rash adventurers who rushed off into the depths
of the forest to strange encounters with tribes known only
to themselves, and whom they would rob of their modest
harvests only to fall victim later to their arrows, dreamers
who set up ephemeral empires in remote valleys; cranks in
lonely outposts who expended a wealth of energy which, in
earlier times, might have been rewarded with a vice-royalty.
And lastly, there were the victims of an intoxication fostered by more powerful men than themselves; their bizarre
predicament is illustrated by what could happen to seekers
of adventure along the Rio Machado, near the edge of the
forests occupied by the Mundé and the Tupi-Kawahib.

The following account, which is clumsily written yet not
without a certain grandeur, comes from an Amazonian
paper, *A Pena Evangelica* (1938).

In 1920, the price of rubber fell, and the *patrão*
(Colonel Raymundo Pereira Brasil) abandoned the
seringaes, which here, along the banks of the Igarapé
São Thomé, were still more or less untouched. Time
passed. Ever since I had left Colonel Brasil's estates,
the memory of those fertile forests had remained in-
delibly engraved on my adolescent soul. I was beginning to recover from the apathy into which we had
been plunged by the sudden fall in rubber prices, and,
being already well hardened and accustomed to the
Bertholletia Excelsa, I suddenly remembered the *cas-
tanhaes* I used to see at S. Thomé.

One day I met my former employer, Colonel Brasil,
in the Grand Hotel at Belem do Para. He still showed
traces of his former wealth. I asked his permission to

go and work 'his' chestnut plantations. And he graciously authorized me to do so; he spoke and said: 'All that has been abandoned; it is a long way away, and the only people left are those who haven't managed to escape. I don't know how they live and the question doesn't interest me. You can go.'

I scraped together a little money, and I asked for an *aviação* [this is the term for goods given on credit] from the firms, J. Adonias, Adelino G. Bastos, and Gonçalves Pereira and Co. I bought a ticket on a steamer belonging to Amazon River and set off for the Tapajoz. At Itaituba, I met up with Rufino Monte Palma, and Melentino Telles de Mendonça. Each of us had fifty men with him. We joined forces, and we succeeded. Soon we arrived at the mouth of the Igarapé São Thomé. There we found a whole sad and abandoned community: old men in their dotage, half-naked women and stiff-limbed and terrified children. When shelters had been built and everything was ready, I assembled my men, together with this whole family, and said to them: 'Here is the *boia* for each one of you —cartridges, salt and flour. In my shanty, there is neither a clock nor a calendar; work begins when we can make out the shapes of our horny hands, and we stop when God sends us night. Those who don't agree will get nothing to eat; they will have to make do with palm-nut gruel and *anaja* salt [when boiled, the buds of the large-headed *anaja* palm tree leave a bitter, salty residue]. We have enough food to last sixty days, and we must make the best of them; we cannot afford to lose a single hour of this precious time.' My associates followed my example, and sixty days later we had 1,420 barrels [a barrel holds about 130 litres] of chestnuts. We loaded and manned the canoes, and sailed down to Itaituba. I stayed there with Rufino Monte Palma and the rest of the group to catch the motorboat, *Santelmo*, which kept us waiting a good fortnight. When we reached the port of Pimental, we embarked with the chestnuts and everything else on the gaiola, *Sertanejo,* and at Belem we sold our chestnuts at 47 milreis 500 per hectolitre [$2.30]. Unfortunately, four men died during the trip. We never went back again. But today, with prices soaring as high as 220 milreis per hectolitre, the highest rate reached during the

1936–7 season, according to the documents in my possession, what tremendous advantages chestnut-gathering offers. Chestnuts are reliable and definite, not like the subterranean diamond and its eternal uncertainties. That, my Cuiaba friends, is how to make a living from Para chestnuts in the State of Mato Grosso.

In sixty days, 150 or 170 people earned a total amount equivalent to a little over 3,500 dollars. But even this may seem a lot in comparison with the plight of the rubber-tappers, whom I saw in the death-throes of their trade during the last weeks of my stay.

36. SERINGAL

The two main species of latex-producing trees, *hevea* and *castilloa*, are called *seringa* and *caucha* respectively in the local dialect. The first is also the most important; it only grows near rivers, and the river-banks constitute loosely defined zones, which, by virtue of some vague governmental authorization, are in the hands not of owners but of 'bosses'; each of these *patrões de seringal* is in charge of a store selling food and miscellaneous supplies; he may own it personally, but he is more usually the representative of an entrepreneur or of a small river-transport company which has a monopoly of all shipping along a particular river and its tributaries. A rubber-tapper is, in the first place, and in the fullest sense, a 'client', and in fact is known as a *freguez*, or client, of the shop in the area where he has settled; from it he undertakes to buy all his supplies, i.e. his *aviação* (already explained in the preceding chapter), and to sell to it all the rubber he collects; in exchange, he receives his equipment and enough supplies for one season, which are debited to his account, as well as being granted a working area known as a *collocação*. This is a system of paths called *estradas*, beginning and ending at his riverside hut, and serving the chief rubber-producing trees, which have already been located in the forest by other employees of the boss: the *mateiro* and the *ajudante*.

Early each morning (the general belief being that it is better to work in the dark), the *seringueiro*, equipped with a *faca*, or curved knife, and a *coronga*, a lamp which he wears attached to his hat in the manner of a miner, follows one of the paths. He makes incisions in the *seringas*, according to delicate techniques known as the 'flag' or 'fish-bone' methods; a wrongly incised tree may give no latex or may become exhausted.

By about ten o'clock in the morning, he will have dealt with 150 to 180 trees; then, after his midday meal, the *seringueiro* goes back along his 'route' and collects the latex which has oozed out since the morning into the zinc cups

417

fixed to the trunks. He pours the contents of these cups into a bag which he has made himself from coarse cotton cloth impregnated with rubber. When he comes home again at about five o'clock in the evening, he starts on the third phase, the 'fattening' of the ball of rubber in course of preparation: the 'milk' is slowly added to a mass of rubber already congealed around a pole slung crosswise over a fire. The smoke makes the latex coagulate in a series of thin, even layers, as the ball slowly revolves on its axis. The ball is considered to be finished when it reaches a standard weight which varies between thirty and seventy kilograms according to the area. A ball may take several weeks to complete if the trees are nearing exhaustion. The balls (which are of many different kinds according to the quality of the latex and the method of fabrication) are deposited along the river-bank and the 'boss' collects them once a year. At the store they are compressed into *peles de borracha*, 'rubber skins', which are roped together in rafts and sent downstream to Manaus or Belem; the rafts inevitably come apart, but are patiently put together again below each waterfall.

So, to simplify an often complex situation, we can say that the *seringueiro* is dependent on the *patrão*, or boss, who in turn is dependent on the shipping company controlling the main waterways. This system is a consequence of the slump in the rubber market which occurred from 1910 onwards, when plantation rubber from Asia began to compete with the Brazilian output. Rubber-tapping in itself no longer presented any interest except for the really needy, but river transport remained profitable, especially since goods are sold on the *seringal* at about four times their market value. The most powerful people gave up rubber but held on to the river-transport business, which allowed them to control the system without risk, since the *patrão* is at the mercy of the transport company either way, whether the latter decides to raise its prices or to withhold supplies. A boss with an empty shop soon loses his clients, who either escape without paying their debts or stay put and die of hunger.

The boss depends on the transport company, and the client depends on the boss. By 1938, rubber was worth fifty times less than the price it had been fetching at the end of the great boom; in spite of a temporary rise in prices during the Second World War, the situation is no better today.

Along the Machado, according to whether he has a bad or a good year, a man many collect between 200 and 1,200 kilos. Taking the most favourable estimate, in 1938 his earnings allowed him to buy about half the quantity of basic goods necessary for survival: rice, black beans, dried meat, salt, rifle bullets, paraffin and cotton fabrics. He made up the difference partly by hunting and partly by running up further debts; he would begin in a state of indebtedness and, in most cases, his position would grow steadily worse until his death.

It would be relevant to quote a typical monthly budget for a family of four, as it worked out in 1938. The variations in the price of rice per kilo will allow the reader, if he wishes, to relate the prices to the international gold standard.

	Price per unit in milreis	*Total in milreis*
4 Kg. cooking fat	10.500	42
5 Kg. sugar	4.500	22.500
3 Kg. coffee	5	15
1 litre paraffin	5	5
4 bars soap	3	12
3 Kg. salt (for salting game)	3	9
20 bullets (0.44 cal.)	1.200	24
4 lb. tobacco	8.500	34
4 books cigarette papers	1.200	6
10 boxes matches	0.500	5
100 gm. pepper (for curing)	3	3
2 heads garlic	1.500	3
4 tins condensed milk (for the baby)	5	20
5 Kg. rice	3.500	17.500
30 litres manioc 'flour'	2.500	75
6 Kg. *xarque* (dried meat)	8	48
TOTAL:		341

An annual budget would have to include cotton fabric, a length of which was worth between 30 and 120 milreis in 1938; shoes, 40 to 60 milreis a pair; a hat, 50 to 60 milreis; also needles, buttons and thread, and medicines, which were consumed in alarming quantities. To give an example, a quinine tablet (one a day was required for each member of the family) or an aspirin cost one milreis. It should be remembered that, at the time, a very good 'season' along the Machado (rubber-gathering lasts from April to September, the forests being impassable during the rainy season) brought in 2,400 milreis (the *fina* was sold at Manaus in 1936 for about four milreis a kilo, of which the producer received half). Even if a *seringueiro* had no young children, and even if he ate only meat obtained by hunting and manioc 'flour' which he had grown and prepared himself in addition to doing his seasonal work, his minimal food budget alone would still use up all the money he could earn during an exceptional year.

Whether or not he was in business on his own account, the boss lived in constant fear of bankruptcy, which was a real danger if his clients disappeared before they had paid back the advances he had made to them. Consequently, his armed foreman would keep a watch on the river. A few days after leaving the Tupi-Kawahib, we had a strange encounter which will remain in my memory as expressing the very essence of the *seringal;* here is the account of the episode as I jotted it down in my travel diary on December 3rd, 1938.

About 10 o'clock, muggy grey weather. Coming towards our canoes is a small *montaria* containing a thin man, his wife—a fat mulatto-woman with frizzy hair— and a child of about ten. They are exhausted and the woman bursts into tears at the end of every sentence. They are returning from a six-day expedition on the Machadinho—eleven *cachoeiras* (falls), one of which, Jaburu, had involved *varação por terra* (carrying the boat)—in search of one of their *fregueses* who has fled with his wife, taking a canoe and his belongings, after receiving an *aviação* and leaving a note to say that 'a mercadoria ê muito cara e não tem coragem pagar a conta' (goods are too dear and I haven't the courage to pay the bill). These people, who are employed by *Compadre* Gaetano, are terrified by their responsibility and are looking for the runaway *freguêz* in order to lay hands on him and get him back to the boss. They have a rifle.

A rifle, usually a Winchester .44, was the weapon used for hunting and, should the need arise, for other purposes too.

A few weeks later, I noticed the following announcement at the entrance to a shop belonging to *Calama Limitada,* at the junction of the Machado and the Madeira:

EXTRAORDINARY LUXURY ARTICLES

including fat, butter and milk
will only be sold on credit
by special authorization from the *patrão.*
Otherwise
they will only be sold on sight!
Money or some other equivalent article

Immediately below, was the following notice:

SMOOTH HAIR

Even for coloured people!
However frizzy or wavy hair may be,
even hair belonging to coloured persons,
it will become smooth through regular use
of the very latest preparation
Alisante
On sale at 'The Big Bottle',
in Uruguayana Street, Manaus

Actually, the people were so inured to sickness and poverty that life on the *seringal* was not always dreary. Gone, no doubt, were the days when high rubber prices made it possible to build wooden inns at river junctions— noisy gambling dens where, in one night, a *seringueiro* would lose the fortune he had taken several years to amass; he would go off next morning to start all over again, after obtaining an *aviação* from a sympathetic *patrão.* I saw one of these ruins, which was still known as the Vatican, a name evocative of past splendours. On Sundays, people had gone there in striped silk pyjamas, soft hats and patent-leather shoes to listen to expert shots performing variations with revolvers of different calibres, like soloists. Now it was no longer possible to buy a fancy pair of pyjamas in the *seringal.* But an ambiguous charm was still lent to the place

by the young women who led a precarious existence as concubines to the *seringueiros*. The expression used to describe
their state was *casar na igreja verde*, 'to get married in the
green church'. This *mulherada,* or group of women, occasionally organized a dance, each of them contributing five
milreis, or coffee or sugar, or lending their hut if it was
somewhat larger than the others, or their lantern filled with
a night's supply of paraffin. They arrived in flimsy dresses,
with their faces made up and their hair done, and as they
came in kissed the hands of their hosts. But their make-up
was not so much intended to create an illusion of beauty
as to give an appearance of health. Under a layer of rouge
and powder they were hiding syphilis, tuberculosis and
malaria. They came in high-heeled shoes from the *barracão,*
where they lived with 'the man', their *seringueiro,* and, although ragged and dishevelled all the rest of the year, for
one evening they appeared spick and span; yet they had had
to walk two or three kilometres in their evening dresses
along muddy forest paths. And in order to get ready, they
had washed in darkness in filthy *igarapés* (streams), and in
the rain, since it had poured all day. There was a staggering
contrast between these flimsy appearances of civilization
and the monstrous reality which lay just outside the door.

The clumsily cut dresses emphasized typically Indian
bodily features: very high breasts set almost under the
armpits, and squashed by the tension of the material, which
had to accommodate a protuberant stomach; small arms
and slender, prettily shaped legs; and very delicate wrists
and ankles. The men, dressed in white trousers, thick shoes
and pyjama jackets, would come forward to invite their
partners. (As has already been explained, the women were
not married. They were *companheiras,* either *amasiadas,*
that is 'keeping house' for a man, or *desoccupadas* 'unat-
tached'.) The man led the woman by the hand to the
middle of the *palanque,* which was made of *babassu* straw
and lit by a noisy paraffin lamp called a *farol.* The couple
would wait for a moment or two to catch the strong beat
of the *caracachá,* or box of nails, shaken by a dancer who
was having a rest; then off they would go: 1, 2-3: 1, 2-3,
etc. Since the hut was built on piles, the floor would rever-
berate under the scraping and shuffling of feet.

The steps they danced were those of another age. Especially the *desfeitera* consisting of refrains, between which
the accordion (sometimes accompanying the *violão* and the

cavaquinho) would stop to allow each man in turn to improvise a couplet full of mocking or amorous innuendoes,
to which the ladies were expected to reply in similar vein.
This was not always easy for them, as they were embarrassed, *com vergonha;* some blushed and avoided the issue,
while others quickly muttered some unintelligible couplet,
like little girls reciting a lesson. Here is a couplet which was
improvised about us one evening at Urupa:

> Um é médico, outro professor, outro fiscal do Museu,
> Escolhe entr'os três qual é o seu.
>
> (One is a doctor, the other a professor, the other a
> museum inspector; choose which one of the three will
> be yours.)

Fortunately, the poor girl to whom it was addressed was at
a loss for a reply.

When a dance lasted several days, the women would
change their dresses every night.

The Nambikwara had taken me back to the Stone Age
and the Tupi-Kawahib to the sixteenth century; here I felt
I was in the eighteenth century, as one imagines it must
have been in the little West Indian ports or along the coast.
I had crossed a continent. But the rapidly approaching end
of my journey was being brought home to me in the first
place by this ascent through layers of time.

PART NINE

The Return

37. THE APOTHEOSIS
OF AUGUSTUS

One stage of the journey had been particularly depressing, my stay at Campos Novos. Cut off from my companions by the epidemic which kept them immobilized eighty kilometres further back, all I could do was wait just outside the post, where a dozen or so people were dying of malaria, leishmaniosis and hookworm, but chiefly of hunger. The Paressi woman, whom I employed to do my washing, demanded not only soap, but a meal: otherwise, as she explained, she would not have had the strength to do the work. This was true: these people had lost all capacity for living. Being too weak and too sick to struggle, they tried to reduce their activities and their needs, so as to reach a state of torpor which would demand a minimum expenditure of physical energy and at the same time dull the realization of their wretchedness.

The Indians contributed to this depressing atmosphere in a different way. The two hostile groups, who had met at Campos Novos and were constantly on the point of coming to blows with each other, were not particularly well disposed towards me. I had to keep a sharp look-out and all anthropological work had become virtually impossible. In normal conditions, fieldwork is already enough of a strain: you have to be up at daybreak, and then remain awake until the last native has gone to sleep, and even sometimes watch over him as he sleeps; you have to try to make yourself inconspicuous, while being constantly present; see everything, remember everything, note everything; display an embarrassing degree of indiscretion, coax information out of a snotty-nosed urchin and be ready to make the most of a moment's obligingness or carelessness; or alternatively, for days on end you have to repress all curiosity and withdraw into an attitude of research because of some sudden change of mood on the part of the tribe. As he practises his profession, the anthropologist is consumed by doubts: has he

really abandoned his native setting, his friends, and his way
of life, spent such considerable amounts of money and
energy, and endangered his health, for the sole purpose of
making his presence acceptable to a score or two of miserable creatures doomed to early extinction, whose chief occupations meanwhile are delousing themselves and sleeping,
and on whose whims the success or failure of his mission
depends? When the natives are definitely ill-disposed, as
was the case at Campos Novos, the situation becomes
worse. They even refuse to let themselves be seen; without
warning, they may disappear for days, having gone off on
some hunting or gathering expedition. In the hope of re-
establishing a contact that was so hardly won, the anthropologist hangs about, marking time and champing at the
bit; he rereads his old notes, copies them out and tries to
interpret them; alternatively he may set himself some finicky
and pointless task, a sort of caricature of his true function,
such as measuring the distance between the hearths or making an inventory of the individual branches used in the
building of the deserted shelters.

Above all, he asks himself questions: Why has he come
here? With what hopes or what objectives? What exactly is
the nature of anthropological research? Is it a normal occupation like any other profession, the only difference being
that the office or laboratory is separated from the practitioner's home by a distance of several thousand kilometres?
Or does it result from a more radical choice, which implies
that the anthropologist is calling into question the system in
which he was born and brought up? It was now nearly five
years since I had left France and interrupted my university
career. Meanwhile, the more prudent of my former colleagues were beginning to climb the academic ladder: those
with political leanings, such as I had once had, were already members of parliament and would soon be ministers.
And here was I, trekking across desert wastes in pursuit of
a few pathetic human remnants. By whom or by what had I
been impelled to disrupt the normal course of my existence?
Was it a trick on my part, a clever diversion, which would
allow me to resume my career with additional advantages
for which I would be given credit? Or did my decision express a deep-seated incompatibility with my social setting
so that whatever happened, I would inevitably live in a state
of ever greater estrangement from it? Through a remarkable paradox, my life of adventure, instead of opening up a

new world to me, had the effect rather of bringing me back
to the old one, and the world I had been looking for dis-
integrated in my grasp. Just as, once they were in my power,
the men and the landscapes I had set out to conquer lost
the significance I had hoped they would have for me, so for
these disappointing yet present images, other images were
substituted which had been held in reserve by my past and
had seemed of no particular importance when they still belonged to the reality surrounding me. Travelling through
regions upon which few eyes had gazed, sharing the existence of communities whose poverty was the price—paid
in the first instance by them—for my being able to go back
thousands of years in time, I was no longer fully aware of
either world. What came to me were fleeting visions of the
French countryside I had cut myself off from, or snatches
of music and poetry which were the most conventional ex-
my life. On the plateau of the western Mato Grosso, I had
renounced, if I were not to belie the direction I had given to
my life. On the plateau of the western Mato Grosso, I had
been haunted for weeks, not by the things that lay all
around me and that I would never see again, but by a
hackneyed melody, weakened still further by the deficiencies
of my memory—the melody of Chopin's Etude no. 3, opus
10, which, by a bitterly ironical twist of which I was well
aware, now seemed to epitomize all I had left behind.

Why Chopin, when I had never been particularly fond of
him? I had been brought up to admire Wagner, and had
discovered Debussy quite recently, but not before Stravin-
sky's *Noces*, of which I heard the second or third performance, had revealed a world which appeared more real
and more substantial to me than the savannahs of central
Brazil, and brought about the collapse of my previous
musical convictions. But at the period when I left France, it
was *Pelléas* which was supplying me with the spiritual sustenance I needed; so why should Chopin, and his tritest
composition, force themselves upon me in the wilderness?
Being more concerned with solving this problem than with
making observations which would have justified me profes-
sionally, I reflected that the progress involved in moving
from Chopin to Debussy is perhaps amplified when it occurs in the opposite direction. The delights which had led
me to prefer Debussy I now enjoyed in Chopin, but in a
form that was so implicit, uncertain and unobtrusive that I
had not noticed them at first and instead had gone straight

to their most blatant expression. I was now accomplishing a twofold progress: through a better understanding of the earlier composer's work, I was coming to recognize in it beauties which would have remained hidden from anyone without a previous knowledge of Debussy. My feeling for Chopin was the result of a surplus, not of a dearth, as would have been the case had I been someone for whom the development of music stopped with Chopin. At the same time, for the arousal of certain emotions, I no longer needed the total stimulus: an indication, an allusion, a premonition of certain forms was enough.

Mile after mile, the same melodic phrase rang through my memory, and I could not get rid of it. It seemed constantly to reveal fresh charms. After beginning very slackly, it appeared to be twisting its thread as if to conceal its approaching termination. The knotting became progressively more inextricable, so much so indeed that one began to wonder if the melody was not about to founder; suddenly, the next note brought complete resolution and the path of escape appeared all the bolder after the dangerous preliminaries which had both rendered it necessary and made it possible; once it had been heard, the notes leading up to it were illuminated with fresh meaning: what they had been seeking no longer seemed arbitrary, but became a preparation for the unsuspected way out. Perhaps, then, this was what travelling was, an exploration of the deserts of my mind rather than of those surrounding me? One afternoon, when everyone and everything was asleep in the overpowering heat, and I was crouching in my hammock under the mosquito net, which protected me from 'pests' —as the South Americans call them—but because of the fineness of its weave made the air even less breathable, I had the idea that the problems bothering me could provide the subject-matter of a play. It was as clear in my mind as if it had already been written. The Indians had disappeared: for six days, I wrote from morning till night on the backs of sheets of paper covered with word lists, sketches and genealogical tables. After which, inspiration abandoned me before the work was completed, and has never returned since. On rereading my scribblings, I don't think there is any cause for regret.

My play was called 'The Apotheosis of Augustus' and took the form of a new version of Corneille's *Cinna*. There were two main characters, who had been childhood friends and had met again at a crucial moment for both of them in their divergent careers. One, who thought he had opted out of civilization, discovers that he has used a complicated means of returning to it, but by a method destructive of the meaning and value of the choice with which he had originally believed himself to be faced. The other, who has been singled out from birth for social life and its attendant honours, realizes that all his efforts have been strained towards an end which dooms them to oblivion; and each, in trying to destroy the other, is seeking, even at the cost of death, to preserve the meaning of his past.

The play began at the point when the Senate, wishing to bestow on Augustus an honour higher than that of emperor, had voted in favour of apotheosis and was preparing to place him among the gods even during his lifetime. In the palace gardens, two guards were discussing the news and trying to forecast what the consequences would be from their particular point of view. Would the policeman's function not become impossible? How could one protect a god who, at will, was able to turn into an insect, or make himself invisible or paralyse people? They discussed the possibility of a strike, and decided that, in any event, they deserved a rise in pay.

The chief of police then arrived on the scene and explained their mistake to them. The police are not entrusted with a mission which differentiates them from those they serve. Being unconcerned with ultimate purposes, they are inseparable from the persons and interests of their masters, and shine with their reflected glory. A police force serving a divinized Head of State itself becomes divine. Everything will be possible for it, as for its master. It will achieve its true nature, so that, in the style of a detective agency motto, it can be said to *see and hear everything without raising suspicion.*

In the next part, various characters emerged from the Senate and commented on the session which had just taken place. Several scenes brought out contradictory conceptions of the transition from the human to the divine; the representatives of important interests speculated about the new opportunities for making money. Augustus, being very much an emperor, was only concerned with the confirmation of his power, at last ensured against intrigues and conspiracies. For his wife, Livia, the apotheosis was the crowning point of his career: 'It was only what he deserved', in other words, the equivalent of the Académie Française . . . Camilla, Augustus' young sister who was in love with Cinna, announced the latter's return after ten years of adventurous living. She wanted Augustus to see him, since she hoped that Cinna's wayward and poetic disposition, which had always been in evidence, would prevent Augustus from opting irrevocably for conventional social regimentation. Livia was against this: Cinna had always exercised a disruptive influence on Augustus' career: he was a madcap and only happy among savages. Augustus was tempted to agree with his opinion; but he was beginning to be perturbed by a series of delegations of priests, painters and poets, all of whom assumed that Augustus' divinity would be tantamount to his expulsion from the world: the priests expected the apotheosis to transfer temporal power into their hands, since they were the official intermediaries between the gods and men. The artists wanted to change Augustus from a person into an idea: to the great dismay of the imperial couple, who could imagine themselves idealized as marble statues larger than life, they proposed instead all kinds of representations in the form of vortices and polyhedra. The confusion was further increased by the conflicting assertions of a bevy of ladies of easy virtue—Leda, Europa, Alcmena and Danaë—who insisted on giving Augustus the benefit of their experience of relationships with the divine.

Augustus then found himself alone, in conversation with an eagle: not the conventional bird, the emblem of divinity, but a wild creature, warm to the touch and foul-smelling. Yet it was Jupiter's eagle, the same eagle which carried off Ganymede, after a bloody fight in which the young boy had struggled in vain. The eagle explained to the incredulous Augustus that the divine nature he was about to acquire would consist precisely in no longer experiencing the feeling of revulsion by which he was now overwhelmed while still a man. Augustus would realize that he had become a god, not by some radiant sensation or the power to work miracles, but by his ability to tolerate the proximity of a wild beast without a sensation of disgust, to put up with its stench and the excrement with which it would cover him. Carrion, decay and organic secretions would appear familiar to him: 'Butterflies will come and copulate on your neck and any kind of ground will seem good enough to sleep on; you will not see it, as you do now, bristling with thorns, and swarming with insects and infection.'

In the second act, Augustus, having been made aware of the problem of the relationship between nature and society through his conversation with the eagle, decided to see Cinna again; the latter in the past preferred nature to society, the opposite choice to the one which had led Augustus to the imperial dignity. Cinna was disheartened. During his ten years of adventure, he had done nothing but think about Camilla, the sister of his childhood friend, and whom he could have married, if he had said the word. Augustus would have been delighted to give her to him. But it would have been intolerable for him to obtain her according to the rules of the social code; he had to win her in defiance of the established order, not through it. Hence his effort to acquire an heretical prestige which would allow him to force society's hand and make it grant him that which it was, in any case, prepared to accord.

Now that he had come back with a halo of glory—the explorer whose presence was in demand at every society dinner—he alone knew that the fame he had bought at such cost was founded on a lie. There was nothing real in all the experience he was credited with having lived through; travelling was a snare and a delusion; the whole thing could appear true only to those people acquainted with the reflection, not the reality. Cinna, jealous of the destiny in store for Augustus, had wanted to possess an empire vaster than his: 'I said to myself that no human mind, not even Plato's, is capable of imagining the infinite diversity of all the flowers and leaves which exist in the world, and that I would get to know them; I would collect the sensations caused by fear, cold, hunger and fatigue, and that all of you who live in snug houses next to well-stocked barns cannot even imagine. I have eaten lizards, snakes and grasshoppers; and I approached these foods, the mere thought of which is enough to turn your stomach, with the emotion of one about to be initiated and the conviction that I was going to establish a new link between the universe and myself.' But after all his strivings, Cinna was conscious of having found nothing: 'I have lost everything,' he said, 'even what is most human has become inhuman for me. To fill the emptiness of the endless days I would recite Aeschylus and Sophocles to myself; I became so permeated with certain lines that now, when I go to the theatre, I cannot appreciate their beauty any more. Every passage reminds me of dusty roads, burnt grass and eyes reddened by the sand.'

The closing scenes of the second act showed the contradictory situations in which Augustus, Cinna and Camilla were caught. Camilla was full of admiration for her explorer, who struggled in vain to make her understand the deceptiveness of travellers' tales. 'Although I might express all the vacuity and insignificance of each of these events, my account would only have to be cast in the form of a story to dazzle and hold the attention. Yet, the experience was nothing; the earth resembled this earth and the blades of grass were the same as in this meadow.' Camilla was outraged by this, being only too aware that, in her lover's eyes, she too was affected in her being by the general failure of interest that he was suffering from: he was no longer attached to her as a person but as a symbol of the only possible link between himself and society. Augustus, for his part, recognized with alarm that Cinna was saying the same as the eagle, but could not bring himself to reverse his decision: too many political interests were involved in his apotheosis, but more important still, he rebelled against the idea that there should be no absolute terminus to provide the man of action with both his reward and his peace of mind.

The third act opened in an atmosphere of crisis; on the eve of the ceremony, Rome was swamped by an onrush of the divine: the walls of the imperial palace cracked and it was invaded by plants and animals. The city was returning to the state of nature as if it had been destroyed by a cataclysm. Camilla had broken with Cinna, thus providing the latter with final proof of a failure of which he was already fully aware. He directed his resentment against Augustus. However vain the undisciplined exuberance of nature might now seem to him in comparison with the denser joys afforded by human society, he wanted to be alone in appreciating its savour. 'It is nothing, I know, but this nothingness is still dear to me since I opted for it.' The idea that Augustus might succeed in combining nature and society, and obtain the former as a bonus with the latter, instead of having to pay for it by renunciation, was intolerable to him. He determined to assassinate Augustus in order to testify to the inevitability of the choice.

At that moment, Augustus called upon Cinna to help him. How could he deflect the march of events which no longer depended on his will, while still remaining faithful to his public image? In a moment of high excitement, they thought they had found a solution: yes, Cinna could assassinate the emperor, as he had planned to do. Thus they would both win the immortality they had dreamed of: Augustus would enjoy the official immortality of books, statues and worship; and Cinna the black immortality of the regicide, and would thus be reintegrated into society while continuing to oppose it.

I cannot quite remember how it was all supposed to end, as the last scenes remained unfinished. I think it was Camilla who involuntarily provided the denouement. Reverting to her initial sentiments, she persuaded her brother that he had misinterpreted the situation and that Cinna, rather than the eagle, was the messenger of the gods. If this were true, Augustus saw the possibility of a political solution. He had only to trick Cinna for the gods to be deceived at the same time. It was agreed between them that the guards would be withdrawn and then Augustus would offer himself as a defenceless victim to Cinna's dagger. But instead, Augustus secretly arranged for the bodyguard to be doubled, so that Cinna did not even get near him. Confirming the course of their respective careers, Augustus was to succeed in his last undertaking: he would be a god, but a god among men, and he would pardon Cinna. But for Cinna, this would be only one more failure.

38. A LITTLE GLASS OF RUM*

The only justification for the dramatic fable described in the preceding chapter is that it illustrates the mental disorder to which the traveller is exposed through abnormal living conditions over a prolonged period. But the problem still remains: how can the anthropologist overcome the contradiction resulting from the circumstances of his choice? He has in front of him and available for study a given society—his own; why does he decide to spurn it and to reserve for other societies—which are among the most remote and the most alien—a patience and a devotion which his choice of vocation has deflected from his fellow-citizens? It is no accident that the anthropologist should rarely have a neutral attitude towards his own group. If he is a missionary or an administrator, we can infer from this that he has agreed to identify himself with a certain system, to the point of dedicating his life to its propagation; and when he practises his profession on a scientific or academic level, one can very probably discover in his past certain objective factors which show him to be ill-adapted to the society into which he was born. In assuming his role, he has tried to find either a practical means of reconciling his allegiance to a group and the reservations he feels with regard to it, or, quite simply, a way of turning to advantage an initial state of detachment which gives him an advantage in approaching different societies, since he is already halfway towards them.

But if he is honest, he is faced with a problem: the value he attaches to foreign societies—and which appears to be higher in proportion as the society is more foreign—has no independent foundation; it is a function of his disdain for, and occasionally hostility toward, the customs prevailing in

* TRANSLATORS' NOTE: Traditionally, French criminals about to be guillotined were offered a last cigarette and a little glass of rum. The author is referring to the significance of rum as discussed in the chapter and to the possible fate of both the anthropologist and mankind as a whole.

his native setting. While often inclined to subversion among his own people and in revolt against traditional behaviour, the anthropologist appears respectful to the point of conservatism as soon as he is dealing with a society different from his own. This is more than just a bias. In fact, it is something quite different: I know some anthropologists who are conformists. But they are so in a derivative way, by virtue of a kind of secondary assimilation of their society to the foreign ones they study. Their allegiance is always given to the latter, and the reason why they have abandoned their initial revolt against their own, is that they make the additional concession to foreign societies of approaching their own as they would like all societies to be approached. There is no way out of the dilemma: either the of giving himself wholeheartedly to these other groups and other groups inspire in him no more than a fleeting curiosity which is never quite devoid of disapproval, or he is capable of giving himself wholeheartedly to these other groups and his objectivity is vitiated by the fact that, intentionally or not, he has had to withhold himself from at least one society, in order to devote himself to all. He therefore commits the very sin that he lays at the door of those who contest the exceptional significance of his vocation.

I was assailed by this doubt for the first time during the enforced stay in the West Indies that I described at the beginning of this book. In Martinique, I had visited rustic and neglected rum-distilleries where the equipment and the methods used had not changed since the eighteenth century. In Puerto Rico, on the other hand, in the factories of the company which enjoys a virtual monopoly over the whole of the sugar production, I was faced by a display of white enamel tanks and chromium piping. Yet the various kinds of Martinique rum, as I tasted them in front of ancient wooden vats thickly encrusted with waste matter, were mellow and scented, whereas those of Puerto Rico are coarse and harsh. We may suppose, then, that the subtlety of the Martinique rums is dependent on impurities the continuance of which is encouraged by the archaic method of production. To me, this contrast illustrates the paradox of civilization: its charms are due essentially to the various residues it carries along with it, although this does not absolve us of the obligation to purify the stream. By being doubly in the right, we are admitting our mistake. We are right to be rational and to try to increase our production and so keep manufacturing costs down. But we are also right to cherish those very imperfections we are endeavouring to eliminate. Social life consists in destroying that which give it its savour. The contradiction seems to disappear when we move from the consideration of our own society to the study of foreign ones. We ourselves are caught up in the evolution of our own society and are, in a sense, interested parties. We are not in a position not to will those things which our situation forces us to carry into effect; when we are dealing with foreign societies, everything is different: the objectivity which was impossible in the first instance is freely granted to us. Since we are no longer agents but spectators of the transformations which are taking place, we are all the better able to compare and evaluate their future and their past, since these remain subjects for aesthetic contemplation and intellectual reflection, instead of being brought home to us in the form of mental anxiety.

By arguing as I have just done, I may have thrown light on the contradiction; I have shown where it originates and how we manage to come to terms with it. But I have certainly not solved it. Is the contradiction, then, a permanent one? It has sometimes been said to be so, and the argument tion displays the predilection we feel for social and cultural tion displays the predilection we feel for social and cultural structures very different from our own—overestimating the former at the expense of the latter—we are said to be guilty of a fundamental inconsistency; how could we proclaim the validity of the foreign societies, except by basing our judgment on the values of the society which has prompted us to engage in research? Since we are permanently unable to escape from the norms by which we have been conditioned, our attempts to put different societies, including our own, into perspective, are said to be no more than a shamefaced way of admitting its superiority over all the others.

Behind the reasoning of these specious critics, there is nothing but a bad pun: they try to pass off the mystification (in which they themselves indulge) as the reverse of mysticism (of which they wrongly accuse us). Archaeological or anthropological research shows that certain civilizations, whether contemporary or extinct, know, or used to know, how to solve certain problems better than we do, although we have endeavoured to obtain the same results. To quote only one example: only during recent years have we discovered the material and physiological principles underlying Eskimo dress and the form of Eskimo houses, and how these principles, of which we were unaware, allow them to live in harsh climatic conditions, to which they are adapted neither by use nor by anything exceptional in their constitutions. So true is this that it also enables us to understand why the so-called improvement that explorers introduced into Eskimo dress proved to be less than useless, and in fact produced the opposite result to what was intended. The native solution was perfect; we could only realize this once we had grasped the theory on which it was based.

This is not where the difficulty lies. If we judge the achievements of other social groups in relation to the kind of objectives we set ourselves, we have at times to acknowledge their superiority; but in so doing we acquire the right to judge them, and hence to condemn all their other objectives which do not coincide with those we approve of. We implicitly acknowledge that our society with its customs and norms enjoys a privileged position, since an observer belonging to another social group would pass different verdicts on the same examples. This being so, how can the study of anthropology claim to be scientific? To re-establish an objective approach, we must abstain from making judgments of this kind. We must accept the fact that each society has made a certain choice, within the range of existing human possibilities, and that the various choices cannot be compared with each other: they are all equally valid. But in this case a new problem arises; while in the first instance we were in danger of falling into obscurantism, in the form of a blind refusal of everything foreign to us, we now run the risk of accepting a kind of eclecticism which would prevent us denouncing any feature of a given culture—not even cruelty, injustice and poverty, against which the very society suffering these ills may be protesting. And since these abuses also exist in our society, what right have we to combat them at home, if we accept them as inevitable when they occur elsewhere?

Behind the two divergent attitudes of the anthropologist who is a critic at home and a conformist abroad, there lies, then, another contradiction from which he finds it even more difficult to escape. If he wishes to contribute to the improvement of his own community, he must condemn social conditions similar to those he is fighting against, wherever they exist, in which case he relinquishes his objectivity and impartiality. Conversely, the detachment to which he is constrained by moral scrupulousness and scientific accuracy prevents him criticizing his own society, since he is refraining from judging any one society in order to acquire knowledge of them all. Action within one's own society precludes understanding of other societies, but a thirst for universal understanding involves renouncing all possibility of reform.

If the contradiction were insurmountable, the anthropologist ought to have no hesitation about the alternative to opt for: he is an anthropologist, and chose to become one; he must therefore accept the mutilation inseparable from his vocation. He has preferred other societies and must suffer the consequences of his preference: his function will be simply to understand these other societies, in whose name he is unable to act, since the very fact that they are different prevents him thinking and taking decisions for them; such behaviour would be tantamount to identifying himself with them. Furthermore, he will renounce all action within his own society, because he is afraid of taking a stand about values which could well recur in different societies, and therefore of allowing his thought to be coloured by prejudice. Only the initial choice will remain, and for that he will admit no justification: it is a pure, unmotivated act, or if motivated at all, can be so only by external considerations connected with the character or life-history of the particular individual.

Fortunately, the situation is not quite as bad as that; after peering into the abyss which yawns in front of us, we may be allowed to look for a way of avoiding it. Such a way can be found, provided we are moderate in our judgments and break the difficulty down into two stages.

No society is perfect. It is in the nature of all societies to include a degree of impurity incompatible with the norms they proclaim and which finds concrete expression in a certain dosage of injustice, insensitiveness and cruelty. If it is asked how this dosage is to be evaluated, anthropological research can supply an answer. While it is true that comparison between a small number of societies makes them appear very different from each other, the differences diminish as the field of investigation widens. We then discover that no society is fundamentally good, but that none is absolutely bad; they all offer their members certain advantages, with the proviso that there is invariably a residue of evil, the amount of which seems to remain more or less constant and perhaps corresponds to a specific inertia in social life resistant to all attempts at organization.

This assertion will surprise readers of travellers' tales who recall with dismay the 'barbarous' customs of some native community or other. Yet such superficial reactions cannot stand up to an accurate appreciation of the facts, once the latter have been set in a wider perspective. Let us take the case of cannibalism, which of all savage practices is no doubt the one that inspires the greatest horror and disgust. First, we must separate off its purely alimentary forms, that is those instances in which the appetite for human flesh is to be explained by the lack of any other animal food, as was the case in certain Polynesian islands. No society is morally protected from such hunger pangs: famine can force men to eat anything, as is proved by the recent example of the extermination camps.

There remain those forms of cannibalism which can be termed positive, since they stem from a mystic, magic or religious cause: for instance, the consumption of a fragment of the body of a parent or of an enemy in order to ensure the incorporation of virtues or the neutralization of power; such rites are usually carried out very discreetly and involve only a small quantity of organic matter which is ground down or mixed with other foods, but even when they are practised in more overt forms it has to be admitted that the moral condemnation of such customs implies either a belief in bodily resurrection (resurrection being jeopardized by the material destruction of the corpse), or the affirmation of a link between the soul and the body, with a corresponding dualism; that is, in either case, convictions similar in nature to those underlying the practice of ritual consumption and which we have no reason to prefer to them. This is all the truer when we consider that the disrespect for the memory of the deceased which cannibals might be accused of is certainly no greater—far from it— than that tolerated by us on the dissecting table.

But above all, we should realize that certain of our own customs might appear, to an observer belonging to a different society, to be similar in nature to cannibalism, although cannibalism strikes us as being foreign to the idea of civilization. I am thinking, for instance, of our legal and prison systems. If we studied societies from the outside, it would be tempting to distinguish two contrasting types:

those which practise cannibalism—that is, which regard
the absorption of certain individuals possessing dangerous
powers as the only means of neutralizing those powers and
even of turning them to advantage—and those which, like
our own society, adopt what might be called the practice of
anthropemy (from the Greek *émein*, to vomit); faced with
the same problem, the latter type of society has chosen the
opposite solution, which consists in ejecting dangerous individuals from the social body and keeping them temporarily
or permanently in isolation, away from all contact with
their fellows, in establishments specially intended for this
purpose. Most of the societies which we call primitive
would regard this custom with profound horror; it would
make us, in their eyes, guilty of that same barbarity of
which we are inclined to accuse them because of their symmetrically opposite behaviour.

Societies which seem savage to us in some respects may
appear humane and kindly when considered from another
angle. Let us take the case of the Plains Indians of North
America, who are doubly significant in this connection, because they practised certain moderate forms of cannibalism
and at the same time offer one of the rare instances of a
primitive community with an organized police system. It
would never have occurred to their police (who were also
a judicial body) to make the culprit's punishment take the
form of a breaking of social ties. If a native had infringed
the laws of the tribe, he was punished by having all his possessions destroyed, including his tent and horses. But at the
same time, the police contracted a debt towards him: it was
their duty to organize collective reparation for the losses
sustained by the culprit as his punishment. This put him
under an obligation to the group, and he had to show his
gratitude to them by means of presents that the whole community—including the police—helped him to assemble, so
that this once again reversed the relationships; and so on
and so forth until, after a whole series of gifts and counter-
gifts, the disorder introduced by the crime was gradually
neutralized and there was a return to the pristine state of
order. Not only are such customs more humane than ours,
they are also more coherent, even if the problem is formulated in terms of modern European psychology; logical-
ly, the 'infantilization' of the culprit implied by the notion
of punishment demands that he should have a corresponding right to a reward, in the absence of which the initial

procedure will prove ineffective and may even lead to results contrary to those that were hoped for. Our system is the height of absurdity, since we treat the culprit both as a child, so as to have the right to punish him, and as an adult, in order to deny him consolation; and we believe we have made great spiritual progress because, instead of eating a few of our fellow-men, we subject them to physical and moral mutilation.

Analysis of this kind, if carried out sincerely and methodically, leads to two results: it introduces an element of moderation and honesty into our evaluation of customs and ways of life very remote from our own, without conferring on them the virtue of absoluteness, which exists in no society. And it removes from our own customs that air of inherent rightness which they so easily have for anyone unacquainted with other customs, or whose knowledge is partial and biased. Consequently, it is true that anthropological analysis tips the balance in favour of foreign societies and against the observer's own; in this sense, it is self-contradictory. But further reflection will show that the contradiction is more apparent than real.

It has sometimes been said that European society is the only one which has produced anthropologists, and that therein lies its greatness. Anthropologists may wish to deny it other forms of superiority, but they must respect this one, since without it they themselves would not exist. Actually, one could claim exactly the opposite: Western Europe may have produced anthropologists precisely because it was a prey to strong feelings of remorse, which forced it to compare its image with those of different societies in the hope that they would show the same defects or would help to explain how its own defects had developed within it. But even if it is true that comparison between our society and all the rest, whether past or present, undermines the basis of our society, other societies will suffer the same fate. The general averageness I referred to above brings out by contrast the existence of a number of ogres, and it so happens that we are among them; not by accident, since if we had not been of their number and had not deserved first prize in this sorry competition, anthropology would not have been invented by us, because we would not have felt the need for it. The anthropologist is the less able to ignore his own civilization and to dissociate himself from its faults in that his very existence is incomprehensible except as an attempt at redemption: he is the symbol of atonement. But other societies too have been tainted with the same original sin; not very many perhaps, and they become increasingly fewer in number as we move down the scale of progress. I need only cite the example of Aztec culture, that open wound in the side of American history, whose maniacal obsession with blood and torture (a universal obsession, in fact, but overt in the case of the Aztecs in the *excessive form* that comparison allows us to define)—however explicable it may be through the need to overcome the fear of death—puts it on a level with ourselves, not because the Aztecs were the only people wicked in this way but because, like us, they were inordinately so.

Yet this condemnation of ourselves by ourselves does not imply that we are prepared to award a certificate of excellence to any particular society, past or present, situated at any specific point in time or space. To do so would be to commit a real injustice, since we should be failing to recognize the fact that, were we part of that society, we would find it intolerable: we would condemn it on the same grounds as we condemn our own society. Does this mean that we must inevitably criticize any form of social organization and glorify a state of nature which social organization can only corrupt? This was Diderot's view when he wrote: 'Beware of him who comes to impose order.' He thought that 'the abridged history' of humanity could be summarized as follows: 'There existed a natural man; an artificial man was introduced into this natural man, and inside the cave there arose continuous warfare which lasts throughout life.' This is an absurd conception. Man is inseparable from language and language implies society. Bougainville's Polynesians (Diderot put forward this theory in his *Supplément au voyage de Bougainville*) were just as much social beings are we are. To maintain any other point of view would be to run counter to anthropological analysis instead of moving in the direction which it encourages us to explore.

The more I consider these problems, the more I am convinced that they admit of no reply other than the one given by Rousseau: Rousseau, who has been so maligned, who is more misunderstood now than ever before and is preposterously accused of having glorified the state of nature—an error that can be attributed to Diderot but not to him— when in fact he said exactly the opposite and is the only

thinker who can show us how to escape from the contradictions in which we are still floundering in the wake of his
opponents; Rousseau, the most anthropological of the
philosophes: although he never travelled to distant lands,
his documentation was as complete as it could be for a man
of his time and, unlike Voltaire, he infused life into it by
his warm-hearted curiosity about peasant customs and popular thought; Rousseau, our master and brother, to whom
we have behaved with such ingratitude but to whom every
page of this book could have been dedicated, had the
homage been worthy of his great memory. We shall emerge
from the contradiction inherent in the anthropologist's position only by repeating, on our own account, the procedure
which allowed Rousseau to move on from the ruins left by
the *Discours sur l'origine de l'inégalité,* to the ample structure of the *Contrat Social,* the secret of which is revealed in
Emile. It was he who taught us that, after demolishing all
forms of social organization, we can still discover the principles which will allow us to construct a new form.

Rousseau never fell into Diderot's error of idealizing
natural man. He is never in any danger of confusing the
natural state with the social state; he knows that the latter
is inherent in man, but that it leads to evils; the only problem
is to discover whether these evils are themselves inherent in
the social state. This means looking beyond abuses and
crimes to find the unshakable basis of human society.

To this quest, anthropological comparison can contribute
in two ways. It shows that the basis is not to be discovered
in our civilization: of all known societies ours is no doubt
the one most remote from it. At the same time, by bringing
out the characteristics common to the majority of human
societies, it helps us to postulate a type, of which no society
is a faithful realization, but which indicates the direction
the investigation ought to follow. Rousseau thought that the
way of life now known as neolithic offered the nearest approach to an experimental representation of the type. One
may, or may not, agree with him. I am rather inclined to
believe he was right. By neolithic times, man had already
made most of the inventions necessary for his safety. We
have already seen why writing can be excluded; to say that
it is a double-edged weapon is not a sign of primitivism;
this is a truth that has been rediscovered by contemporary
cyberneticians. In the neolithic period, man knew how to
protect himself against cold and hunger; he had achieved

leisure in which to think; no doubt there was little he could do against disease, but it is not certain that advances in hygiene have had any other effect than to transfer the responsibility for maintaining demographic equilibrium from epidemics, which were no more dreadful a means than any other, to different phenomena such as widespread famine and wars of extermination.

In that mythic age, man was no freer than he is today; but only his humanness made him a slave. Since his control over nature remained very limited, he was protected—and to some extent released from bondage—by a cushioning of dreams. As these dreams were gradually transformed into knowledge, man's power increased and became a great source of pride; but this power, which gears us, as it were, to the universe, is surely little more than our subjective awareness of a progressive welding together of humanity and the physical universe, whose great deterministic laws, instead of remaining remote and awe-inspiring, now use thought itself as an intermediary medium and are colonizing us on behalf of a silent world of which we have become the agents.

Rousseau was no doubt right to believe that it would have been better for our well-being had mankind kept to 'a happy mean between the indolence of the primitive state and the irrepressible busyness of our self-esteem', that such a position was the 'best for man' and that he only emerged from it through 'some unhappy chance', this being, of course, the advent of mechanization, a doubly exceptional phenomenon, since it was both unique and of late occurrence. It nevertheless remains clear that this intermediary position is by no means a primitive state, since it presupposes and admits of a certain degree of progress; and that no known society offers an exceptionally accurate representation of it, even if 'the example of the savages, who have almost all been found at this stage, would seem to confirm that the human race was intended always to remain in it.'

The study of these savages leads to something other than the revelation of a Utopian state of nature or the discovery of the perfect society in the depths of the forest; it helps us to build a theoretical model of human society, which does not correspond to any observable reality, but with the aid of which we may succeed in distinguishing between 'what is primordial and what is artificial in man's present nature and in obtaining a good knowledge of a state which no longer exists, which has perhaps never existed, and which will probably never exist in the future, but of which it is nevertheless essential to have a sound conception in order to pass valid judgment on our present state'. I have already quoted this remark to bring out the significance of my study of the Nambikwara. Rousseau's thought, which was always in advance of his time, does not dissociate theoretical sociology from research in the laboratory or in the field, which he recognized as being necessary. Natural man did not precede society, nor is he outside it. Our task is to rediscover his form as it is immanent in the social state, mankind being inconceivable outside society; this means working out a programme of the experiments which 'would be necessary in order to arrive at a knowledge of natural man' and determining 'the means whereby these experiments can be made within society'.

But the model—this is Rousseau's solution—is eternal and universal. Other societies are perhaps no better than our own; even if we are inclined to believe they are, we have no method at our disposal for proving it. However, by getting to know them better, we are enabled to detach ourselves from our own society. Not that our own society is peculiarly or absolutely bad. But it is the only one from which we have a duty to free ourselves: we are, by definition, free in relation to the others. We thus put ourselves in a position to embark on the second stage, which consists in using all societies—without adopting features from any one of them—to elucidate principles of social life that we can apply in reforming our own customs and not those of foreign societies: through the operation of a prerogative which is the reverse of the one just mentioned, the society we belong to is the only society we are in a position to transform without any risk of destroying it, since the changes, being introduced by us, are coming from within the society itself.

By taking as our inspiration a model outside time and place, we are certainly running a risk: we may be underestimating the reality of progress. It is as if we are asserting that men have always and everywhere undertaken the same task in striving towards the same objective and that, throughout history, only the means have differed. I confess that this view does not worry me; it seems to be the one most in keeping with the facts, as revealed by history and anthropology, and above all it appears to be more fruitful.

Enthusiastic partisans of the idea of progress are in danger of failing to recognize—because they set so little store by them—the immense riches accumulated by the human race on either side of the narrow furrow on which they keep their eyes fixed; by underrating the achievements of the past, they devalue all those which still remain to be accomplished. If men have always been concerned with only one task—how to create a society fit to live in—the forces which inspired our distant ancestors are also present in us. Nothing is settled; everything can still be altered. What was done, but turned out wrong, can be done again. 'The Golden Age, which blind superstition had placed behind [or ahead of] us, is *in us*.' The brotherhood of man acquires a concrete meaning when it makes us see, in the poorest tribe, a confirmation of our own image and an experience, the lessons of which we can assimilate, along with so many others. We may even discover a pristine freshness in these lessons. Since we know that, for thousands of years, man has succeeded only in repeating himself, we will attain to that nobility of thought which consists in going back beyond all the repetitions and taking as the starting-point of our reflections the indefinable grandeur of man's beginnings. Being human signifies, for each one of us, belonging to a class, a society, a country, a continent and a civilization; and for us European earth-dwellers, the adventure played out in the heart of the New World signifies in the first place that it was not our world and that we bear responsibility for the crime of its destruction; and secondly, that there will never be another New World: since the confrontation between the Old World and the New makes us thus conscious of ourselves, let us at least express it in its terms—in the place where, and by referring back to a time when, our world missed the opportunity offered to it of choosing between its various missions.

39. TAXILA

At the foot of the Kashmir mountains, between Rawalpindi and Peshawar, the archaeological site of Taxila lies a few kilometres from the railway line. I went there by train, which led to my being the involuntary cause of a minor drama. There was only one first-class compartment of a fairly old type—sleep four, seat six—simultaneously reminiscent of a cattle-truck, a drawing-room and—because of the protective bars on the windows—a prison. A Moslem family was already in possession, when I got in: a husband, with his wife and two children. The lady was in purdah: although she made an attempt to isolate herself by crouching down on her bunk wrapped in her *burkah* and with her back obstinately turned towards me, the promiscuity eventually appeared too shocking and the family had to split up. The wife and children went off to the 'Ladies Only' compartment, while the husband continued to occupy the reserved seats and to glare at me. I managed to take a philosophical view of the incident; it was in fact less upsetting than the spectacle which greeted me on my arrival; the waiting-room, in which I had to spend some time before my carriage came, opened on to another room with brown wooden panelling and a score or so of commode chairs set along the walls, as if in preparation for the meetings of some association of enterologists.

One of those little horsedrawn vehicles called a gharry, in which you sit with your back to the coachman and are in danger of being thrown overboard at every jolt, took me to the archaeological site, along a dusty road lined with low adobe houses, between eucalyptus trees, tamarisks, mulberry bushes and pepper plants. Orange and lemon groves lay around the bottom of a hill of bluish stone, dotted with wild olive trees. I passed peasants dressed in pastel colours —white, pink, mauve and yellow—and wearing turbans shaped like flat cakes. I finally arrived at the administrative buildings surrounding the museum. It had been agreed that I would make a brief stay, just long enough to visit the deposits. However, since the 'official and urgent' telegram sent from Lahore the previous evening to warn of my arrival did not reach the director until five days later because of floods in the Punjab, I might just as well have come unannounced.

The archaeological site of Taxila, which once bore the Sanskrit name of Takshasilâ—the town of the stone-cutters —occupies a double circular declivity, ten or so kilometres deep, formed by the converging valleys of two rivers, the Haro and the Tamra Nala (the Tiberio Potamos of ancient times). The two valleys and the ridge between them were inhabited without interruption for ten or twelve centuries, from the founding of the oldest excavated village, which dates from the sixth century B.C., to the destruction of the Buddhist monasteries by the white Huns who invaded the Kushan and Gupta kingdoms between A.D. 500 and 600. To go up the valleys is to journey down through the course of history. Bhir Mound, at the foot of the central ridge, is the oldest site; a few kilometres upstream is the town of Sirkap, which reached its heyday under the Parthians, and just outside the enclosure, the Zoroastrian temple of Jandial, which was visited by Apollonius of Tyana; further away still is the Kushan city of Sirsuk and, on the heights all around it, the Buddhist monuments and monasteries of Mohra Moradu, Jaulian and Dharmarâjikâ, bristling with statues which were originally of unfired clay but were accidentally preserved by being baked in the flames lit by the Huns.

Around the fifth century B.C., there was a village there which was incorporated into the Achemenedean empire and became a university centre. In 326 B.C., in the course of his march towards the Jumna, Alexander stopped for a few weeks at the very spot now occupied by the ruins of Bhir Mound. A century later, the Maurya emperors reigned over Taxila, where Asoka—who built the largest stupa—encouraged the implantation of Buddhism. The Maurya empire collapsed with his death in 231 B.C., and was replaced by the reign of the Greek kings of Bactria. About 800 B.C., the Scythians settled in the area, and then they in turn gave way to the Parthians, whose empire, about A.D. 30, extended from Taxila to Doura-Europos. It is generally thought that Apollonius' visit took place about this time. But for two hundred years the Kushan communities had already been on the move from the north-west of China, which they left about 170 B.C. to advance as far as

the province of Bactria, the Oxus, Kabul and finally northern India, which they occupied about A.D. 60, remaining for
a time in the neighbourhood of the Parthians. The Kushan
fell into decline as early as the third century and were wiped
out by the Hun invaders two hundred years later. When
Hsüan Tsang, the Chinese pilgrim, visited Taxila in the
sixth century, he found no more than traces of its vanished
splendour.

At the centre of Sirkap, whose quadrangular plan and
absolutely straight streets are marked out on the ground
by the ruins, there is a monument which reveals the full
significance of Taxila: it is the altar known as the altar of
'the two-headed eagle', on the base of which are three
porticoes carved in low relief: one has a pediment in the
Graeco-Roman style, the other is bell-shaped in the Bengali
manner and the third follows the archaic Buddhist style of
the gates of Bharhut. But even so, we would be underestimating Taxila if we thought of it only as the place
where, for several centuries, three of the greatest spiritual
traditions of the Ancient World, Hellenism, Hinduism and
Buddhism, lived side by side. The Persia of Zoroaster was
also present and, with the Parthians and Scythians, the
civilization of the steppes, which here combined with Greek
inspiration to create the most beautiful ornaments ever to
come from the hands of a jeweller; and these memories had
not yet been forgotten when Islam invaded the country,
never to leave it again. With the exception of Christianity,
all the influences which moulded the Old World come together here. Distant springs have mingled their waters. I
myself, a European visitor meditating on the ruins, represent the missing tradition. Where better than on this site,
which offers him a microcosm of his culture, could an inhabitant of the Old World, renewing the links with his past,
meditate on his destiny?

I was wandering one evening within the precincts of Bhir
Mound, which were defined by a bank of rubble. This
modest village, of which only the foundations survive, does
not rise above the level of the little geometrical streets along
which I was walking. I had the feeling of looking down on
the plan of the village from a great height or a great distance and this illusion, which was encouraged by the absence of vegetation, added an additional depth to the
perspective of history. These houses were once inhabited
perhaps by the Greek sculptors who followed Alexander,

the creators of the art of Gandhara and who inspired the ancient Buddhists with the courage to make images of their god. Something gleaming at my feet made me stop: it was a small silver coin loosened by the recent rains and bearing the Greek inscriptions, MENANDR BASILEUS SÔTEROS. What would the West be like today, if the attempt to unite the Mediterranean world and India had had any lasting success? Would Christianity or Islam have come into being? It was chiefly the presence of Islam which troubled me, not because I had spent the previous months in a Moslem setting. Here, while I was looking at the great monuments of Graeco-Buddhist art, my eyes and my mind remained obsessed with the memory of the Mogul palaces that I had devoted the last few weeks to in Delhi, Agra and Lahore. Since I knew little of the history and literature of the East, its crafts made a powerful impact on me (as had happened among the primitive peoples I had visited without knowing their language) and offered me the one salient feature it was possible for me to reflect upon.

After Calcutta, with its seething poverty and sordid suburbs, which seemed merely to transpose the musty profusion of the tropics on to a human level, at Delhi I had hoped to find the serenity of history. I had visions of myself installed in some antiquated hotel up against the ramparts, as at Carcassonne or Semur, where I could meditate in the moonlight; when I was asked to choose between the new and the old town, I had no hesitation in selecting at random a hotel situated in the latter. Imagine my surprise when the taxi travelled a distance of thirty kilometres or so across a featureless landscape, which might have been either an ancient battlefield with ruins jutting up here and there through the vegetation, or an abandoned building-site. When we finally arrived at the so-called old town, I was even more disillusioned; like everywhere else, it was a sort of English garrison. I was to learn during the next few days that instead of having the past concentrated within it over a small area, as is the case with European towns, Delhi was like an exposed stretch of windswept scrubland, over which the monuments were scattered like dice on a gaming-table. Each sovereign had tried to build his own town, and had abandoned and demolished the previous one in order to make use of the building materials. There was not one, but twelve or thirteen Delhis, lying dozens of kilometres from each other on a plain which was also dotted with tumuli, monuments and tombs. Islam was already beginning to surprise me by an attitude towards history, which was both the reverse of ours and self-contradictory: the desire to found a tradition was accompanied by a compulsion to destroy all previous traditions. Each monarch had tried to create something imperishable by abolishing time.

So, like a sensible tourist, I set about traversing these enormous distances in order to visit monuments each one of which seemed to be built in the desert.

Red Fort is less a monument than a palace, combining vestiges of the Renaissance (such as mosaics in *pietra dura*) with incipient Louis XV, a style which in this instance seems to have sprung from Mogul influences. In spite of the richness of the materials and the decorative refinement, I remained unsatisfied. There was nothing architectural in the whole thing, to correct the impression that it was only a palace: it was rather like a collection of tents, erected in a hard material in a garden which itself was no more than an idealized encampment. All the decorative ideas seemed to be derived from the textile arts: there were marble baldaquins resembling the folds of a curtain, and *jali* which were really (and not metaphorically) 'lacework in stone'. The marble canopy over the imperial throne was a replica of a collapsible wooden one with draperies; it was no more an integral part of the audience-chamber than the original would have been. Even Humayun's tomb, archaic though it is, produced in the visitor the uneasy feeling that some essential element was lacking. The whole edifice created an impressive mass, every detail was exquisite, but it was impossible to discover any organic link between the parts and the whole.

The Great Mosque—Jamma Masjid—which dates from the seventeenth century, is more pleasing to the Western visitor both in structure and colour. One can almost agree that it was conceived and planned as a whole. There, on payment of four hundred francs, I was shown the oldest copies of the Koran, a hair from the Prophet's beard fixed by a wax pellet to the bottom of a glass-lidded box filled with rose petals, and his sandals. A worshipper, a poor man, came close to get the benefit of the display, but the official in charge pushed him back with horror. Perhaps he had not paid his four hundred francs, or perhaps the relics were too highly charged with magic power to be seen by a believer.

To sense the appeal of this civilization, one has to go to Agra. There is nothing that cannot be said about the Taj

Mahal and its easy, coloured-picture-postcard charm. One can make ironical remarks about the procession of young British newly-weds who were granted the privilege of spending their honeymoon in the pink sandstone temple on the right, and the elderly, no less Anglo-Saxon spinsters who will cherish until their dying day the memory of the Taj sparkling under the stars and reflecting its white shadow in the Jumna. This is the 1900 aspect of India; but when one comes to think about it, one realizes that it is based on deep-seated affinities rather than on historical accident and the fact of conquest. No doubt the Europeanization of India took place around 1900, and signs of this can be seen in its vocabulary and Victorian customs ('lozenge' for sweet, and 'commode' for closed stool). But conversely, one begins to understand here that the turn of the century was the West's 'Hindu period'; it was marked by great displays of wealth, indifference to poverty, a liking for languid and over-elaborate shapes, sensuality, a love of flowers and perfumes, and even by tapering moustaches, curls, frills and furbelows.

When I visited the famous Jain temple in Calcutta, which was built in the nineteenth century by a millionaire in a park full of statues—some of cast-iron daubed with silver, others marble of crude Italian workmanship—it seemed to me that its alabaster pavilion encrusted with a mosaic of mirrors and reeking with perfume was the most ambitious possible expression of our grandparents' conception in their younger days of a high-class bordello. But in formulating this thought, I was not blaming India for building temples that looked like brothels, but rather blaming our civilization for not providing any other place where we could assert our freedom and explore the limits of our sensuality, such functions in fact being appropriate to a temple. The Hindus, our Indo-European brothers, seemed to reflect an exotic image of ourselves; they have evolved in another climate and in contact with different civilizations, but their private temptations are so identical with our own that at certain times, such as the 1900 period, these temptations also come to the surface again in European society.

There is nothing like this at Agra, where the different influences of medieval Persia and classical Arabia have been at work, in a form that many people think conventional. Yet I defy any visitor who still retains some freshness of approach not to be overcome with emotion as he enters the

precincts of the Taj, and at the same time steps straight
back, over great distances and periods of time, into the
world of the Arabian Nights; the effect is less subtle, no
doubt, than at Itmadud Daulah, that pearl, jewel or treasure
in white, beige and yellow; or at Akbar's pink tomb, haunted
only by monkeys, parrots and antelopes, in the heart of a
sandy landscape where the very pale green of the mimosa
trees merges into the colour tones of the ground, and, in the
evenings, the scene is enlivened by green parrots and tur-
quoise-coloured jays, peacocks in cumbersome flight and the
chatter of monkeys sitting around the tree-boles.

But, like the palace at Red Fort and Jehangir's tomb in
Lahore, the Taj remains a marble imitation of a draped
scaffolding, with the supporting poles for the hangings still
quite visible. At Lahore, there are even mosaic copies of
hangings. The various storeys do not form a structure; they
are merely repetitions. One may wonder about the underlying reason for this aesthetic indigence, in which can be
detected the origin of the current Moslem contempt for the
plastic arts. At the University of Lahore, I met an English
lady, married to a Moslem, who was in charge of the Department of Fine Art. Only girls were allowed to attend her
lectures; sculpture was forbidden, music had become a
clandestine activity and painting was taught as a social
accomplishment. Since the separation between India and
Pakistan followed the religious frontier, there had been an
intensification of austerity and puritanism. Art, I was told,
'had gone underground'. The official attitude was determined perhaps not so much by a desire to remain faithful to
Islam as by the urge to repudiate India: the destruction of
images was a harking back to Abraham, but with quite
recent political and national implications. Trampling art
underfoot was a way of abjuring India.

Idolatry—if we give the word its exact meaning, which
implies the personal presence of the god in his image—is
still very much alive in India; it exists in the reinforced concrete basilicas of the outer suburbs of Calcutta, where the
priests of recent cults, with shaven heads, bare feet and
yellow robes, receive worshippers in the very modern offices surrounding the shrine while sitting at their type-
writers administering the profits from their last missionary
tour of California; it is equally present in the slums at Kali
Ghat: 'This is a seventeenth-century temple,' I was told by
the business-like guide-priests; however, it was overlaid with

nineteenth-century ornamental tiles. At the time of my
visit, the shrine was closed, but if I were to come back one
morning, and stand at a precise spot which was pointed
out to me, I would be able to catch a glimpse of the goddess through a half-open door, between two pillars. Here,
as in the great temple of Krishna on the bank of the
Ganges, the temple was the mansion of a god who was only
accessible on feast days: the ordinary form of worship consisted in camping in the corridors and picking up from the
sacred servants any available gossip about the master's
state of mind. I decided just to stroll around in the vicinity,
along alleys crammed with beggars waiting for free distribu-
tions of food by the priests, a practice which served as an
alibi for a highly mercenary trade in coloured pictures and
plaster statuettes of the divinities, while here and there
could be seen more direct evidence of divine presences: a
red trident and stones standing on end against the intestinal
trunk of a banyan signified Siva; an altar painted red all
over, Laksmi; a tree, the branches of which were bedecked
with innumerable offerings—pebbles and scraps of material
—was inhabited by Ramakirshna, who can cure barrenness;
and a flower-covered altar concealed Krishna, the god of
love.

In comparison with this religious art, which is both
shoddy and incredibly alive, the Moslems could offer only
their one official painter, Chagtai, an English water-colourist
using the Rajput miniatures as his inspiration. Why did
Moslem art collapse so completely once it had passed its
peak? It went from the palace to the bazaar without any
transitional phase. This must have been a result of the rejection of images. Being deprived of all contact with reality,
the artist perpetuates a convention which is so anaemic that
it can be neither rejuvenated nor refertilized. Either it is
sustained by gold or it collapses completely. At Lahore, the
scholar who accompanied me had nothing but contempt for
the Sikh frescoes which adorned the fort—'Too showy, no
colour scheme, too crowded'—and no doubt they were a
far cry from the fantastic ceiling of mirrors in the Shish
Mahal which sparkles like a star-studded sky. But as is so
often the case when one compares contemporary India with
Islam, they were vulgar, ostentatious, folk-like and charming.

Apart from forts, the Moslems built nothing in India except temples and tombs. But the forts were inhabited

palaces, whereas the tombs and temples are unoccupied ones. Here too one can realize how difficult it is for Islam to conceive of solitude. It sees life as being first and foremost a communal affair, and a dead man is always inserted into the framework of a community which has no participants.

There is a striking contrast between the splendour of the mausoleums, with their vast dimensions, and the skimpily conceived tombstones they house. The tombs themselves are minute and the dead must feel rather short of space. The halls and galleries surrounding them are of no use except for the enjoyment of passers-by. In Europe, tombs are in proportion to their occupants: mausoleums are rare and art and ingenuity are brought to bear on the tomb itself, in order to make it sumptuous and comfortable for the dead.

In Islam, the tomb divides up into a splendid monument, from which the dead man cannot benefit, and a niggardly abode (itself half-visible cenotaph, half-concealed burial place) in which the deceased seems to be imprisoned. The problem of repose in the beyond is given a doubly contradictory solution: on the one hand, excessive and ineffectual comfort, and on the other real discomfort, the first providing a compensation for the second. This seems to be symbolic of Moslem culture which accumulates the most subtle refinements—palaces made of precious stones, fountains of rose-water, dishes of food coated with gold leaf and tobacco mixed with pounded pearls—and uses them as a veneer to conceal rustic customs and the bigotry permeating Islamic moral and religious thought.

On the aesthetic level, Islamic puritanism, abandoning the attempt to abolish sensuality, has been content to reduce it to its minor manifestations: scents, lacework, embroidery and gardens. On the moral level, the same ambiguity is noticeable: there is a display of toleration, accompanied by an obviously compulsive kind of proselytizing. The truth is that contact with non-Moslems distresses Moslems. Their provincial way of life survives, but under constant threat from other life-styles freer and more flexible than their own, and which may affect it through the mere fact of propinquity.

Instead of speaking of genuine toleration, it would be more accurate to say that in so far as Moslems are tolerant, this attitude marks a perpetual victory over themselves. By recommending toleration, the Prophet put them in a state of permanent crisis, resulting from the contradiction between the universal significance of the revelation and the acceptance of the plurality of religious faiths. This is a 'paradoxical' situation in the Pavlovian sense, giving rise to anxiety on the one hand and complacency on the other, since Moslems feel that, thanks to Islam, they can overcome the contradiction. They are mistaken, however: as I heard an Indian philosopher say one day, Moslems pride themselves on believing in the universal value of great principles, such as liberty, equality and toleration, and then cancel out the credit they would like to be given for this by asserting in the same breath that they are the only people to practise such principles.

One day, at Karachi, I found myself in the company of a group of Moslem scholars and academic leaders. As I listened to them extolling the superiority of their system, I was surprised to observe how insistently they came back to a single argument: namely, its *simplicity*. The Islamic legal system is better than the Hindu as regards matters of inheritance, because it is simpler. The way to get round the traditional ban on usury is simply for a banker and his client to enter into a partnership agreement and the interest accruing to the former will be no more than his share of the joint profits. As regards agrarian reform, the Moslem law relating to the inheritance of arable land can be applied until the land has been adequately divided up, and then its application can be stopped—since this law is not an article of dogma—in order to avoid parcelling out the land into too many smallholdings: 'There are so many ways and means . . .'

The whole of Islam would, in fact, seem to be a method for creating insurmountable conflicts in the minds of believers, with the proviso that a way out can subsequently be found by adopting extremely simple (but oversimple) solutions. With one hand they are rushed to the brink of danger; with the other they are held back at the edge of the abyss. If a man is worried about the virtue of his wives and daughters while he is away campaigning, what simpler solution could he find than to veil them and lock them away? This explains the development of the modern *burkah* which, with its complicated cut, its braid-edged slits for the eyes, its snap-fasteners and cords, looks like some orthopaedic ap-

paratus; the heavy material of which it is made allows it to
follow the exact contours of the body while at the same
time concealing it as completely as possible. But this merely
leads to a shifting of the threshold of anxiety, since a man
is disgraced if another man as much as brushes against his
wife, and the problem becomes even more worrying. Two
thinks emerge from a frank discussion with young Moslem
men: first, they are obsessed with the problem of prenuptial virginity and subsequent fidelity; secondly purdah,
that is the segregation of women, which in one sense puts
obstacles in the way of amorous intrigue, encourages it on
another level by enclosing women in a world of their own,
with the intricacies of which they alone are conversant.
Men who used to break into harems when young have good
reasons for keeping a sharp watch once they themselves are
married.

The Hindus and Moslems of India eat with their fingers.
The former do so delicately and deftly, picking up the food
in a piece of *chapati:* this is the name of the large pan-
cakes which are cooked very quickly by flattening them
against the inside wall of an earthenware jar buried in the
ground and filled a third of the way up with hot embers.
The Moslems have turned eating with the fingers into a
system: it is not done to hold a bone to gnaw off the flesh.
Using the only available hand (the left one being unclean,
since it is reserved for intimate hygiene), the eater kneads
and tears at the meat; and when he is thirsty, his greasy
hand seizes his glass. In observing these table manners,
which are certainly as good as any others but, from the
Western point of view, seem almost deliberately slovenly,
one wonders if, instead of being a relic of a bygone age,
they are not a consequence of a reform laid down by the
Prophet: 'Do not do as other peoples do who eat with a
knife.' He may have been prompted by the same, no doubt
unconscious, desire for systematic infantilization, and for
homosexual imposition of the community through the promiscuity involved in post-prandial cleansing rituals, when
all the men wash their hands, gargle, belch and spit into the
same basin, thus participating, with terribly *autistic* indifference, in the same fear of uncleanliness associated with
the same exhibitionism. The desire to be indistinguishable
from each other is accompanied, however, by the need to
be conspicuous as a group. Hence the institution of purdah:

'Let your women be veiled so that they can be recognized as being different from other women.'

The Islamic sense of fraternity rests on a cultural and religious basis. It has no economic or social character. Since we all have the same god, the good Moslem is a man who is ready to share his hookah with a road-sweeper. The beggar is indeed my brother, but chiefly in the sense that we commune in the same fraternal approval of the inequality between us. Hence those two, sociologically remarkable, species, the Germanophil Moslem and the Islamized German. If one were looking for a barrack-room religion, Islam would seem to be the ideal solution: strict observance of rules (prayers five times a day, each prayer necessitating fifty genuflexions); detailed inspections and meticulous cleanliness (ritual ablutions); masculine promiscuity both in spiritual matters and in the carrying out of the organic functions; and no women.

These anxious men are also men of action; being caught between incompatible sentiments, they make up for their feelings of inferiority by those traditional forms of sublimation, with which the Arab soul has always been associated; jealousy, pride and heroism. But their determination to keep themselves to themselves, and their combination of parochialism with chronic rootlessness (Urdu has been appropriately termed a 'military camp' language), which are basic causes of the setting up of the state of Pakistan, cannot be adequately explained by the community of religious faith and historical tradition. Pakistan is a contemporary social fact and must be interpreted as such: it arose from a collective moral crisis which imposed an irrevocable choice on thousands of individuals, forcing them to abandon their lands, often their wealth, occasionally their relations, professions and plans for the future, the land of their forebears and their ancestral tombs, in order to be Moslems among Moslems, and because they only feel at ease with their own people.

This great religion is based not so much on revealed truth as on an inability to establish links with the outside world. In contrast to the universal kindliness of Buddhism, or the Christian desire for dialogue, Moslem intolerance takes an unconscious form among those who are guilty of it; although they do not always seek to make others share their truth by brutal coercion, they are nevertheless (and this is more serious) incapable of tolerating the existence of others as others. The only means they have of protecting themselves against doubt and humiliation is the 'negativization' of others, considered as witnesses to a different faith and a different way of life. Islamic fraternity is the opposite of an unadmitted rejection of infidels; it cannot acknowledge itself to be such a rejection, since this would be tantamount to recognizing that infidels existed in their own right.

40. THE KYONG

I am only too well aware of the reasons for the uneasiness I felt on coming into contact with Islam: I rediscovered in Islam the world I myself had come from; Islam is the West of the East. Or, to be more precise, I had to have experience of Islam in order to appreciate the danger which today threatens French thought. I cannot easily forgive Islam for showing me our own image, and for forcing me to realize to what extent France is beginning to resemble a Moslem country. In Moslems and French people alike, I observe the same bookish attitude, the same Utopian spirit and the stubborn conviction that it is enough to solve problems on paper to be immediately rid of them. Behind the screen of a legal and formalist rationalism, we build similar pictures of the world and society in which all difficulties can be solved by a cunning application of logic, and we do not realize that the universe is no longer made up of the entities about which we are talking. Just as Islam has kept its gaze fixed on a society which was real seven centuries ago, and for the problems of which it then invented effective solutions, so we are incapable of thinking outside the framework of an epoch which came to an end a century and a half ago, and which was the one period when we were in tune with history—only too briefly, however, since Napoleon, that Mohammed of the West, failed where the other succeeded. Like the Islamic world, the France which emerged from the revolution suffered the inevitable fate of repentant revolutionaries, which is to become the nostalgic preservers of a state of things with regard to which they once stood in a dynamic relationship.

In our attitude towards the peoples and cultures still dependent on us, we are caught in the same contradiction as that which afflicts Islam in dealing with its protégés and the rest of the world. We seem to be incapable of realizing that principles, which were fruitful when it was a matter of ensuring our own development, may not be venerated by others to the point of inducing them to renounce these same principles for their own use, through the sheer gratitude we think they owe us for having been the first to invent them. Similarly, Islam, which invented toleration in the Near East, finds it difficult to forgive non-Moslems for not abjuring their own religions in favour of Mohammedism, when the latter enjoys the overwhelming superiority over all other faiths of respecting them all. In our case, the paradox lies in the fact that the majority of the dependent populations we are concerned with are Moslem, and that the cultural steamrolling to which both they and we are prone has too many features in common for us not to be antagonistic to each other—on the international level, I mean, since the differences spring from a confrontation between two bourgeoisies. Political oppression and economic exploitation have no right to look for excuses among their victims. However, if France, with her 45 million inhabitants, generously offered equal rights of citizenship to 25 million Moslem citizens, even though a large proportion of them are illiterate,* this would be no bolder a step than the one which saved America from remaining an insignificant province of the Anglo-Saxon world. When the citizens of New England decided a century ago to authorize immigration from the most backward regions of Europe and the most impoverished strata of society and to allow themselves to be swamped by the invasion, they gambled and won, and the stake was just as important as the one we refuse to risk.

Shall we ever be able to take the risk? Is it likely that, by combining, two regressive forces will reverse their trends? Instead of saving ourselves, we might rather be confirming disaster if, through reinforcing our mistake with an error symmetrical to it, we resigned ourselves to narrowing down the heritage of the Old World to the ten or fifteen centuries of spiritual impoverishment of which its western half has been both the setting and the agent. At Taxila, in Buddhist monasteries bristling with statues because of the influence of Greece, I was aware of the slim opportunity of remaining united which is open to our Old World; the schism is not yet complete. A different future is possible, the very future that Islam opposes by erecting its barrier between the West and the East, which, without it, would perhaps not

* This remark, like several others, is out of date; but it must be remembered that this book was written in 1954-5.

have lost their attachment to the common ground in which their roots are set.

No doubt, both Islam and Buddhism, in their different ways, have been opposed to this oriental basis, at the same time as they have been in opposition to each other. But, to understand the relationship between them, we must not compare Islam and Buddhism in the historical forms they had assumed by the time they came into contact with each other, since one had been in existence for five centuries and the other for nearly twenty. In spite of this discrepancy, we must think of each when it was in the full flower of its existence, which, in the case of Buddhism, smells as fresh in its earliest monuments as it does today in its more humble manifestations.

I cannot dissociate in my memory the peasant temples of the Burmese frontier from the Bharhut stelae dating from the second century B.C., the scattered fragments of which are to be found in Calcutta and Delhi. The stelae, carved at a time when, and in a region where, no Greek influence had yet been felt, provided me with an initial cause for wonderment; to the European observer, they seem to be outside time and place, as if their sculptors, being in possession of some machine for abolishing time, had concentrated three thousand years of art history into their work and—standing midway between Egypt and the Renaissance—had succeeded in encapsulating in a single moment developments which began at a period they could not possibly have known and ended with the conclusion of another that had not yet begun. If any art has a right to be called eternal, this is surely it: it may have been produced five thousand years ago, or it may date only from yesterday, there is no way of telling. It is akin to the pyramids and to our domestic architecture; the human shapes engraved in the pink, close-grained stone could step down and mingle with the society of the living. No statuary gives a deeper feeling of peace and familiarity than this, with its chastely immodest women and its maternal sensuality which delights in contrasting mother-mistresses with sequestered girls, both of which types are in opposition to the sequestered mistresses of non-Buddhist India: it expresses a placid femininity which is also suggested by the temple priests whose shaven heads make them indistinguishable from the nuns, with whom they form a kind of third sex, half parasitical and half captive.

If Buddhism, like Islam, has tried to control the excesses of primitive cults, it has done so by means of the unifying reassurance implicit in the promise of a return to the maternal breast; by this approach, it has reintegrated eroticism within itself, after divesting it of frenzy and anguish. Islam, on the contrary, has developed according to a masculine orientation. By shutting women away, it denies access to the maternal breast: man has turned the female world into a closed entity. No doubt, by this means, he too hopes to attain serenity; but he makes it depend on a principle of exclusion: women are excluded from social life and infidels from the spiritual community. Buddhism, on the other hand, conceives of its serenity as a form of fusion: with woman, with mankind in general, and in an asexual representation of the divinity.

It would be impossible to imagine any greater contrast than that between the Sage and the Prophet. Neither is a god, and that is the only point they have in common. In every other respect, they are opposed to each other: one is chaste, the other potent, with four wives; one is androgynous, the other bearded; one peaceable, the other bellicose; one exemplary and the other messianic. But at the same time, there is a gap of 1,200 years between them; and it is unfortunate for the consciousness of the West that Christianity which, had it emerged later, would have been able to effect a synthesis between them, should have appeared 'avant la lettre'—too soon—not as an *a posteriori* reconciliation between two extremes, but as a transition from one to the other: the middle term of a series which, because of its internal logic and geographical and historical factors, was destined thereafter to develop in the direction of Islam; since the latter—Moslems triumph on this point—represents the most evolved form of religious thought, although not necessarily the best; I would even say that it is, for this reason, the most disquieting of the three.

Mankind has made three major religious attempts to free itself from persecution by the dead, the malevolence of the Beyond and the anguish of magic. Over intervals of approximately five hundred years, it originated in turn Buddhism, Christianity and Islam; it is a striking fact that each stage, far from constituting an advance on the previous one, should be seen rather as a regression. For Buddhism, there is no Beyond: its whole teaching can be summarized as a radical criticism of life, such as humanity would never again be capable of, leading the sage to deny all meaning to beings and things: it is a discipline which abolishes the universe, and abolishes itself as a religion. Christianity, yielding again to fear, restored the other world, with its hopes, its threats and its last judgment. It only remained for Islam to bind this world to the other world: temporal and spiritual were brought together. The social order acquired the prestige of the supernatural order, and politics became theology. In the last resort, the spirits and phantoms, which superstition had always failed to bring to life, were replaced by masters who were only too real, and who were furthermore allowed to monopolize an after-life which added its burden to the already crushing weight of life here below.

This example justifies the anthropologist's ambition always to go back to the sources. Man never creates anything truly great except at the beginning; in whatever field it may be, only the first initiative is wholly valid. The succeeding ones are characterized by hesitation and regret, and try to recover, fragment by fragment, ground that has already been left behind. Florence, which I visited after New York, did not produce any first effect of surprise: in its architecture and plastic arts, I recognized the Wall Street of the fifteenth century. When I came to compare the Primitives with the Renaissance masters and the Siena painters with those of Florence, I had an impression of decline: the latter did precisely everything they ought not to have done. And yet they remain admirable. The grandeur inseparable from beginnings is so undeniable that even mistakes, provided they are new creations, can still overwhelm us with their beauty.

Now I can see, beyond Islam, to India, but it is the India of Buddha, before Mohammed. For me as a European, and because I am a European, Mohammed intervenes with uncouth clumsiness, between our thought and Indian doctrines that are very close to it, in such a way as to prevent East and West joining hands, as they might well have done, in harmonious collaboration. I had been on the point of committing the error of those Moslems who declare themselves to be Christian and Western and see the frontier between the two worlds as running along their eastern border. The two worlds are closer to each other than either is to the Moslem anachronism. Rational evolution would have been the converse of what actually occurred historically:

Islam cut a more civilized world in two. What appears modern to it belongs to a bygone age; it is living with a time lag of a thousand years. It was able to accomplish a revolutionary mission, but since this mission affected a backward section of mankind, Islam fertilized actuality and sterilized potentiality: it brought about a form of progess which is the reverse of a project.

If the West traces its internal tensions back to their source, it will see that Islam, by coming between Buddhism and Christianity, Islamized us at the time when the West, by taking part in the crusades, was involved in opposing it and therefore came to resemble it, instead of undergoing—had Islam never come into being—a slow process of osmosis with Buddhism, which would have Christianized us still further, and would have made us all the more Christian in that we would have gone back beyond Christianity itself. It was then that the West lost the opportunity of remaining female.

In the light of this, I can achieve a better understanding of the ambiguous nature of Mogul art. The emotion it arouses is not in the least architectural: it relates to poetry and music. But surely it was for the reasons just mentioned that Moslem art was to remain phantasmagorical. The Taj Mahal has been described as 'a marble dream'. This guidebook expression conceals an extremely profound truth. The Moguls dreamed their art; they literally created *dream*-palaces; they did not build, but transcribed. It follows that their monuments are disturbing both because of their lyrical quality and because of an appearance of insubstantiality, as if they were castles made of cards or shells. They are not palaces solidly anchored to the ground, but rather scale-models trying in vain to reach the status of existence through the preciousness and hardness of their materials.

In the temples of India, the idol *is* the divinity; the temple is its dwelling-place; its real presence makes the shrine precious and awe-inspiring and justifies the precautions taken by the devout, such as the bolting of the doors except on those days when the god receive his worshippers.

In comparison with this conception, Islam and Buddhism react in different ways. The former banishes idols and destroys them; its mosques are bare, and have only the congregation of believers to enliven them. The latter substitutes images for idols, and has no scruples about their numbers, since no image is in fact the god but merely evokes him and the more there are, the more the imagination is stimulated. Whereas the Hindu sanctuary houses an idol, the mosque is deserted except for men, and the Buddhist temple shelters a host of effigies. The Graeco-Buddhist centre, where one has difficulty in picking one's way through a mushrooming profusion of statues, chapels and pagodas, prepares one for the humble *kyong* along the Burmese frontier with its rows of identical mass-produced statuettes.

In September 1950, I happened to find myself in a Mogh village in the Chittagong hill tracts; for several days I had been watching the women take food every morning to the priests in the temple; during the siesta period, I could hear the beating of the gong which regulated the rhythm of the prayers and childish voices intoning the Burmese alphabet. The *kyong* stood just outside the village at the top of a little wooded hillock like those that Tibetan painters love to depict in the backgrounds of their pictures. At the foot of the hill was the *jédi*, that is the pagoda: in such a poor village it was no more than a circular, earth construction, rising in seven concentric tiers, and set in a square enclosure surrounded by bamboo fencing. We had taken off our shoes to climb the hillock, and the fine, damp clay felt soft under our bare feet. On either side of the slope, we could see pineapple plants which had been torn out the day before by the villagers, who were shocked that their priests should take the liberty of growing fruit when their needs were provided for by the lay population. The top of the hill had the appearance of a little square, surrounded on three sides by open-sided straw shelters containing enormous bamboo objects, covered with multicoloured paper-like kites, and which were used as decorations for processions. On the fourth side stood the temple, which was built on stilts, like the village huts to which it was very similar, except that it was bigger and had a square-shaped structure with a thatched roof rising above the principal building. After the climb through the mud, the prescribed ablutions seemed quite natural and devoid of any religious significance. We went into the temple. The only light, apart from the rays filtering in through the thatch walls, came from the lantern formed by the central structure just above the altar, which was hung with standards made of rags or rush-matting. Fifty or so brass statuettes were piled up on the altar, at the side of which hung a gong: on the walls were a few pious coloured lithographs and a stag's skull. The floor, which was made of thick bamboo canes split lengthwise and plaited, had been polished by the constant rubbing of bare feet and was springier than a carpet. A peaceful barn-like atmosphere pervaded the place and there was a smell of hay in the air. The simple and spacious room which was like a hollowed-out haystack, the courteous behaviour of the two priests standing next to their beds with straw-mattresses, the touching care with which they had brought together or made the instruments of worship—all these things helped to bring me closer than I had ever been before to my idea of what a shrine should be like. 'You need not do what I am doing,' my companion said to me as he prostrated himself on the ground four times before the altar, and I followed his advice. However, I did so less through self-consciousness than discretion: he knew that I did not share his beliefs, and I would have been afraid of debasing the ritual gestures by letting him think I considered them as mere conventions: but, for once, I would have felt no embarrassment in performing them. Between this form of religion and myself, there was no likelihood of misunderstanding. It was not a question of bowing down in front of idols or of adoring a supposed supernatural order, but only of paying homage to the decisive wisdom that a thinker, or the society which created his legend, had evolved twenty-five centuries before and to which my civilization could contribute only by confirming it.

What else, indeed, have I learned from the masters who taught me, the philosophers I have read, the societies I have visited and even from that science which is the pride of the West, apart from a few scraps of wisdom which, when laid end to end, coincide with the meditation of the Sage at the foot of the tree? Every effort to understand destroys the object studied in favour of another object of a different nature; this second object requires from us a new effort which destroys it in favour of a third, and so on and so forth until we reach the one lasting presence, the point at which the distinction between meaning and the absence of meaning disappears: the same point from which we began. It is 2,500 years since men first discovered and formulated these truths. In the interval, we have found nothing new, except—as we have tried in turn all possible ways out of

the dilemma—so many additional proofs of the conclusion
that we would have liked to avoid.

This is not to say that I am not also aware of the dangers
of overhasty resignation. This great religion of non-knowl-
edge is not based on our inability to understand. It bears
witness to that ability and raises us to a pitch at which we
can discover the truth in the form of a mutual exclusiveness
of being and knowledge. Through an additional act of bold-
ness, it reduces the metaphysical problem to one of human
behaviour—a distinction it shares only with Marxism. Its
schism occurred on the sociological level, the fundamental
difference between the Great and the Little Ways being the
question of whether the salvation of a single individual
depends, or does not depend, on the salvation of humanity
as a whole.

However, the historical solutions offered by Buddhist
morality face us with two chilling alternatives: anyone who
gives an affirmative reply to the question shuts himself up
in a monastery: anyone who replies in the negative can
achieve easy satisfaction in the practice of egotistical virtue.

Yet injustice, poverty and suffering exist; they supply a
mediatory term between the two alternatives. We are not
alone, and it does not depend on us whether we remain
deaf and blind to mankind, or believe exclusively in the
humanity within ourselves. Buddhism can remain coherent
while agreeing to respond to appeals from outside. It may
even be that, over a vast area of the world, it has found
the link that was missing from the chain. If the last phase
of the dialectic leading to illumination is legitimate, then
all the others which preceded and resembled it are legitimate too. The complete denial of meaning is the end point
in a succession of stages each one of which leads from a
lesser to a greater meaning. The final step, which cannot
be achieved without the others, validates them all retro-
actively. In its own way and on its own level, each one
corresponds to a truth. Between the Marxist critique, which
frees man from his initial bondage—by teaching him that
the apparent meaning of his condition evaporates as soon
as he agrees to see things in a wider context—and the Buddhist critique which completes his liberation, there is
neither opposition nor contradiction. Each is doing the
same thing as the other, but on a different level. The transition from one extreme to the other is guaranteed by all the
advances in knowledge that man has accomplished in the

last two thousand years, thanks to an unbroken movement of thought going from East to West, and then from West to East—perhaps for no other reason than to confirm its origin. As beliefs and superstitions dissolve when one thinks in terms of the real relationships between men, ethics gives way to history, fluid forms are replaced by structures and creation by nothingness. It is enough to fold the initial process back upon itself to discover its symmetry; its parts are superimposable one upon the other: the completed stages do not destroy the validity of those that went before; they confirm it.

As he moves about within his mental and historical framework, man takes along with him all the positions he has already occupied, and all those he will occupy. He is everywhere at one and the same time; he is a crowd surging forward abreast, and constantly recapitulating the whole series of previous stages. For we live in several worlds, each truer than the one it encloses, and itself false in relation to the one which encompasses it. Some are known to us through action; some are lived through in thought; but the seeming contradiction resulting from their coexistence is solved in the obligation we feel to grant a meaning to the nearest and to deny any to those furthest away; whereas the truth lies in a progressive dilating of the meaning, but in reverse order, up to the point at which it explodes.

This being so, as an anthropologist, I am no longer the only one to suffer from a contradiction affecting humanity as a whole and containing its own inherent cause. The contradiction remains only when I isolate the extremes: what is the use of action, if the thought guiding it leads to the discovery of the absence of meaning? But this discovery is not immediately accessible: I have to arrive at it by thought, and I cannot do so in one go. Whether there are twelve stages, as in the Boddhi, or whether they are more or less numerous, they all exist together, and in order to reach this conclusion, I am constantly called upon to live through situations each one of which demands something of me: I have a duty to men, just as I have a duty to knowledge. History, politics, the economic and social world, the physical world and even the sky surround me with concentric circles, from which I cannot escape in thought without ceding a fragment of my person to each one of them. Like a pebble striking water and making rings on

the surface as it cuts through, in order to reach the bottom
I too must take the plunge.

The world began without man and will end without him.
The institutions, morals and customs that I shall have spent
my life noting down and trying to understand are the
transient efflorescence of a creation in relation to which
they have no meaning, except perhaps that of allowing
mankind to play its part in creation. But far from this part
according man an independent position, or his endeavours
—even if doomed to failure—being opposed to universal
decline, he himself appears as perhaps the most effective
agent working towards the disintegration of the original
order of things and hurrying on powerfully organized matter towards ever greater inertia, an inertia which one day
will be final. From the time when he first began to breathe
and eat, up to the invention of atomic and thermonuclear
devices, by way of the discovery of fire—and except when
he has been engaged in self-reproduction—what else has
man done except blithely break down billions of structures
and reduce them to a state in which they are no longer
capable of integration? No doubt he has built towns and
cultivated the land; yet, on reflection, urbanization and
agriculture are themselves instruments intended to create
inertia, at a rate and in a proportion infinitely higher than
the amount of organization they involve. As for the creations of the human mind, their significance only exists in
relation to it, and they will merge into the general chaos, as
soon as the human mind has disappeared. Thus it is that
civilization, taken as a whole, can be described as an extraordinarily complex mechanism, which we might be tempted
to see as offering an opportunity of survival for the human
world, if its function were not to produce what physicists
call entropy, that is inertia. Every verbal exchange, every
line printed, establishes communication between people,
thus creating an evenness of level, where before there was
an information gap and consequently a greater degree of
organization. Anthropology could with advantage be
changed into 'entropology', as the name of the discipline
concerned with the study of the highest manifestations of
this process of disintegration.

Yet I exist. Not, of course, as an individual, since in this
respect, I am merely the stake—a stake perpetually at risk
—in the struggle between another society, made up of

several thousand million nerve cells lodged in the ant-hill of my skull, and my body, which serves as its robot. Neither psychology nor metaphysics nor art can provide me with a refuge. They are myths, now open to internal investigation by a new kind of sociology which will emerge one day and will deal no more gently with them than traditional sociology does. The self is not only hateful: there is no place for it between *us* and *nothing*. And if, in the last resort, I opt for *us*, even though it is no more than a semblance, the reason is that, unless I destroy myself— an act which would obliterate the conditions of the option—I have only one possible choice between this semblance and nothing. I only have to choose for the choice itself to signify my unreserved acceptance of the human condition; in thus freeing myself from an intellectual pride, the futility of which I can gauge by the futility of its object, I also agree to subordinate its claims to the objective demands of the emancipation of the many, to whom the possibility of such a choice is still denied.

Just as the individual is not alone in the group, nor any one society alone among the others, so man is not alone in the universe. When the spectrum or rainbow of human cultures has finally sunk into the void created by our frenzy; as long as we continue to exist and there is a world, that tenuous arch linking us to the inaccessible will still remain, to show us the opposite course to that leading to enslavement; man may be unable to follow it, but its contemplation affords him the only privilege of which he can make himself worthy; that of arresting the process, of controlling the impulse which forces him to block up the cracks in the wall of necessity one by one and to complete his work at the same time as he shuts himself up within his prison; this is a privilege coveted by every society, whatever its beliefs, its political system or its level of civilization; a privilege to which it attaches its leisure, its pleasure, its peace of mind and its freedom; the possibility, vital for life, of *unhitching*, which consists—Oh! fond farewell to savages and explorations!—in grasping, during the brief intervals in which our species can bring itself to interrupt its hive-like activity, the essence of what it was and continues to be, below the threshold of thought and over and above society: in the contemplation of a mineral more beautiful than all our creations; in the scent that can be smelt at the heart of a lily and is more imbued with learn-

ing than all our books; or in the brief glance, heavy with
patience, serenity and mutual forgiveness, that, through
some involuntary understanding, one can sometimes exchange with a cat.

October 12th, 1954–March 5th, 1955

INDEX